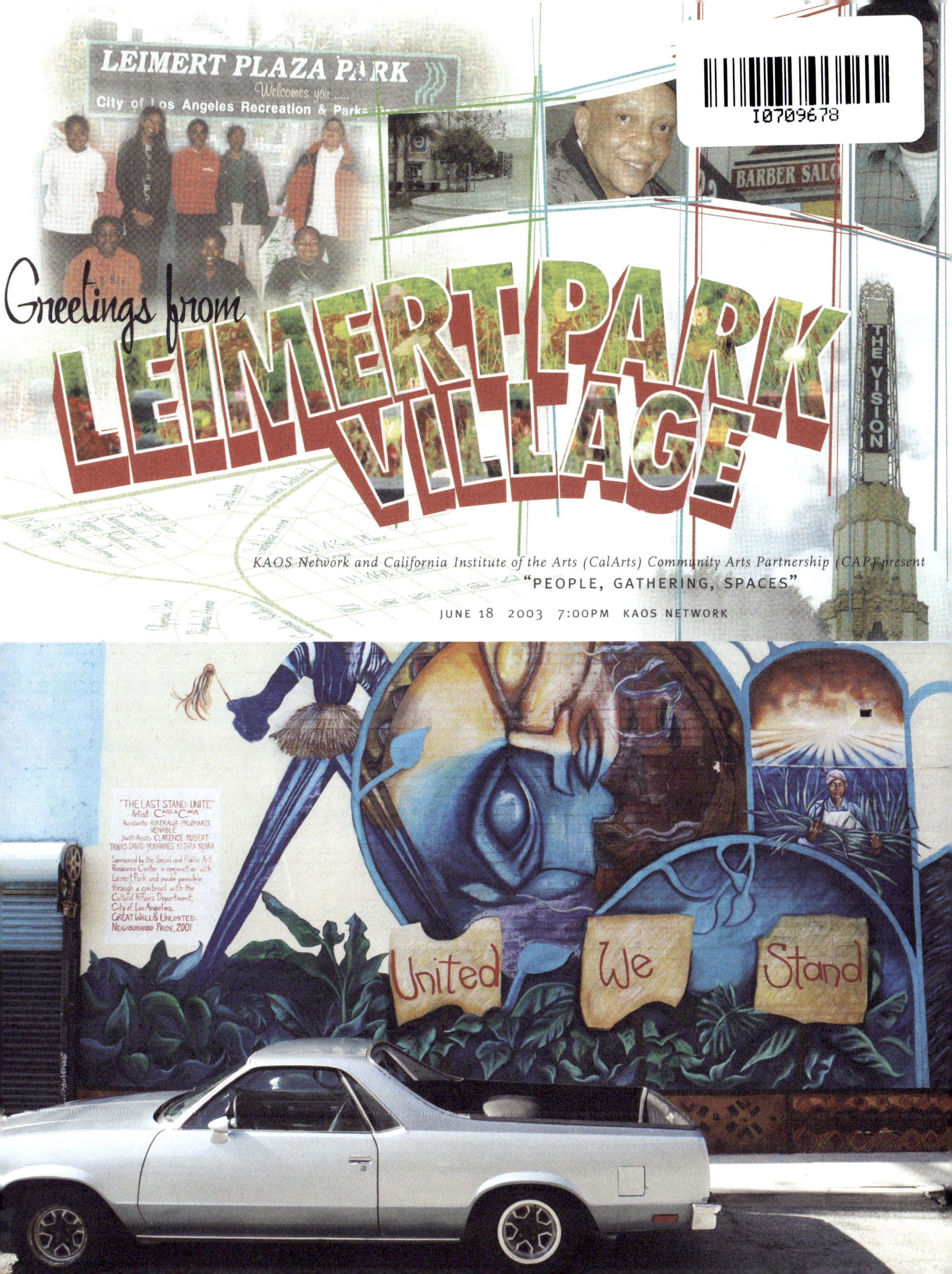

LEIMERT PLAZA PARK
Welcomes you .....
City of Los Angeles Recreation & Parks
I0709678
BARBER SALON
THE VISION
Greetings from
LEIMERT PARK VILLAGE
KAOS Network and California Institute of the Arts (CalArts) Community Arts Partnership (CAP) present
"PEOPLE, GATHERING, SPACES"
JUNE 18 2003 7:00PM KAOS NETWORK
"THE LAST STAND UNITE"
Artist: CARLA CARR
Assistants: KIKEKAUA PALOMARES
VENABLE
Youth Assts: CLARENCE ROBERT
TRAVIS DAVID YOHANNES KITARA KEARA
Sponsored by the Social and Public Art
Resource Center in conjunction with
Leimert Park and made possible
through a contract with the
Cultural Affairs Department,
City of Los Angeles.
GREAT WALLS UNLIMITED:
NEIGHBORHOOD PRIDE, 2001
United We Stand

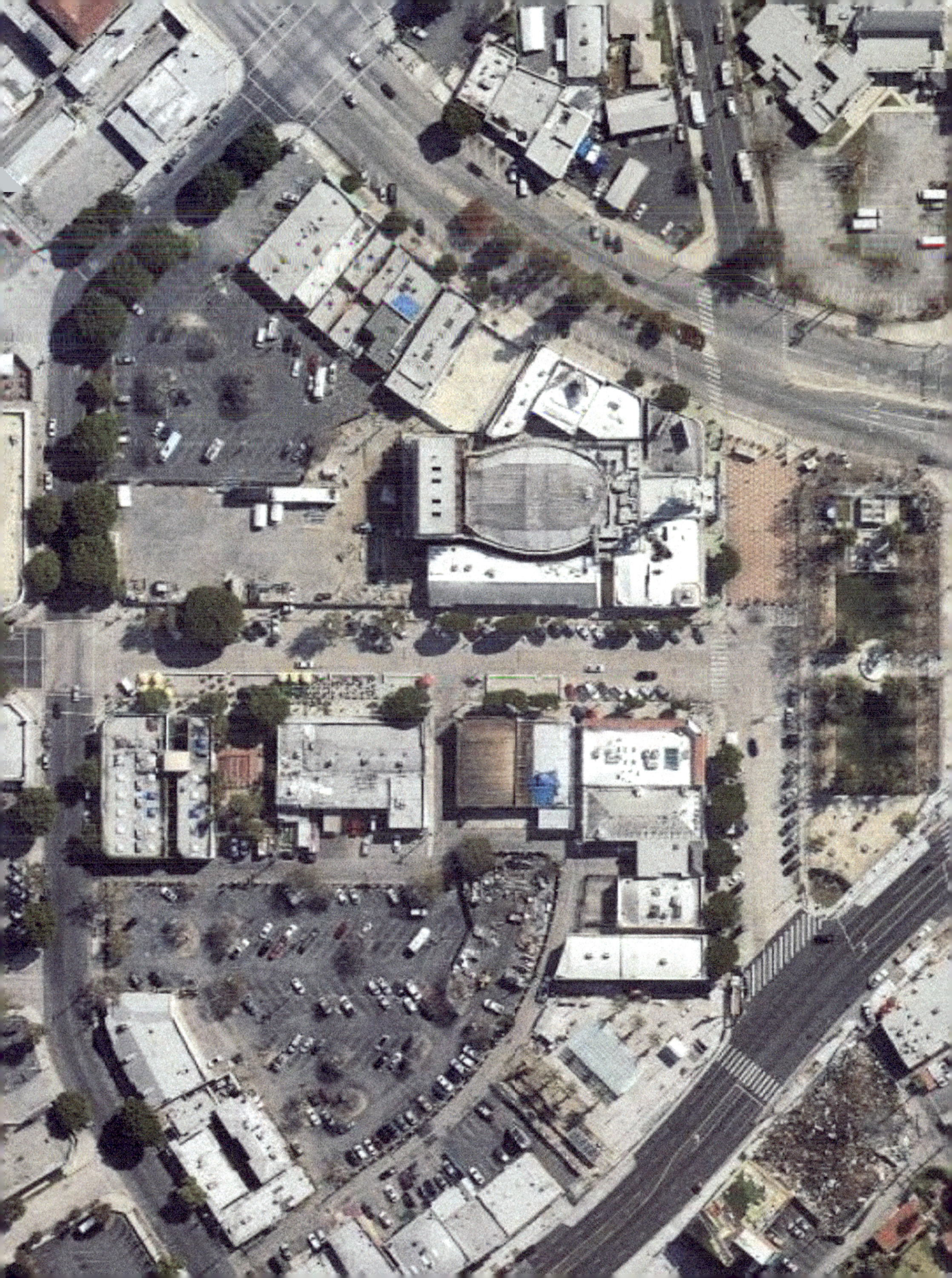

KAOS THEORY

THE AFRO—KOSMIC ARK OF BEN CALDWELL

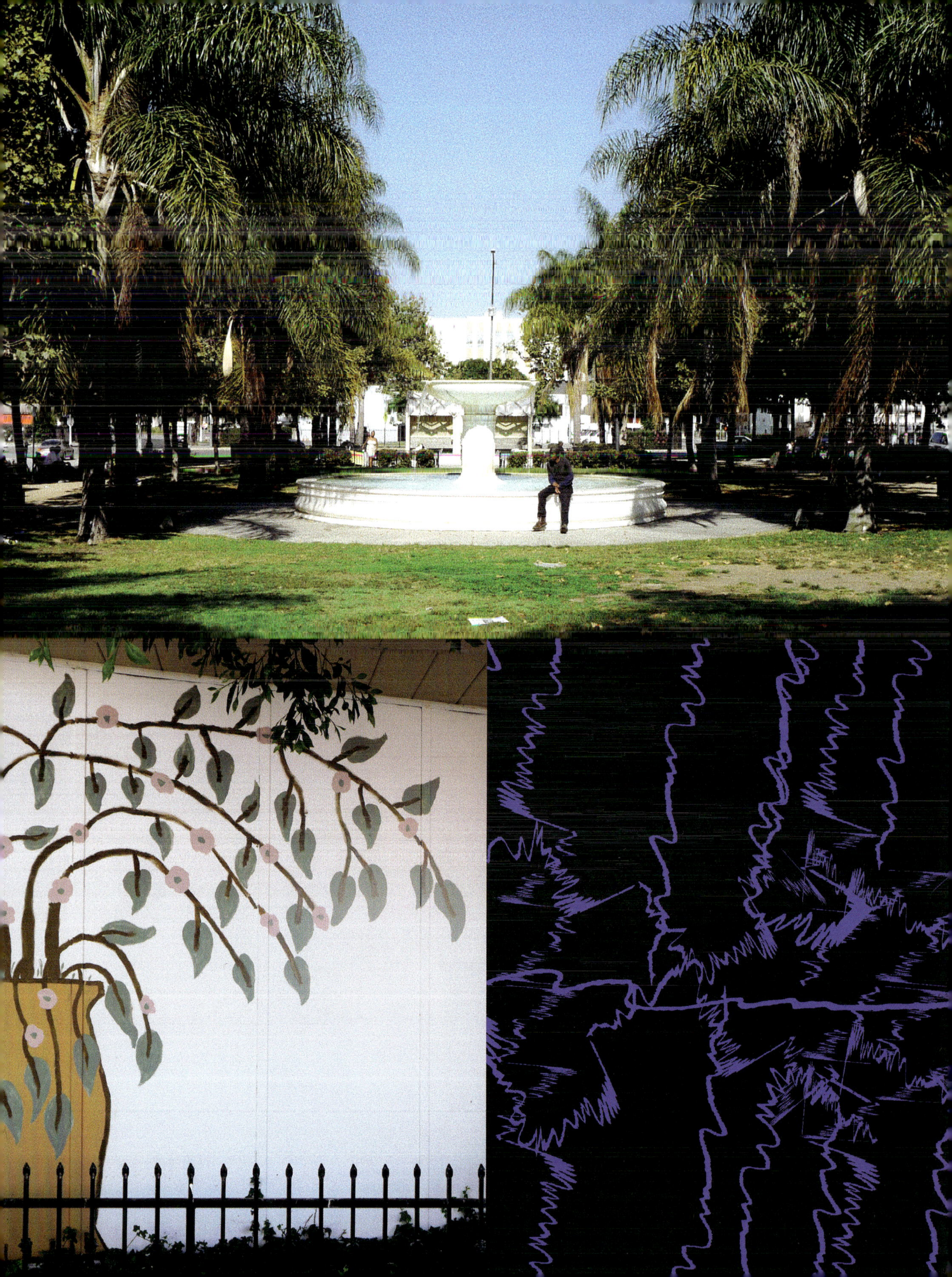

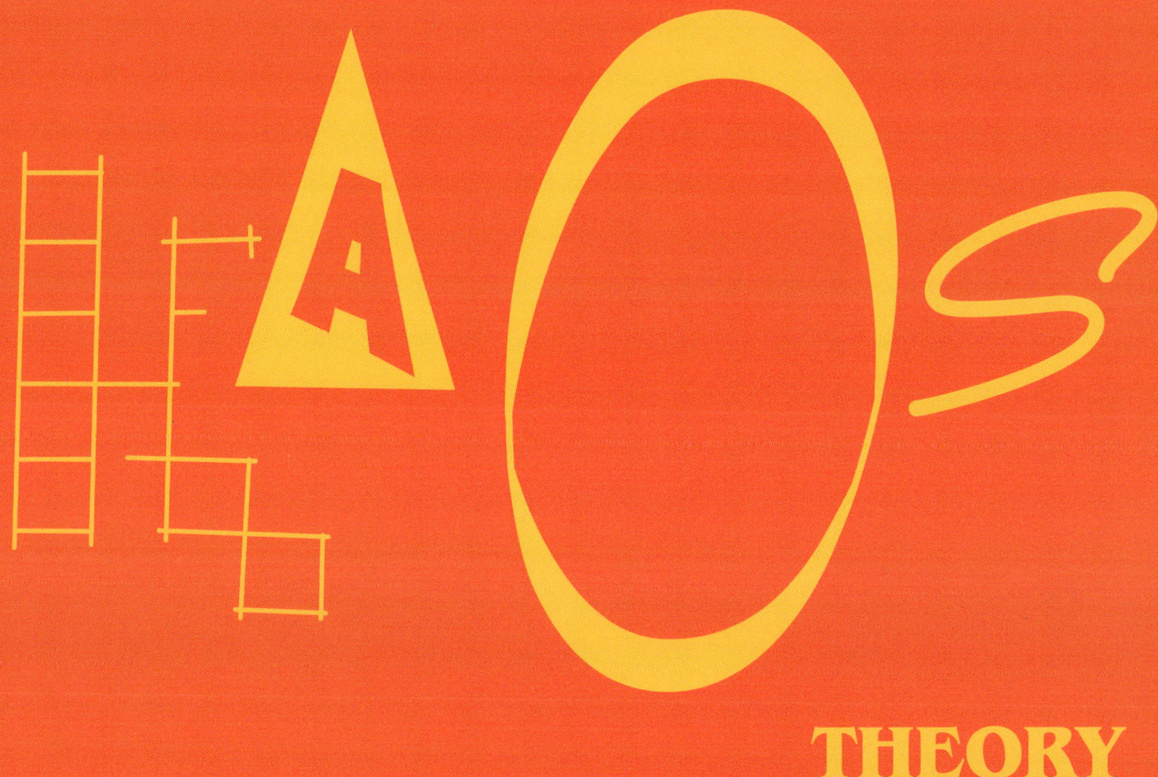

CHAOS

THEORY

ROBESON
TAJ
FRAZIER
WITH
BEN
CALDWELL

ANGEL
CITY
PRESS

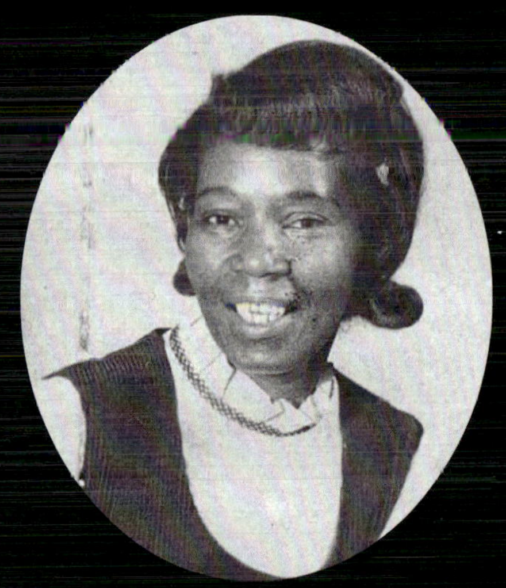

FOR
MAMIE T.

One day I went and asked my mother for my own garden, and she did let me have my own little plot. I loved it and took care of it well ... I would pull the grass in my garden ... I would patrol the rows on my hands and knees for any worms and bugs, and I would kill them and bury them. And sometimes when I had everything straight and clean for my things to grow, I would lie down on my back between two rows, and I would gaze up in the blue sky at the clouds moving and think all kinds of things.   —Malcolm X, *The Autobiography of Malcolm X*

CONTENTS

QR codes throughout the book link to videos that enhance the text.

The life of any artist is inevitably filled with models of different sorts. There are objects (living or still), that one attempts to render. There are artistic works that arrest you in ways both overt and mysterious. And, there are the artists/creators themselves.

Artistic models (the flesh-and-blood makers) matter because life is finite. And, in the end, we're all stardust. Combine this with an anti-black universe, and models (particularly for Black folks) aren't just the difference between success and failure, but life and death. It's a minefield out here.

So one discovers the work of Artist X. This frames what's possible, sets the terms of excellence. If one's fortunate, you develop some conscious understanding of why the work captured your attention in the first place. If one is blessed (and herein lies the difference between viewers and those with aspirations to become artists themselves), meeting Artist X is an opportunity to seek, not just answers, but questions. The questions driving Artist X—blessings upon blessings—become a template for more personal interrogations, the sort one spends a lifetime attempting to answer.

Ben Caldwell was my Artist X. Meeting (and ultimately coming to know) him has been an extended "hanging with 'Trane" moment for me.

I attended Howard University in the early '80's and, despite having gone there to study architecture, I increasingly found myself in the film department. Plus, I'd spent my previous two years in D.C. taking advantage of the Circle theaters which were, at that time, the most sophisticated repertory film chain in the U.S. That, plus the American Film Institute and the plethora of universities in D.C., had given me an opportunity to see some of pretty much everything cinema had to offer.

So when I found myself standing in the doorway of a studio at HU, checking out Ben's job talk, I was curious at best. And, being the harsh judge that I am, not particularly expecting to be impressed. I couldn't have been more wrong. Seeing *I & I: An African Allegory* (Ben's 1977 thesis project from UCLA) was like being struck by lightning. I, quite literally, had never seen anything like it. And I can't overstate its impact on me. Its combination of modalities, from the theatrical to ritual performance, interspersed with abstract sequences, was simply overwhelming. It was a fully realized jazz cinema. Plus, I simply had never considered the possibility, much less existence, of a Black experimental filmmaker.

There's a sequence in *I & I* composed entirely of black-and-white still images that triggered such a shift in my thinking, that I'm still working out its implications forty years later. Check out my *APEX* (2013) if you think I'm exaggerating. There's this staccato montage of images that demonstrated conclusively the possibility of imposing on cinema the feel and flow of Black music. For that alone, it's forever on my list of most electrifying moments in cinema. But there was something else, much more subtle, paradigm shifting, that took me a moment to fully grasp its implications. In addition to images of Black folks, Ben used still images of white people in his montages. That was unexpected. How was it Black cinema, when fully half of its content was made up of images of white folk? Perhaps from our vantage it is hard to appreciate how unprecedented this was. Take my word, *it does not compute*. And, didn't I recognize several images by the super famous, super white photographer, Diane Arbus? *Head explodes*.

And then he was gone.

The following year, Ben was back. He'd been hired, and I naturally fell into his orbit. Over the course of a couple of years, Ben impacted me in more ways than I can even touch on here. But a few things:

Ben once told me, "I used to read the liner notes on jazz albums and every time I saw the word 'music,' I scratched it out and substituted 'cinema'." *Head explodes*.

He once said, "Black music is densely codified African Philosophy." *Head explodes*.

One winter evening, after helping Ben with a video shoot, we found ourselves schlepping through the snow, having dropped off the gear. Ben invited me up to his apartment and unexpectedly, offered to show me this other film he was working on, *The Nubian* (1980). He set up a projector and we screened it on the wall of his living room. It's on a very short list (along with *2001: A Space Odyssey* and Kenneth Anger's *Scorpio Rising*) of the most memorable, most primordially magical experiences of projected moving images I've had.

Ben described his attempt to create a film not simply about a healer, but a film that actually functioned to heal the viewer. And seeing *The Nubian* made certain fundamental questions explicit. Does cinema have any potential therapeutic value? And how might this work with or against some supposedly artistic value? How might cinema inform or catalyze things like self-sufficiency, well-being or mutual aid? Why spirituality matters in these endeavors?

The Nubian had these color fields. You'd have a character talking and then suddenly there'd just be red on the screen, vibrating in a certain kind of way. What I came to grasp was the difference between representing something and presenting something. Of the possibilities of the concrete-yet-material dimensions of cinema. Cinema as light, fundamentally. Cinema like rhythm, both the least-material but most-felt of things. And yet, how these concerns were never mutually exclusive. Not an either/or proposition. How "our way" was forever contingent, improvisatory.

Ben, slowly but assuredly, taught me how to think. Not only about the task at hand and how to identify the task, but to consider the relationship between task and mission. How one's conceptualization of a mission overdetermines what enacting those goals might look like. And most importantly, how these questions are long term, marathons rather than sprints.

In a way, Ben let me in on a secret. He wasn't just a filmmaker, or even just an artist. He was creative practice profoundly bound up with the lived, and specifically spiritual, circumstances of Black folks' lives. And in doing so, he challenged me to think beyond my drive for success (artistic or commercial), or my still formulating metric of what "mastery" might look like.

Ben showed me a terrain, pointed out the horizon, and sent me on my way.

THE VILLAGE

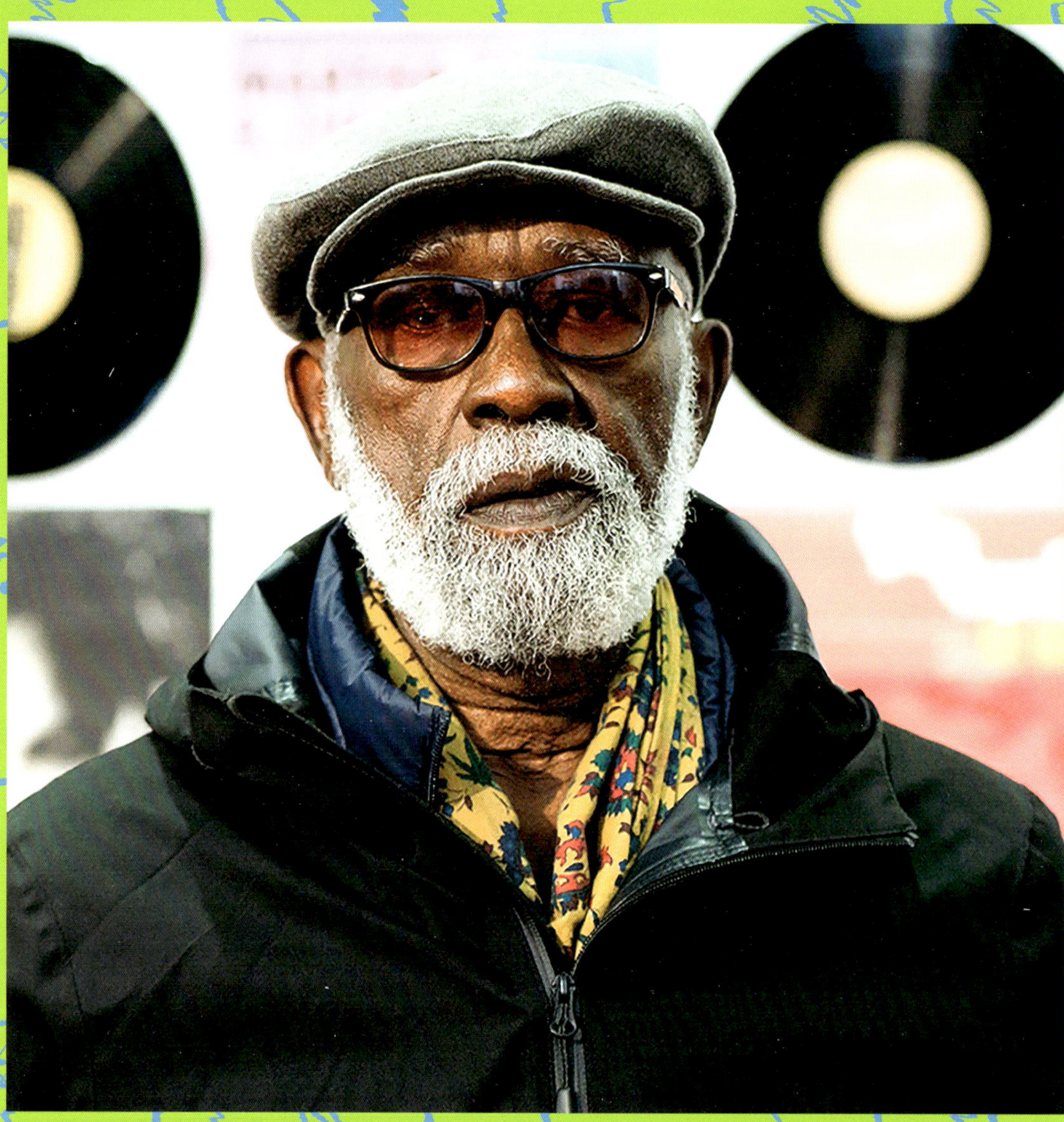

OCTOPUS

For this fantastic voyage, make your way to Leimert Park Village, what locals refer to as "the Village." It is a cultural center of Black Los Angeles. A bustling enclave located within the Crenshaw-Leimert Park neighborhood. Pull it up on the map on your phone. **Type in the coordinates above.**

At some point in your visit, you will run into him. Either on the block or in his studio/lab. Or perhaps you will just sense his vibes and energy. You will certainly feel it if it's Sunday. This is when the Village comes together for their art walk, drum circle, and marketplace.

Roll through. He'll be there. Dark-skinned, silver-bearded man.

He has a distinctive yet low-key style. Baseball cap, black shades. Often clad in an artful t-shirt. He will be wearing comfortable shoes, probably sneakers.

From his perch, he has observed the neighborhood's cycles of life. Multiple generations making a way, living just enough, just enough for the city. There, outside 4343 Leimert Blvd., he has stood, arms crossed, taking in the Village's sounds and sights. The park just across the plaza. The Degnan and Crenshaw Strips. The People's Street, with its Adinkra symbols etched into the pavement, a block that he and others pushed the city to close off to automobiles. This is where children play, where community members assemble, where the drum circle percussionists and dancers congregate.

When you chat with him, you'll find he's very personable. Knowledgeable about a wide range of subjects, yet chill and modest. He enjoys a good laugh and can find humor and irony in the most serious of subjects. He's also very comfortable with people of different backgrounds and walks of life.

Some people remark that he speaks in a manner they would expect from a Native chief or shaman, due to his baritone voice and his relaxed and deliberate dialogue. He demonstrates appreciation for the weight and texture of each word and value for both word and breath. There is an acknowledgment of the power of pauses, breaks, intonations, and exhalations. "All communicate different frequencies and are reminders of being alive" he explains, "reminders that speech and dialogue are ancient arts of supreme alchemy."

People have given him many titles: Filmmaker. Artist. Educator. Technologist. Business owner. Activist. Community leader. He is a polymath that a journalist once described as "the octopus of Leimert Park."

He is a friend, collaborator, and mentor to many. And, most significantly, a father and grandfather.

He is also a caretaker of the Village and its traditions of art and community. He has kept his ear to the neighborhood's pulse, helping support and steward its different generations, dynamically pushing each one to seed and nurture new cycles of growth and patterns of purpose.

Like all elders, he has stories to share. Of love, aspiration, toil, strife, introspection. The mysterious magic of the unknown. The aliveness of the world and the great universe—each part in its abundance, its opacity. And the luminary essence that connects all, even in degeneration, decay, death.

"There is an art to these processes we call life," he states in a meditative manner.

You mull over this.

Did you say art or arc, you inquire?

He grins.

And there you have it.

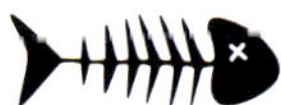

Ben Caldwell is a filmmaker, multimedia artist, cultural entrepreneur, community activist, and educator. He is also the founder of KAOS Network, a media-arts lab and commercial enterprise located in the Village, on the corner of West 43rd Place and Leimert Boulevard. For fifty years, Ben has fashioned a life dedicated toward artistic expression, collaboration, and the stewarding of creative community.

Ben was born and raised in New Mexico. He first drew prestige as a filmmaker in the 1970s. His work was part of a movement of films produced and shot by filmmakers attending the University of California, Los Angeles, from the late 1960s to the late 1980s—a group that was later dubbed "the L.A. Rebellion" (also referred to as the Los Angeles School). This cadre produced avant-garde, often low-to-medium-budget films with small crews, which were anchored in nuanced depictions of Black and Afro-diasporic life and whose range of diverse and experimental styles pushed the bounds of cinema. With this community, Ben developed a distinctive style of filmmaking, one that built on his earlier practice of painting and mixed-media photography. His films fused archival images and footage with staged shots, fragmented and non-linear narrative sequences, photographs, painting, animation, vibrant sonic landscapes and back-beats, and a percussive editing style—disparate pieces blended into cinematic dream sequences that transport viewers across different histories, memories, geographies, and traditions of culture. It is a visual style that corresponds with that of Ghanaian-British filmmaker John Akomfrah, both artists visually mining, recontextualizing, and juxtaposing the audiovisual archive of the twentieth century with film and other media in a manner that "show[s] the interconnectedness of many ideas" and which "blur[s] the lines of the traditional cinematic genres of dramatic, documentary, and journalism." In so doing, Ben's films, like those of Akomfrah, point out "that the cinematic form is also in question, and that to create new formal cinematic structures is also in keeping with the futuristic traditions of African culture and art-making."

Ben began to expand his oeuvre to other types of media, technology, and creative formats in the 1980s. This includes forays into video, multimedia performance, public access television, telecommunications, new media digital technologies, and, most recently, urban interactive and speculative community-based art, as well as design and future-facing technologies such as augmented and virtual reality and autonomous vehicles. Whereas it has become convention to separate media and art into distinct realms, Ben's practice subverts these disciplinary demarcations and socially engineered boundaries. No technology or media of representation is off limits to him. Ben approaches all media and technology with a point of view, methodology, and palette that is Afro-diasporic and shaped by his experiences as an artist, ethnographer, technologist, and music lover who was raised in the American Southwest. He remains devoted to discovering how emerging technologies and media can communicate new registers of feeling, expression, and instrumentation and serve as tools to mentor, instruct, and support the artistic growth of others.

In 1984, Ben established **VIDEO 3333**, a community art and technology incubator, media education center, and screening and performance space that he later renamed **KAOS Network**. Located in a storefront in the southeast corner of Leimert Park Village and financed through teaching, grants, and independent commercial productions and events, KAOS Network is an axis for innovative artistic expression and technological creativity. It is a place where different genres of art, media, music, technology, philosophy, and culture converge.

This is most especially the case among local youth and young adults. The most well-known example is **Project Blowed**, a hip-hop open-mic workshop and performance collective. For this group and other creative syndicates, KAOS Network is a transformative space, what writer Lynell George described in a *Los Angeles Times* article as a "media-arts sanctuary." What these people admire most about Ben is his enduring openness to each new generation and their different and new modes of expression, art, and belonging. Inside KAOS Network, their cultures and creativity are treated with value and respect. They are also encouraged to celebrate their ancestors and understand the power of art and culture as instruments of empowerment and healing. Media arts and creative community, Ben often asserts, are intergenerational resources for imagination and collaboration, and furthermore are weapons and remedies for the souls and spirits of oppressive, war-torn societies. "Artists should have the same role in the community as doctors or lawyers," he insists. "They should be there on the street; you should be able to drop in and see them, interact with them."

KAOS Network's mission of using art, media, and culture as sources for community formation and healing extends a long and living tradition in Los Angeles, most centrally among its Black, Brown, and Asian American inhabitants. This

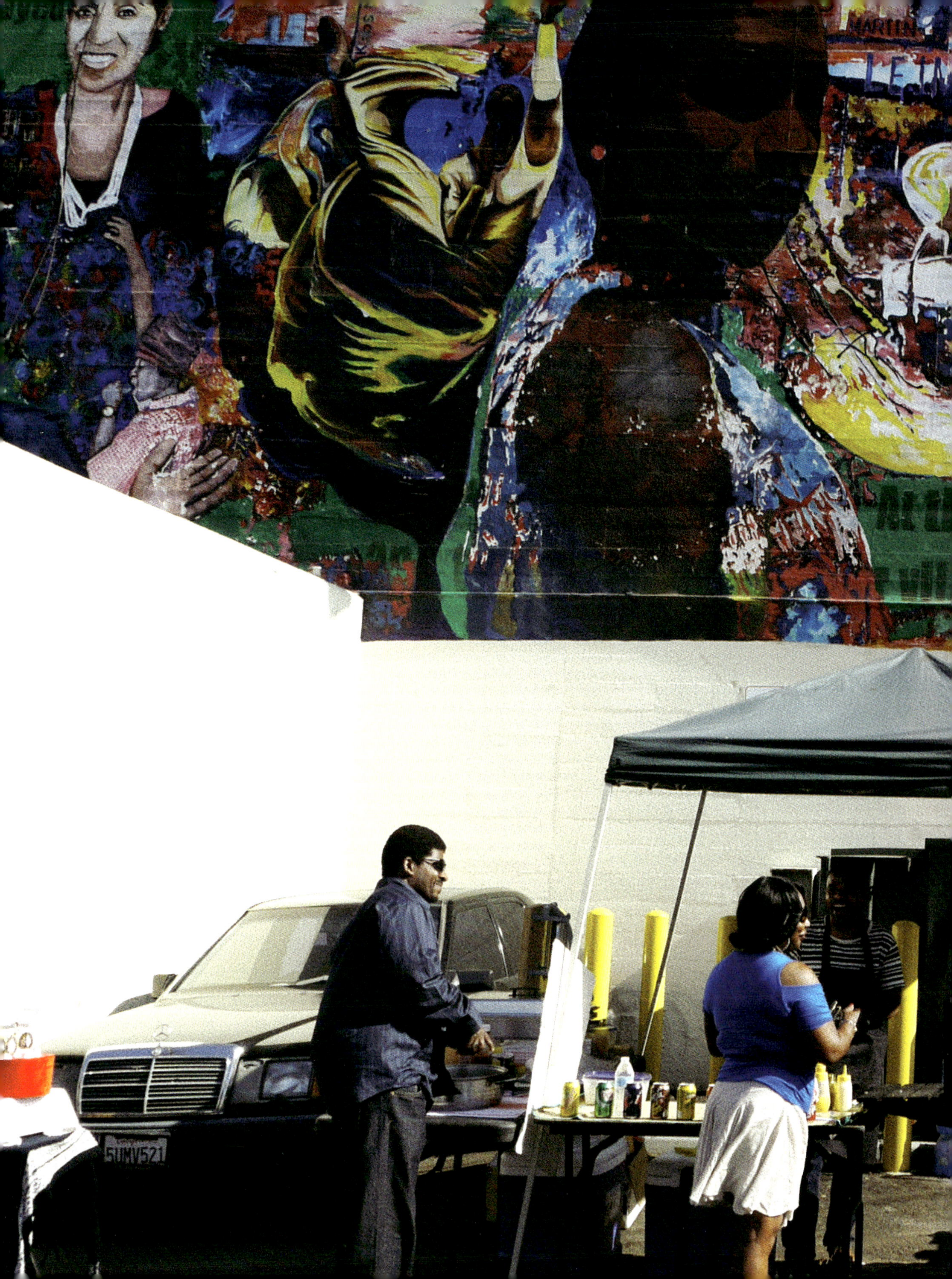

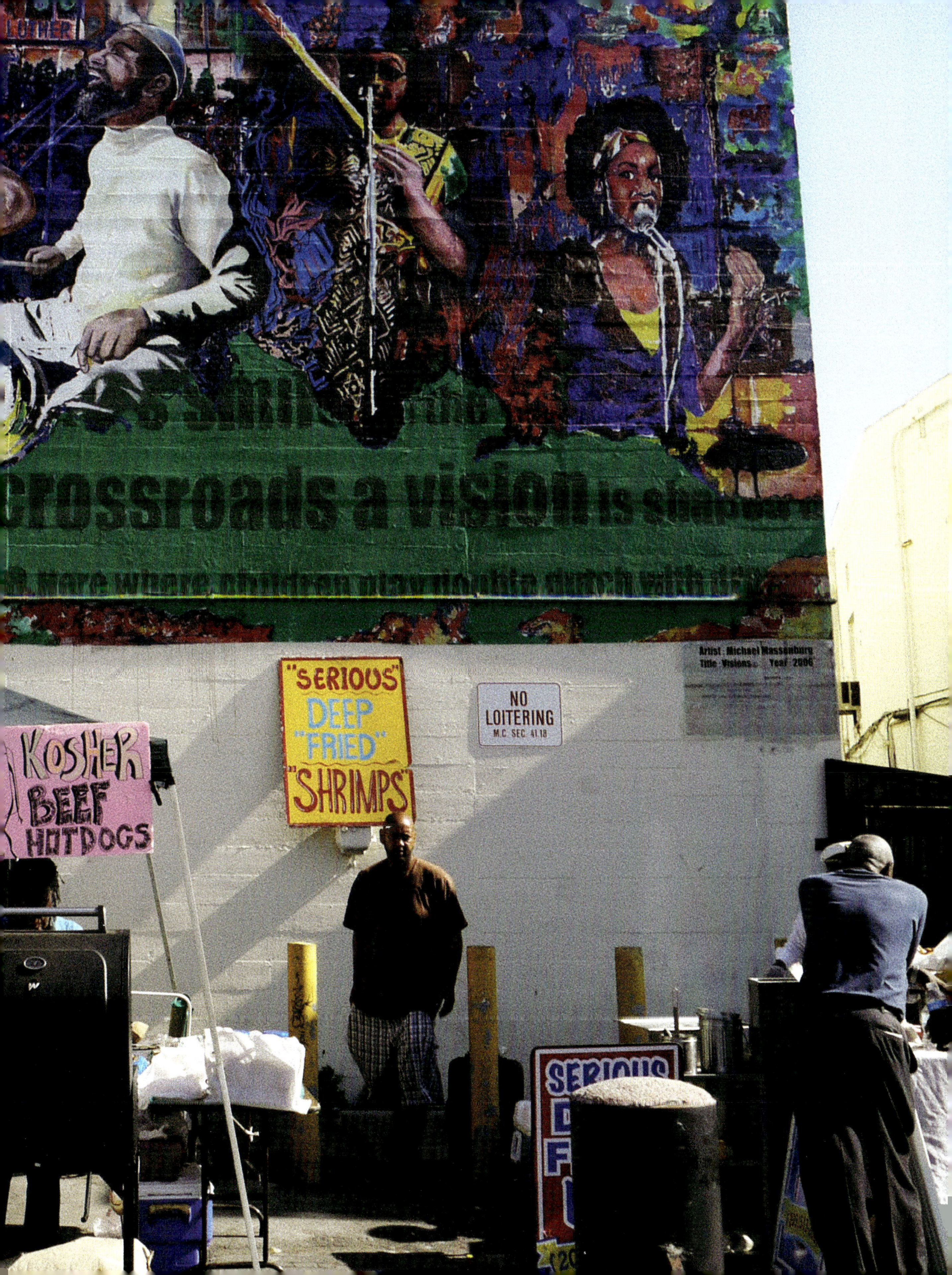
crossroads a vision is shaped
Artist : Michael Massenburg
Title : Visions Year : 2006
"SERIOUS"
DEEP
"FRIED"
"SHRIMPS"
NO LOITERING
M.C. SEC. 41.18
KOSHER BEEF HOTDOGS
SERIOUS

is a tradition devoted to the power and utility of art, media, and culture, and committed to empowering and training each new generation of artists to seize the means of art/media production and create works born of their own unique vision. "This is important to me," Ben explains, "to demonstrate and participate in a self-sustaining system for producing and distributing art, and one that prioritizes supporting and activating the community in which I reside."

Ben's use of media arts to stimulate healing and foster community is best understood as **KAOS theory**, a philosophy of life and creative exploration. Ben believes that there is no easy separation between life, art, and media. Human bodies can become mountains, there is movement in still images, walls can speak. He maintains that media and art at their highest forms are foregrounded by communally constituted ethics and ancestral systems of belief, knowing, and love. These are animated via inspired human expressive exercises and rituals that are utilitarian, imaginative, inventive, and improvisatory, and which echo and reveal the dynamism, dissonance, and truths of physical, ecological, ancestral, and cosmic worlds. They prompt individual and collective searching and experimentation. And they embolden people to develop malleable capacities of navigating existence and open themselves to wide spectrums of being, perception, sensation, cognition, communication, and becoming.

For Ben, art and artistry are not tethered to the created object or final product. Instead, the actual work of art is in the creative act itself; that is the power of wielding art as a social force. Art, he maintains, is capable of more than just representing and creating an impression of life experience and an artist's emotional state. *It has the ability to produce new social relations among people and activate their desire and will to change the conditions of their lives—to struggle for a different reality and work to transform it.* And in Ben's view, there is no art or media more powerful than that produced in and with community. Overemphasis on the master work (what is conventionally described as "the masterpiece") and the artist as a master worker or savant downplay the spaces where art and a creative mindset are nurtured and nourished. These are social spaces that in the best circumstances serve as convivial sites of co-creation; places where everyone involved is encouraged to play and listen to one another and to themselves, and where everyone experiences sensations of fulfillment, joy, connection, and healing—where everyone is made better. It is for this reason that Ben's artistic practice has gone beyond just making films and media art, and has been centered around mentoring and instructing people to be their own artists. The creative act, then, refers to this magical process of bearing witness to the world and using art, media, and creative expression to change the world and people's experiences in it.

Ben's ideas about the higher power and purpose of art and media intersect with writer adrienne maree brown's concepts of emergence and emergent strategy. Emergence, brown explains, is an "adaptive, relational way of being" that "see[s] the world in life-code—awakening us to the sacred systems of life all around us," and which aspires to "apply the brilliance of the world around us to our efforts to coexist in and with this world as humans ... to turn our legacy towards harmony." This idea reverberates in much of what Ben says, does, and creates. It is his conviction that artistic and creative exploration is a process of unfolding, whereby the mysteries of the unknown, unseen, and unheard are made vibrant. People stretch themselves, their imaginations, and their relations with other humans and forms of life. And in so doing, new possibilities of inhabiting and interacting and coexisting and loving are revealed. This is what we refer to in this book as *the ark*—the emergent strategies and practices of endurance and imagination and love that are central to our lives.

> ***Ark: a vessel or sanctuary that serves as protection against extinction.***

In Judeo-Christian traditions, "ark" refers to the ship built by Noah to save his family and two of every kind of animal from the Flood. The term is now commonly used to signify the beliefs, resources, and traditions a person mobilizes to sustain themselves and endure. In Los Angeles and other places, the term also serves as a shorthand for Black community-centered practices of music and performance, as well as for Pan-African and Afro-speculative notions of history, diasporic community, and alternate realities. Myth and science fiction have played a significant role in this, where the ark has periodically come to symbolize spaceships, intergalactic exploration, time travel, technology, and creative searching, experimentation, and self-realization. Several of the prime articulators of this have been musicians. Sun Ra's Arkestra. Horace Tapscott and the Pan Afrikan People's Arkestra (who are more commonly known as "the Ark"). Lee Scratch Perry's Black Ark recording studio. Parliament-Funkadelic's P-Funk Mothership. Janelle Monae's *The ArchAndroid*.

Our notion of "ark" extends on this tradition. But it also works as a double entendre for that of an "arc." This word, too, is helpful in framing Ben's creative life.

> ***Arc: a part of the circumference of a circle or other curve; a curved shape, or something shaped like a curve; a curving trajectory; to move with a curving trajectory; a luminous electrical discharge between two electrodes or other points; (in a novel, play, or movie) the development or resolution of the narrative or principal theme.***

Ben's friends and family say that his true artistry lies in his capacity to spark connections between people and different systems of thought, aesthetics, and culture. They describe him as a "consummate connector," "a human Internet ... a network of human connections," and colloquially as the plug—an electric arc personified where different energies collide, converge, and discharge currents of high density and voltage.

This book explores the ark and arc of Ben's creative life—the forces, belief systems, cultural practices, and people that have shaped and sustained him (ark);

the historical bend of cultural networks and traditions of which he is a connective part and to which he has served as an electric spark, caretaker, and custodian (arc).

"I want to start at the point when I first had thought, but no words to describe it," Ben explains, "Waaaaahhhhh [he breathes with a sound mimicking the wind]. So, the next step is to really describe something that might be fictional . . . to try to find a way to describe the un-wooordly [stretches the word] descriptions of the world before we are cognizant of how to speak."

As Ben relays above, to appreciate his experience and that of the other people who have contributed to KAOS Network requires more than words, more than just sifting through celluloid film and videotape, multiple exposures and slides, digital files and manila folders. It is to orbit around satellites, frequencies, spectrums, and collages of information, wisdom, memory, and imagination. It is to be migration, wind, breath, atmosphere.

So, fasten your seatbelt for a journey through this cross-cutting elsewhere. Keep in mind that our starting coordinates begin not with Ben, but with the village communities of his ancestors. After that, we will make pit stops within a constellation of villages, historical settings, and circuits of community. At each stop are stories of outlaw-creative-cooperative efforts for survival, inspiration, and emergence. And in each story space, and place matter to a great extent.

Our goal is not to fossilize and freeze in time and space these places of origin, migration, and arrival, but rather to embrace them as intertwined and in correspondence. We insist that there are dynamics of movement and connection across these spaces and places—a parallelism that complicates prevailing narratives of the American Southwest and twentieth-century Black American life. "I was raised in New Mexico. My family was a migrant family, so we had a lot of Southern roots. And then we also had a lot of the Voodoo [Vodun] things that [were] passed down through the South by way of Texas," Ben explained in a 1979 cable television news program. "I don't know what that has to do with giving me a historical perspective, but that's the thing that got me involved in wanting to discover what specifically makes us tick as Black people, you know?" Ultimately, this book privileges space and place as conduits for understanding creative acts of artistic expression, community formation, and the making and remixing of environment, physical space, and human relations—i.e., the creative acts of placemaking and place-stewarding.

You should be warned, this book has an unconventional format and irregular narrative rhythm that may differ from historical texts, artist retrospectives, biographies, and community organization histories that you've experienced before. Like Ben's films, this book's unexpected ruptures and mixtures require you to suspend your expectations and learn from what happens when they are disrupted.

Narrative history, archival materials, ephemera, visual art, Internet-linked digital media, and poetic-proverbs are our storytelling instruments. With these materials, we compose the narrative-collage-media-map that is in your possession. We desire for the book's different elements to be experienced not as supplements to the narrative, but as vital to its constitution. These materials play an essential role in communicating the depths of the KAOS Network collective's thinking, experiences, and unique forms of interaction and collaboration. They, furthermore, augment our attempt to enact the artistic and ideological project that we envision within this book. Via both its form and content, this book is offered to you as a work of art, remembrance, and tribute—a volume of imagination and ancestral homage that may ask a lot of some readers, but will hopefully inspire new ways of knowing, thinking, reading, listening, experiencing, and creating.

What is KAOS? It refers to the dynamic and disordered—yet interconnected, imbricated, and spiraling—cycles of coexistence, healing, and emergence that are ever-present in Ben's life and that of other people. Of the parts that don't comprise the whole, but which twist, rub against, and blur into one another to fashion unique bends, ripples, bulges, swells, arches. It is, moreover, a framework—albeit a critically masculine one—for the ancestral and cosmic strategies of living, volition, struggle, and loving that this group of alchemist-sentinels have conjured and deciphered. All while navigating the catastrophe of global racial capitalism and Euro-American empire, as well as the universe's chaotic forms and storms of change. KAOS is a reminder that enveloping many expressive cultures and formations of community and family are patterns of love, kinship, and stewardship.

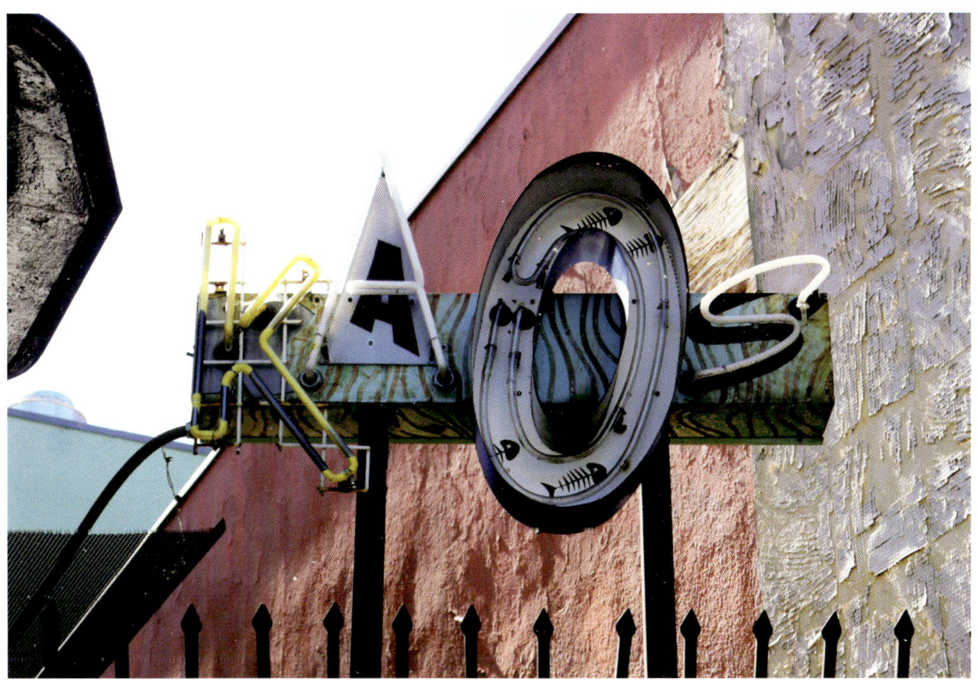

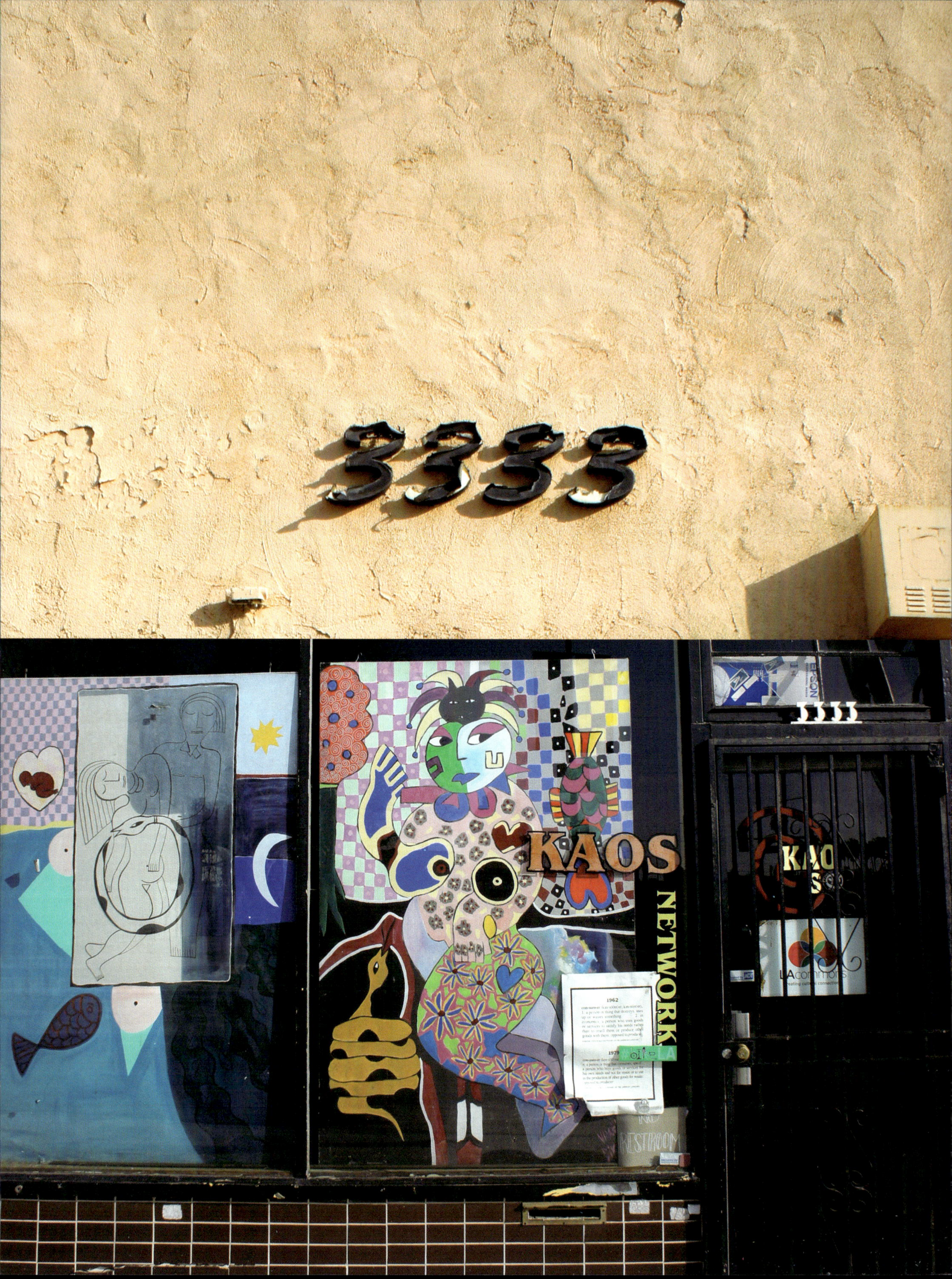

3333
KAOS
NETWORK
KAOS
LAcommons
RESTROOM

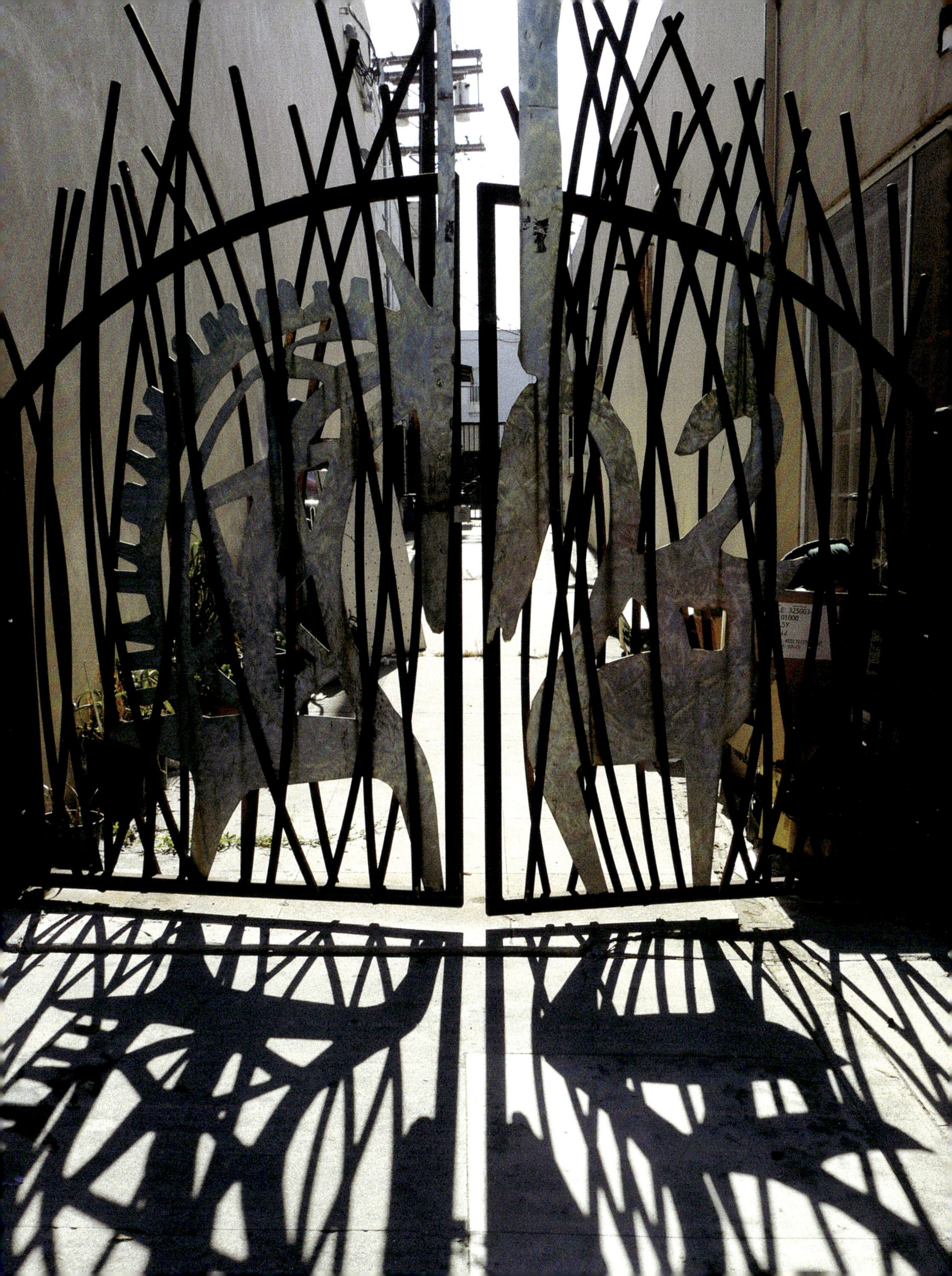

cha· os
/ kā äs/
noun
1.	A state of extreme confusion and disorder; (late 15th century) denoting a gaping void or chasm, later formless primordial matter via French and Latin from Greek khaos 'vast chasm, void'
2.	(Physics) A dynamical system that is extremely sensitive to its initial conditions
3.	(Greek mythology) The most ancient of gods: the first created being, from which came the primeval deities Gaia, Tartarus, Erebus, and Nyx
4.	The formless and disordered state of matter before the creation of the cosmos; the personification of the infinity of space preceding creation of the universe

NEW MEXICO

STATE OF MIND

*Laying on the earth—
dreaming.*

*The ground beneath,
adjacent, around.*

*Staring up at the sky
at night.*

*Your eyes adjust.
Counting stars.*

*The starlight are like
laser beams that touch every
one of your body microbes.*

*There's a star for every
cell in your body.*

*And it's talking
to you.*

*The feeling
of being propelled
through space.*

*And you're stuck on
this massive ball that's
moving a million miles an
hour, and we're playing like
it isn't. It's spinning and
rotating at a speed that's
unbelievable but we're
making our minds feel like
it isn't.*

*Is it really real?
This is an interesting
thing.*

*The preverbal,
prewritten, un-sense of what
space is like, since you don't
have a sense of what it is
supposed to be.*

*You haven't been
taught it yet.*

*Maybe what we see is
the world in the way that it
really is.*

*That there is a lot of
trans-movement like an
ocean out there in front of us,
and around us.*

*And that's what this
whole ball is being propelled
through.*

*And as we pass minds,
bodies—it has the swish
effect.*

*Like a car passing
another. Sometimes it's like
a jet-plane.*

*Another time it's like a
fish moving slowly.*

*But there's still that
movement.*

*And that movement
engages your body, because
your body is moving in a kind
of dynamic movement too.*

*Your body is
very similar to the space,*

*And the space
is very similar to your body.*

*And all these people
are synchronous with that.*

*And the whole job
when you start growing up as
a kid is to accentuate those
feelings, intuitions, ways of
seeing:*

*Into what breaks down
to the commonalities of
culture.*

*And that really leads us
to New Mexico.*

*—Ben Caldwell
"Input 2.STE-066"*

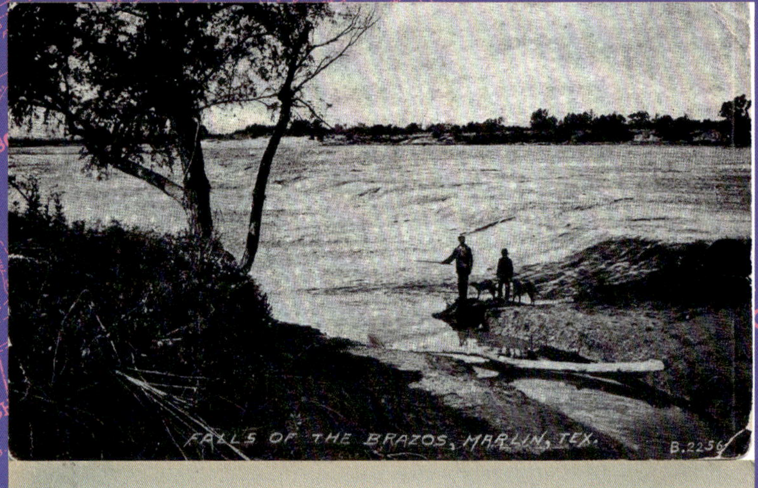

CHAPTER 1

Falls of the Brazos, Marlin, Tex.

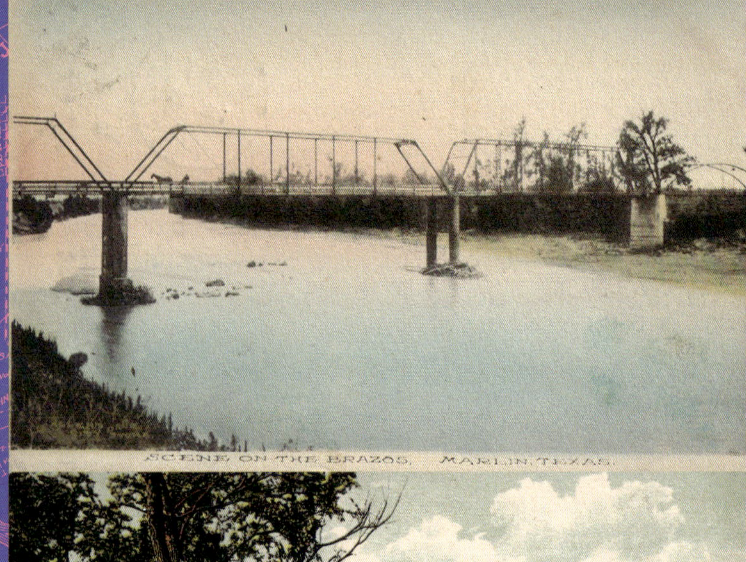

Scene on the Brazos, Marlin, Texas.

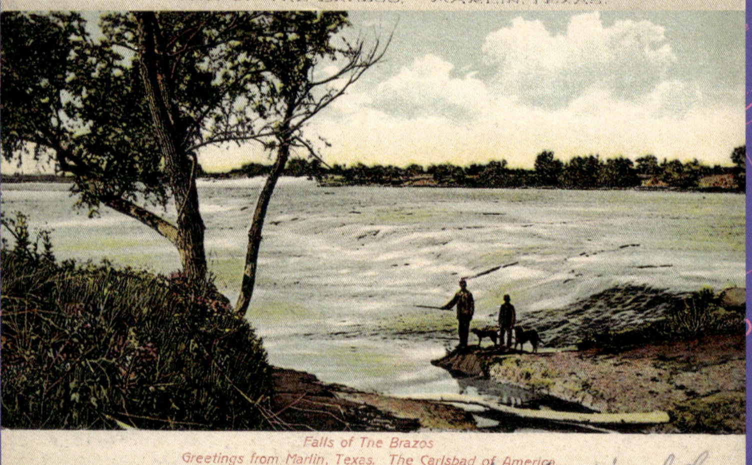

Falls of The Brazos
Greetings from Marlin, Texas. The Carlsbad of America.

TULLI HOPPIN'

Before Ben there was Mamie. And long before Ben and Mamie there was John.

Texan, son of sharecroppers. A forty-year-old migrant farmer and laborer who, in the spring months of 1942, found himself standing in southwest New Mexico, staring at the Mimbres River.

John's first impression of the river was that it was nothing spectacular. A dry stream cutting through chaparral, split by underground stems and roots.

Yet he did not take the Mimbres River's appearance for granted. He knew that rivers could seem tranquil and serene and then, without warning, decimate and overpower.

He was also enchanted by all that surrounded the river. Yuccas, mesquite bushes with their sweet hanging fruit, and on the ground a patch of goat head plants with yellow flowers and intimidating thorns. As he looked around him, he saw tumbleweeds running across the horizon and jackrabbits darting in and out of the bushes.

He was raised along the Brazos—Texas's longest river. It stretched from New Mexico's border through Texas and emptied into the Gulf of Mexico at Freeport. It was near this river that John learned to fish, farm, write, and read; where he and other children climbed maple and ash trees, hopped, ran, and tooled around through fields of bluestem, prairie grass, and wildrye. This was where his parents and the county's first generation of free Black men and women attended church and made a life. *Los Brazos de Dios*—the river of heavy tangles of vines and undergrowth, guarded by oak and cedar elm.

Highbank, John's hometown, owed its name to the Brazos. The small farming village that locals nicknamed "Brazos's Bottom" was developed in the mid-to-late nineteenth century just east of the Brazos's high banks. Taylor and Charity Waits, John's parents, migrated to this town located in the southeastern quadrant of Falls County, Texas, just after the end of the American Civil War.

Up until the late 1820s, Wacos, Tawakonis, Anadarkos, Comanches, and later Cherokees inhabited the area. Anglo and Hispano invasion and encroachment propelled the tribes into violent struggles with one another and with the influx of Euro-American slaveholders and poorer white settlers who came to the region seeking to seize and exploit its most abundant natural resource: uncultivated nutrient-rich, waxy soil. To execute this illicit land grab, these white people forged a cross-class alliance and waged a crusade of murder, terror, and dispossession against the indigenous communities. Those who survived the genocide and plunder were forcibly removed to Oklahoma and other states, or compelled to assimilate into the white settler communities that christened the area as "Falls County" after the United States's victory in the Mexican-American War.

Taylor Waits came to Falls County sometime between 1866 and 1869. The sapwood-complexioned preteen traveled there with his mother, Dina; elder siblings Albert and Louis; younger siblings Dora, William, and Drayton; Cesar, Dina's husband; and the family's former enslavers, Samuel J. and Senia Waite. At the time, Taylor and his family's last name was Waite, not Waits. With the abolition of slavery, the newly freed family had opted to use their former enslavers' surname.

Taylor was born in 1856 in Scott County, Mississippi. He was one of sixteen persons enslaved by Edmund and Phanuel Waite, Samuel Waite's parents. The Waite family had built their wealth through landholding, cotton-farming, and slaveholding, first in Alabama and later in Mississippi. On the Waite farm, Taylor and the other enslaved people picked cotton and tended to hogs, chickens, and other livestock. Taylor, like his mother, Dina, was mixed-raced, a distinction that clearly caught the eye of several census-takers who, during his adult years, listed him and several of his children as "mulatto."

When Edmund Waite died in 1861, Samuel inherited his father's estate. This included Taylor's family. The heir's stretch as a slave-owner, though, was short-lived. After a brief and humiliating stint in the Confederate Army's Mississippi Volunteers Infantry, and amid Union forces beginning to occupy the South, Samuel and Senia Waite fled to Texas with their family. With the Confederacy's defeat on the horizon, Texas offered slaveholding families like the Waites the possibility of rebuilding their wealth via cheap, abundant land and a social and economic environment committed to the continued exploitation of poor people and Black labor.

Thus, although legally "free" at the end of the Civil War, Taylor's family was coerced to join the Waites on their westward journey and resume working for their former owners. Their freedom was severely constrained by the 1866 Black Codes, a series of laws that restricted the freedom of ex-slaves and free Blacks to move, own land, marry, and bear arms. For Taylor, the most impactful of these laws was that of "apprenticeship." It enabled the Waites to retain control of Taylor and all their other former slaves under the age of twenty-one, under the pretext that this group required guardianship until they reached an adult age. Dina consequently served as a domestic worker inside the Waite household, while Taylor, Albert, Louis, and Cesar worked outdoors tilling the land, handling the livestock, and making repairs.

On his twenty-first birthday, Taylor left the Waite household. He worked first for a local blacksmith, learning how to forge and weld iron, steel, and other metals into gates, tools, furniture, weapons, and other objects. Once he earned enough money, he married Charity Stuard, a Black woman and former slave whose family, like Taylor's, had migrated to Texas from Mississippi.

Over the next forty years, the couple conceived and raised ten children. Charity delivered their ninth child, John Thomas, on Thursday, April 11, 1901.

In the years that followed, they nurtured their brood. These were not easy times, and they struggled. But they worked to set a solid foundation for their children. And they relinquished the last name of Taylor's former enslavers, "Waite," simplifying it to "Waits." Besides its true-to-life, sobering meaning, "Charity Waits" had a crisper, more resounding ring to it.

Falls County's economy was centered around raising livestock, especially cattle, and agricultural production, predominantly cotton, wool, corn, and sugarcane. The Waits family was in a similar predicament as most Black residents—they were cotton farmers who tilled land they did not own. They were part of a mass of tenant farmers and sharecroppers who either paid rent to a landowner for a house and farmland, which they then used to farm the crops of their choice, or farmed a landowner's selected crops in exchange for lodging and a share of what they raised. It was an exploitative arrangement that perpetuated Black poverty and dependence on an colonial labor system undergirded by instability, inequality, and racial violence and oppression.

The Waitses worshiped at **Zion Rock Baptist Church**. John and his siblings detested Zion Rock's sweltering heat; the space at midday felt more like David's oven than his hill. But they loved the spectacle of service: parishioners' swaying torsos and resounding stomps; the onlookers squeezed between doorways and windows, transfixed and raptured by the Holy Word; the believers lost in prayer and devotion who were called upon to testify to His power; the congregants assembled at "Corner Hole" to witness Pastor Reverend P. Williams baptize the flock; the ringing of the church tower's bell to broadcast a churchgoer's transition into the ancestral world. There was survival and community-building in these different rituals of fellowship and faith. The cumulative effect was a sensation of collective autonomy, self-determination, and sanctitude—a feeling of fantastic, celestial protection and purpose that lifted both worshippers and God's temple above the Brazos's waters and surrounding fields.

Zion Rock also helped its congregants anchor and steer themselves through the white man's abyss of humiliation, abuse, and violence. In Falls County, and throughout Texas, acts of barbarity and terror at the hands of white armed patrols, vigilance committees, disgruntled white mobs, and white citizens took different forms: public execution, lynching, race riots, home bombings, the shooting down of people attempting to vote. Sometimes this viciousness could appear random and precipitated by little to nothing. But it was systematic and systemic, a fundamental weapon of ensuring white advantage and Black deprivation.

Amid this, the Waitses guided their children and instilled in them faith in higher, otherworldly possibilities. John's childhood was filled with deep-blue skies, powerful wind, and days spent sprinting through stalks of corn, hunting for possums and wild rabbits, combing through orchards for pecans.

As a teen and young man, he enjoyed venturing to Wood Street, a one-block red-light district in Marlin, the county's administrative center and largest city. There, he and his brother Charlie would listen to the live performances of Henry "Ragtime Texas" Thomas, Huddie "Lead Belly" Ledbetter, Blind Lemon Jefferson, Willie Johnson, and Sam "Lightnin'" Hopkins. On songs like "Ain't No More Cane on the Brazos," these singers exchanged memories and tales about their people's hard times in the cane and cotton fields just a short distance away:

> *Ain't no more cane on the Brazos, oh, oh, oh*
> *They done ground it all into molasses, oh, oh, oh*
> *Oughta come on the river in 1904*
> *You could find a dead man on every turn row.*
> *Oughta come on the river in 1910*
> *They was driving the poor women just like the men.*

Songs like this were part of a work-song tradition created by Black inmates serving time in Texas prisons. The prisoners worked on chain gangs that were leased out to public construction projects and crop plantations along the Brazos River. To manage time and ensure the consistency of each person's labor and participation, the inmates cultivated and improvised songs that were incorporated into their work—songs whose rhythm, cadence, repetitive nature, and percussive organization provided a metered pattern and pacing for singing and working. So, while the message of the songs was significant—and often veiled and disguised— what was also essential were the songs' participatory and metered foundation. Keeping time, or better put, *keeping in time* with the labor of those around you, and working well together, was a vital, though not singular, aspect of the prisoners' music.

When performed by Wood Street's musicians and singers, inmate songs like "Ain't No More Cane on the Brazos" and "Go Down, Old Hannah" were reminders of several things: That the condition and fate of the Black prisoner was an extension of that of the enslaved African in the Americas. That the state of U.S. Black life post-Reconstruction was not that far off or dissimilar to that of the antebellum period. And of Black people's continued vulnerability in a societal (dis)order not of their making.

But this was not all. The music was also evidence that these people had endured and could sporadically transcend the white man's stormy and overwhelming yank. Hence, while the songs aired the folks' dreadful, still undetermined, situation in this country, the communal fellowship and connection the music fostered, along with the inner momentum and conviction and cunning they transmitted, communicated something else. It was the expression of a collective inner drive and an ancestral Eden; a cosmic pulse of other worlds and a people's utilitarian and wondrous efforts to beam their minds and carry bodies there.

John's love for baseball, most especially his skill as a pitcher, enabled him to actualize how the music made him feel. There were several things he admired about pitching: the poise and grit required of good pitchers on the mound; the mysterious communication that occurred between pitchers, catchers, and basemen; and the skill required to correctly read and respond to the body language of batters and players on base. What he revered most was that when the game

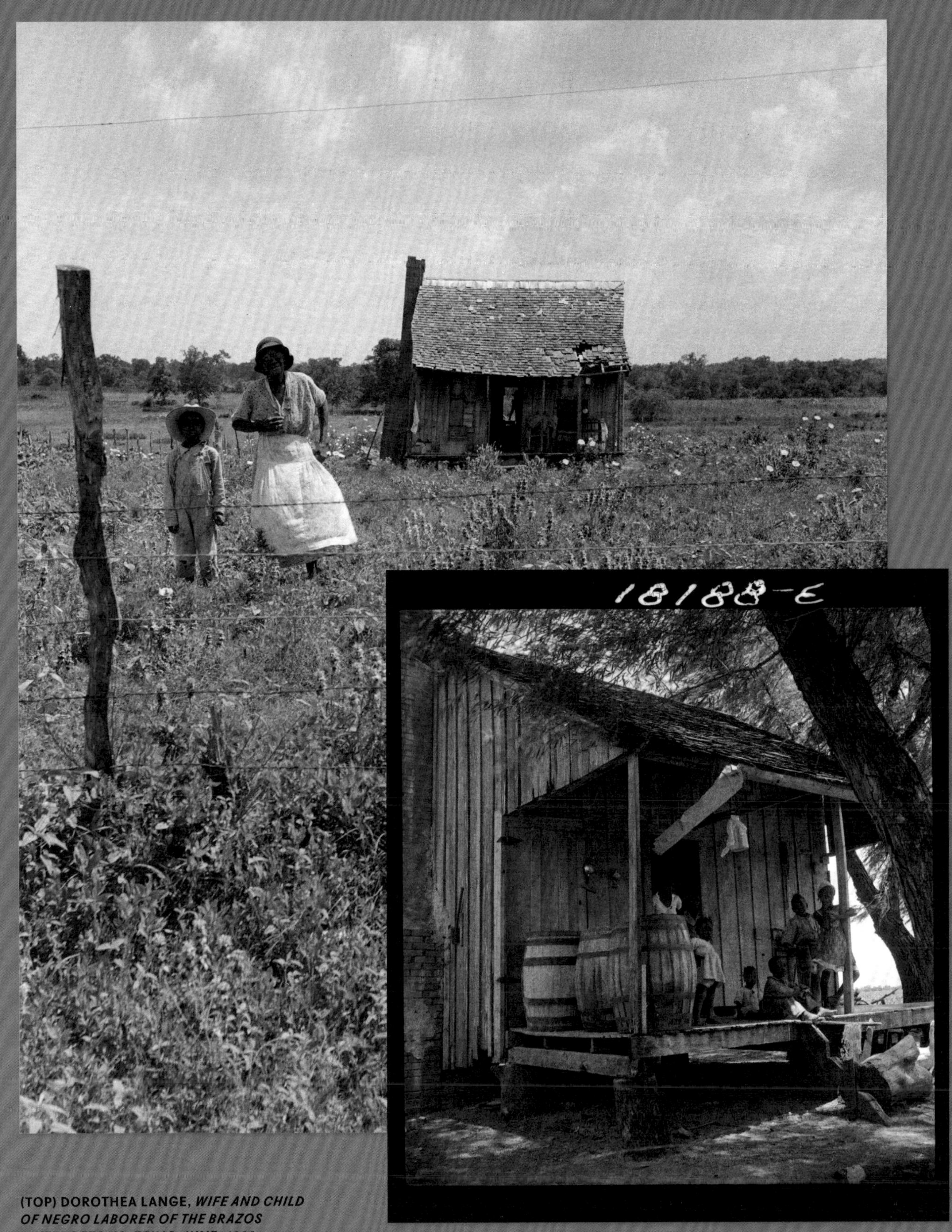

(TOP) DOROTHEA LANGE, *WIFE AND CHILD OF NEGRO LABORER OF THE BRAZOS RIVERBOTTOMS, TEXAS,* JUNE, 1938
(BOTTOM) DOROTHEA LANGE, *WATER BARRELS ON PLANTATION CABIN IN BRAZOS RIVERBOTTOMS,* JUNE 1938

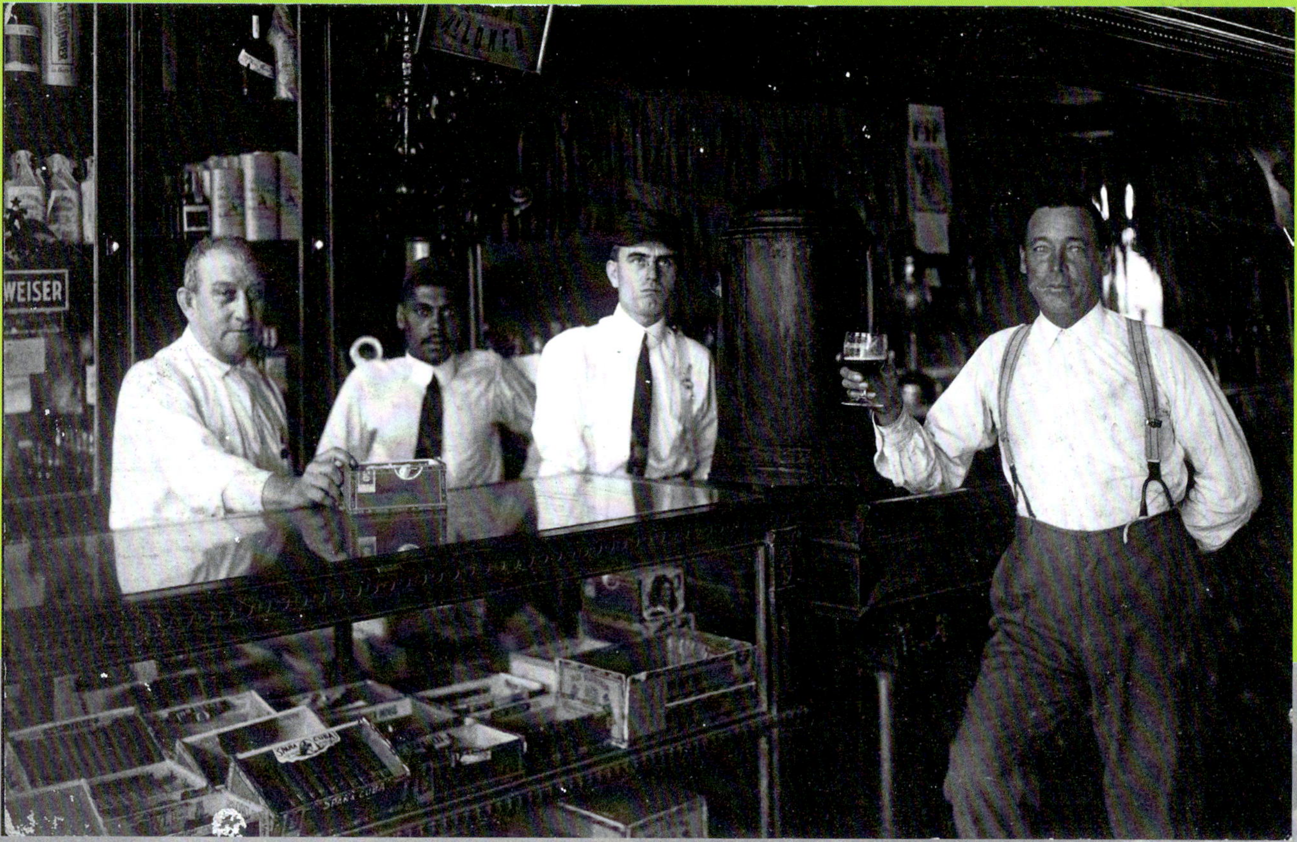

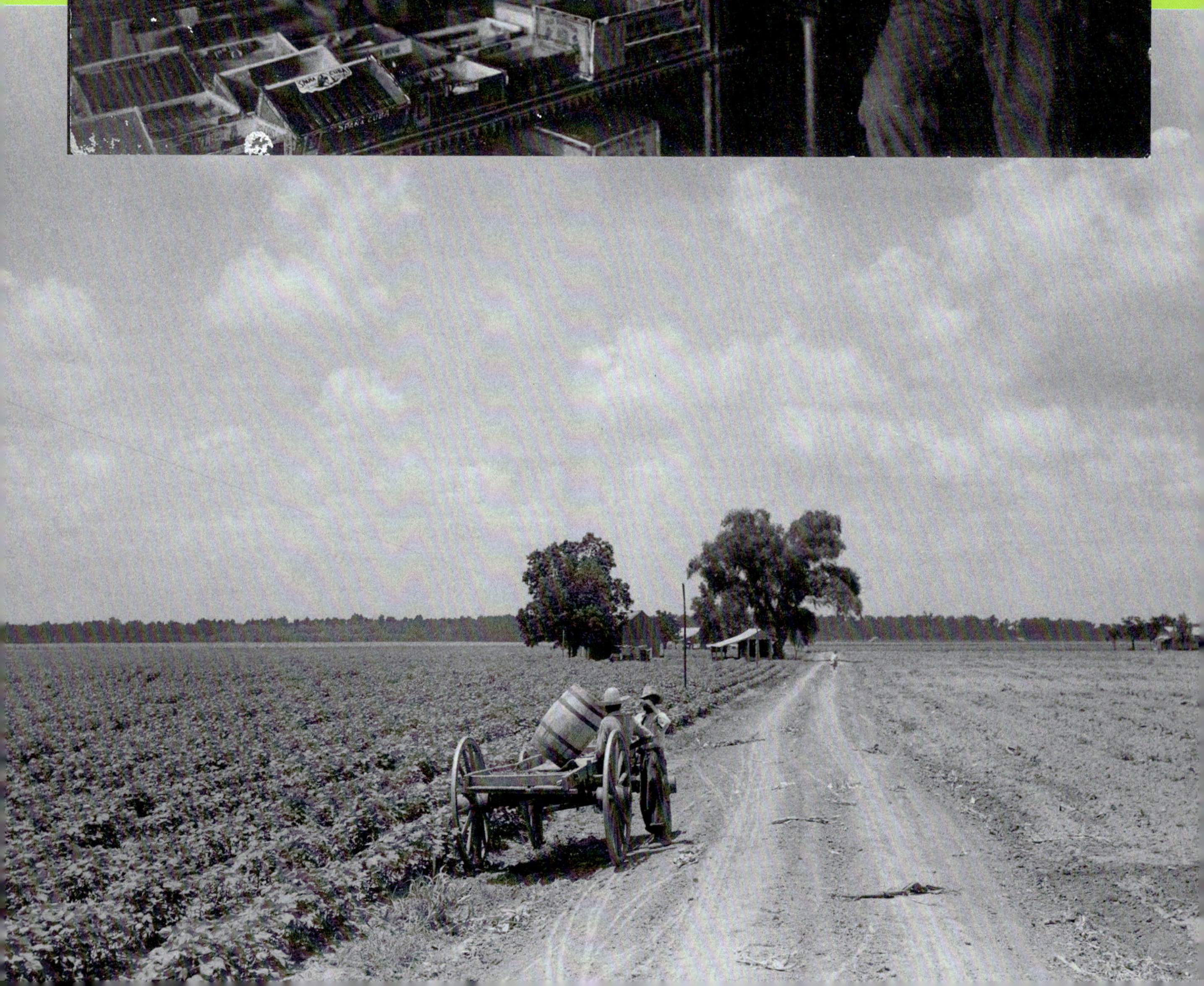

slowed down, it was the pitcher who stood center stage, who initiated the game's choreography, its art of *keeping in time and space*. Great pitching required an intimacy with one's environment and surroundings and with human actions and reactions. These were key elements in a pitcher's ability to forecast what was to come. To understand and capitalize on the game's ebbs and flows called for a spiritual relationship to the game and everything that exceeded the game. Then you harnessed that into an outdoor exercise that was a mixture of exhibition, play, strategy, and fortune.

Baseball was big in Falls County. For years, Marlin, the county's largest city, hosted several major league teams' spring training camps. And by John's teenage years, the city had its own minor league team. He dreamed of being a world-class professional ballplayer for these teams, but Black men were excluded from the leagues. When a minor league for Black Texan men was finally established in 1919, it was too late. By then he had thrown his arm out, an injury that ended his baseball ambitions.

John farmed, sometimes traveling as far as Oklahoma for seasonal jobs. Throughout the 1920s, he and other workers weathered the storm of boll weevils, the infamous migratory snout beetle from Veracruz, Central Mexico, that laid havoc to cotton plants, buds, and bolls (along with millions of dollars of revenue) throughout the U.S. South and Southwest. The bug made quite an impression; in songs and wisecracks, workers joked about the beetle's resilience:

> *The boll weevil is a lil' bug, from Mexico, they say,*
> *He come try this Texas soil, and think he better stay*
> *Looking for a home—just looking for a home.*
> *The farmer took the boll weevil and put him in the sand,*
> *Boll weevil said to farmer, I'll stand it like a man,*
> *For it's just my home—it's just my home.*
> *First time I see de weevil, he on the eastern train,*
> *Next time I see de weevil, he on the Memphis train,*
> *Looking for a home—just looking for a home.*

That the song offered an extension of grace for this otherwise destructive creature is noteworthy. Black workers, likewise, could relate to the beetle's search for belonging. They could empathize with its undignified portrayal. They, too, knew the feeling of having to shoulder the blame for catastrophes not of their making.

Some even speculated that the planter elite was to blame for the beetle's devastation. In a 1930s Works Progress Administration (WPA) interview, John Love, a formerly enslaved man who became one of Highbank's first mail carriers, reasoned that in preparing the land for harvesting, cotton planters killed off various beetle-eating bug species. Love maintained that the planters had thus tilted the ecosystem away from its natural state of coexistence and juxtaposition:

I know why that boll-weevil came. They say he comes from Mexico, but I think he's always been here. Away back yonder a spider lived in the country, especially in the [Brazos] Bottoms. He lived on the cotton leaves and stalks, but he didn't hurt it. These spiders ate up all the insects. When they [the farmers] didn't plow deep and planted cotton in February, it made it bad for the insects. Then when they [the farmers] got to plowing deep, and it was colder and the trees were all cut, they plowed up all the spiders and the cold killed them [the spiders]. When they [the farmers] planted later, there weren't any spiders left to eat up the boll-weevil.

Love may have not been wrong. But what he and his farming peers were also experiencing was the beginning of a tectonic economic and cultural shift that was altering the landscape of Southern cotton farming. A mix of factors was creating new challenges for cotton farmers: altering power dynamics among the planter class, crop overproduction, falling prices, cotton plant breeders' development of hybrid varieties and increasing use of pesticides, the rising tide of mechanical harvesting, and the ascension of nylon and other man-made fibers as alternative fabrics for clothing.

At 141 pounds and just over five-foot-five, Waits was perceived as scrappy and serious among the farmers. But the gray-eyed, reddish-brown-haired young man was also charming. Or so thought the teenage Roselia Martin when she first spotted him.

She had grown up in Marlin, the third of seven children. The fifteen-year-old's life, however, changed drastically after she learned that she was pregnant with the child of Donnie Moody, a young man from nearby Bremond. Their relationship was short-lived, dissolving not too long after their daughter Mamie's birth in January of 1928.

John swiftly stepped in to provide Roselia and her infant with emotional and monetary support. Moreover, by Mamie's first birthday, she and her mother had moved in with him.

With time, John became the most reliable presence in the little girl's life. It was for this reason that Mamie bestowed him with the title of "Daddy" and later just "Dad." She also took his last name and middle initial as her own. Decades later, when anyone asked about her middle name and what the "T" stood for, Mamie's reply was simple: "Nothin'. Just 'T.'"

To support his newly formed family, John continued to pick cotton and sugarcane while also breaking horses, herding cattle, and doing odd jobs. But the 1929 stock market crash and subsequent worldwide economic depression hit Highbank hard. Falls County's total number of farms, as well as the total value produced by farms, dropped. With it went cotton's value, which decreased by fifty-seven percent. Hog, cattle, and sheep farms saw growth, but livestock was an industry that did not require significant masses of workers. And as jobs and crop production decreased, so too did the county's population, the first decline since its formation.

As the economy worsened, Roselia and John's relationship began to crumble. She cared for him but was not looking to be anyone's housewife or old lady. She was irked by a nagging feeling that her joy, pleasure, and dreams were being interrupted by the needs of others. She was barely twenty years old, yet she had promised her life away.

The breaking point came in 1936. Early in the year, over the course of one day, a massive fire burned down most of Highbank's business district. Then in September, a tropical storm roared through the region—the second major one within a span of two months.

It had formed in Mexico's Bay of Campeche. Within days, the storm made its way into Texas, the rainfall becoming widespread over the southern and central regions of the state. Portions of central Texas were hit hard, especially the Brazos River and Highbank.

Torrential downpour filled the Brazos to record levels, eventually cresting at forty-one feet. In nearby Waco, just forty-five miles north of Highbank, the surging river overflowed East Waco's banks, bursting through a levee and flooding the city, resulting in $1.5 million worth of property damage and leaving two thousand residents homeless.

While the structural devastation in Highbank wasn't nearly as bad, the storm's impact on the village's quality of life was more severe. Simply put, many of the businesses that survived the fire were wiped out by the storm. Decades later, resident Robert Falsone recalled, "The water was deep enough in front of the house for a motorboat . . . There were bales of ginned cotton . . . and displaced people spent the night sleeping on the bales."

Highbank never recovered. Neither did John and Roselia's relationship. Just after Mamie's eighth birthday, the couple decided to separate. John took full custody of Mamie. Roselia would visit her periodically, but the visits became less frequent after Roselia moved to Amarillo. Still, every Christmas, Roselia made it her mission to return to Highbank to see Mamie.

Tougher times followed. Farming jobs became so scarce that families took in lodgers or combined their households to compensate for loss of income. John and ten-year-old Mamie were one of these families. They moved into the household of Willie Lee and Prince Anna Carr and their three sons. John and Willie Lee supported the household with income earned from working with the WPA. They built roads, painted buildings, and performed other odd jobs. Prince Anna cared for the children and maintained their merged households.

Together, the Waitses and Carrs formed a unique family structure. Their decision was necessitated by the dire socioeconomic conditions that poor Black families were made to endure. Yet living together also provided both families with a kinship that linked the adults and children for the duration of their lives. Mamie and the Carr boys grew to view and treat one another as siblings. And Prince Anna, Willie Lee, and John formed a working and parenting triad.

Even amid their new household arrangement, things didn't improve significantly. Over the course of the mid-to-late 1930s, tragedy and death beset John and his new chosen family. In a span of three years, two of Willie Lee's brothers died—one from tuberculosis and the other killed in a knife attack. In 1938, Charity Waits, John's mother, passed away, followed months later by Mamie's birth father, Donnie Moody. One year later, John's family was again rocked by the sudden passing of his elder sister Earsie.

It was as if the boll weevil had descended again, the enormity of these accruing deaths compounded by the weltering hollowing out of Highbank—its main street vacant, its communal life emaciated.

Is there an elegy for a settlement's final gasp? Is there a requiem that commemorates the village's last breath before it joins the graveyard of drowned dark Brown towns? Is there an incantation that can raise the dead and their communal life?

For the Waits and Carr families, the signs were clear. In 1941, both families packed their belongings, loaded up a car, and joined the massive exodus of Black folk fleeing the South in pursuit of better employment opportunities, education, and quality of life. After months spent working seasonal jobs in central and western Texas and a brief period living out of their car, they secured permanent work in El Paso County with Frank and Ruth Brown Owen, one of the region's most prominent cotton-farming families. The work schedule was grueling: twelve hours per day, six days per week. Their family made a home in Canutillo, Texas, and built a community with other families there and in Fabens, a nearby town.

When John wasn't working, he took Mamie on daylong driving excursions. Sometimes they rode into El Paso. They would wander through the city, venturing across the bridge at Stanton Street, crossing the Rio Grande and U.S.-Mexico border into Ciudad Juárez. Other times, they drove northwest into New Mexico, then west along US 80, stopping for walks in Berino, Vado, and other near-empty ghost towns that reminded John of Highbank. It was during one of these excursions that John learned about work opportunities at an airfield just sixty miles west of Las Cruces. On a subsequent drive, he decided to visit the area. This is how he came upon New Mexico's Mimbres River.

Mamie took great delight in these drives and the stories her father shared, especially his tales about Highbank. He rarely said, "I love you." But his unceasing tenderness towards her conveyed his deep devotion. Her favorite moments were when they stopped the car for walks in the empty desert or prairie lands. Sometimes Prince Anna would collect different textures of soil and taste them, pointing out the soils' distinct and contrasting flavors. The Carr boys would search around for snake holes, lizards, scorpions, and rabbits. And occasionally, John would goad Mamie to run with him. Enveloped by New Mexico's open fields full of barbed wire, creosote bushes, yucca, and black grama grass, John chased the teenager. They laughed wildly as the day became evening, the sky shifting from cornflower to cobalt.

TEXAS STATE DEPARTMENT OF HEALTH
BUREAU OF VITAL STATISTICS
STANDARD CERTIFICATE OF BIRTH

B. O. V. S. FORM B

07300

2939

(1) PLACE OF BIRTH

County of *Falls* Registration District No. ______ File No. *249*

Register No. ______

City *Highbank* (No. ______ St., ______ Ward)

(2) FULL NAME OF CHILD *Mamie Moody* — If child is not yet named, make supplemental report, as directed.

(3) Sex of Child *girl*

(4) Twin, triplet, or other (To be answered in event of plural births)

(5) Number in order of birth

(6) Legitimate (Yes or No) *no*

(7) Date of Birth *Jan* (Month) *18* (Day) *1928* (Year)

FATHER	MOTHER
(8) FULL NAME *Donnie Moody*	(14) FULL MAIDEN NAME *Rosa Lee Martin*
(9) RESIDENCE Post Office Address *Highbank*	(15) RESIDENCE Post Office Address *Highbank*
(10) COLOR *Negro* (11) AGE AT LAST BIRTHDAY *22* (Years)	(16) COLOR *Negro* (17) AGE AT LAST BIRTHDAY *16* (Years)
(12) BIRTHPLACE *Bremond*	(18) BIRTHPLACE *Highbank*
(13) OCCUPATION *Farming*	(19) OCCUPATION *Farming*
(20) Number of children born to this mother, including present birth *1*	(21) Number of children of this mother now living *1*

(22) CERTIFICATE OF ATTENDING PHYSICIAN OR MIDWIFE*

I hereby certify that I attended the birth of this child, who was born alive ~~stillborn~~ at *1* A. M. on the date above stated

*When there was no attending physician or midwife, then the father, householder, etc., should make this return. A stillborn child is one that neither breathes nor shows other evidence of life after birth.

(Signature) *Lizzie Oliver* (Physician or Midwife)

Address *Highbank*

Give name added from a supplemental report ______, 192___

(23) Filed *July 16*, *1928* *Gertrude Ray* Registrar.

No. ______

8-128-200m

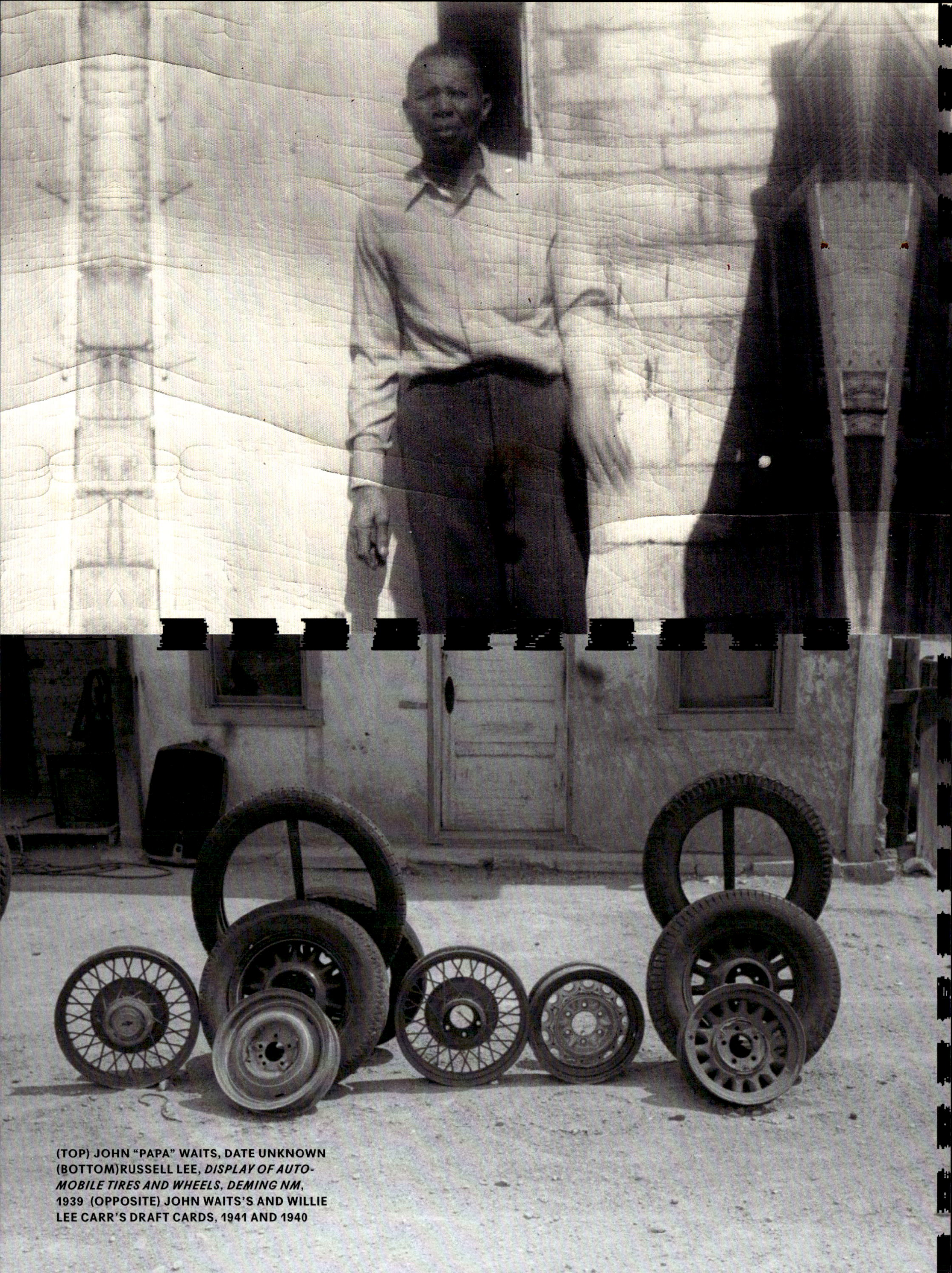

(TOP) JOHN "PAPA" WAITS, DATE UNKNOWN
(BOTTOM) RUSSELL LEE, *DISPLAY OF AUTO-
MOBILE TIRES AND WHEELS, DEMING NM*,
1939 (OPPOSITE) JOHN WAITS'S AND WILLIE
LEE CARR'S DRAFT CARDS, 1941 AND 1940

REGISTRATION CARD—(Men born on or after February 17, 1897 and on or before December 31, 1921)

SERIAL NUMBER	1. NAME (Print)			ORDER NUMBER
T 1671	JOHN (First)	THOMAS (Middle)	WAITS (Last)	T 11560

2. PLACE OF RESIDENCE (Print)

OWEN FARM (Number and street) — TORNILLO (Town, township, village, or city) — EL PASO (County) — TEXAS (State)

[THE PLACE OF RESIDENCE GIVEN ON THE LINE ABOVE WILL DETERMINE LOCAL BOARD JURISDICTION; LINE 2 OF REGISTRATION CERTIFICATE WILL BE IDENTICAL]

3. MAILING ADDRESS — SAME

[Mailing address if other than place indicated on line 2. If same insert word same]

4. TELEPHONE (Exchange) (Number)

5. AGE IN YEARS — 39

DATE OF BIRTH — APR. (Mo.) 11 (Day), 1902 (Yr.)

6. PLACE OF BIRTH — REAGAN (Town or county) — TEXAS (State or country)

7. NAME AND ADDRESS OF PERSON WHO WILL ALWAYS KNOW YOUR ADDRESS

WILLIE LEE CARR — TORNILLO, TEXAS — P.O. Box 65

8. EMPLOYER'S NAME AND ADDRESS

FRANK OWEN JR. TORNILLO, TEXAS

9. PLACE OF EMPLOYMENT OR BUSINESS

OWEN FARM (Number and street or R.F.D. number) — TORNILLO (Town), EL PASO (County), TEXAS (State)

I AFFIRM THAT I HAVE VERIFIED ABOVE ANSWERS AND THAT THEY ARE TRUE.

John Waits (Registrant's signature)

D.S.S. Form 1 (Revised 1-1-42) (over) ☆ GPO 16—21630-1

SERIAL NUMBER	1. NAME (Print)			ORDER NUMBER
171	Willie (First)	Lee (Middle)	Carr (Last)	2032

2. ADDRESS (Print)

R.F.D. no. 2 (Number and street or R.F.D. number) — Chilton (Town) — Fall (County) — Texas (State)

3. TELEPHONE (Exchange) (Number)

4. AGE IN YEARS — 30

DATE OF BIRTH — Nov. (Mo.) 14 (Day), 1909 (Yr.)

5. PLACE OF BIRTH — MART (Town or county) — McLennan (State or country)

6. COUNTRY OF CITIZENSHIP — U.S.A.

7. NAME OF PERSON WHO WILL ALWAYS KNOW YOUR ADDRESS

Mrs. (Mr., Mrs., Miss) Prince (First) Anna (Middle) Carr (Last)

8. RELATIONSHIP OF THAT PERSON — wife

9. ADDRESS OF THAT PERSON

R.F.D. no. 2 (Number and street or R.F.D. number) — Chilton Falls (Town) — Texas (State)

10. EMPLOYER'S NAME

W.P.A. (McLennan-Headquarters)

11. PLACE OF EMPLOYMENT OR BUSINESS

Chilton (Number and street or R.F.D. number) — Falls (Town) — Texas (State)

I AFFIRM THAT I HAVE VERIFIED ABOVE ANSWERS AND THAT THEY ARE TRUE.

Willie Lee Carr (Registrant's signature)

REGISTRATION CARD
D.S.S. Form 1 (over) 16—17105

*How do you describe gravity before you know
what that is?*

*How do you describe light?
Color? Feelings? Taste?
Your position in the universe?
Your position with your family?
Your mother, your siblings?
The community around you?*

*Including the insects.
Cuz' you pay real, personal, close attention to
details as a kid.
You watch little ants crawling around, little
roaches, little grasshoppers.
Snakes, lizards.
The grains of dirt.
The grains of dirt that ants make.
The ants look like grains of dirt moving.
All that out there in the desert, that's supposed
to have nothing in it.*

Appearance of the desert can make it seem empty, like there is nothing going on.

There are millions of things going on.

When you really focus and see all the movement that nature has in the rocks, the sand, the ants, the bugs.

How it's all interconnected.

How it appears when there's something that nature wants.

You see a lot of activity around the things that have died or passed on, that are part of the transition of nature from one thing to another.

That's enchantment.

To see the basic elements of life happen before you, in simple ways.

—Ben Caldwell
"Input 5.STE-069"

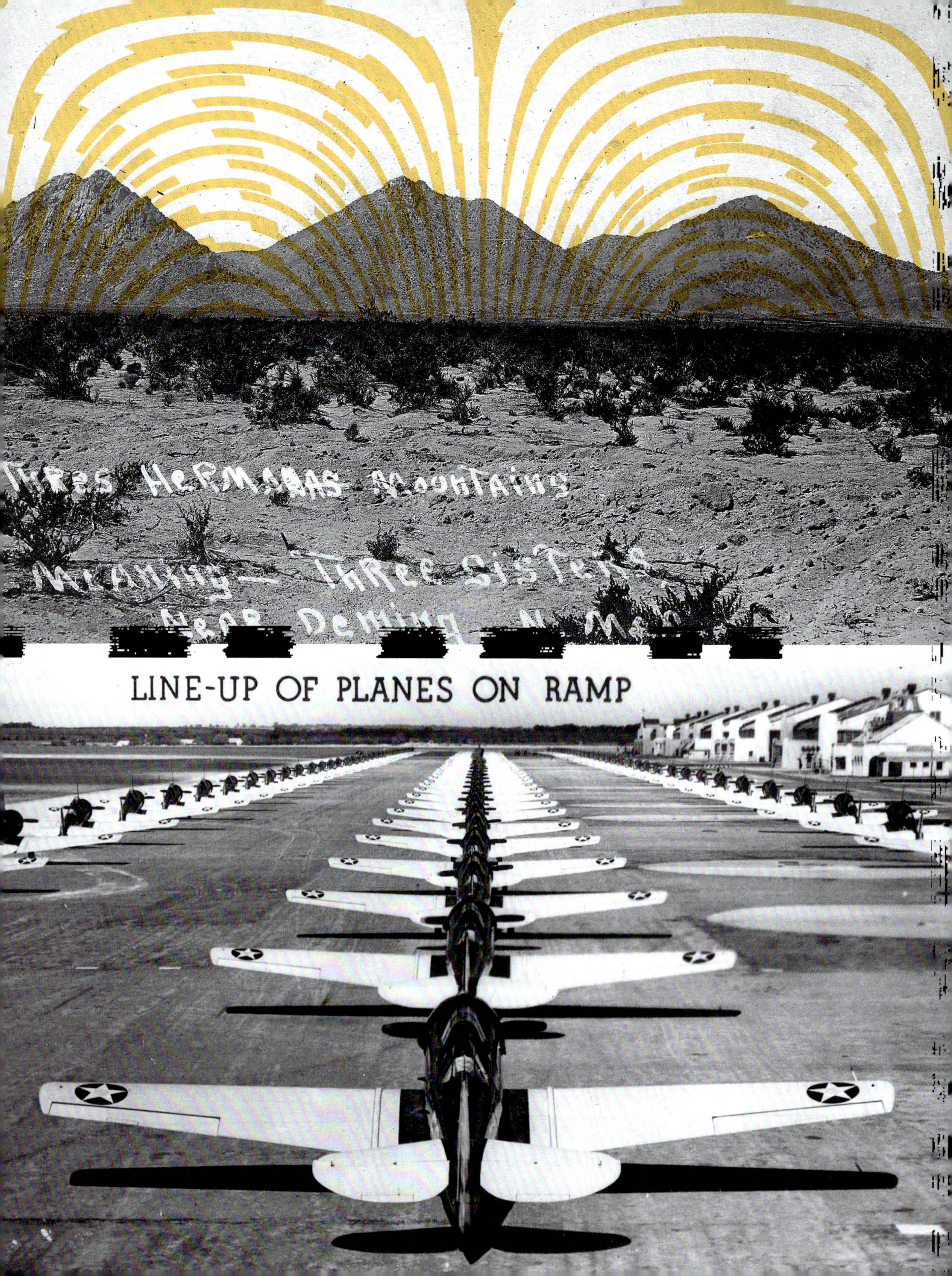
ThRee HeRMANAS MoUNTAINS
MEANINg — ThRee SiSTeRS
NEAR DeMINg — N. Mex
LINE-UP OF PLANES ON RAMP

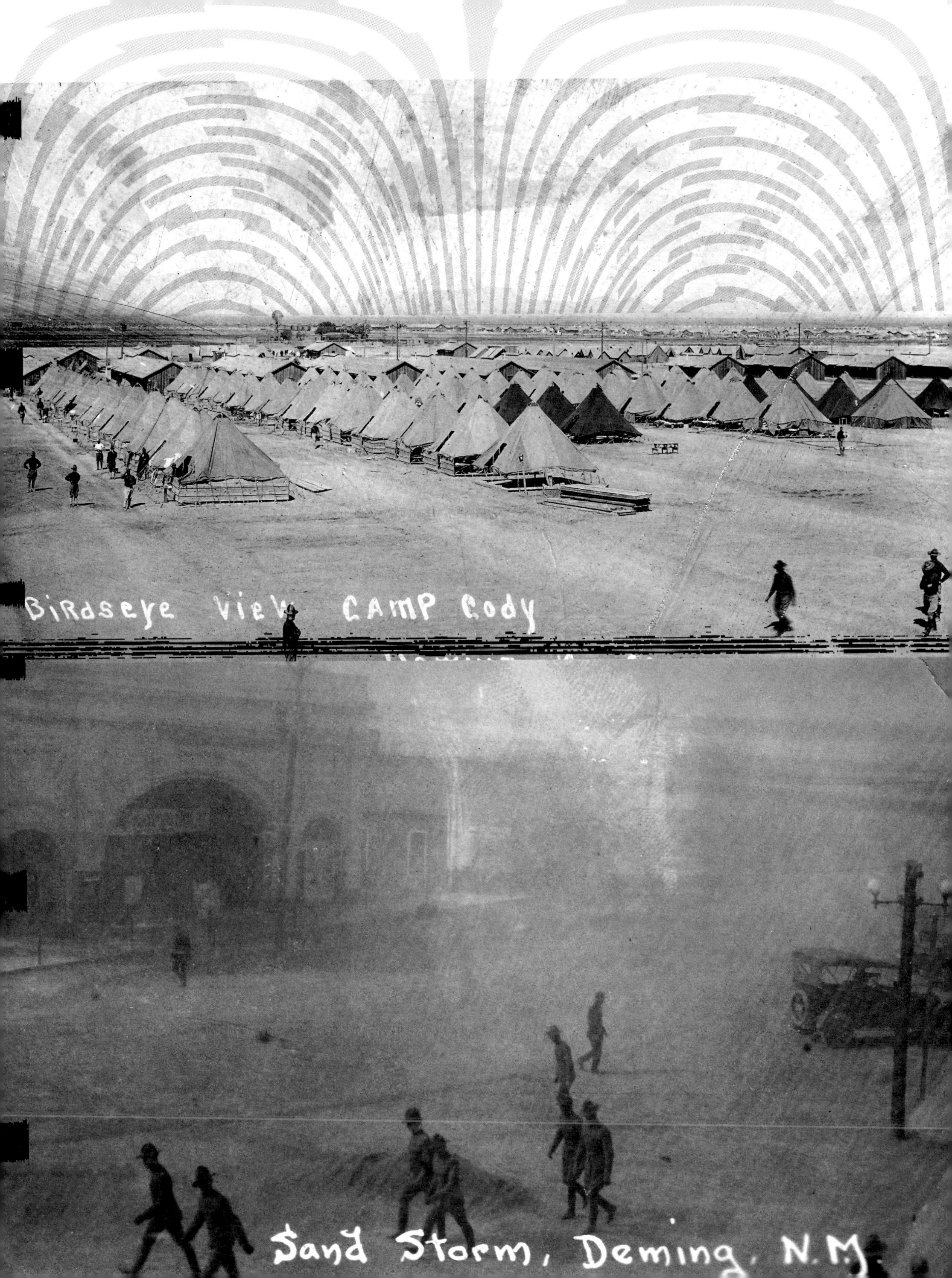
BiRDseye VieW CAMP CoDy
Sand Storm, Deming, N.M.

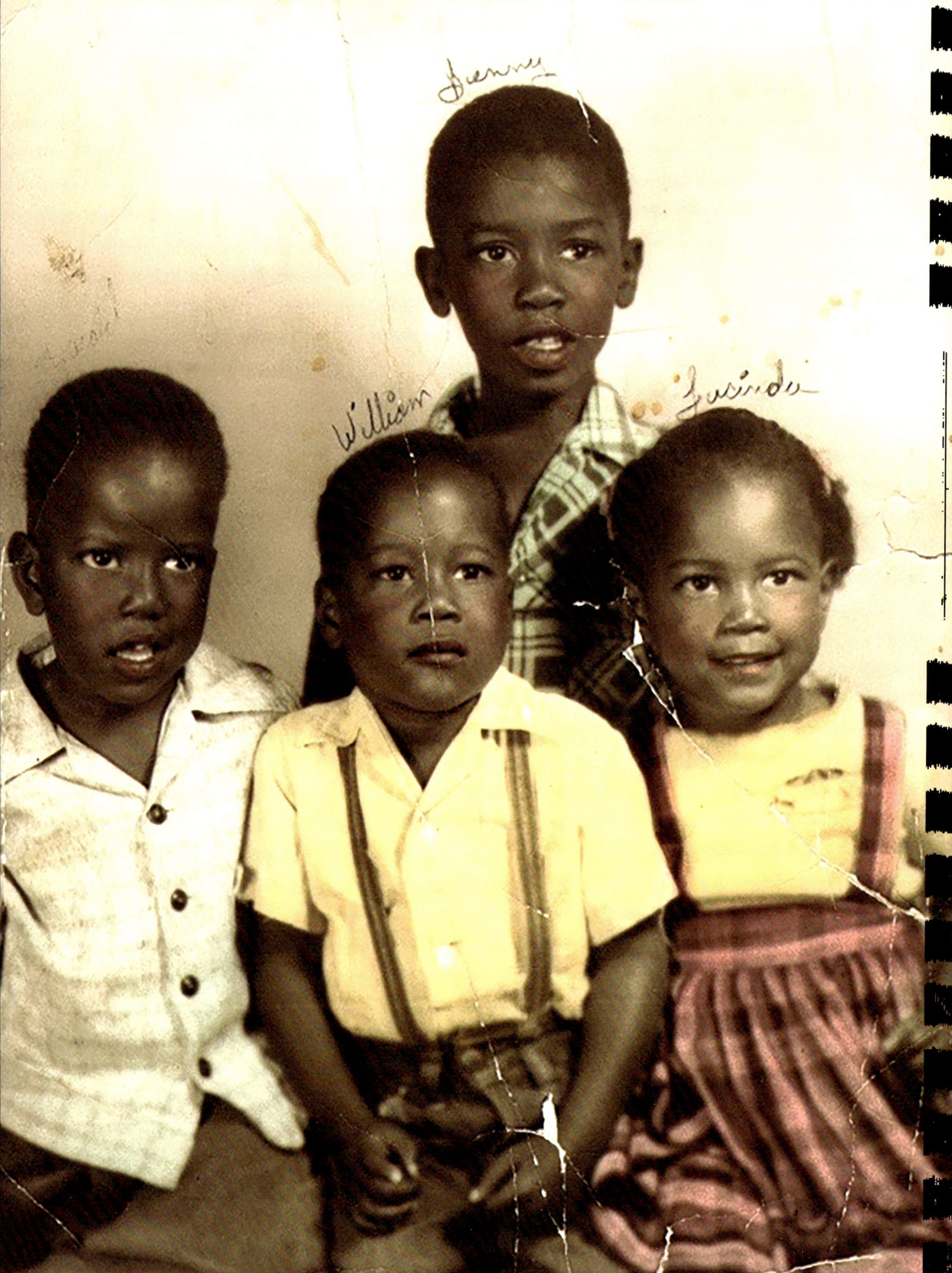
Danny
William
Lucinda

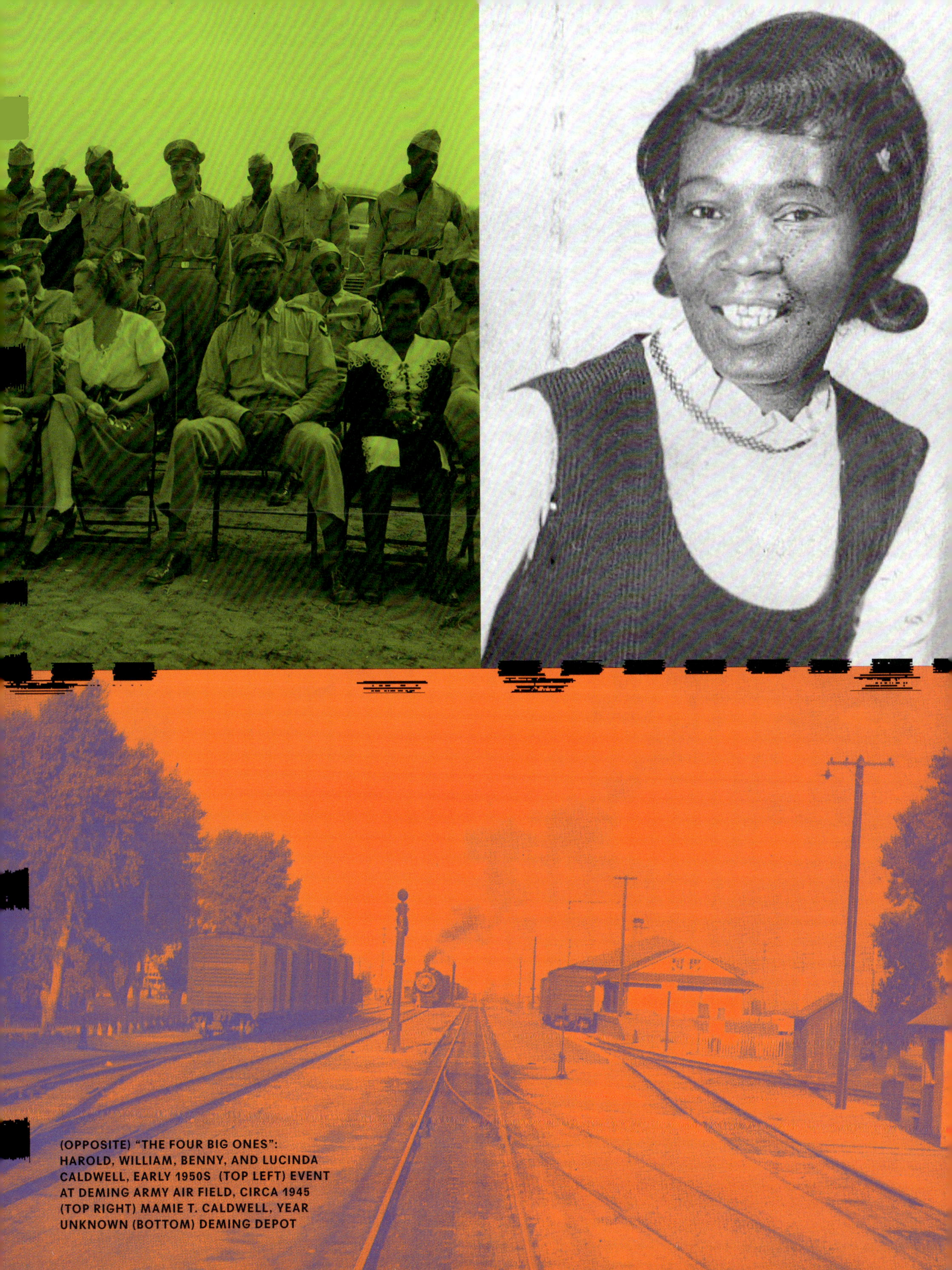

(OPPOSITE) "THE FOUR BIG ONES":
HAROLD, WILLIAM, BENNY, AND LUCINDA
CALDWELL, EARLY 1950S (TOP LEFT) EVENT
AT DEMING ARMY AIR FIELD, CIRCA 1945
(TOP RIGHT) MAMIE T. CALDWELL, YEAR
UNKNOWN (BOTTOM) DEMING DEPOT

CHAPTER 2

DEM'·(ING) FOLKS

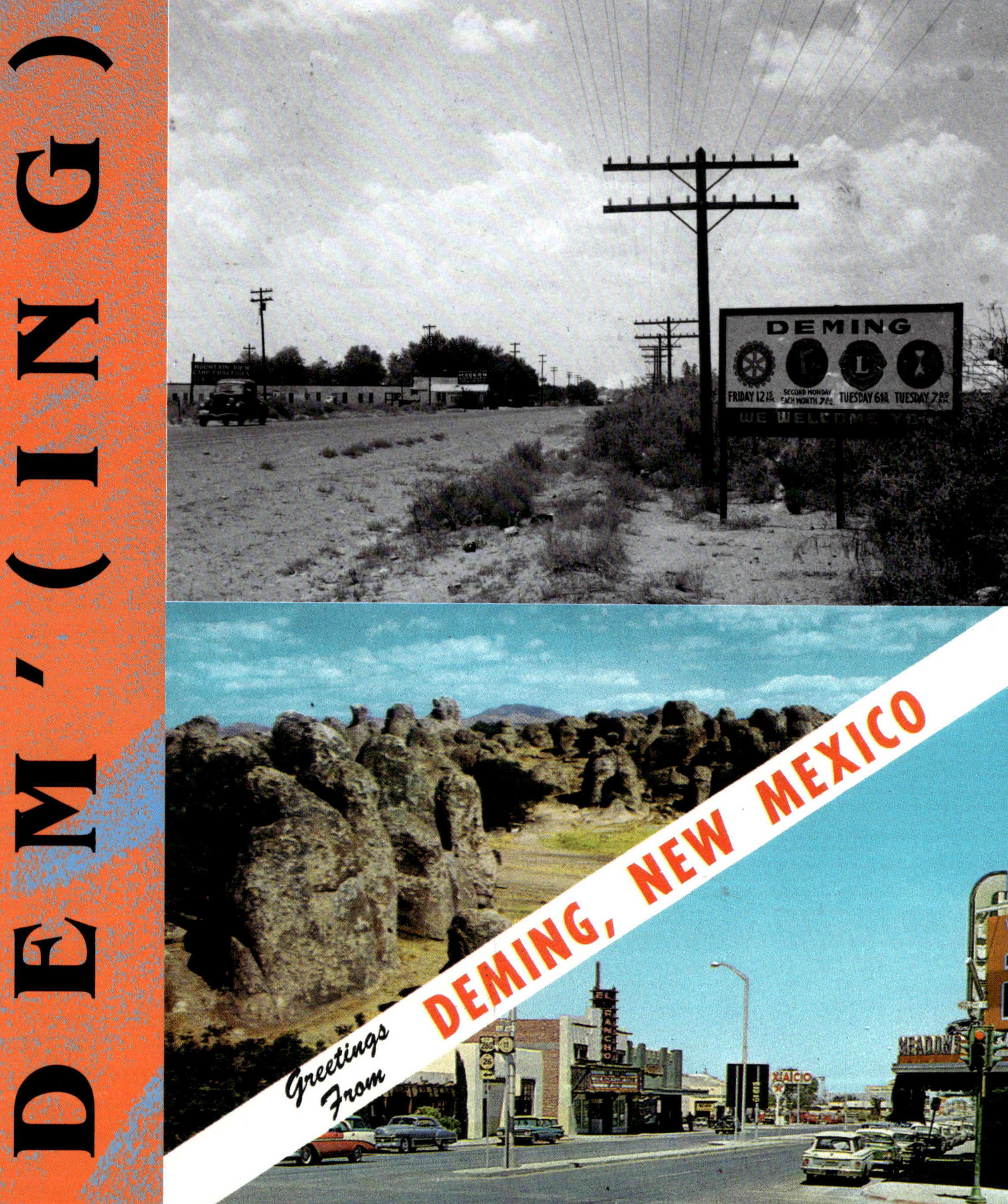

When Mamie T. Waits started working in Deming Army Airfield's laundromat, she knew little about how the soldiers spent their days. She did know that the airfield opened in November 1942 to prepare pilots, bombardiers, and navigators for the windy skies of World War II's European and Pacific fronts. And she knew that the airfield's soldiers enjoyed indulging in day-long baseball games and quartet renditions of melancholic, Southwestern tunes like "The Deming Field Complaint" and "Dem Deming Blues."

But the sixteen-year-old didn't know that the cadets' training exercises entailed flying Beech-built AT-11 planes. Or that the pilots maneuvered these planes through the gorgeous Florida mountains until they reached a precision bombing range—Sierra County earth west of where the Trinity atomic bomb was tested. And it wasn't until she met the father of her first child that she learned the bombing range's center was a bullseye surrounded by four concentric circles tattooed into the land.

"From up high," he told Mamie during one of their evening walks, "It looks like the grooves in a record, or the ripples in water when you skip a stone, or even the symbols etched in those rocks at Pony Hills."

How he came to learn about the bullseye circles is a mystery. He never saw it with his eyes. He couldn't have. Black troops were not included in the airfield's aerial and bombing exercises. The Black detachments did provide ground and technical support for these drills. However, they were segregated from white cadets. They were relegated mostly to unskilled and semi-skilled positions: military police, truck drivers and transporters, barrack supervisors, and those managing and distributing supplies and equipment. Alongside them were the common folk who serviced the base as cooks, bakers, mechanics, carpenters, construction workers, and cleaning staff—people like Mamie.

John was not thrilled when Mamie started working at the airfield. But he thought twice about pushing back.

Three years earlier, she wanted a gold tooth. John refused. She begged. When that didn't work, she made threats: "I'll sneak out and GET ONE!" Like always, he relented. In Juarez, a dentist shaved away at her right central incisor to create room for the gold frame. The dentist then carefully layered dental cement onto her natural crown before attaching a gold-capped tooth—at its center was the shape of a heart. Over her lifetime, this became her calling card. In the middle of a conversation, a child would point it out, their eyes fixated on the glimmering jewel. Once Mamie had her own children, their friends suspected that the family's modest home and belongings couldn't hide the truth. "Mrs. Mamie must be loaded," they reckoned. "Only rich people have gold teeth!"

So when Mamie told John about being hired at the laundromat, he just nodded. *That's an uphill march not worth the climb*, he thought. Plus, she had stopped attending school. It was time for Mamie to get a job.

She already knew the base grounds well. She had first visited in the spring of 1942, when John and Willie Lee were hired as construction workers to help build the base. Over five months the men commuted there, first from Tornillo, Texas, and later from Vado, New Mexico. Alongside hundreds of other men, they smoothed down rutted fields and barren land, installed tarmacs, and constructed barracks.

After work, they often stopped by the Night Owl, what Black folks more commonly called the Big House. Located just behind the Harvey House depot hotel, the Big House was a mix of a juke joint, inn, barbershop, and brothel. There, they mingled with an assortment of folk: toilers, domestics, mine workers, cowboys, horse-breakers, hoboes, pros, call boys, gigolos. From this group, they learned that although only a few Black people lived in Deming, the small town was a decent place to live. Furthermore, Deming's low cost of living and proximity to mining, farming, cattle-ranching, and conservation work made it a place where a resourceful Black man could potentially own land and raise a family without much trouble or constraint at the hands of white folk. It didn't take long to convince John and Willie Lee. By 1943, this working-class village, located just thirty miles from the U.S.-Mexico border, was their family's new home.

On US 80 (later replaced by Interstate 10) billboards beckoned drivers to "STOP AT DEMING, NEW MEXICO, 'The Friendly City' IN THE KINGDOM OF THE SUN." Yet up until the late 1930s and 1940s, most Black migrants were not convinced. Previous eras had seen small waves of Black migration to Deming and the surrounding areas, but most of these folk didn't stay. They came primarily to supply temporary, oftentimes seasonal, work for mines, large-scale commercial and independent farms, cattle ranches, sheepherders, railroads, and military forts. World War II, however, produced a boom in military defense jobs and other industries, and this drew families like the Waitses and Carrs to New Mexico.

Mamie's first friend at the airfield was Virginia Lee Coleman, or "Miss Virginia," as Mamie called her due to their eleven-year age gap. Despite the age difference, Virginia and Mamie were thick as thieves. In hushed voices, they mused over the good-looking men posted at the airfield. Most of them were polite, some even flirtatious. It was still surprising when the dark-skinned soldier from Miami approached them in the post exchange and asked Mamie out on a date.

His name was Walter Harris. He was twenty-six years old. Medium-build, thick full lips, gentle brown eyes, baritone voice, and incredibly shy. Their first date was at the Luna Theatre, where Mamie's father worked. They watched *The Story of Dr. Wassell*, a World War II drama about a naval doctor who is forced to care for and lead a U.S. brigade after a Japanese attack leaves the troops stranded in the Dutch East Indies. They sat upstairs, in the balcony area with the neon sign designating where Black people were allowed to sit. They spent the entirety of the movie holding hands while staring directly at the screen, too nervous to

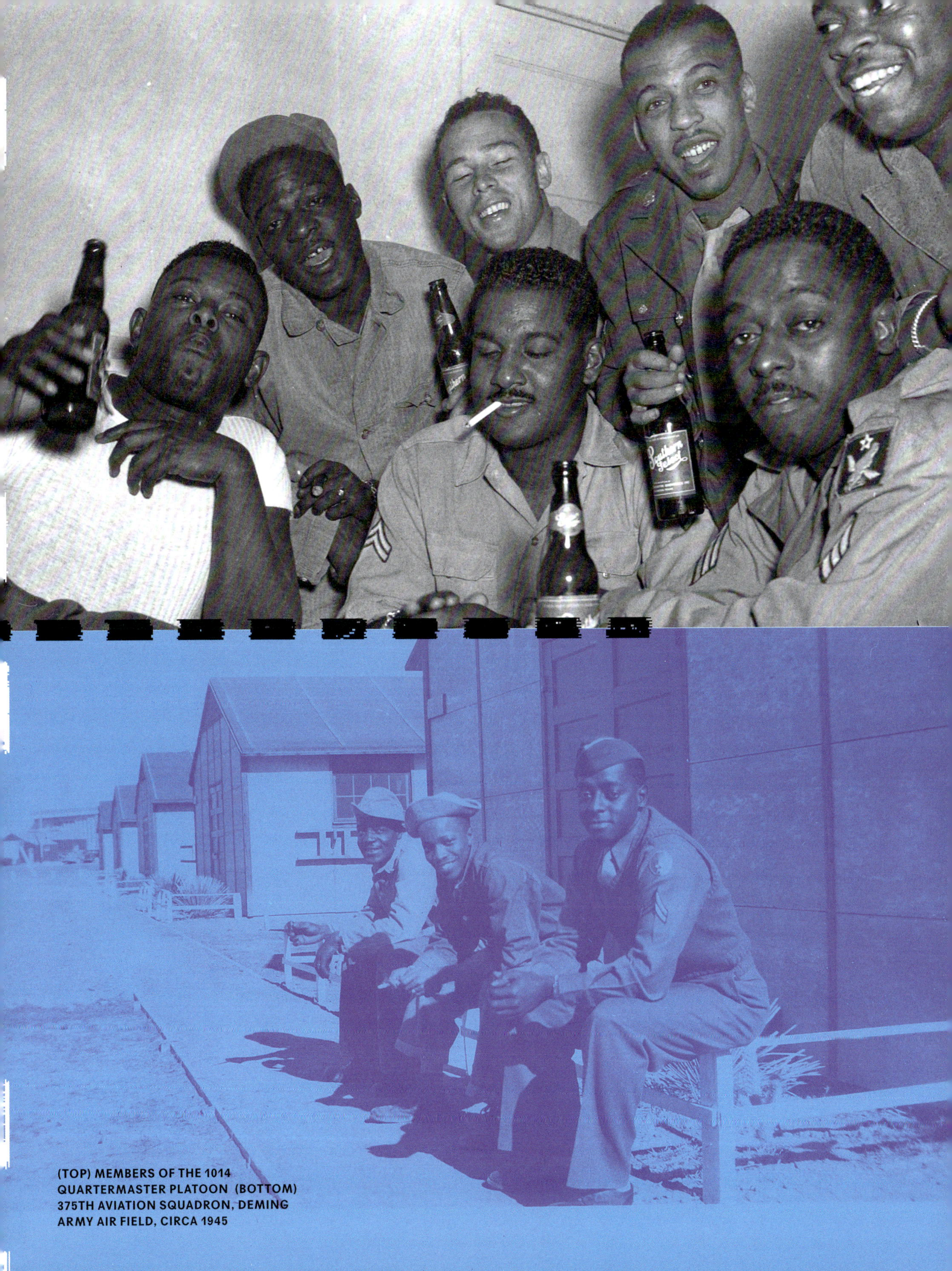

(TOP) MEMBERS OF THE 1014
QUARTERMASTER PLATOON (BOTTOM)
375TH AVIATION SQUADRON, DEMING
ARMY AIR FIELD, CIRCA 1945

steal a glance at one another. When the film ended, they said goodbye and went home separately. On their second date, Walter approached Mamie's father in the projectionist booth and communicated his interest in Mamie. After some thought, John gave his approval. "You can walk Mamie *to* the movie, but not home," he said. "That's my job."

The wide-eyed young couple spent the summer watching movies, going on long walks, and basking in New Mexico's unending skies and mandarin-violet sunsets. It was a sweet, whirlwind romance. In the fall, Walter asked for her hand in marriage, and she accepted. John wasn't happy about it, but he reluctantly gave his approval. Walter could now walk Mamie home.

However, the lovers' intentions to marry were put on hold when Walter's squadron was ordered to leave Deming. He promised Mamie he would return. A month later, Mamie learned she was pregnant.

On Thursday, August 30, 1945, she gave birth to her first son. His arrival came just three weeks after the U.S. military detonated atomic bombs in Japan, killing hundreds of thousands of people and subsequently ending World War II. Mamie named him Benny Ray.

Mamie mailed Walter a picture of their baby. Again, Walter promised to return. This time he kept his word. When he was discharged, he contacted Mamie to arrange a visit to see Benny. But her father rejected the idea. "Walter should just move on," John countered. John didn't provide much reasoning, but he was insistent that she listen. And for some reason, she did. It was one of the most difficult decisions of her life.

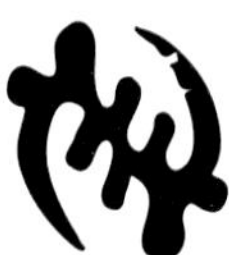

Robert Thomas Caldwell Jr. arrived in Deming in 1946. The third child of Ada Hill and Robert Caldwell Sr., he was born in the fall of 1918 in Des Moines, Iowa, two years after the family moved there from Savannah, Missouri. The move was prompted by Robert Sr.'s employment as a stationary engineer and boiler operator at Hawkeye Portland Cement Company, a job that provided the family with a decent quality of life. Throughout their lives they resided in rented homes, primarily located in the River Bend neighborhood, just a few minutes' walk from the Des Moines River. This was a working-class and lower-middle-class community, composed of Blacks and first- and second-generation white immigrants who worked as carpenters, porters, office clerks, janitors, freighters, and domestic workers.

Their lives were a far cry from that which Ada and Robert Sr. had experienced growing up as the children of formerly enslaved people. The couple consequently insisted that their children prioritize their studies. Their kids were no angels, but all of them completed high school.

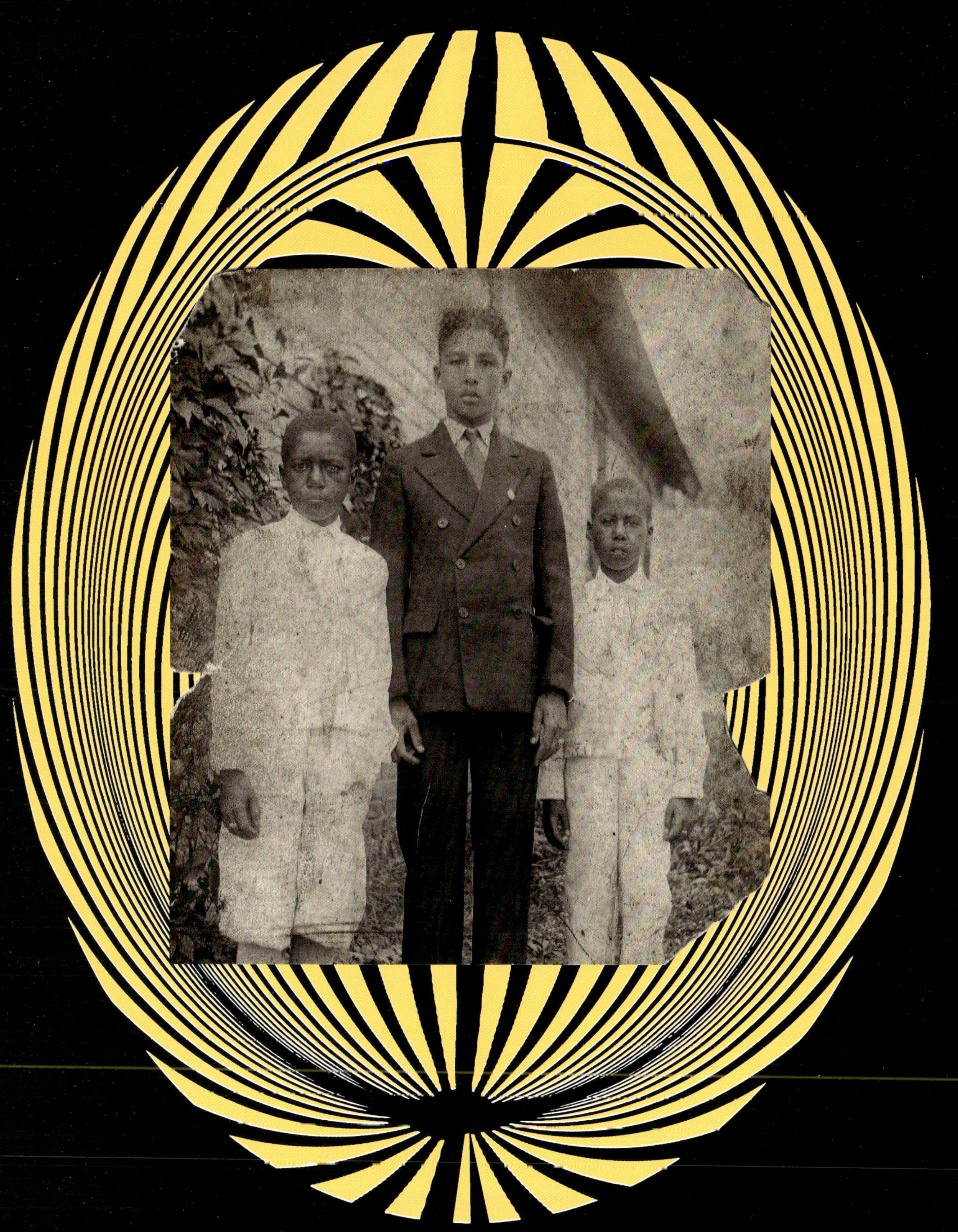

ROBERT, HAROLD, AND WILLIAM
CALDWELL, MID-TO-LATE 1920S

Robert, Jr., or "Bob" as he was more commonly known, was bright and serious. Some said he was born with the eyes of an elder, that his intense glare could burn a hole in the sun. He was a quick study and a leader, comfortable, confident, and apt at cajoling others to follow him. But he had a quick temper and an unrelenting will that made it difficult for him to back down from confrontation. It was for this reason that his parents enrolled him at a local boxing gym. He needed a healthy space to release his frustration and grow thicker skin.

But no gym could extinguish Bob's fire. The only person with even the slightest ability to do so was Harold, Bob's elder brother. The boys were best friends, forging the tightest of bonds. Good times were had swimming and skipping rocks at the river, fighting other neighborhood boys, chasing after girls outside the Crescent Beauty School on Center Street.

They were together when their innocence was stolen on a hot Sunday afternoon in July of 1930. They were traveling home with friends from a swimming hole when a white pharmacist, A. C. Rist, alleged that he saw a member of the boys' group stealing apples from the tree in his yard. Without warning he fired a .32 caliber revolver at the teens, striking Harold in the hip. Harold thankfully only suffered a slight flesh wound. Rist would later tell the police and newspapers that "he had been pestered all summer by boys stealing his fruit and garden products," as if this justified his act of attempted murder. He must have been on to something; the courts ruled that for a white adult male, the penalty for committing a casual act of near-fatal violence against unarmed Black teenagers was a three-hundred-dollar fine.

The boys were forever changed after the incident. Harold made light of it, a chuckle here and there, a ruse for his blues. Bob was more reserved, more tense. The differences in their transformations, though, didn't prevent them from deducing the same, quintessentially American, lesson. For a measly apple, their lives could be stolen with impunity.

Five years later, tragedy struck again. In the early hours of June 16, 1935, Harold's mangled body was discovered near the railroad tracks in Numa, a small town in Appanoose County, Iowa. It was found alongside the similarly disjointed and disfigured body of his Civilian Conservation Corp (CCC) mate, Patrick Bettis. Their fellow CCC companion, Orlando Anderson, was found four hundred yards away, unconscious, with his arms and legs broken, suffering from extreme shock and hypothermia; by the day's end, he, too, was dead.

How the three young men were killed is a mystery. The police report claimed that all three fell from a train while "bumming a ride" home for weekend leave from their CCC camp. But the Caldwell family didn't accept this account. They believed that the boys' death was not an accident, some fortuitous calamity in the middle of the night. It was whispered that something else had transpired. ***Three fellas riding the Rock Island Line north on a Saturday night all just happen to "fall" off a moving train? Hell nah. We wasn't born yesterday. Somebody threw them boys from the train.***

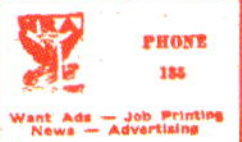

CENTERVILLE DAILY IOWEGIAN
AND CITIZEN

THE WEATHER
Mostly cloudy and cooler with showers probable in extreme east portion tonight. Tuesday partly cloudy and cooler.

ASSOCIATED PRESS WIRE SERVICE   CENTERVILLE, IOWA, MONDAY, JUNE 17, 1935   CITIZEN ESTABLISHED 1864—IOWEGIAN 1883   VOL. 42, NO. 142

TRAIN KILLS THREE YOUTHS

Twelve Persons Killed in Accidents in Iowa

AUTO MISHAPS TAKE 7 LIVES OVER WEEKEND

Three Youths Killed by Train; Two Persons Drowned

(By The Associated Press)

Iowa counted today an accident toll of 12 lives.

Seven persons were killed in automobile accidents. Two were drowned. Three negro youths were killed when they either fell from or were struck by a train.

The automobile and drowning accidents are:

Otto Bartz, Aurelia, Ia.

Grace Bartz, Aurelia, Ia.

Mr. and Mrs. George E. McIninch, St. Poseph, Mo.

David C. McIninch, St. Joseph, Mo.

Mr. and Mrs. J. E. Burnett, Charles City.

Frank Joudle, 28, Fort Dodge.

Lee A. Smith, Ottumwa.

Bartz and his sister were killed when a tire blew out on their auto near Aurelia, causing it to overturn. They were driving to Hanover, Ia., to attend a picnic.

Cars Collide.

The McIninch car in which the family was driving north on a vacation trip collided with one driven by Gus Dubberke of Hubbard on highway 65, south of Hubbard.

The impact hurled both cars against a cement bridge. The two men were killed outright. Mrs. McIninch died shortly afterward in an Iowa Falls hospital. Occupants of the other car escaped serious injury.

George E. McIninch was a St. Joseph company official and a former mayor.

Burnett's automobile and one driven by Charles Boers, president of the Rock Island, Ill., Western league baseball club, collided head on highway 6 east of South Amana.

Mrs. Helen Burnett, daughter-in-law of the victims, suffered a skull fracture. She was taken to an Iowa City hospital in a critical condition. Mrs. Beers suffered a leg fracture, and Beers and his son were cut and bruised. Mr. and Mrs. Harold Burnett of Mishawaka, Ind., riding with the Burnets, suffered serious injuries.

Three Killed.

A train crew found the bodies of the Negro youths along the Rock Island railroad tracks near Numa, Iowa. They were wearing CCC uniforms. A letter addressed to Walter Brown of Kansas City was found in the pocket of one youth, but Brown later appeared at his camp at Liberty, Mo. Brown and three other camp members had week-end leaves. They were Patrick Bettis, Orlando Anderson and Harold Caldwell, all of Des Moines. The bodies have been tentatively identified as theirs.

Joudle, Fort Dodge farmer, drowned while swimming in an abandoned pit five miles west of Fort Dodge. He was not married.

Smith fell from a dam abuttment into the Des Moines river at Ottumwa and drowned. Surviving are his widow and eight children.

Grand Jury To Consider Case Against Waley

Tacoma, Wash., June 17 (AP)—While department of justice agents continued their search for William Mahan, a grand jury was called into session for Wednesday to consider the cases of Harmon M. Waley, ex-convict, and his young wife, reported by federal agents to have confessed their part in the $200,000 kidnaping of George Weyerhaeuser, lumber fortune heir.

Reports that Mrs. Waley, now held with her husband in the county jail at Olympia, was to become a mother, were denied today by officers but they appointed a physician to examine the woman.

Youths Plan Swim Down Mississippi

Janesville, Wis., June 17 (AP)—With plans for the initial plunge of their 2,500 mile swim down the Mississippi river from St. Paul set for next Monday, three youthful Janesville, Wis. adventurers today headed for the Twin Cities and the prospects of a thrilling summer.

Robert Shultis, Donald Slawson and Cecil Sanders, all 20 years old, look forward to the endurance trip down the "Father of the Waters" as New Orleans not only as an unusual experience but as an opportunity to challenge existing marathon records for the distance.

SERVICES SET FOR CCC BOYS

Third Train Victim Is Identified.

Funeral services for two of the three Des Moines Negro CCC youths killed early Sunday when struck by a Rock Island train near Numa, Ia., will be Wednesday.

The services for Harold Caldwell, 19, of 1124 Bluff st., will be at 9 a. m. at St. Ambrose cathedral. Those for Orlando Anderson, 18, of 1141 School st., will be at 2 p. m. at Corinthian Baptist church.

Both will be buried at Glendale cemetery.

The third Negro killed in the accident was identified as Patrick Bettis, jr., 1101 Second st. His parents, two sisters and a brother survive.

Sunday night the body was believed that of Walter Brown, Kansas City, Mo., later found in the camp at Liberty, Mo., from which the three were on leave.

No inquest will be held. Four officers from the CCC camp arrived at Centerville, Ia., to act as a board of investigation.

TRUCK RAMS BRIDGE.

FAIRFIELD, IA. — Seven head of cattle were killed here late Monday when a truck loaded with cattle and driven by Walter Harpke of Watseka, Ill., skidded and was wrecked on Cedar creek bridge on Primary 1 four miles south of here.

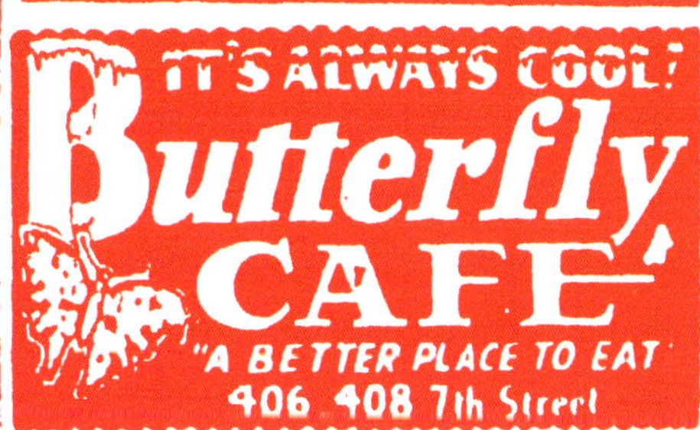

BODIES FOUND EARLY SUNDAY NEAR TRACKS

Facts of Case Closed To Public by Death of Entire Party

In the dark of the night, probably either shortly before or after midnight, three colored youths of the Civilian Conservation Corps from Liberty, Mo., Camp No. 1728 had a rendezvous with death along the Rock Island right of way at Numa, Iowa.

Early dawn revealed two horribly mangled bodies strewn along the tracks for a distance of 400 yards and another youth lying near the tracks dying as the result of a broken leg and arm, and exposure through the long hours of the night.

Injuries Fatal

The dead were Orlando Anderson, Harold Caldwell and Patrick Bettis, all of Des Moines. Anderson, who was rushed to St. Joseph's hospital and by Coroner Hugh Johnson, died at 1:45 p.m. Sunday. Dr. J. C. Donahoe sought to rally Anderson in the hope that the youth could throw some light on the mystery that completely enshrouds the death of the three C. C. C. camp men. However, shock and long hours of exposure, coupled with his injuries, had put Anderson beyond recovery and he never regained consciousness that mercifully closed his last hours.

Facts Unrevealed

The meager story, so far as it can be pieced together, is that three youths from the Liberty camp obtained week end leave privileges and are supposed to have set out for Des Moines. Presumably they were on the Golden State Limited or possibly the Apache. What happened at Numa no one will ever know. Whether the boys started to get off the train and fell, whether they were waiting in Numa to catch a train and stumbled, whether someone forced them to get off the train while it was traveling at high speed, whether one started to fall, grabbed the boy nearest him and this lad grabbed the third and all fell to their death, is mere conjecture.

Two Facts Known

Two things are known definitely now. Three youths left the Liberty camp Saturday and Saturday night or early Sunday morning. All three met their deaths by falling or being thrown from a train at the Arbogast mine at Numa.

State and wire reports today to the effect that there were four in the party were not correct. There were only three. Further state and wire reports, that one of the men killed was Walter Brown of Kansas City, were not correct. Brown is alive and at the Liberty camp and talked from there over the phone to his commanding officer here today. This left the identity of the third man, Bettis, unknown for a time.

Two Mutilated

While Anderson was not mutilated severely, his two companions were crushed beyond identification, except by records. One of the dead men stumbled next to Brown and had some of Brown's possessions. This led to the first belief that Brown had been killed, and the incorrect state reports.

There will be no inquest held locally, according to County Coroner Johnson. Local action was made unnecessary by the arrival here of Civilian Conservation Corps officers from Missouri, including Captain M. Clark of Company 3748, Capt. G. L. Riddle of Company 1728, Lt. Rinehart Becker, and Lt. Floyd Shinn. These men constitute an officers board of investigation and their inquest is sufficient to meet legal requirements in such cases.

Report

The officers reported to the Iowegian this morning that their only conclusion was that the three men met their death as the result of a railroad accident at Numa on the night of June 15 or morning of June 16. Further than that they reported they could not determine. Because there were only three men involved and all three died without being able to speak, there are no known living witnesses to be obtained in the case. Just what happened probably never will be known — except that three youths bound on a week end holiday—had a rendezvous with death instead.

Condition of Dean Resident Serious

Dean, Ia. (Special)—The condition of Mrs. Ed. Davis, who resides north of here, remained critical today.

Friends of Mrs. Davis were shocked Friday to learn of her sudden illness. She became ill while picking strawberries in the garden Friday morning, and lost consciousness after returning to the house. A doctor was called, and pronounced her condition serious.

---

of the Iowa DeMolay opened here today with nearly 400 representatives from all parts of the state present.

Three degrees will be presented starting at 7:15 p.m. The Muscatine chapter will have charge of the initiatory degree; the Davenport chapter of the DeMolay degree and the Davenport alumni chapter of the majority service.

The three-day session will be in charge of Norman J. Guster, of Dennison, state master councilor.

Women Barred From Working in Mines

Geneva, June 17 (AP)—The international labor conference today unanimously adopted an agreement prohibiting women from working under ground in mines.

be sufficient to bring stabilization of world monies.

MISSOURI WEATHER

Partly cloudy in northwest, local thundershowers in east and south portions tonight and possibly Tuesday morning; cooler Tuesday and in north portion tonight.

lulu is expected to take slightly more than the nine hours, 13 minutes consumed on its westward hop due to accelerated headwinds and also to additional flight observations.

Flood Releases Body of Woman

Benkelman, Neb., June 17 (AP)—The body of Mrs. Harold Mosier, 34, who lived on a farm 13 miles south of here, was found near Benkelman today and hope was abandoned for finding her 8 year old daughter safe after flood waters last night swept them from their farm.

(AP)—Divers were prepared to go beneath the waters of Vineyard Sound today for $100,000 in hijackers' cash, believed to be on the hulk of the rum runner John Dwight, which lay in 15 fathoms of water off Nashawena Island.

The ship was scuttled in 1923 after at least eight of her crew had met apparently violent death. The bodies of the eight, faces battered, drifted ashore on a foggy morning 12 years ago, shortly after the coast guard sighted her sinking.

Farmers Forced To Use Cradles To Cut Barley

Monett, Mo., June 17 (AP)—Old fashioned cradles are being used by some farmers in Barry county to harvest a barley crop predicted to produce 30 bushels to the acre if it can be saved. Some fields are so wet that horses bog down to their knees.

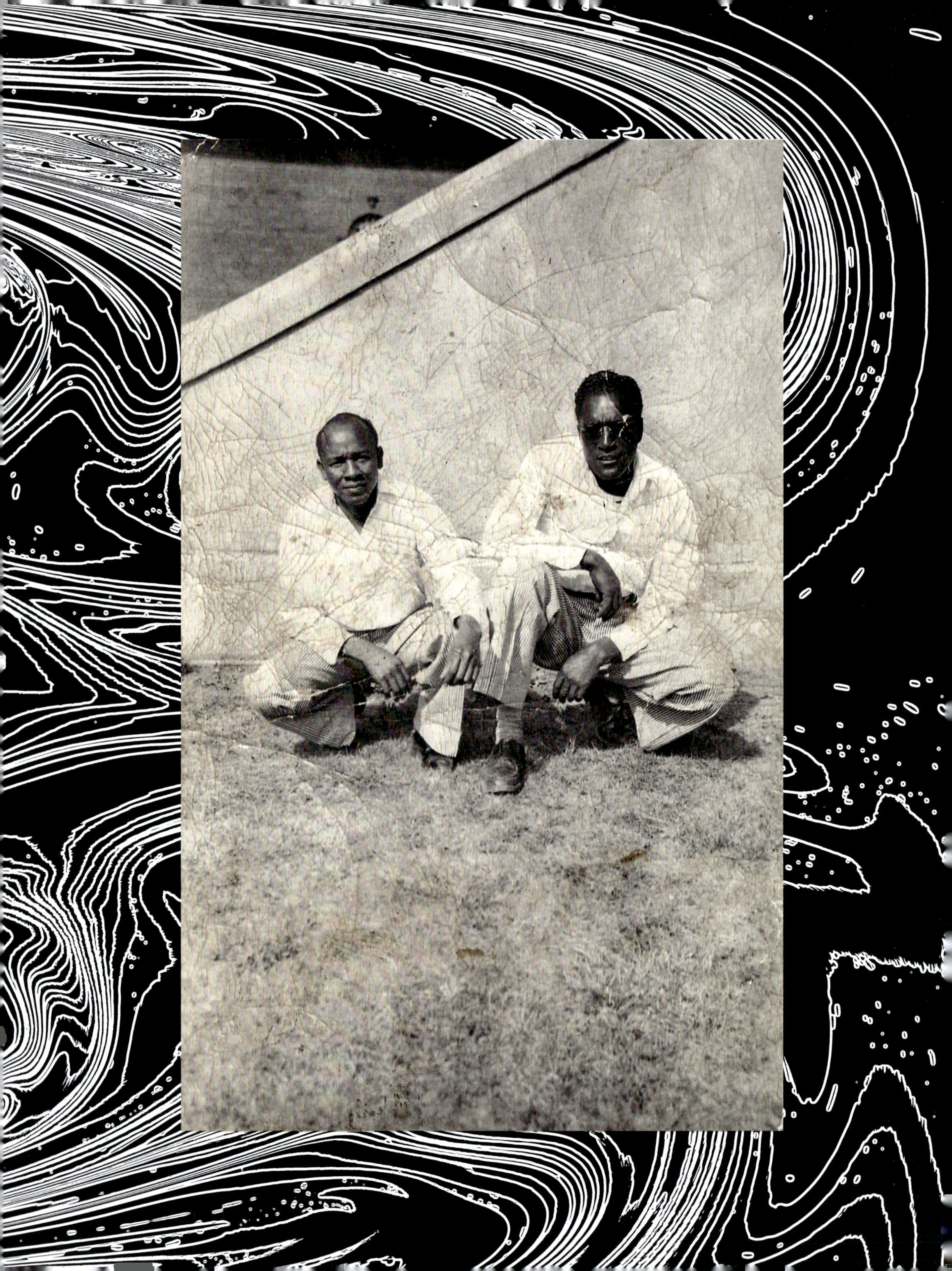

Still, beyond their families and communities, no one else blinked an eye when the police and CCC investigators, just two days after the tragedies, declined an inquest and ruled the deaths accidental. On a Wednesday in mid-June, three families buried their sons' mutilated bodies, young men slaughtered in the springtime of their lives. Harold was two months shy of his twentieth birthday.

The Caldwell family was devastated by grief, especially Bob. It derailed him and lit a rage inside of him that perhaps never subsided. He took some of this hostility out on opponents in the ring. From 1935 to 1938, he built up a solid record of victories as a middleweight boxer, his fists pummeling anyone and anything that stood before him. He began to drink. And he developed a rap sheet of petty crimes: carrying a concealed weapon, stealing a lead pipe from an unoccupied house, threatening a neighbor with a "chicken jar" (a mason jar used to water chickens). Each time, he avoided jail. But this only lasted for so long. After he and two other young men robbed a man of twenty-three dollars, he was arrested and sentenced to ten years in the Anamosa State Penitentiary.

For thirty months, he languished inside a cell. His main comfort was reading novels about the American Old West. When he was paroled in April of 1941, he left Iowa and never looked back.

When Bob met Mamie, he was working as a foreman for Southern Pacific Railroad. He was living inside a railroad outfit car with two other men in Gage, a town fifteen miles west of Deming. Mamie was taken aback by this mysterious, dark-skinned, stony-faced man with maroon-colored eyes and silky hair. Her father questioned what she saw in Bob. "He's almost as old as me," John proclaimed. This time, Mamie did not heed her father's command. In 1947, she married Bob and moved with Benny into Bob's railroad car.

That Benny's first real home was a railroad car seems fitting. Deming, his hometown, was a creation of the railroad industry, its name adopted from that of Mary Ann Deming Crocker, wife of railroad baron Freddie Crocker. The village was established in 1881 as the point that connected two expanding railroads: the Southern Pacific Railroad being constructed from the west, and the Atchison, Topeka & Sante Fe Railway being extended from the northeast. The fusing of these two lines created North America's second transcontinental railroad, a development that was key to the region's economic integration into national and international markets. This vast rail network further intensified the conflicts and convergence of peoples and cultures in the Southwest, a growing population that included the already settled Hispanos, Mexicans, and Indians (Pueblo, Zuni, Navajo, and Apache), along with ever-increasing numbers of Anglo, Asian American, and African American migrants.

Mamie frequently found her young son outside the railcar, lying on the desert floor, gazing into the sky, enamored with its never-ending depth and volume. For Benny, the stars were bright lights that moved and sometimes flew towards him, the ground beneath him simultaneously propelling him in their direction. It felt both scary and exhilarating, the feeling of there being nothing between him, nature, and the cosmos except for gravity and his body—a sensation that communicated he was a product of a place where the ground was always moving.

There was no better reminder of this than living inside a railroad car. *No one else he knew lived in a home with wheels!* His fascination with the railroad car was also stirred by his father's work. Benny frequently traveled with Bob to his jobs in Hurley, a small town just north of Deming. The journey usually consisted of them riding past the Chino Mine in Santa Rita. To Benny's young eyes, this open-pit copper quarry's depth seemed gargantuan, as if it was a towering mountain that had been inverted into the ground. Riding alongside the mine, it was hard to distinguish what it resembled most: a massive gulley that led to the center of the earth? Or a mountaintop and the dark sky turned upside down, the upended replica of his view lying on the desert floor?

Long before the mine and surrounding region were seized by railroad developers, miners, military personnel, and conquistadors, it was inhabited by others: the Athapaskan-speaking people whom the Spanish called "Apaches" (Chiricahua, Gileños, Mescalero, Mimbreño, Ndendahe, and other peoples). Before that, there was the indigenous prehistoric Pueblo civilization that Western archaeologists later designated as "Mimbres Indians" (Mimbres meaning "willow," the name first adopted by nineteenth-century Hispano settlers to describe the river and nearby mountain ranges, on account of the cottonwood and willow trees that aligned the river). Yet, for the most part, the village's chroniclers gave little attention to these groups' lifeways and legacy in the region.

Take the Apaches. Outside of the aged tomahawks, hatchets, and spear points that Boy and Girl Scouts found on hikes at the City of Rocks and in the surrounding areas, their perceptions of the Apaches mirrored that of white America. In folklore and popular culture, the group was villainized as both savages and anti-hero renegade-outlaws. Their unsuccessful twenty-five-year (1861–1886) war of resistance against U.S. occupation was portrayed as the final stage in the taming of the Wild West and consolidation of America's project of frontier expansionism.

The Mimbres peoples, on the other hand, were given far less attention, reduced to an enigma by a relatively small group of people. This was the case primarily among anthropologists, artifact traders, and hiking enthusiasts who sought out the Mimbres people's systems of meaning in the group's vibrantly adorned black-on-white painted pottery and in the petroglyphs that they had carved into the terrain at Pony Hills and Frying Pan Canyon, two areas just north of Deming, along the Butterfield Trail.

The misrepresentation and symbolic erasure of these Native communities was an echo of a broader, region-wide distortion. Central to Spanish conquistador and Anglo American militarial/colonial settlement of the Southwest was disowning the fact that the land had been inhabited by Native peoples, and later by settlers, laborers, and enslaved peoples, most of whose bloodlines and cultures were a fusion of Native, Spanish, and African peoples and traditions. One of the

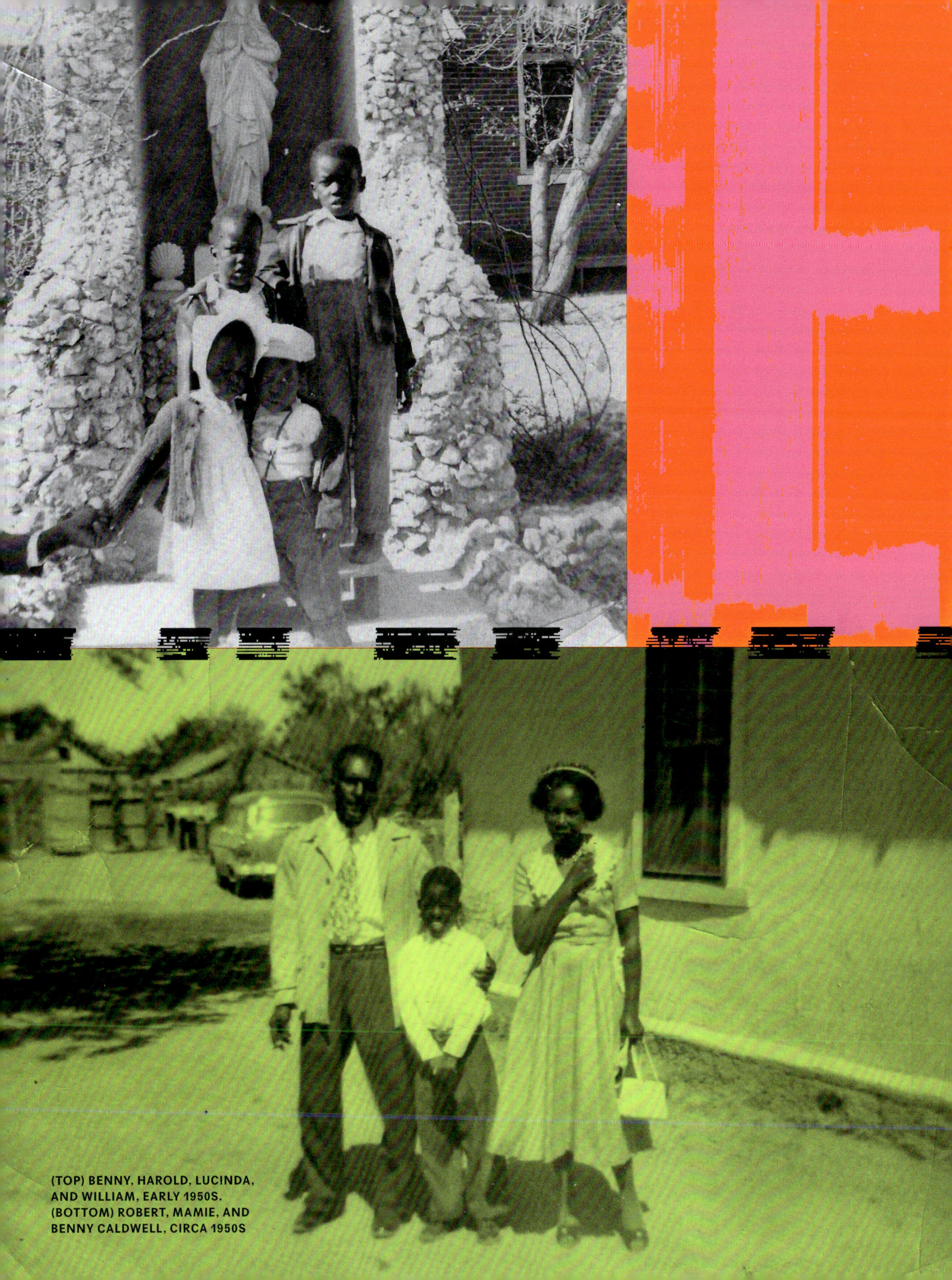

(TOP) BENNY, HAROLD, LUCINDA, AND WILLIAM, EARLY 1950S. (BOTTOM) ROBERT, MAMIE, AND BENNY CALDWELL, CIRCA 1950S

most notable examples was Mustafa Azemmouri, an enslaved North African, Arabic-speaking explorer more commonly known as "Esteban" and "Estevanico" in American Southwestern histories and folklore. Azemmouri was one of the first non-Native peoples to explore the region, journeying through much of northern Mexico and the American Southwest during the late 1520s and 1530s.

Deming, like many American villages, was good at forgetting. In the civic lot on Platinum and Spruce Streets, where Benny's Little League baseball team held barbecues, sat the old jail where just two generations earlier seventeen of Mexican general Francisco "Pancho" Villa's soldiers were imprisoned after they raided the nearby town of Columbus. Six of these soldiers were ultimately hung on scaffolding on this land—the same terrain where, just a decade later in the 1920s, a local branch of the Ku Klux Klan called upon its members to (albeit unsuccessfully) murder Deming's Mexican, Jewish, and Catholic residents. However, such history lessons were not the norm for most folks' dinner table conversations and civic association meetings.

Still, as Mamie, Bob, and John Waits put down roots in the village, Benny absorbed other important lessons. In a span of fifteen years, he went from being Bob and Mamie's sole child to the big brother of twins Harold and John, twins Lucinda and William, and siblings Robert, Michael, Richard, Gary, and David.

To cover the bills, Mamie cleaned hotel rooms for several years before she was hired to work the conveyor at Auburn Rubber Company. Bob continued to work for Southern Pacific for a short period but was fired after a dispute with a coworker. In the early 1950s, he spent another year in prison after writing and cashing a bad check at a gas station. The harsh sentence for such a minor infraction heightened his rage at the world. The combination of this and alcohol turned the fire that burned inside him into a Molotov cocktail, ready to scorch anything in his path. Consequently, throughout the Caldwell children's childhood, Bob had trouble keeping long-term employment and primarily earned income from seasonal work at the cotton gin.

Bob and Mamie raised their children to be upstanding, work hard, and always carry themselves with a sense of dignity and pride. Mamie was carefree for the most part, but she constantly encouraged the children to look out for one another and make the most of what they had been blessed with. Bob was more rigid and domineering, always demanding that the kids adhere to a strict code of discipline and respect, even when it clashed with his own behavior. But he also insisted that they not allow people to take advantage of them and that they must fight back when treated unfairly. Having a developed and sharp mind, he insisted, was fundamental in ensuring that they could survive and not be afraid of struggle.

Benny enjoyed helping Bob tend to the family garden and accompanying him on his social outings at the Big House. The garden provided Benny with a hands-on view of the cycles of life: soil, water, and sunlight nourishing the herbs and vegetables; creatures, big and small, feeding on what was harvested as well as on one another, their excrement and carcasses later returning nutrients back to earth. Benny gleaned a lot from watching and helping facilitate this process. The Big House, on the other hand, was a bastion for the vernacular culture and traditions that his father, grandfather, and other Black migrants brought with them to Deming. Benny relished being a fly on the wall there, listening to the adults trade stories, jokes, and crude tales as they sipped tequila and Oso Negro.

Benny's most important schooling, however, came from years of shadowing his grandfather, John Waits, around town. By the mid-1950s, John was known throughout Deming for being industrious and entrepreneurial. Among many jobs, he worked as a firefighter, dry-cleaner employee, manager of a restaurant, janitor and projectionist at two movie theaters, manager of a local minor league baseball team, seasonal cotton farmer, and handyman. His fair-skinned complexion also enabled him to gain social status, particularly among members of Deming's Anglo middle class, who assumed that he had some Spanish ancestry. John eventually leveraged his reputation to purchase real estate; one property became Mamie and Bob's primary residence.

The Caldwells lived at the corner of Tenth and Pine Streets, next to a gas station and just across from US 80/US 70, two highways that, taken together, stretched from California to North Carolina. The family's adobe home was on Deming's westside, just south of the railroad tracks that divided the town. It was an area that locals considered "the white side" of town, the neighborhood composed primarily of working-class Czech and Polish families with a small number of Hispanos. Benny and his siblings' first friends were the children of these families—youngsters like the Nemec kids (John, Carol, Jimmy, and Danny), Tico Martinez, Terry McGraw, and Larry Jackson. And they partied with their Hispano and Mexican neighbors at the League of United Latin American Citizens hall, located just around the corner from their home.

Living on the westside also required the Caldwell kids to be mentally and physically tough. On Benny's first day at school, students threw rocks at him and repeatedly referred to him as "that nigger." The jeers and catcalls persisted for days. Benny's initial experience with name-calling, though, did not last for too long. It was brought to a halt after he coldcocked a boy on the playground. But it wasn't the end. Racism was durable and finely honed. Even in small-time Deming.

The town's power structure was a microcosm of the broader region: Anglo and Hispano middle classes and a small group of wealthy elites at the top of the food chain; working-class Anglos and Hispanos struggling with one another in the middle; and at the bottom, poor and working-class Mexicans, Blacks, and Indios. This racial and economic order shaped where people lived, their employment options, where their children attended school, and even where and how they shopped. So, Blacks, Indios, and Mexicans could purchase food and goods from some white-owned businesses, but they were not allowed to fraternize inside. They were also prevented from accessing the municipal swimming pool; it allowed Black children one day a week to swim, but Mexicans and Indios were excluded entirely. And although Deming schools were integrated before the 1954

Brown v. Board of Education decision, it was only in 1947 that the school board allowed Black male students to compete on white sports teams.

This context was the backdrop for John's decision to manage the Deming Merchants, the town's minor league baseball team. He believed that athletic competition could bring together youth, young adults, and communities of different racial, ethnic, and socioeconomic backgrounds. He set it upon himself to organize teams that pulled from all of Deming's talent, from all sectors of the village. Over the 1950s and early 1960s, the Merchants played teams in New Mexico, Texas, Arizona, and northern Mexico.

The 1955 team was one of John's most talented teams. It included pitcher Sammy Pacheco, a Korean War vet whose Spanish ancestors' time in the U.S. Southwest dated back to 1734, and whose grandfather raised the American flag at Las Cruces when the United States government took possession of the Rio Grande Valley in 1847. Another pitcher, Louis Quarrel, was also a talented first baseman of Spanish and Mexican descent; his family had worked in the mines in Carlton and at Cooke's Peake. The Smith brothers, "Big Joe" (Joe) and "Little Joe" (José) were outstanding hitters from Oklahoma and the team's lone American Indian players. And then there was the team's most gifted athlete, who also happened to be its youngest—Colonius "Pee Wee" Newton, Miss Virginia's eldest son, a teenage athletic phenom who John recruited back when Newton was in middle school.

John was a tireless manager, but his title included numerous duties beyond just coaching and instruction. He raised money for uniforms, transported players to games, petitioned the city to allocate resources for boys' and girls' sports, and mentored ballplayers daily at Rabbit Park, a rocky, weed-filled sandlot on the northside. Benny was always trailing along nearby. The lad loved watching his grandfather in action. Furthermore, hanging with the town's big fish came with perks: free soda pop or candy from a shopkeeper; traveling out of state with the Merchants as their batboy; and the most coveted prize of all, never having to pay to watch movies at the two cinemas where John worked as a projectionist.

During the summer, Benny spent whole days watching Hollywood films at the El Rancho Theatre and Spanish-language films at the Luna Theatre. And he always viewed the films from the projector's booth, seated right next to John.

For most movie-goers, projecting a film seems like a simple process. But for John and his grandson-apprentice, the alchemy behind it all was undeniable. Inside the projector, the film reel's images (or "frames") were paused for a fraction of a second in front of the projector's lens assembly and its arc lamps, the latter of which served as the device's light source. The arc lamps produced a high intensity light by creating an arc or, better put, an "electric arc," between carbon electrodes in air. This process generated extraordinary heat, especially when bringing the unenclosed lamps into contact with the extremely flammable nitrate-composed 35mm film.

Benny marveled at the arc lamp's power. The chemical equation wasn't hard to figure out: ***Nitrate + Light/Spark = Bomb.*** More than once, Benny watched with dread and amazement as sparks flashed, film burned, and John, the farmer-fireman-businessman-manager-projectionist, calmly prevented a catastrophe.

John's coolness under pressure and skill in transforming celluloid into animated moving image made a long-lasting impression on Benny. Moreover, it was these truths—from the projectionist booth, his parents' garden, the railroad car, and the desert—that reverberated throughout Benny's life. In the decades that followed, he strove to stay attuned to these messages' echoes, vibrations, patterns. ***Without warning, they would radiate from the most unexpected phenomena: water, wind, land, light, nature, sound, voice, music, dance, body, spirit. This was the region's magic and its most vibrant media.*** This is what made it a unique place and space to grow up in.

Amid the Southwest's peculiar spheres and mediums of attraction, impression, and coexistence, Benny first discovered the grandeur and mystical properties of all that surrounded him. It was also where he first discovered himself.

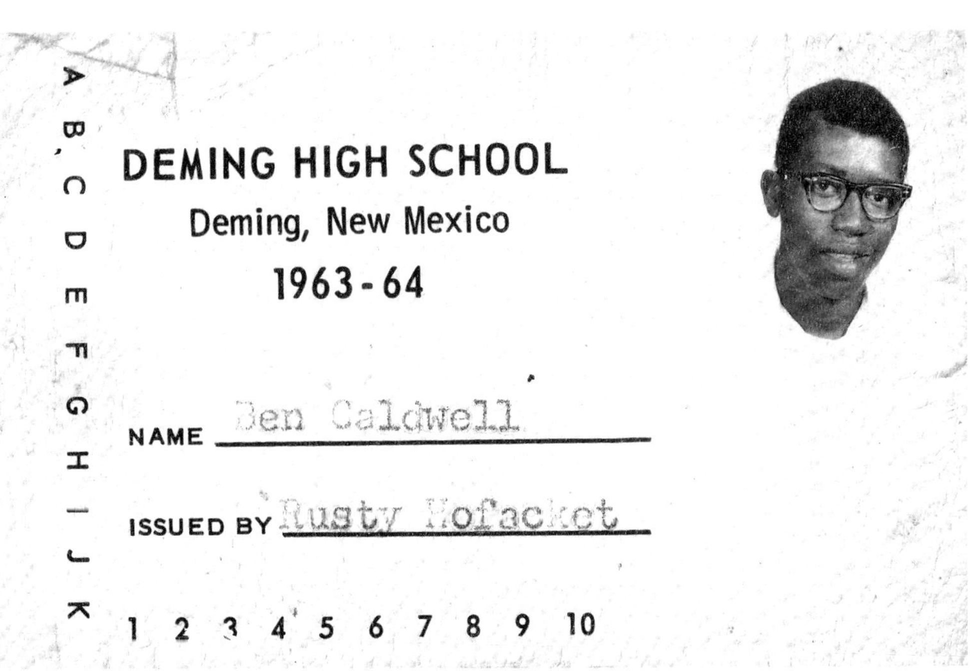

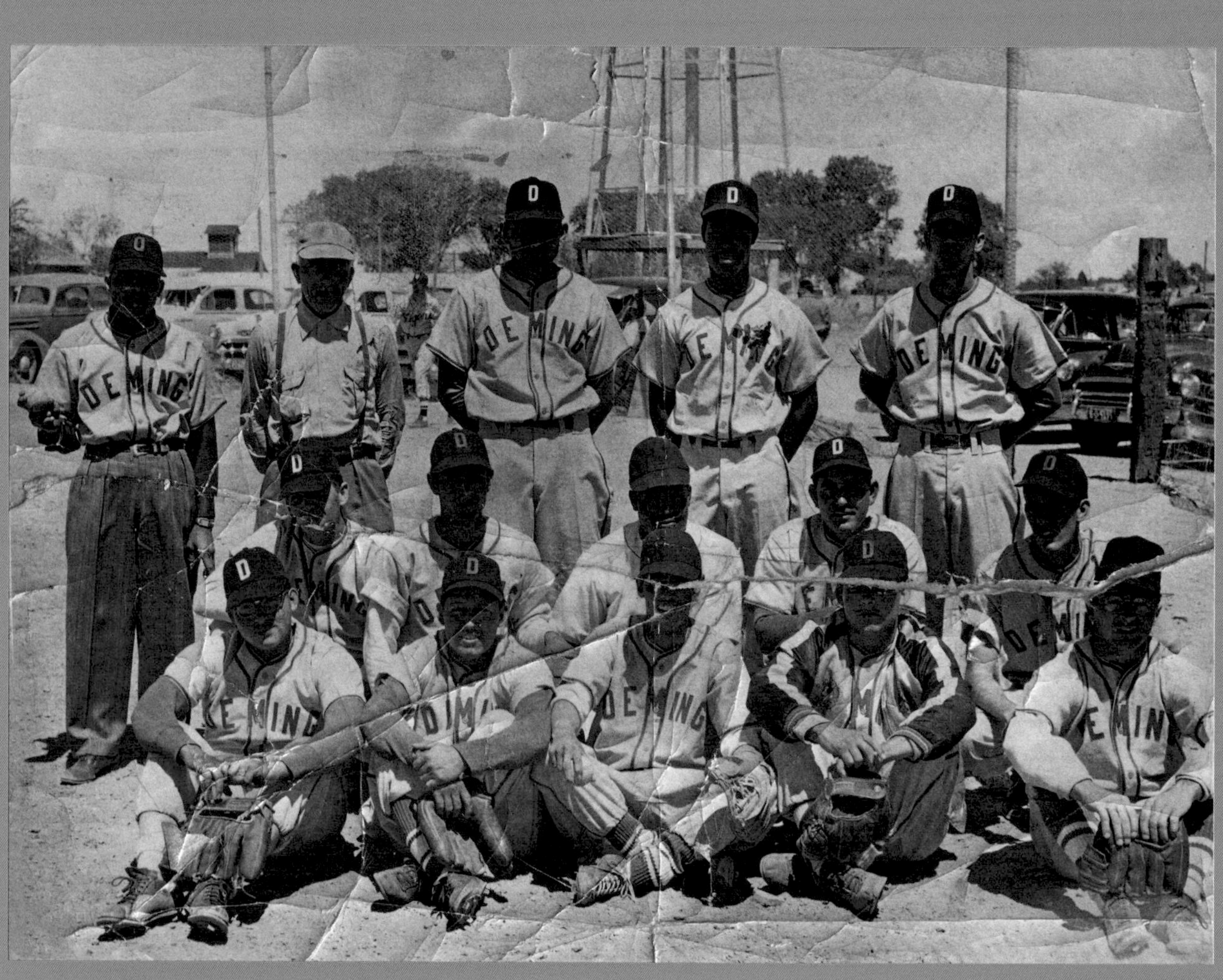

JOHN WAITS (BACK ROW, LEFT) AND
THE DEMING MERCHANTS, MID 1950S
(OPPOSITE) LUNA THEATRE (LEFT)
AND EL RANCHO THEATRE (RIGHT),
DEMING, NEW MEXICO, 1945

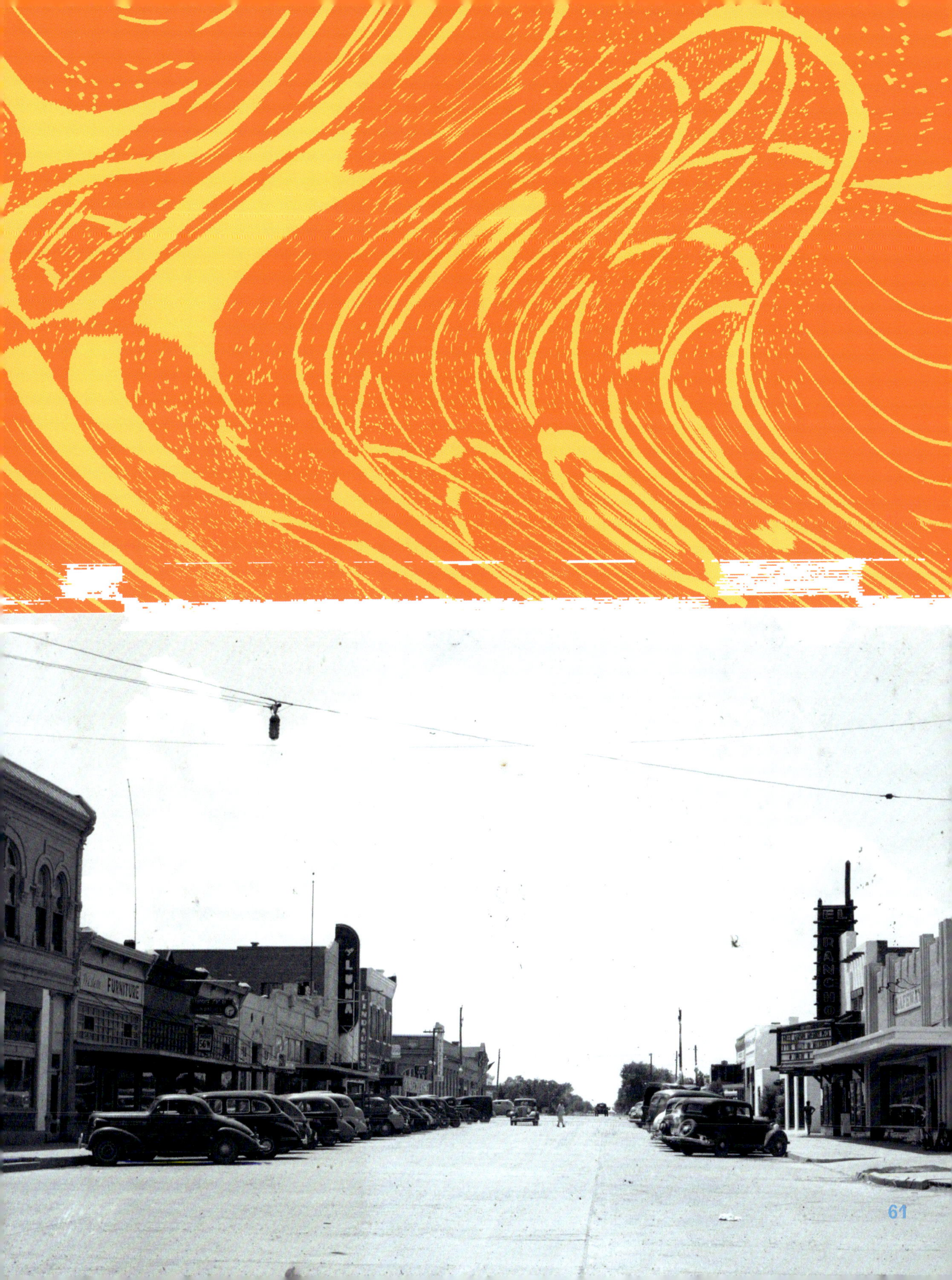

am· ka
/ähm-kä/
noun/verb (Swahili)
1.   Awake
2.   Wake up; get up
3.   Arise; rise up

A M

We used to talk about how the birds can do these extraordinary maneuvers where they'll all change the formation, something that even airline pilots couldn't do . . . They just somehow knew how to do that. And it would be a mystery to us, but it was at a higher level and a lot of cultures still operate on that level, so it was almost that here we are with wonderful mechanized U.S.A. we've lost that. And in a certain sense some of the music was trying to recapture, I guess you could say, that ethos.

—David Amram (discussing his relationship with Thelonious Monk)

Running
The real country way
with our shoes off
In the desert, in
the sand

Jump over the tullis,
which were really bushes,
tumbleweeds
Run over gravel,
feeling the heat in the ground.

Hating cement. Loving
the sand.
Sand is forgiving
Hot on the top
But as you put your
feet down in it

Desert dirt, not sand
dirt around oceans
Different kind of
consistency
Not as rough on
your feet

*Waiting for school to
let out
Take off your shoes
Start testing*

*A gravel road,
a sandy area where we play
baseball
Rocks and thorns
Try to run over
the top of them without
feeling*

*Make your feet strong
End of the summer your
feet are calloused
Enough to not be
bothered by too much*

*Run around without
shoes
Getting grounded with
the earth
Getting in tune with
mother nature*

*—Ben Caldwell
"Input 8. ZOOM001"*

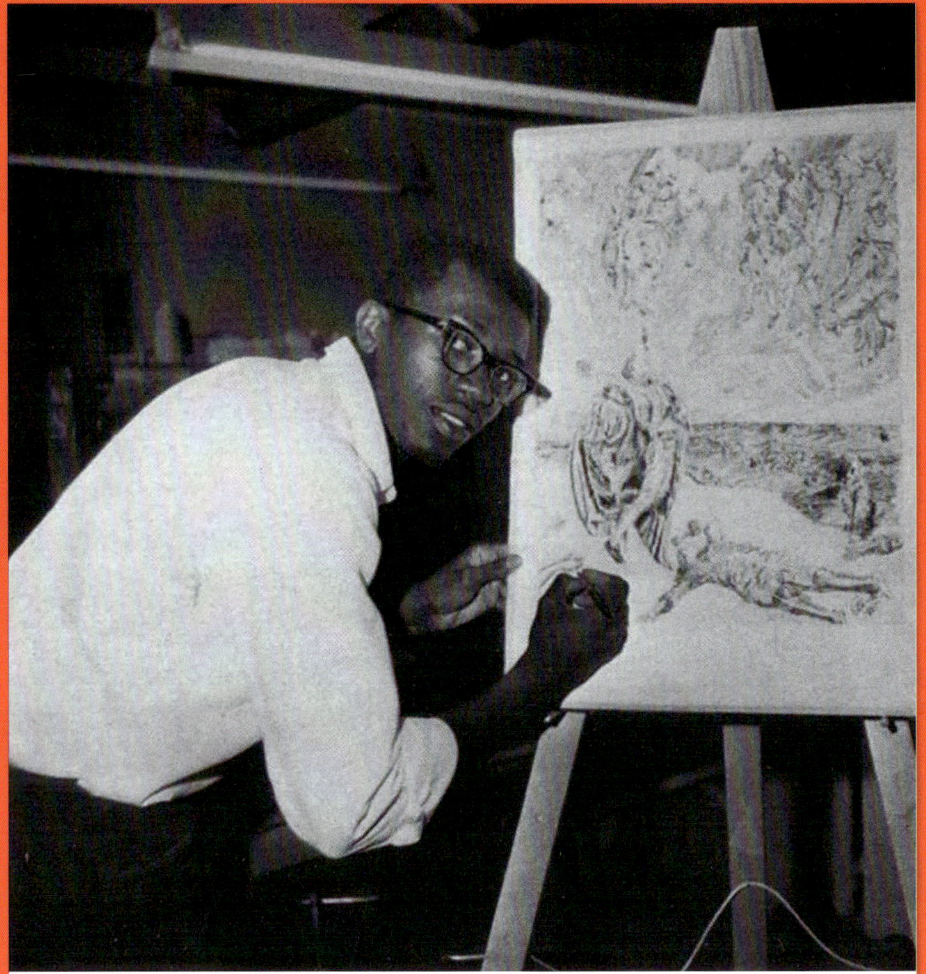

Below left: "I love art; it's the only thing I've ever enjoyed in my life," Benny Caldwell said in a Wildcat interview. It really all started as a hobby, but now Benny wants to make it a career. He's been painting for little more than a year now and has finished nine paintings. Four of these were on display in the DHS library. One of his most popular paintings is of the late John F. Kennedy which took five months to complete. Here he displays one of his pen and ink drawings of the surrealistic style.

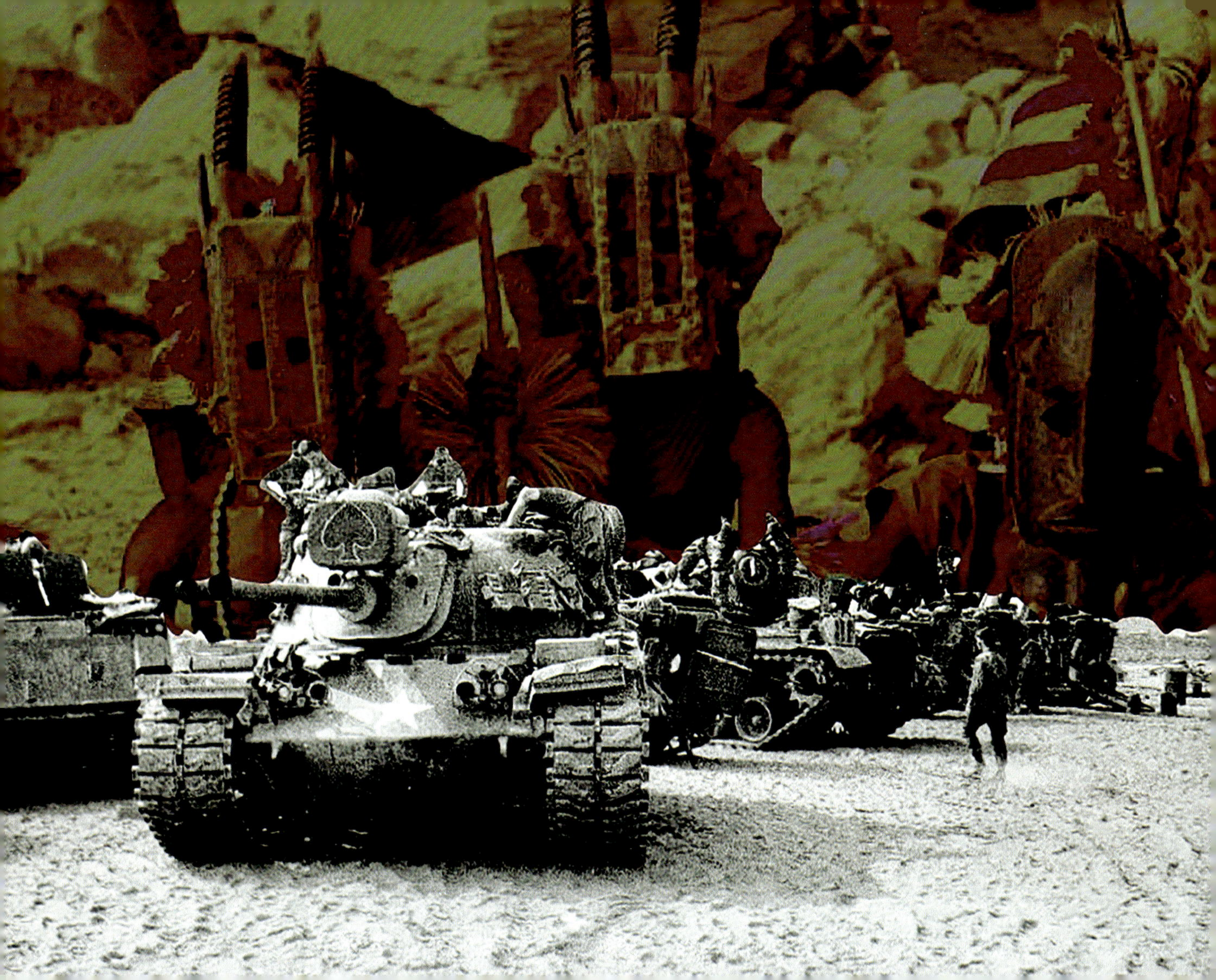

I KNOW YOU

{BUFFALO SOLDIER}

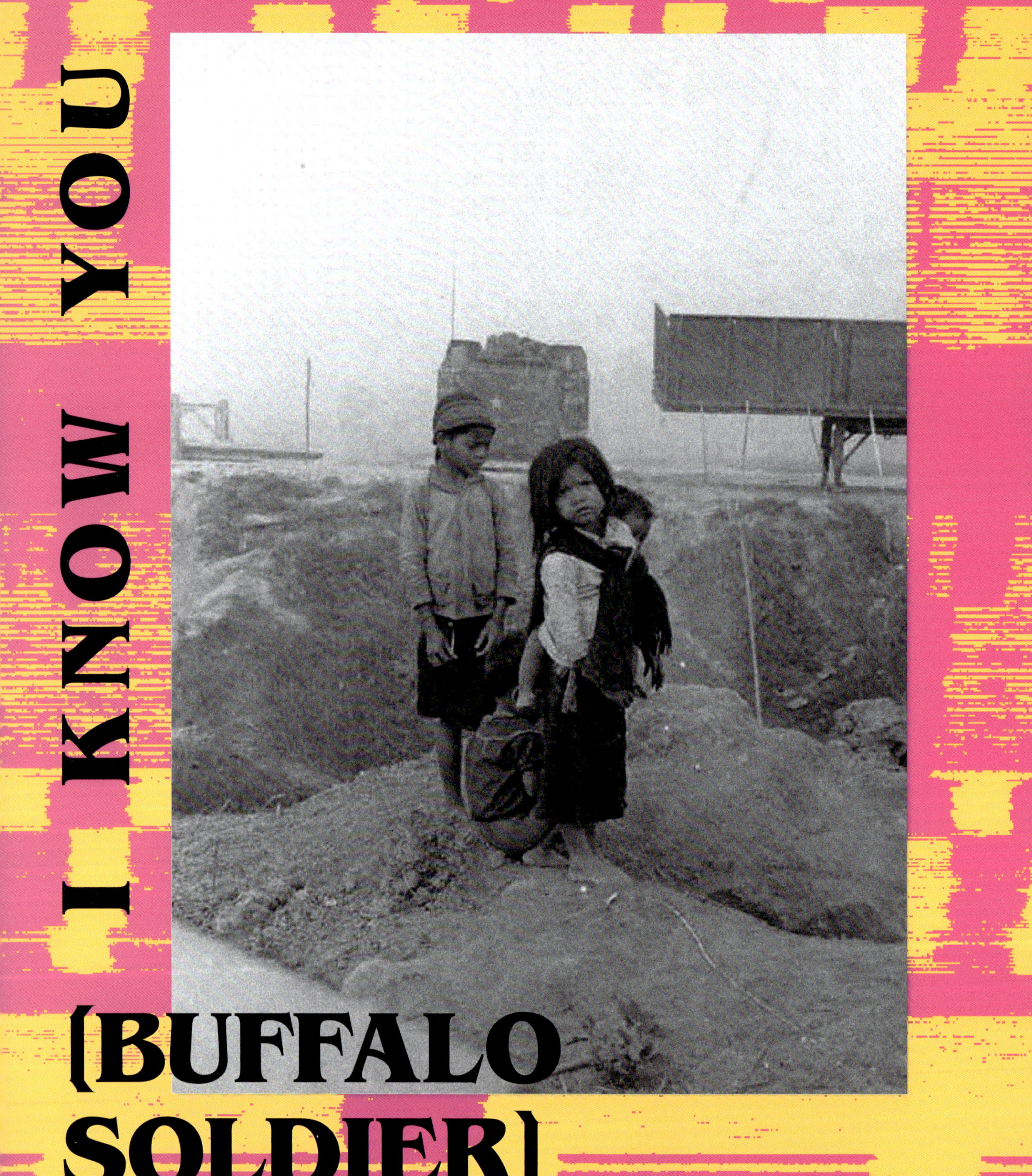

JUNE 1965 – AUGUST 1967

aptured. His cage was a military cattle boat. His penitentiary was a 609-foot long P-2 troopship, or a slave-ship, if you asked him. His warden was the U.S. Army.

Just two years earlier, in June of 1965, Benny Caldwell was graduating from high school. That was a happy day for the wide-eyed young man. A day where the furthest thing from his mind was the idea that he might end up imprisoned within the steel walls of the *USS Gen. Nelson M. Walker*, a military transport ship.

He aspired to be a professional artist. He had doodled as a child, drawing pictures for his siblings. And he had grown up surrounded by visual references: the stained glass images, Biblical oil paintings, statues, rituals, and stations of the cross in Deming's Holy Family Catholic Church; the representations etched in stone at Pony Hills and on the Mimbres pottery; the comic books, photography and science books, and general-interest magazines he thumbed through in the local library; and, of course, the Luna and El Rancho Theaters' constant flow of films and New Mexico's dynamic skies and environment.

But in high school, Benny got serious. He quit sports and prioritized developing his talent as a painter and an animator. Anything that required art, he did. Painting backdrops for plays and prom, portraits of iconic figures, landscape images—anything.

Yet after graduation, he didn't know how to make his dream manifest. He was the descendant of migrant workers. No person in his family was an "artist" (or at least earned a living as one). So, Benny did what everyone else he knew did. He looked for work.

First, he tried to get work cleaning windows. He was unsuccessful. Then he asked about a retail job. Same response. And this rejection was not the last. Benny next tried to get hired bagging groceries at the El Rancho Supermarket. He was good friends with the owner's daughter and attended church with the family, so he assumed he was a shoo-in for the job. "We don't have any jobs available," the man informed Benny. Days later, Benny learned that the man had hired one of Benny's former classmates, and a middle-school dropout at that!

Benny noticed the trend. Only young white males had the jobs to which he applied. He was twenty years old, imprisoned by his skin. The town that had raised him felt like a prison cell.

He finally landed a job in a factory stacking hundred-pound bags of beans. It paid well, but it was grueling and backbreaking. Next, his former coach got Benny a job weighing trucks. This, too, was hard labor that paid well. For months, Benny weighed trucks, dug ditches, and occasionally moonlighted hauling hides onto transporter vehicles, sometimes earning several hundred dollars a night. In less than a year's time, he saved up enough money to leave Deming.

In early 1966, he moved to Phoenix, Arizona, to attend the Phoenix School of Art. His parents and extended family, especially his grandfather John Waits, were not too happy about his decision. He was the eldest, they asserted, and needed to stay to help raise his siblings and support the family's financial needs. But Benny's mind was made up. He reasoned that Phoenix was not too far from Deming, they had family who already lived there, and his acceptance into art school was an opportunity he couldn't pass up.

The new environment was just what Benny needed. He spent his first semester studying animation with instructors who transformed his ideas about proportionality and depth of field. Moreover, Arizona's skies and topography offered him a different palette of colors, textures, and features to seek inspiration from. There was so much to appreciate, ranging from the state's iconic saguaro cactus, adobe architecture, and mountain ranges to the symbolism of his new home city's name. Phoenix—the mythical Egyptian bird associated with the sun, which overcomes darkness when it cyclically burns to death at night and is reborn from its own ashes in the morning sky. Renewal and rebirth. This is what the city of Phoenix offered Benny.

He decided to change his name. He was done being Benny. Now he was just Ben.

Six months into his new life, it all got ruined. In June, he received a letter from President Lyndon B. Johnson:

SELECTIVE SERVICE SYSTEM ORDER TO REPORT FOR INDUCTION
You are hereby ordered for induction into the Armed Forces of the
United States and to report at
<u>HQ, US Army Garrison FORT BLISS, TX</u>

The news punched him in the gut. He didn't want to go to war. As a teen, he and his buddy Steve Gonzalez Duran talked about joining the Marines and traveling the world together. And Steve was true to his word. He enlisted and was deployed to Vietnam a few months before Ben began his senior year of high school. But one year later, twelve days before Ben's twentieth birthday, Steve returned to Deming in a coffin, killed in action in Quang Tin province.

So, when Ben received his draft papers, he went into action, hoping to counter the letter's instructions. A doctor advised that Ben's sports-related injuries, in particular a bum right knee that had never fully healed, might prevent him from being inducted. A college counselor recommended that he immediately transfer to Arizona State University (ASU). "They're less likely to draft you if you're attending a college than a trade school," the man said. When the day came for Ben to report for his induction and medical evaluation, he prayed that he would be ruled ineligible and that his nightmare would end.

Six months to the day that he fled Deming, Ben was captured by the U.S. Army. He was sent to Fort Hood, a military base halfway between Austin and Waco, for training as part of the 2nd Armored Division. He was assigned to the 2nd Squadron of the 1st Cavalry (2/1 Cavalry or 2/1 Cav) and trained with C Troop, a contingent of scouts tasked with gathering information, tracking, and reporting enemy activities, engaging the enemy, and helping secure and transport ammunition.

For Ben, all of the drills and lessons didn't veil the truth. The military base was not a training ground or site for the making of men; it was a prison. He consequently determined that in order to survive, he needed to become someone else—some*thing* else.

It was as if the spirit of his father, Bob Caldwell, took over Ben's body. Throughout Ben's year of training at Fort Hood, he called upon his father's brash and defiant spirit to help him endure the prison of the military camp, the prison of being drafted into a war of which he wanted no part. For thirteen months, Ben didn't take shit from anyone. **I will kick everyone's ass until they kick me out**, he reasoned. He measured people up, goading them to test him. He rarely smiled or laughed and never conceded anything to anyone, no matter how slight. When a superior officer assigned him to the cleaning crew detail, his response was **FUCK THAT.** Ben's mandate was simple: **I set the territory. You all tiptoe around it.** And, oddly enough, most folks left him alone.

In short, it was at Fort Hood that Ben forged a robust psychological armor, its sole purpose to aid him in withstanding the conditions of the military, and moreover the war. The materials for this armor were the lessons and take-no-prisoners attitude that his father instilled in him. Yet this created quite a paradox for the young soldier, because Ben's relationship with Bob was complicated. As the eldest child responsible for helping care for his younger siblings, Ben always reasoned that his father's tough-love approach was beneficial. But Bob's anger could make him unreasonable, especially during arguments. When Ben was fifteen, he and Bob got into a physical altercation. The fight demonstrated to Bob that he was no longer the physically dominant of the two. Hence, when Bob and Ben got into another argument a year later, rather than come to blows, Bob responded with an artful counterattack: he had the police arrest Ben. The teenager sat in a holding cell overnight until Bob bailed him out.

It was the jail that came to Ben's mind when he learned he had been drafted. It was the jail that he was reminded of throughout his time at Fort Hood. And he couldn't escape that memory. A year after being drafted, Ben had another experience that conjured up the feeling of being locked up in that jail cell. It was July of 1967, the middle of a summer that was filled with Black people participating in uprisings throughout the country in response to police brutality, unemployment, housing inequality, and systemic racism. Ben had just completed military training and was on his way to Oakland, California. His unit had received word that they were to be deployed from there during the second week of August.

En route to California, Ben stopped for a couple of days in Phoenix to see friends. His arrival in Phoenix, however, coincided with three nights of uprisings in Tucson and Phoenix after the Tucson police arrested a fourteen-year-old Black teen. Just minutes after disembarking from the bus that brought him to the city, Ben was stopped and assaulted by the Phoenix police. They threw him onto a car hood, assuming he was part of the uprisings. It was only after he showed his military identification that they let him go. The following day, the police stopped Ben again. This time the officer pointed a double-barreled shotgun at his temple.

It was the memory of cold steel pressed against his flesh that flooded Ben's body as he stepped aboard the *USS Gen. Nelson M. Walker* during the first weeks of August 1967. From the ship's deck, he watched California disappear into the horizon. The sky was painted pink and violet, with hints of orange at the top and deep indigo at the base, just where the atmosphere met the sea.

It was then that he sensed a new awareness—a feeling of composure and earnestness tempered with the need to be wide awake. Eyes fully open to the grim realities that awaited him. Basic training is over, he acknowledged. So, in preparation for the battlefields of war, he again morphed into Bob, the one person Ben knew who had outlasted a prison cell.

SEPTEMBER 1967 – DECEMBER 1967

He had reinjured his right knee. Two months in Vietnam's Central Highlands could do that.

The knee wasn't in great shape when his unit arrived in Da Nang's harbor in the last days of August. Twenty days of traveling at sea had stiffened it. That the 2/1 Cavalry's first day in Vietnam—his birthday, no less—required them to journey two hundred miles south, through a monsoon, also didn't help. When his unit finally landed at Camp Enari, located just south of the city of Pleiku, Corporal SP4 Ben R. Caldwell marked his first night there in memorable fashion. He and his unit-mate Willie Wells toasted Ben's twenty-second birthday and numbed the throb in Ben's knee by guzzling a bottle of Johnnie Walker Black.

For the next month, their tank traversed through the foggy, dense canopy jungle and the steep, slippery terrain of the Central Highlands. They steered over mountains and hills, through thick brush and mosquito-laden forest, and across heavy, thick mud and moist, compost-like soil. Each man carried a fifty-pound-plus rucksack, several days' rations, an M16 rifle with 500 rounds of ammunition, a .45 caliber automatic pistol, two smoke grenades, and several canteens of water. There were also several M60 machine guns and grenade launchers inside the tank. The men slept little and stopped mainly to eat, rest, and repair their tank's chain track when it got stuck in the mud or a ditch, detached from the tank, suffered a mechanical problem, or just conked out.

Men in Service

Army Private First Class [B]enny R. Caldwell, 21, son of [M]r. and Mrs. Robert T. Caldwell, 106 South 10th, arrived [at] Qui Nhon, Vietnam, Aug. 30, [w]ith the 1st Cavalry Regiment's [2nd] Squadron, now assigned to [th]e 4th Infantry Division.

The squadron, which sailed [fr]om Oakland (Calif.) Army [Te]rminal Aug. 12, was previously part of the 2nd Armored Division at Ft. Hood, Tex.

While in Vietnam, the squadron will participate in "Operation Francis Marion," a search and destroy operation in the Viet Cong-infested Central Highlands.

He is a member of the squadron's Troop C near Pleiku.

Ben Caldwell in Vietnam

Mrs. Mamie Caldwell received a card last week from her son, Ben R. Caldwell, stating that he had arrived in Vietnam.

He said that their ship had landed at Quinhon and that he was then at Dnira, close to Pleiku.

Caldwell's ship sailed from the states on Aug. 7. They stopped in Okinawa for a short while enroute, he wrote that the people were small people, were very friendly and that he enjoyed their stay there.

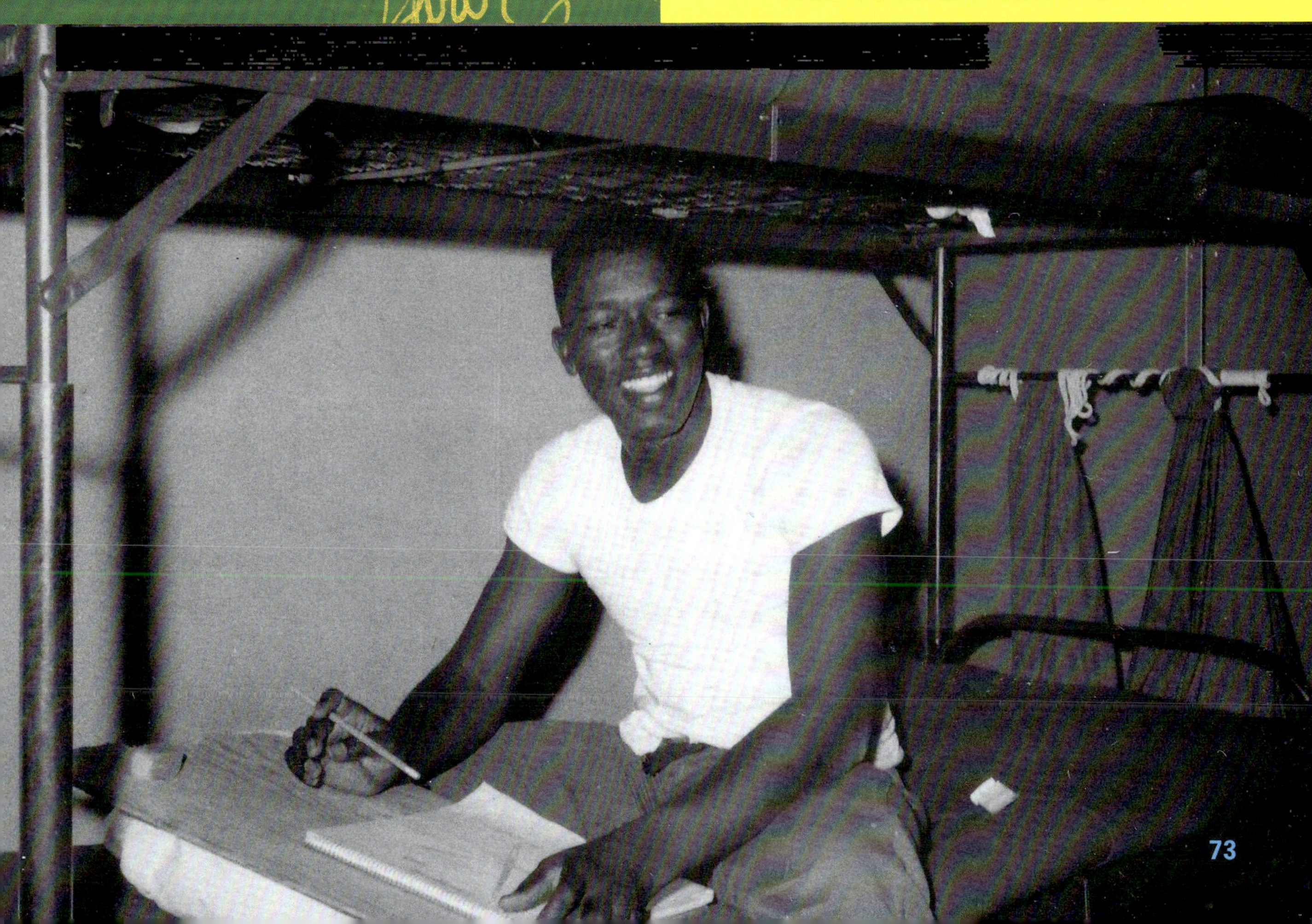

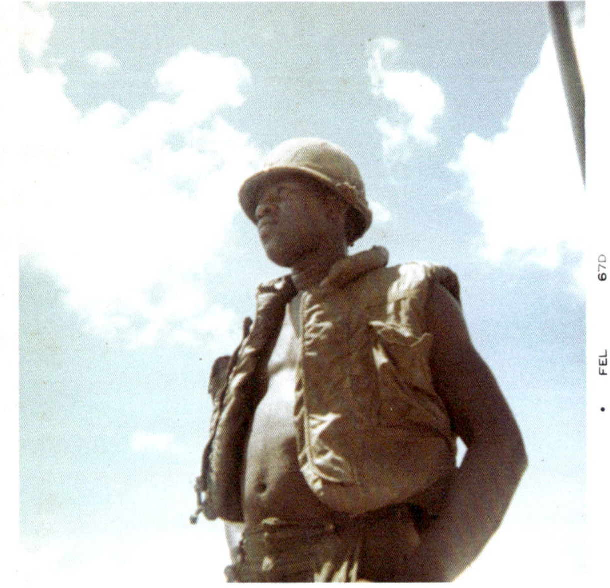

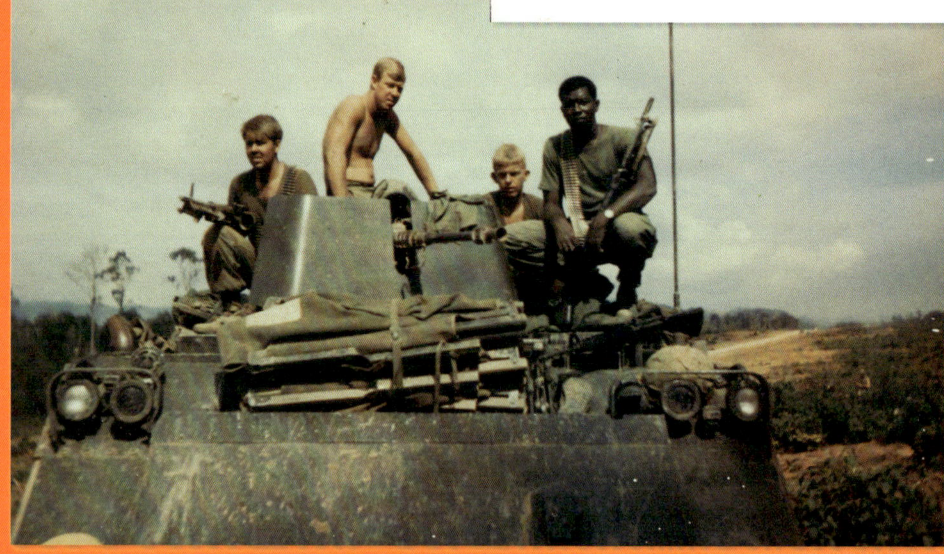

(TOP) BEN CALDWELL'S ARMY-ISSUED
CODE OF CONDUCT CARD (CENTER) BEN
CALDWELL (BOTTOM) BEN AND MEMBERS
OF THE SECOND SQUADRON OF THE FIRST
CAVALRY, PLEIKU, VIETNAM, MAY 1968

The 2/1 Cav's first mission was to assist the 4th Infantry Division in its frontier guard and combat operations along Vietnam's borders with Cambodia and Laos, mostly in Pleiku Province. The 4th Division was in the final throes of OPERATION FRANCIS MARION, a six-month campaign to secure these borders and stifle the North Vietnamese Army (NVA) and the National Liberation Front (NLF or Viet Cong) regiments' efforts to infiltrate the area with large numbers of troops. The operation had already proven arduous and costly, resulting in over 1,600 NVA/NLF deaths, 300 U.S. military deaths, 100 South Vietnam army deaths, and thousands of critical injuries on both sides. Ben's unit joined the 4th Division during the operation's final month, as the 4th Division was experiencing significant personnel turnover, losing seasoned soldiers for untested, newly arrived troops. The 2/1 Cav also arrived at a time when the 4th Division's tactical area of operations was increased significantly, encompassing Kon Tum and Pleiku Provinces, along with parts of Phu Bon and Daklak Provinces.This meant that both divisions were responsible for covering more ground and thus were stretched even thinner, most importantly with the 2/1 Cav's inexperienced troops.

Each day they conducted reconnaissance and search-and-destroy missions alongside armored vehicles. Ben was sickened by the missions. They required platoons to infiltrate and set traps within enemy territory to draw them out and violently ambush them. In late September, he felt a sense of relief after his unit finally set up base in Kon Tum, in a bombed-out villa.

What was unavoidable, however, was his dread of killing and being killed. During his first month on the tank, Ben was thrown from its top. How he ended up with only slight bruises was a mystery to his unit. But for Ben, what was even more puzzling was the feeling of being thrown from the vehicle, the feeling of flight. Everything seemed to slow down. And midair he felt an intensity of focus, an odd clarity of awareness and direction. It was as if spirits were guiding his physical movement and calming his nerves.

This feeling contrasted with the other moments of crises and fear: the loud pinging echo that rang out inside Ben's tank as it was hit by several rounds of NVA gunfire; the long hours of human silence intertwined with nature's noise posted in dense wilderness. These sounds, perceptions, and sensations left the platoon edgy and jumpy.

Their distress was heightened by back-to-back tragedies. First, a B Troop armor intelligence specialist was killed in a fluke accident with a vehicle. A week later, a member of the 4th Division's artillery unit was crushed between two tanks. This occurred just as the unit received news that tactical air and helicopter gunships had killed forty-nine NVA and Viet Cong soldiers along a trail southeast of Pleiku, just miles away from where the 2/1 Cav was posted.

One day, Ben's unit came upon the bodies of several dead Viet Cong soldiers. As they searched the corpses, Ben found a photograph inside one of the soldiers' pockets. It was a black-and-white photo of two smiling young Vietnamese children seated in a canoe, the elder child's arm wrapped around the neck of the other. They were surrounded by calm water, the younger child's unclothed body suggesting that the children had gone swimming or intended to do so after taking the picture.

For some reason, Ben decided to keep the photo. In the weeks that followed, he sometimes stared at the picture. Ben periodically asked himself these unanswerable questions. He knew it was wrong for him to keep the image. Neither the photograph nor the memory it captured were his. But he kept it anyway. And it haunted him.

The photograph was a reminder that Ben, too, was a colonizer, a conquistador—an apostle of American empire and its reign of napalm, bloodshed, and destruction in Southeast Asia. He was now both prisoner and prison guard. Successor to the Reconstruction-era 9th Cavalry Regiment, one of the Army's four segregated African American regiments in the aftermath of the U.S. Civil War. These were the troops who, in the late nineteenth century, served at New Mexico's frontier forts scouting, killing, and forcibly relocating incarcerated Apaches. The Black regiments that came to be known as "Buffalo Soldiers."

Ben looked where he could for an escape from the feeling of being trapped within the military, trapped within the hellhole of war. A battery-operated portable record player; several rhythm and blues, soul, and jazz records; and two books, James Michener's *The Source* (1965) and Malcolm X and Alex Haley's *The Autobiography of Malcolm X* (1965). These were the resources Ben relied on to withstand the unknown circumstances of each day.

Except for the blues music performed and played at Deming's Big House, Ben hadn't grown up listening to much recorded Black music. In Deming, if Black music was played on jukeboxes, record players, or radios, it was primarily that which had been filtered through white pop and country music singers. Elvis Presley and Pat Boone singing cover versions of R&B songs originally performed by Black artists like Big Mama Thornton, Fats Domino, Nat King Cole, Little Richard, and Ivory Joe Hunter. But after Ben left Deming, Black music became an essential part of his life. His record player and several records were the most vital personal items he brought with him to the Central Highlands. This music opened Ben to other worlds and possibilities. He and Willie Wells would share a joint and listen to the songs of Ike and Tina Turner, Nancy Wilson, Aretha Franklin, James Brown, Motown and Stax Records compilations, Willie Bobo, Chico Hamilton, Ramsey Lewis, and the Impressions. Melodies, tempos, and lyrics served as the soldiers' scripture; in their view, the parables of life and alternative futures were revealed through the music's spectrums of sound, color, depth, and emotion.

When he was not listening to music, Ben was reading and internalizing the messages of his two books, especially Malcolm X's autobiography. The book had been published in the months following Malcolm's 1965 assassination. Ben first read it in the summer of 1967, during basic training. He finished it inspired by the Muslim leader's ideological and spiritual evolution and Malcolm's efforts to galvanize Black people within the international struggle against white supremacy, global oppression, and Euro-American imperialism.

What especially stood out was Malcolm's, as well as Muhammad Ali's, condemnation of the Vietnam War and America's military campaigns throughout the world. Ben thought to himself: **How could anyone take the U.S. government's rhetoric about democracy and world peace seriously when what the U.S. practiced was violence against rice farmers, workers, and families in Southeast Asia? Violence against Black children, protestors, and everyday people in the United States?**

Reading Malcolm was a reminder to Ben that he and other soldiers were trapped within a war that pitted poor colonized peoples against one another. Both sides' frontlines were made up of the most exploited and expendable groups. This was especially the case for Ben, Willie Wells, and the more than 300,000 Black troops that served in Vietnam. They were disproportionately undereducated, unemployed, and working class. Once conscripted, they were more likely to be assigned to high-risk combat units, experience racial bias and discrimination, and be killed in combat, yet the least likely to be promoted. And if they survived the war, they were more likely to receive dishonorable discharges and military imprisonment, as well as experience post-traumatic stress disorder.

Ben was also drawn to Malcolm X by the similarities in their upbringings. Both men's fathers were charismatic, militant men whose unbending ways were burdensome on their wives and children. And both men's mothers demonstrated gifts of intuition and foresight that they passed on to their children. It was this perceived connection between him and Malcolm that led Ben to periodically reread the sections of Malcolm's autobiography that detail his childhood. Ben's favorite part was when Malcolm described a garden his mother allotted to him:

> *One day I went and asked her for my own garden, and she did let me have my own little plot. I loved it and took care of it well. . . . I would pull the grass in my garden. . . . I would patrol the rows on my hands and knees for any worms and bugs, and I would kill them and bury them. And sometimes when I had everything straight and clean for my things to grow, I would lie down on my back between two rows, and I would gaze up in the blue sky at the clouds moving and think all kinds of things.*

Ben would sometimes drift off and replay this sequence in his mind. It felt familiar, as if it described his childlike self. He would hear Malcolm's voice in his head, and then be transported back to Deming, back to his parents' home, back to the fields where he and his siblings had played. It also left him with a gnawing sensation. It was these aspects of his identity and legacy—***the best parts of*** *him*—that the war and white supremacy were trying to stamp out until he, too, was one of the slaughtered. `

Ironically, it was the knee—not the book or records—that saved Ben's life the first time. In late October, it swelled up and gave out, leaving him unable to walk. He was transported back to Camp Enari and then to Cam Rahn Air Base. "You shouldn't be walking," the doctor asserted. "You need to see a specialist." Ben fell asleep, anxious to learn where he was headed to next. He was startled hours later by the screams of troops being brought into the patient ward. A helicopter sent in to evacuate several Marine casualties and wounded soldiers had been shot down by NVA rocket rounds. Both the pilot, the gunner, and six soldiers were killed, and forty-five troops were seriously wounded.

In early November, he was transported to the Philippines by air ambulance and then to the 249th General Hospital at Camp Drake in Asaka, Japan. The doctors wanted to operate, but Ben adamantly refused to allow them to cut him open. He didn't trust their opinion, perceiving it as a quick-fix effort to get him back on the battlefield. **Isn't there an alternative remedy?** he asked. They ultimately relented, advising an intensive regiment of physical therapy, and cautioning that the knee might never fully heal.

The two months spent rehabbing the knee afforded Ben a period of much-needed introspection. He had been raised in a society and culture that fetishized war, that celebrated it in movies, popular culture, and history. But war was not thrilling or grand or heroic. It was lonely, terrifying, merciless.

He kept awakening to a recurring thought: **I am not a soldier. I am an artist. I am not a soldier. I am an artist.** This evolved into an incantation that he often recited to himself. It was a reminder of who he once was, and more crucially the person who he felt he needed to become. **Artists create**, he thought. **No matter the circumstance.**

JANUARY 1968 – MAY 1968

Ben rejoined the 2/1 Cav in mid-January. His knee hadn't fully healed and never would. But his doctors ruled him capable of returning to active duty.

It didn't take long for platoon members to notice that he seemed different. Less stern, more humorful; less irritable, more serene. He was like a cool breeze now, his attitude frequently lighthearted and seeking connection.

The platoon, on the other hand, was shell-shocked. While he was away, the 2/1 Cav had been pulled deeper into the war. In November, they fought at Đắk Tô, a rural district northwest of Kon Tum. Amid the three-week battle, upwards of 2,000 people from both sides were killed and nearly 4,000 were wounded, mostly NVA and NLF soldiers. The dead included twenty-year-old PFC Everett Maxwell, a member of Ben's unit. Then, in the month that followed, four other 2/1 Cav members were killed, one in a tragic cargo aircraft crash that killed twenty-six people.

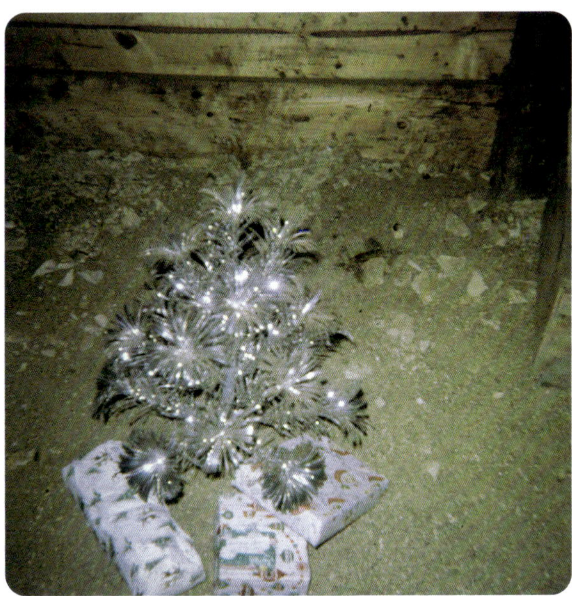

The scale of NLF and NVA soldiers killed in battle outweighed that of U.S. and South Vietnamese forces by a ratio of more than ten to one. Still, this gross disparity didn't shift the war's dynamics in favor of the U.S. The NLF and NVA continued to successfully recruit troops, keeping their regiments organized and intact and launching assaults on U.S. and South Vietnam platoons.

The NLF and NVA's strategic advantage over the allied forces became public knowledge after the NLF and NVA launched the Tet Offensive, a series of surprise attacks throughout South Vietnam that became one of the war's largest military campaigns. Ben had been back a mere three weeks when his squadron's base, Kon Tum Airfield, was attacked in the midnight hours of January 30, 1968. Over several days, the 2/1 Cav and various other squadrons repelled NLF and NVA ground and rocket attacks, ultimately securing the base. But the 2/1 Cav suffered losses, as four of its members were killed during the attack.

Weeks later, a 2/1 Cav tank ran over an improvised explosive device; the explosion ripped one soldier's leg off. This violent act triggered Ben in a way that was different from previous incidents. For the first time ever, he didn't just feel anxiety, fear, and depression. He felt rage. He felt ready to kill, the pent-up adrenaline of surviving death all bottled up and ready to burst. But then, just as quickly, everything seemed to slow down. He felt an intensity of focus, a clarity of awareness and direction.

Ben felt this sensation again after his unit detained a man that they presumed to be an NVA spy or scout. Fearing a looming NVA attack, Ben's commanding officer called in for aerial support. Hearing this, the detainee mounted an escape, running off through the brush. "SHOOT! SHOOT!" the sergeant instructed. Ben didn't want to kill this man. Once again, he felt the intensity of focus, the clarity of awareness and direction. Again, everything seemed to slow down, the man's movements appearing to be in cinematic slow-motion. Ben could see, hear, and feel everything: the bright-green, canopy-stretched leaves ahead of them, the slight wind on his back, the jungle's calm interrupted by his unit's threatening advance. He lifted his rifle … aimed at the man's legs … fired. The bullets hit the ground just yards away from the fleeing man's feet. Thirty yards in the distance, the man slipped away unharmed, hidden within the wilderness. Some fifteen minutes later, the man returned. But he was joined by his family and several other members of his village. It was then that Ben's unit realized the man had run off to rescue his family and warn his village of the impending attack. The sergeant quickly called off the bombing raid.

Before reuniting with his unit, Ben bought a black-and-white Polaroid camera and several Instamatic Kodachrome color cameras. Once back in Kon Tum, he put the devices to use. He shot the countryside of the Central Highlands: the hills and emerald-green mountains, enveloped by clouds and rich, chest-nut-brown soil; a farmer's dwelling composed of wood and rusted steel, with a woman standing in its doorway as two men guided a wagon pulled by dairy cows; aerial shots of the Kon Tum Airbase and its fields of grassy flatlands. He also shot photographs of his unit and the Vietnamese communities that lived in the areas surrounding the airbase. These images depicted moments of stillness and slight movement: soldiers resting and taking a breather inside or outside their tanks, or in the villa, or in a bomb shelter; Vietnamese farmers gradually hauling wood and other supplies on cow-led-carriages; the white-painted exterior of the brothel where U.S. troops patronized the services of Vietnamese sex workers, many of whom were refugees who had fled different regions of Vietnam; and the Central Highlands' sky at twilight, abundant with bright and dark pinks, violets, and oranges, layered above dark treetops that resembled horizon.

Pictures of the sky, the land, the animals, the people of Kon Tum, and the young American men drafted into killing, occupying, and colonizing—these were the focus of Ben's introduction to camerawork. It was a documentation of *the quiet* intimate life and relations that surrounded him—the war and Central Highlands' expressive inner character. And when taking each picture, he became more purposeful, more introspective. He would lean into his ability, his super-power—the capacity to linger within his heightened adrenaline state, to orbit the chaos around him rather than be subdued and subjugated by it. When he slowed things down, he was able to tap into his intensity of focus, and this provided him with greater clarity of awareness and clearer sense of direction, determination, and purpose.

It was this artistic practice and drive—like his injured knee months earlier—that saved his life the second time around. He got so wrapped up in this state of creative flow that he purchased a Yashica J-3 35mm, a prosumer camera. It became a recurring joke among his unit that he had abandoned his M16 for the image-making devices. "If you thought I was a good shot with the rifle, well, wait till you see me with this," Ben cracked back. But his lightheartedness veiled

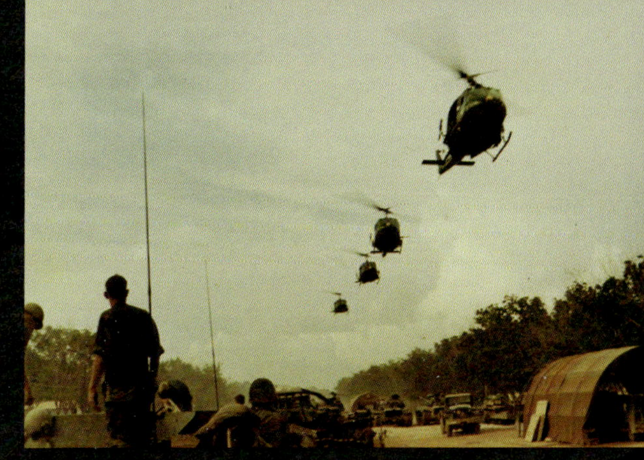

This was an A-Cav, which was hit with
or ran over a land mine, and then
caught on fire, three men lost
their life on this. Then afterwards
they were cleaning it out, and
a bunch of hand gernade went
off.

June 68

P.S. The man in the flerk was <u>the</u> only
man left. The Blast blew him
50 feet in the air, and when he
hit ground he was running.

4

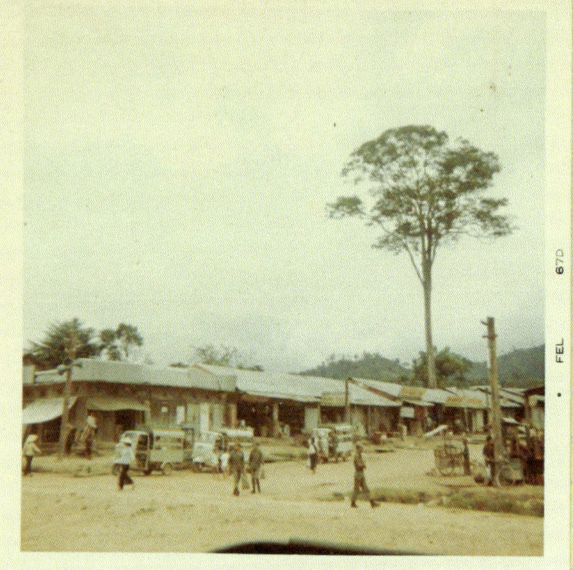

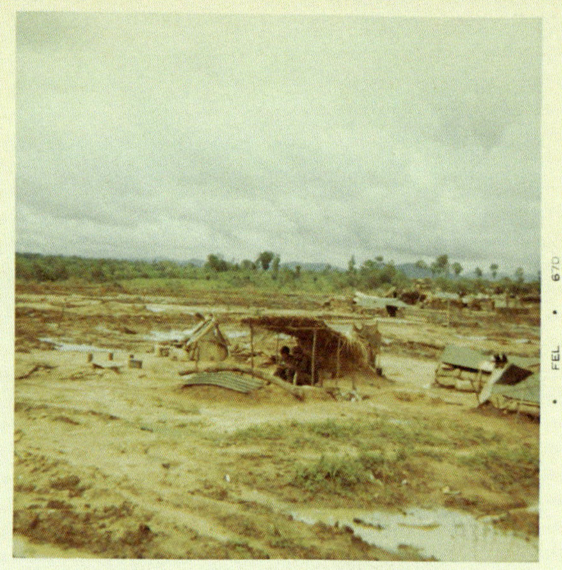

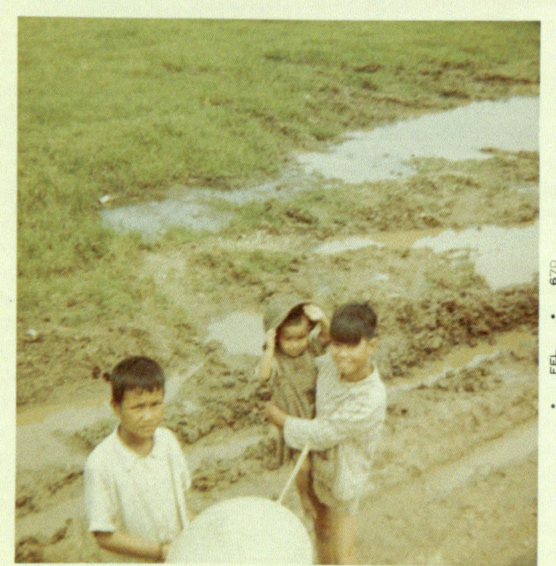

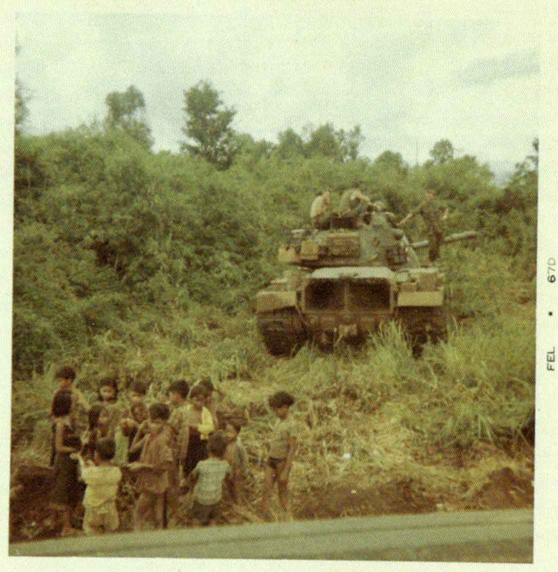

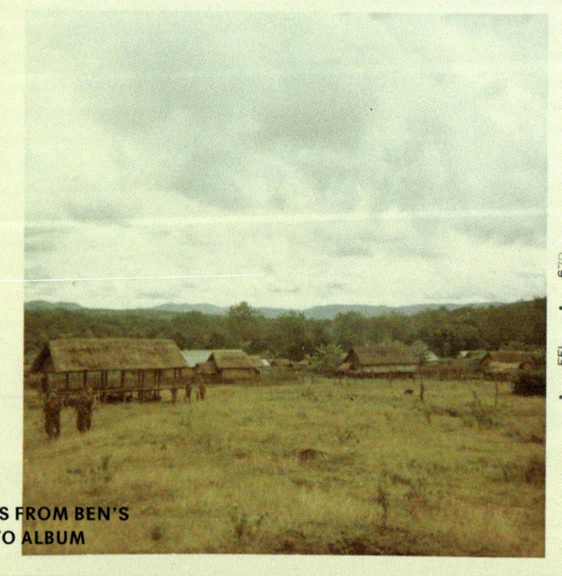

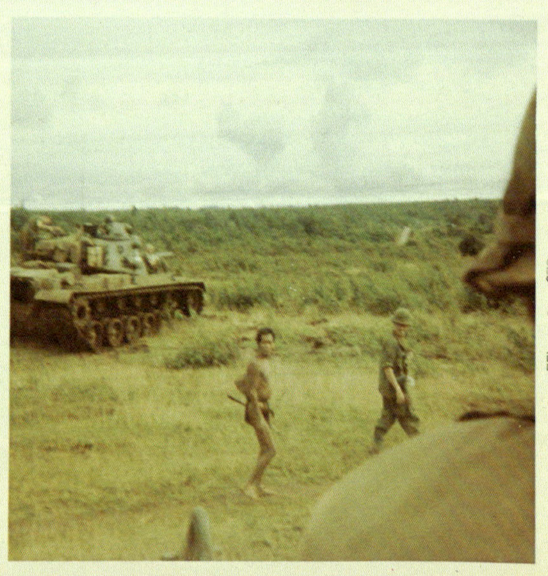

PAGES FROM BEN'S
PHOTO ALBUM

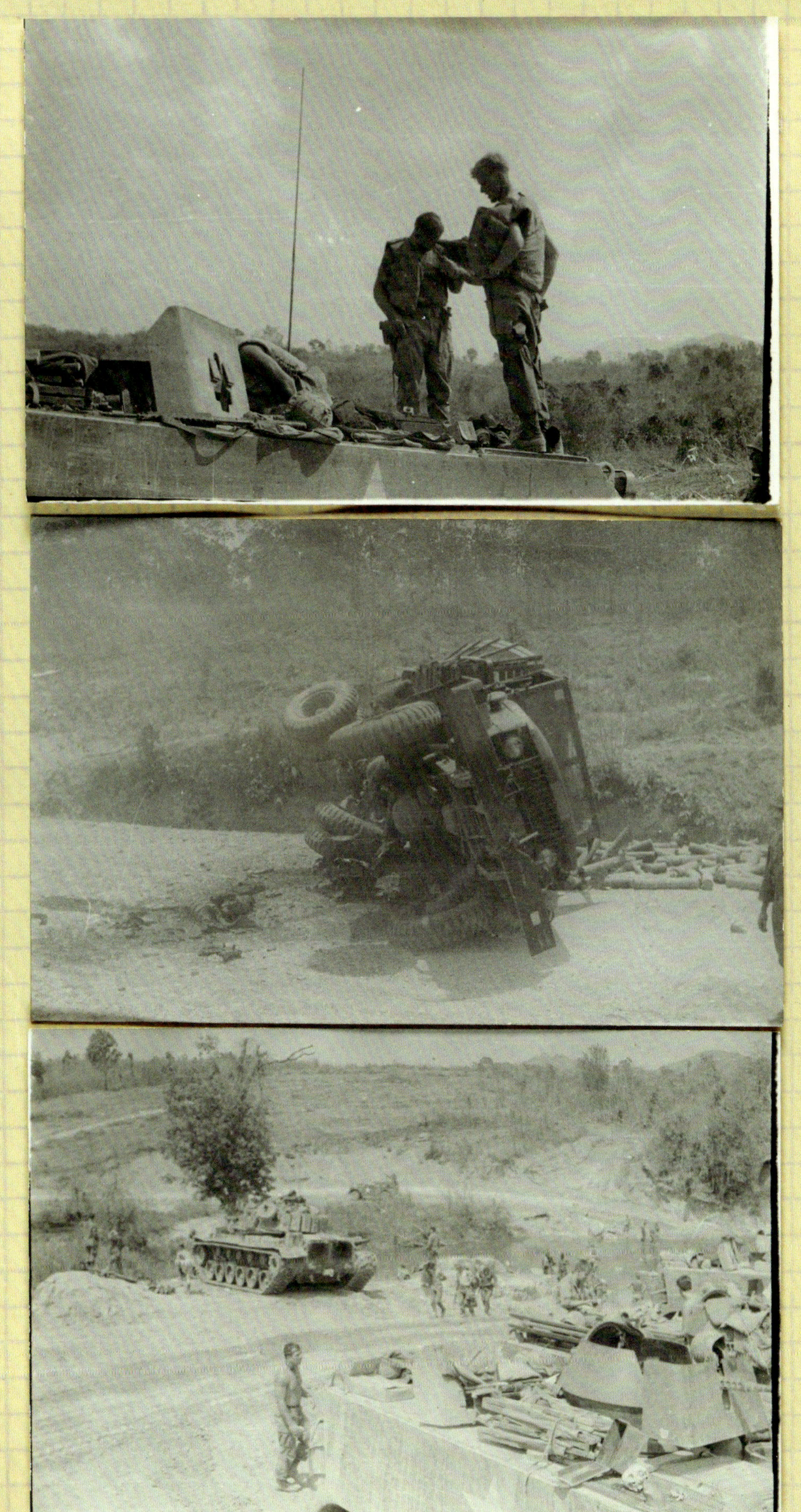

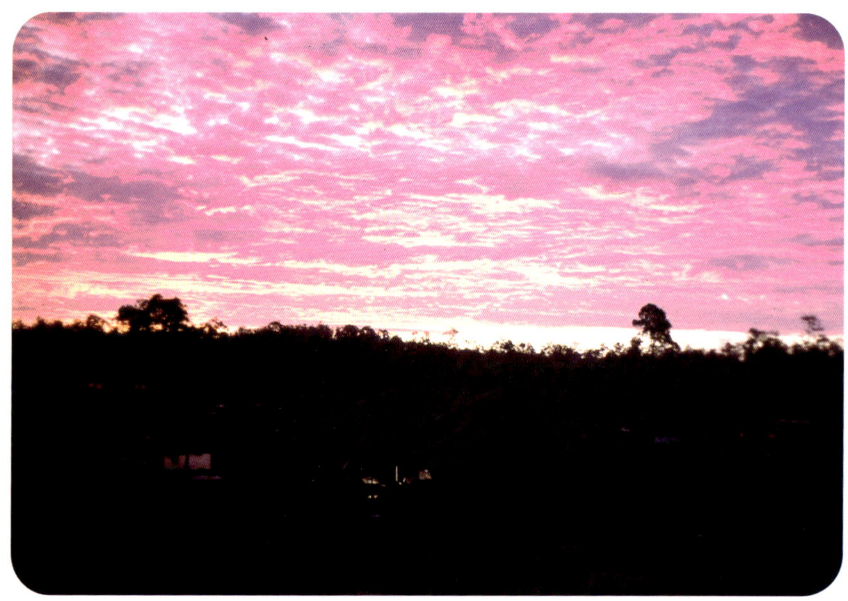

something else that was motivating him to shoot—the photograph of the two Vietnamese boys in the canoe, the dead soldier's picture.

Ben often photographed the Montagnards (also known as the Degar people). These were the indigenous peoples and ethnic minorities who inhabited Vietnam's Central Highlands. Near 800,000 resided in South Vietnam, most of them refusing to choose sides in the war. While some members were recruited by the North and South Vietnamese militaries and provided supplies and information, what the majority demanded was control and autonomy over their ancestral lands. Montagnard villages near American bases, however, constrained the U.S. forces' capacities, while those members who lived near Vietnam-Cambodia border areas were used by the NLF and Viet Cong to provide supplies and information.

A year earlier, in July of 1967, the 4th Division was charged with relocating forty-eight Montagnard villages away from the border areas west of Pleiku and Kon Tum. Over the summer months, the division moved 8,000 Montagnards to South Vietnamese resettlement centers; there, the Montagnards were to receive land and construction materials to develop new villages while receiving aid from the South Vietnam government. But the aid never came. Consequently, by the winter, the Montagnards had fled the centers, perceiving them more as prisons than as spaces to rebuild their communities. Still, amid this exodus, 15,000 Montagnards continued to live in the areas adjacent to the 2/1 Cav's and the 4th Division's base camps.

They were beautiful people, their peaceful and earnest disposition reminding Ben of his mother and siblings. Even amid war, they did not deviate from their customs of life and community.

Sometimes, as he watched the Montagnards, Ben was transported through time and space. Different settings and people would come into his view. His

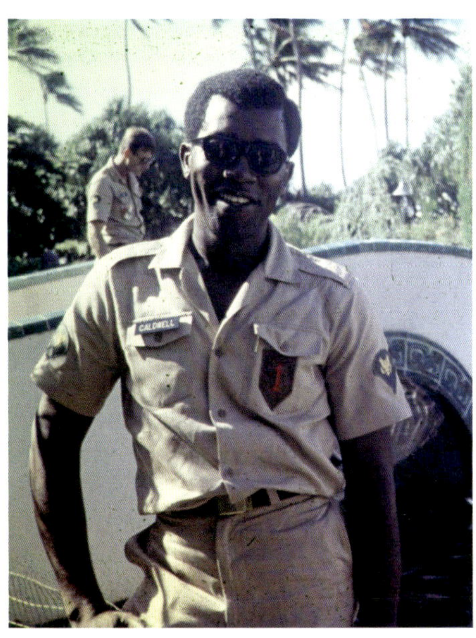

(OPPOSITE) KON TUM, VIETNAM, 1986 (RIGHT) CORPORAL SP4 BEN R. CALDWELL, TOKYO, JAPAN, 1967.

hometown of Deming and the people who composed it. The Pueblo peoples who cared for the land long before that New Mexico village existed. Esteban, the enslaved North African explorer who trekked through the Greater U.S. Southwest, both conquistador-scout and healer to some of the Native people he encountered.

What also came to Ben's mind was the state of life in the U.S.—Black people in the streets of Phoenix, Detroit, Newark, and other cities, struggling for justice and freedom, dispirited by the murder of Dr. Martin Luther King Jr. and America's unjust activities at home and abroad.

One of Ben's photographs plainly captured his feelings about the war. The photo displays two Montagnard women calmly walking down the road, surrounded by U.S. military trucks driven by American soldiers. A soldier riding shotgun looks down at the women. He smokes a cigarette, observing them. The women, however, are oblivious and disinterested in his gaze. They walk barefoot, with straw packs on their back, eyes directed to the ground and what lies ahead. The image encapsulated a feeling that Ben sensed daily: **Here we are in this beautiful space, driving loud mega-ton tanks, killing trees, tearing up the earth to build roads and bridges and pipelines, cutting up their space. Every place we touch, everything we touch—we're aggressive, we're violent.** Tanks, barbed wire fences, military vehicles, bomb shelters—the technologies and material icons of American imperialism—versus bare feet on muddied soil, a determined and dignified presence of mind, and the Montagnards' resolve and more enriched expression of being human.

Ben's interest in the Montagnards was not a one-way affair. A group of Montagnard children frequently followed him around the base camp; decades later, he described the kids as his "guardian angels." He often gave them candy

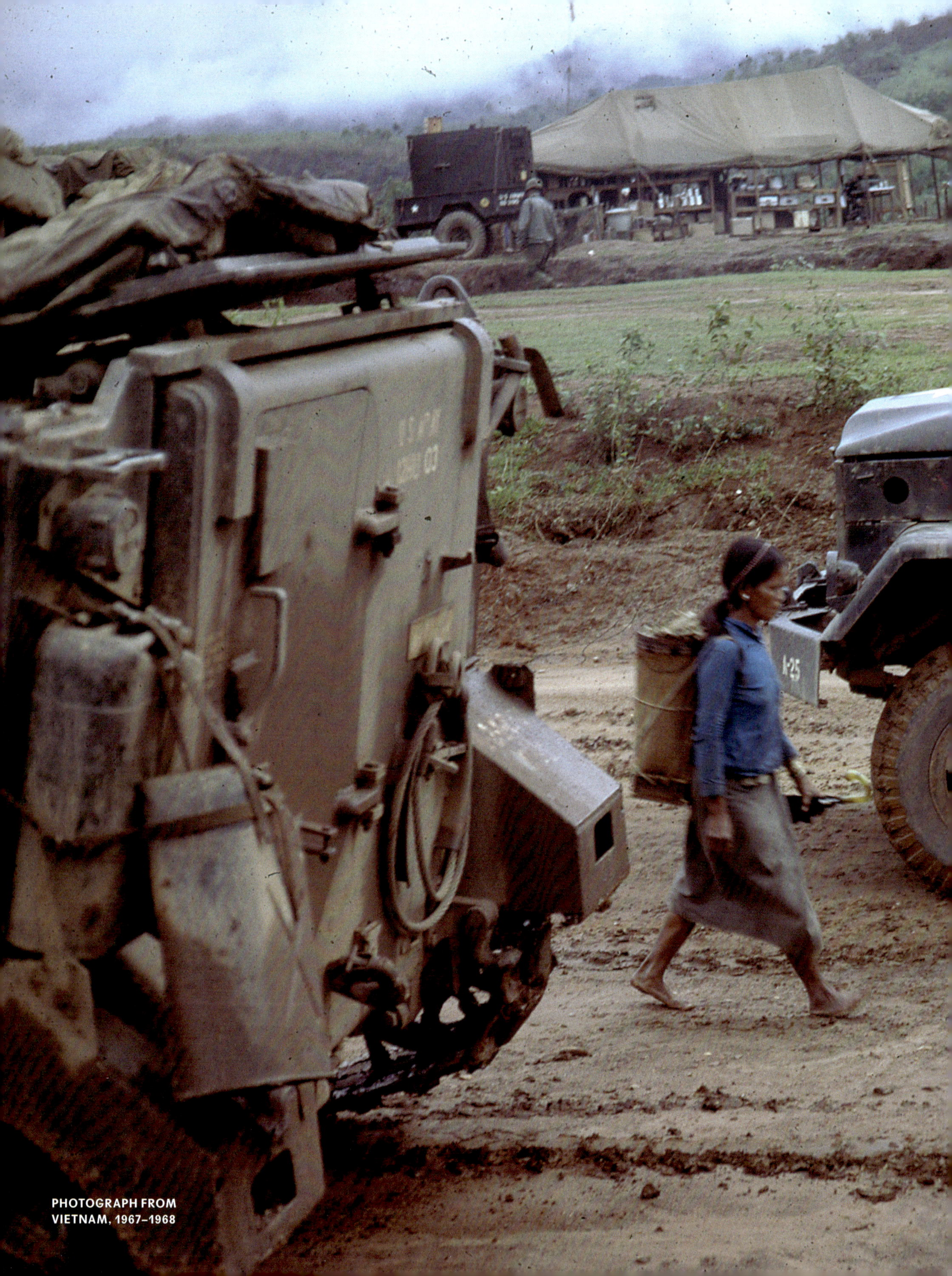

PHOTOGRAPH FROM
VIETNAM, 1967–1968

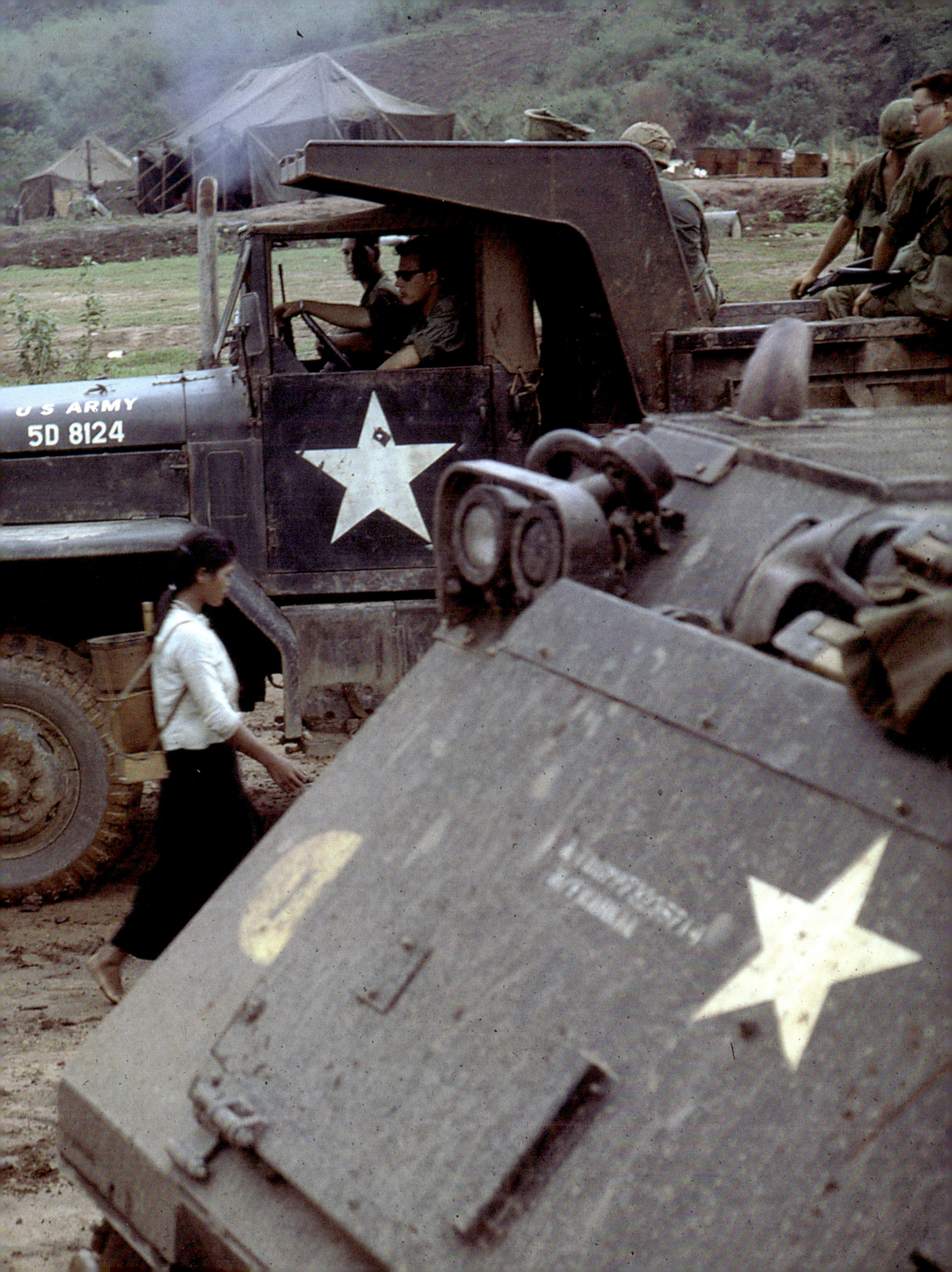
U S ARMY
5D 8124

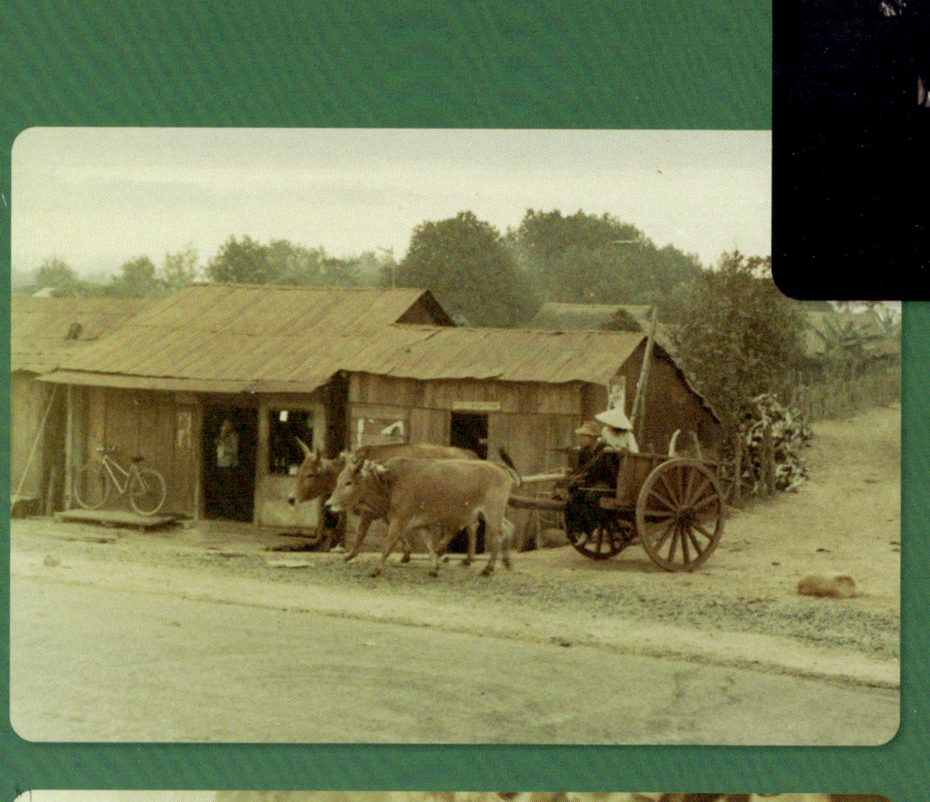

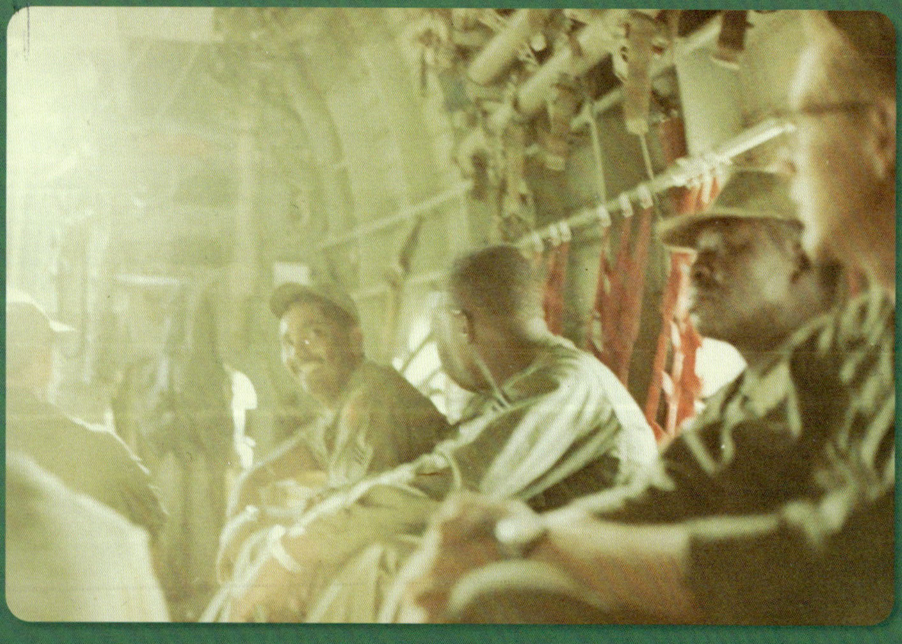

and goofed around with them. One morning, Ben was inside a bomb shelter, dozing off. He awakened to see a small group in the shelter's entryway, peeking in. Still half-asleep, he squinted, trying to make out the three small figures perched against the doorway's frame. The bright daylight behind them contrasted with the bomb shelter's dark interior.

The children were quiet and composed. Ben sat up. They continued to stare. Then the small girl in the middle spoke up. "I know you." **"Uhhh . . . what?"** he replied. He couldn't believe his ears. "I know you," the child responded. "You're Ben. We know you." He smiled. Then the child who was hugging the side of the shelter's entrance smiled back. Ben slowly raised his camera. The children stared back. *Click*—he snapped a picture. And then the girl walked off, the other children in tow.

AUGUST 1968 – JULY 1969

Ben returned to the United States in August of 1968. His arrival in San Francisco contrasted with his departure one year earlier. The beautiful Bay Area horizon of 1967 was replaced with bustling crowds, noise, youthful energy, and debris. He also couldn't help but compare the Haight Ashbury with the manicured rice fields and tranquil farming communities of the Central Highlands and the symmetrical grace and subtlety of Asaka. **Even the reefer here is trash**, Ben thought.

He spent the next month reacclimating to civilian life. He visited Deming, surprising his mother and siblings on a rainy afternoon. Several weeks later, he returned to Phoenix. To support himself, he got jobs as a school janitor and printing assistant. He also immediately enrolled in Phoenix Community College.

Life as a working student had its highs and lows. He was happy to be out of the military, but he couldn't easily shake off the psychosis of war. He was easily startled when people approached him without warning, his body tightening up in a defensive posture. When he took tests in college, sometimes his hands trembled. His mind anxiously contemplated that if he failed college, he would be redeployed to Vietnam.

His still photography class was the main space where he felt at peace. The professor, Allen Ayers Dutton, was an eccentric instructor and self-taught photographer. He also shared several commonalities with Ben. Dutton was born and raised in the U.S. Southwest (Arizona) and was a military veteran, having served in North Africa and the Middle East during World War II. Dutton also started out as a painter before he turned to photography as his primary means of creative expression.

Dutton's class introduced Ben to the basics of exposure, aperture, shutter speed, and ISO sensitivity. In lectures he highlighted the work of photographers Edward Weston, Alfred Stieglitz, Ansel Adams, Minor Martin White, Frederick Sommer, Harry Callahan, Aaron Siskind, Garry Winogrand, and Lee Friedlander. This group offered Ben different models to explore the possibilities of photography, in particular Callahan's use of multiple exposures (the superimposition of two or more exposures to create a single image), White's and Stieglitz's philosophical images of natural phenomena, Adams's and Weston's landscape images of the American West, and Sommer and Dutton's photographs of Arizona's desert areas.

One of Ben's first projects documented Black life in Phoenix and Deming. It was composed of black-and-white photographs of his family and residents of both cities. One standout image was of a teenage boy on a bicycle, his upper body slung over the bike's handlebars. An American flag hangs from the back of the bike. Some people read the photograph as a depiction of U.S. patriotism and American pride. But the teenager's quiet, pensive facial expression and bent-over, subdued body language disrupts the narrative of U.S. nationalism and American exceptionalism. His face and body communicate a skeptical disposition that clashes with the flag's conventional symbolism and ascribed meanings. The location where the photograph was taken is also important—the Phoenix courthouse and jail. For Ben, the juxtaposition of the flag, the youth, and the jail was symbolic of the tensions and contradictions of American citizenship and national belonging for Black Americans.

The photograph that captured Dutton's attention, however, was a self-portrait of Ben. It was shot along the riverbed of the Salt River, a waterway which runs two hundred miles east through Phoenix, past Scottsdale and Mesa, into Arizona's White Mountains. For most of the year, the riverbed that wound through the cities was dry, except for when there was heavy rainfall. It reminded Ben of Deming's Mimbres River.

He went there on an early Sunday morning in mid-July. He placed his camera on the tripod and set its timer, then walked into the riverbed and laid down. He let his body soak into the soil. It was reminiscent of his days as a tyke outside Mamie and Bob's railroad car. He stretched his arms out and opened his eyes as wide as he could. **Click**—the camera snapped.

Ben remained in this position for a few minutes. He had set up the camera for a double exposure. This meant he needed to take another picture, which would be automatically superimposed on the first. **Will this work?** he asked himself. He had never taken a double exposure before. And although he would be able to see a miniature version of the finished product in its negative format, he would only see it in its full scope when he developed it. He stood up, returned to the camera, looked at the riverbed through the lens, and made up his mind. **Click.**

He saw the result in the college's darkroom. The black-and-white photograph displayed him lying in the riverbed. He was gazing up with his feet pointed in the direction of the camera. But the overlay of the second exposure made it look like Ben's body was submerged in the riverbed's earth, as if he was one with the empty river. "You've got something here," Dutton remarked after Ben handed in the assignment. Ben just nodded. What he loved most about the photograph wasn't merely its composition. It was that it looked just as it had in his dreams.

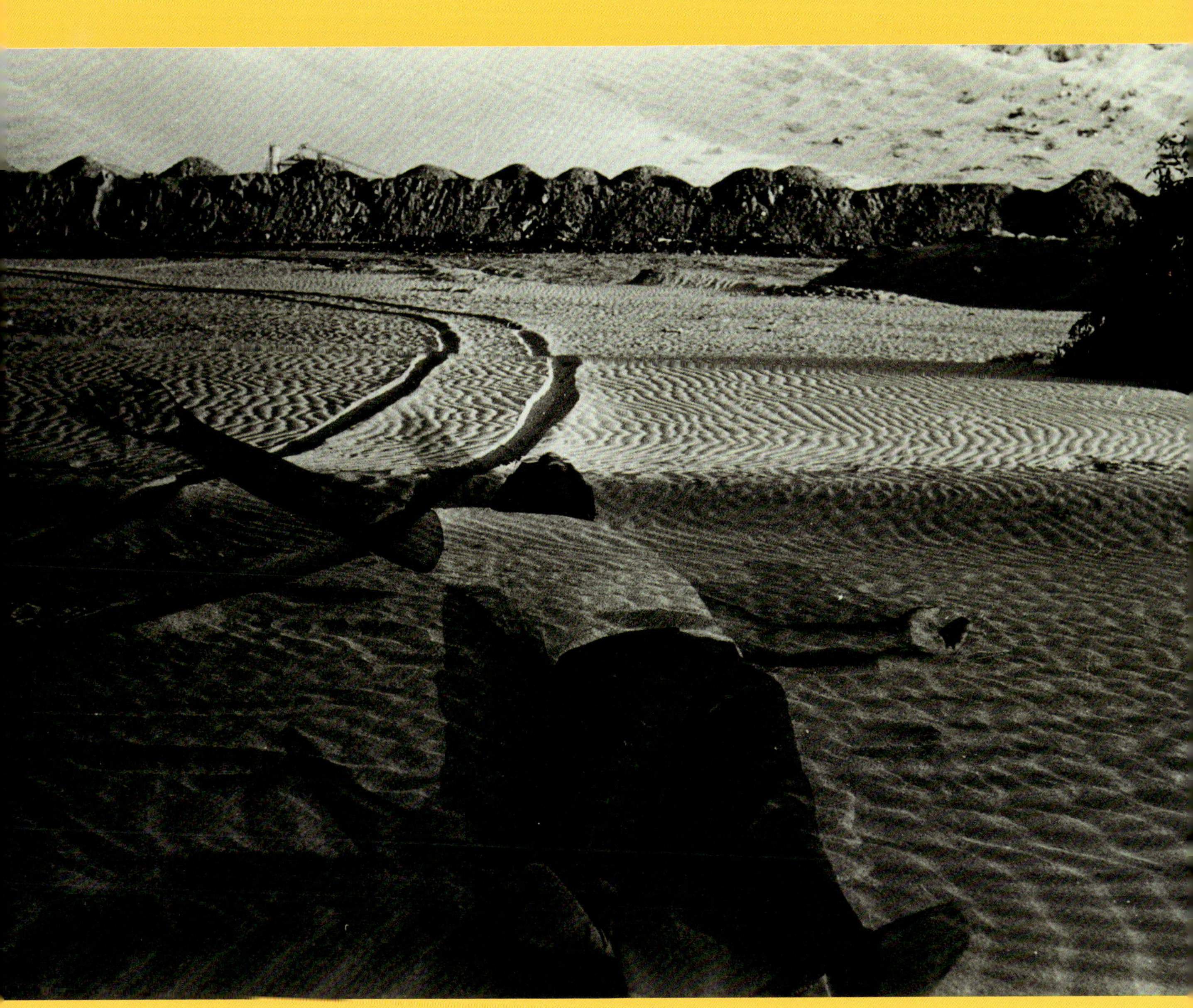

SELF-PORTRAIT, AMKA SERIES, SALT
RIVER, PHOENIX, ARIZONA, 1969

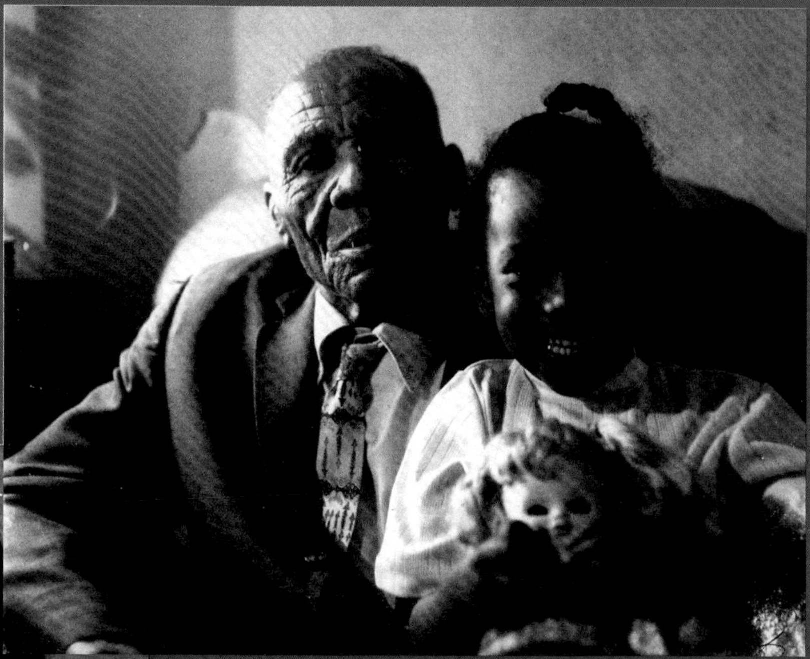

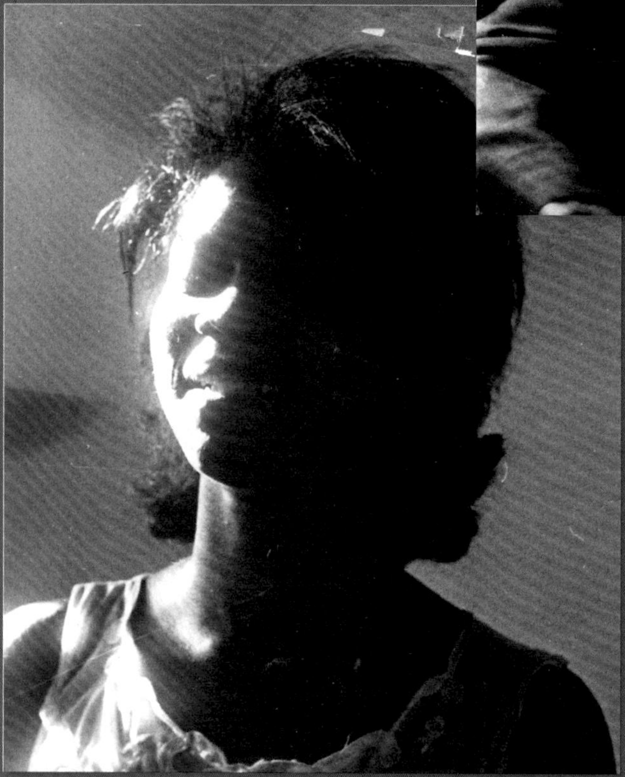

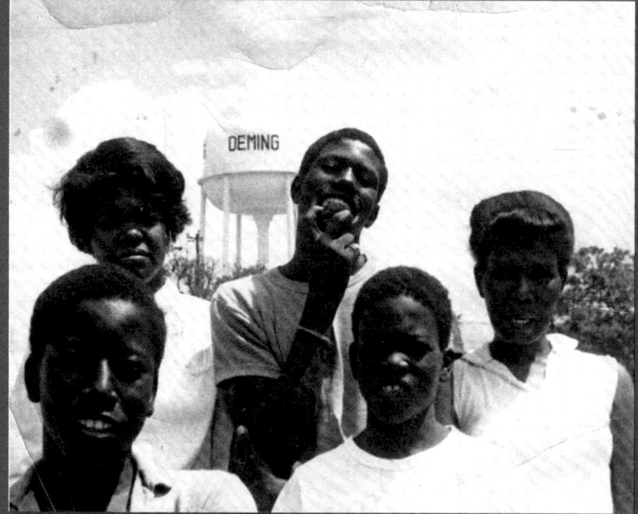

(TOP) *JOHN WAITS AND TONYA KING,*
1970 (CENTER) *LUCINDA,* 1969 (BOTTOM)
MAMIE AND CALDWELL FAMILY, 1969
AMKA SERIES, PHOENIX AND DEMING

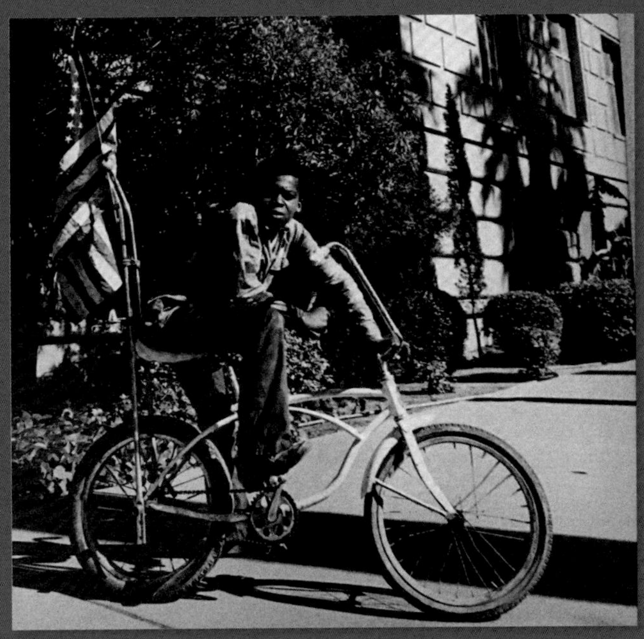

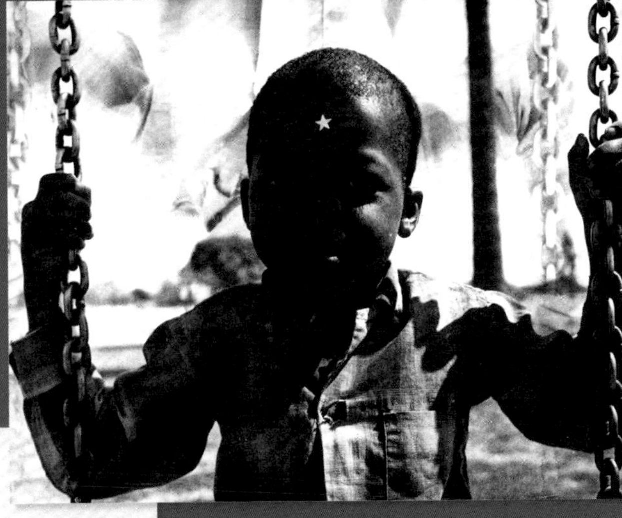

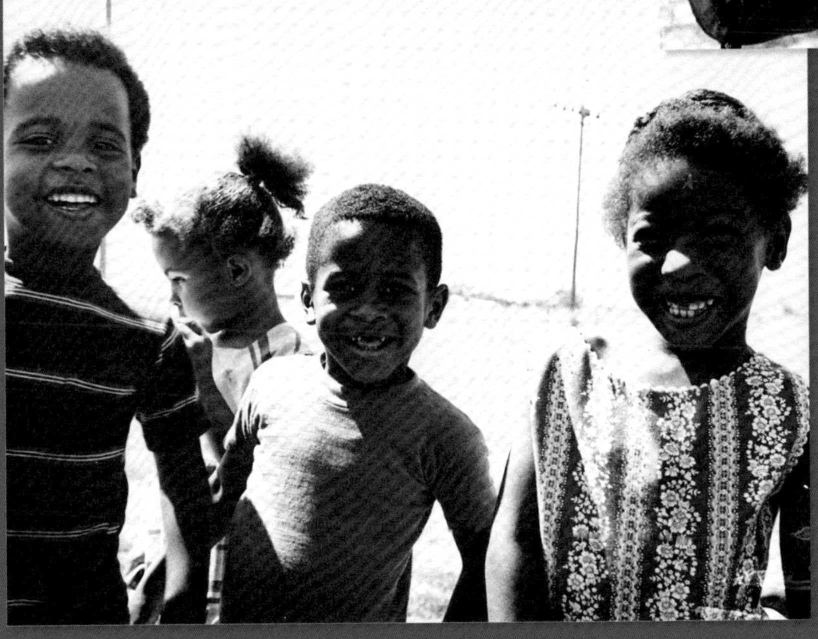

(TOP) *AMERICAN FLAG BOY*, 1969
(CENTER) *BOY ON SWING*, 1970 (BOTTOM)
SMILING CHILDREN, 1970 *AMKA SERIES,
PHOENIX AND DEMING*

Hiding between the
seats. Being afraid.
Of arc lamps and how
they fire up.
Of movies that
were playing.

Learning how to *not*
be afraid.
The *Monster of the
Black Lagoon*, *Godzilla*,
50-Foot Woman and Man.
The upstairs,
near where the projectors
were.

*That being the
Black side, the Black side
of town.
My grandfather's
incessant cough.*

*The wonderful movies
that we were able to see
and watch the transition.
The Mexican movies.
The theater.
Was my babysitter,
too.*

*—Ben Caldwell
"Input 3.STE-067"*

CHAPTER 4

EMANCIPATE

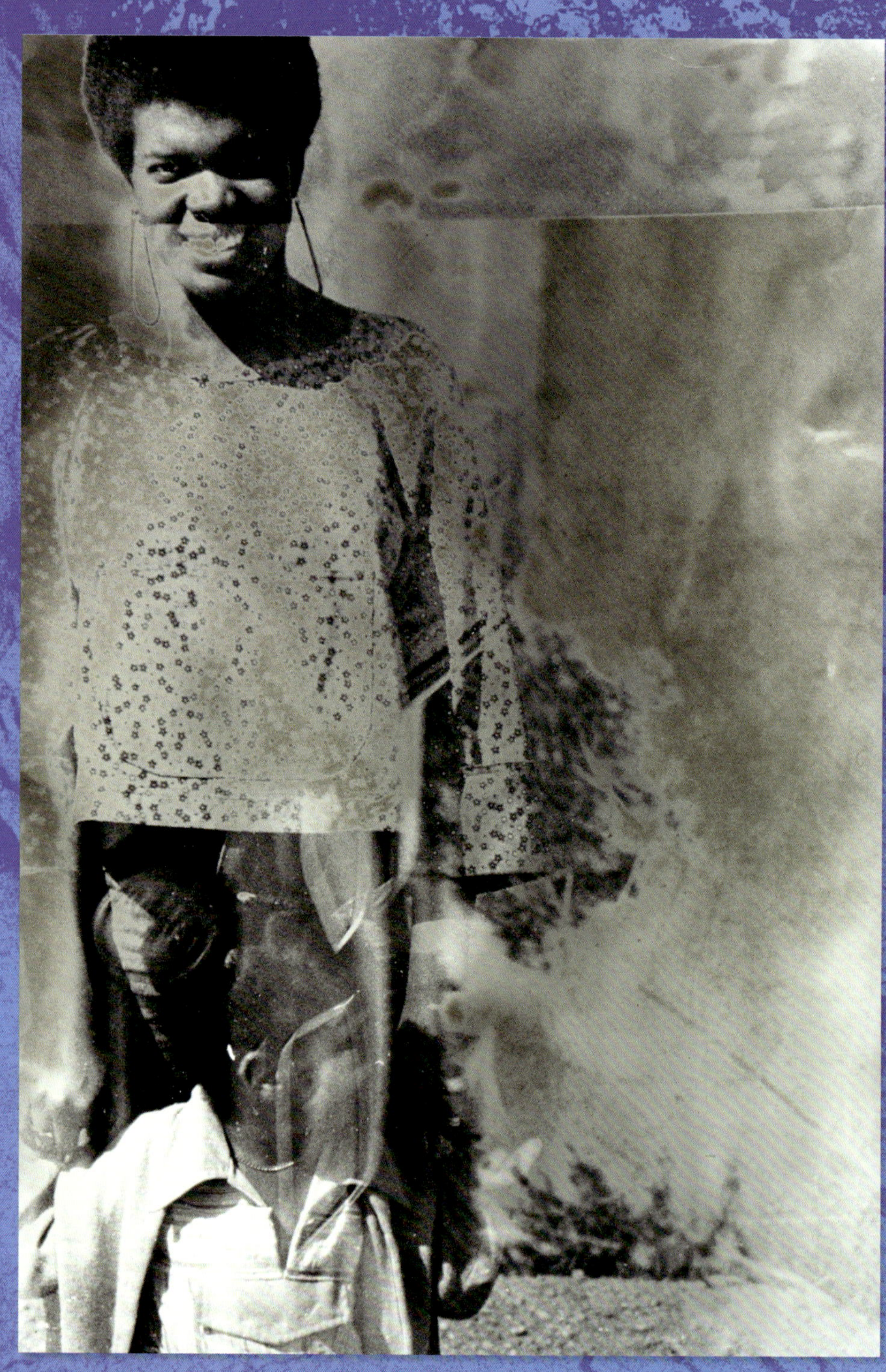

THE (I)MAGE

Pamela Nedd took rest seriously. She had been that way since childhood. Her parents, Norma Jean Burch and Ernest Eugene Nedd Sr., never had a problem getting their eldest child to bed. Their son might persist. But Pam knew when it was her time, often crawling into bed of her own volition.

Decades later, she had a rule that even her husband couldn't break: *No one but God wakes me up.* And for the most part, Ben adhered to her instructions. He would exit their room without waking her and keep their Westwood apartment quiet so that she could linger in bed.

They had met years before in Phoenix at a scholarship fundraiser in honor of a young man killed in a car accident. Pam and the deceased were both members of Phoenix's Careers for Youth Club, an organization committed to exposing high-school-aged Black academic achievers to different industries and professional networks. Pam had allowed the club to use her parent's home on West Mohave Street for the memorial.

When Ben walked in, accompanying one of the club's members, Pam was immediately intrigued by him. Her curiosity was cemented furthermore after they spoke. Ben was confident, patient, passionate about making art, and came across like no one else she knew. *He doesn't sound like other guys I know*, Pam thought. *He sounds like a Mexican.*

Ben, likewise, was smitten with her. Pam was beautiful, vibrant, incredibly smart, and had a lovely smile. But within months, their courtship was interrupted by his induction. They stayed in touch, talking over the phone whenever he had free time. They even arranged for him to come visit her before he was shipped out to Vietnam. The visit, however, had been a train wreck, mired by the police harassment he experienced throughout his stay.

Over the course of 1967 and 1968, they communicated in writing. His letters were sweet and endearing, so much so that she excused his grammar and spelling errors, a big no-no in Pam's book.

When he returned from Vietnam, he had to compete for her heart. She was promised to another man. When the engagement folded, Ben put on the full court press. They were married on December 23, 1969, at First Institutional Baptist, the first African American church established in Phoenix.

Their first years of marriage were a whirlwind. Pam worked as a high school English instructor while Ben was completing his degree at Arizona State University (ASU). He also accepted a position at ASU as the director of the Black House, an on-campus cultural center established for Black students. Leading the Black House gave the couple hands-on experience running a cultural arts space. For the next few years, they organized talks and conferences and hosted

(OPPOSITE) PAMELA AND DARA CALDWELL, FROM *DARK SHADOWS MOVING UNDER BROKEN GLASS* 1977

Ben R. Caldwell
Nov. 8, 1968

Dear Pam,

Now we are about 30 mins from Japan. We are real high, and it's down right beautiful. So beautiful we can't believe it. The sun is just setting and were looking down on the Clouds, which are a beautiful-lovely-lovely-color. It is just unbelievable. All the variations of Color, and these planes seems to be sitting here between the world of which we know of — and never never end,

performances by Bill Cosby and bands including War and Earth, Wind, and Fire. The experience strengthened their relationship and prepared them for their next life transition: relocating to Los Angeles.

In 1972, Ben was admitted into the filmmaking graduate program at the University of California Los Angeles (UCLA). Once there, he was drawn into a collective of emerging filmmakers interested in creating alternative cinematic approaches, styles, and narratives to that of the predominant Hollywood model, one that would offer more complex and empowering depictions of Black people and other non-white groups on the screen. It was with this village of artists that he contributed his skills as a cameraman and photographer, and produced and directed his first films.

It took Pam a bit longer to develop deep friendships in their new city. It felt good when she joined the Black Woman Mwanzo collective, a group convened to create an anthology exploring the histories and experiences of African American women. It was with these women that Pam found community, especially with sisters Pamela and Carol Jones. They formed a study group, reading about and discussing Pan-Africanist thought, African history, and diasporic Black struggles against European and American Empire. Pam and the Jones sisters also sang together, their friends likening the trio's sound to that of the Pointer Sisters.

It was Pam's village of sister-friends who cleaned, organized, and prepared her and Ben's home for the birth of the couple's child, Dara Mariama, on June 25, 1974.

The meaning behind the baby's name perfectly summed up Pam and Ben's feeling about the child: "beautiful gift of God." And Dara was sweet as can be. Chocolate brown. Big, bright eyes. But even after being home for several months, she was unwilling to adhere to Pam's sleep mandate. For the first time in Pam's life, she did not dictate her own sleep schedule; Dara did. One late night/early morning, Pam was awakened by the baby's screams and cries. Pam went to her, frustrated and worn down. She picked up Dara and the baby stopped crying and looked Pam directly in the eyes.

Pam and Ben's new reality instantly set in. Stewarding Dara through her first stages was the ultimate gift and responsibility. ***Our baby is not a thing. She's not a doll. She's something way beyond what we expected her to be—she's a BEING, a SPIRIT, a POWER, an ESSENCE.*** Before the baby, Pam was sleepwalking through life. Then Dara Mariama woke her up.

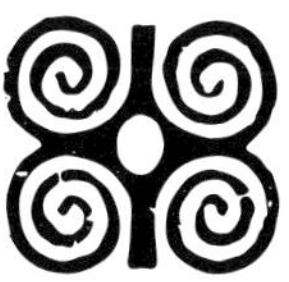

(OPPOSITE, TOP) PAMELA NEDD, 1965 (OPPOSITE, BOTTOM) BEN'S LETTER TO PAM, 1967

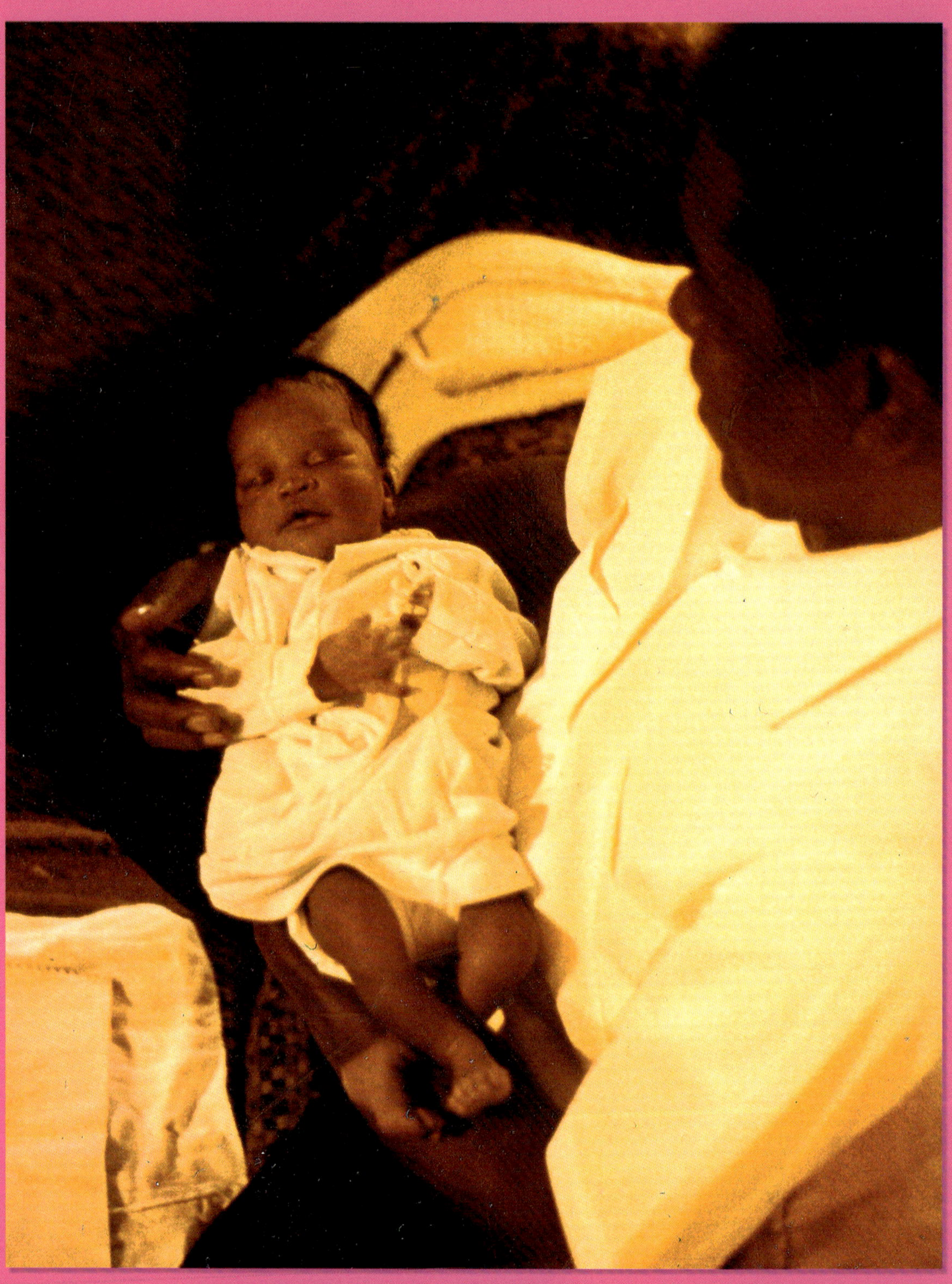

DARA IN THE ARMS OF HER
GRANDFATHER, ERNEST NEDD, 1974

In the years foreshadowing Dara's birth, similar messages were taking shape and reverberating throughout her father's art. This was a period of immense creative exploration and growth for Ben. In the fall of 1969, he transferred from Phoenix College to ASU. He dropped his business and economics major for photography and philosophy in ASU's Department of Fine Art.

Several faculty members were influential in shaping Ben's evolving artistic approach. The former department chair Harry Wood and newcomer Eric Kronengold lectured on the presence of the occult and supernatural themes in art. While Wood, the elder statesman, explored these subjects within the history of painting, Kronengold frequently engaged Ben in discussions regarding surrealist interventions within photography.

Ben also drew inspiration from his former professor Allen Dutton's Arizona landscape series, black-and-white photos that highlighted the curvy, expansive, and unfilled terrain of the Southwest's deserts and mountain ranges. Dutton reasoned that to survey the region's vast openness and its juxtaposition of mountain vistas, dirt roads, wide skies, and slender waterways was akin to considering the mysteries of outer space. "It's about becoming more comfortable getting to a place where there are no answers," he surmised. Dutton also introduced Ben to the black-and-white landscape photographs and conceptual approach of photographer Minor White. Beyond being impressed with White's technical mastery of light and shadow, Ben was intrigued by the photographer's philosophical ideas about the connections between nature and spirituality and, furthermore, regarding photography as a process of "conscious discovery" where photographic scenes were organized around expressing and revealing important messages to both photographer and viewers. Thus, when Dutton brought White to Phoenix to give several lectures in 1969 and 1970, Ben took full advantage, sharing his evolving work with White and soaking up White's numerous insights.

Ben's practice was also informed by his relationships with Professors Roosevelt "Rip" Woods and J. Eugene Grigsby, two artists who joined ASU's faculty in the mid-1960s. Grigsby was a painter, multimedia artist, and prominent arts educator whose lectures enhanced Ben's understanding of the links between Native American, African, and African American art. Woods, on the other hand, was a painter and printmaker who taught courses in drawing, painting, and silk-screening. Ben was drawn to Woods's art. It made satirical commentary about being Black in America—polarizing images that some people found to be insightful, and others saw as offensive. Ben also connected with Woods's approach to artmaking, which Woods attributed to his childhood. Woods encouraged Ben to tap into those elements within himself, to submerge himself within his subconscious mind and memory when creating art.

Ben's undergraduate thesis, *AMKA (The Awakening)* fused these lessons into a series of multimedia photographs. In the images, Black women symbolize the desert and its planetary and celestial energy. Simultaneously, the desert is portrayed as emblematic of the cosmic feminine.

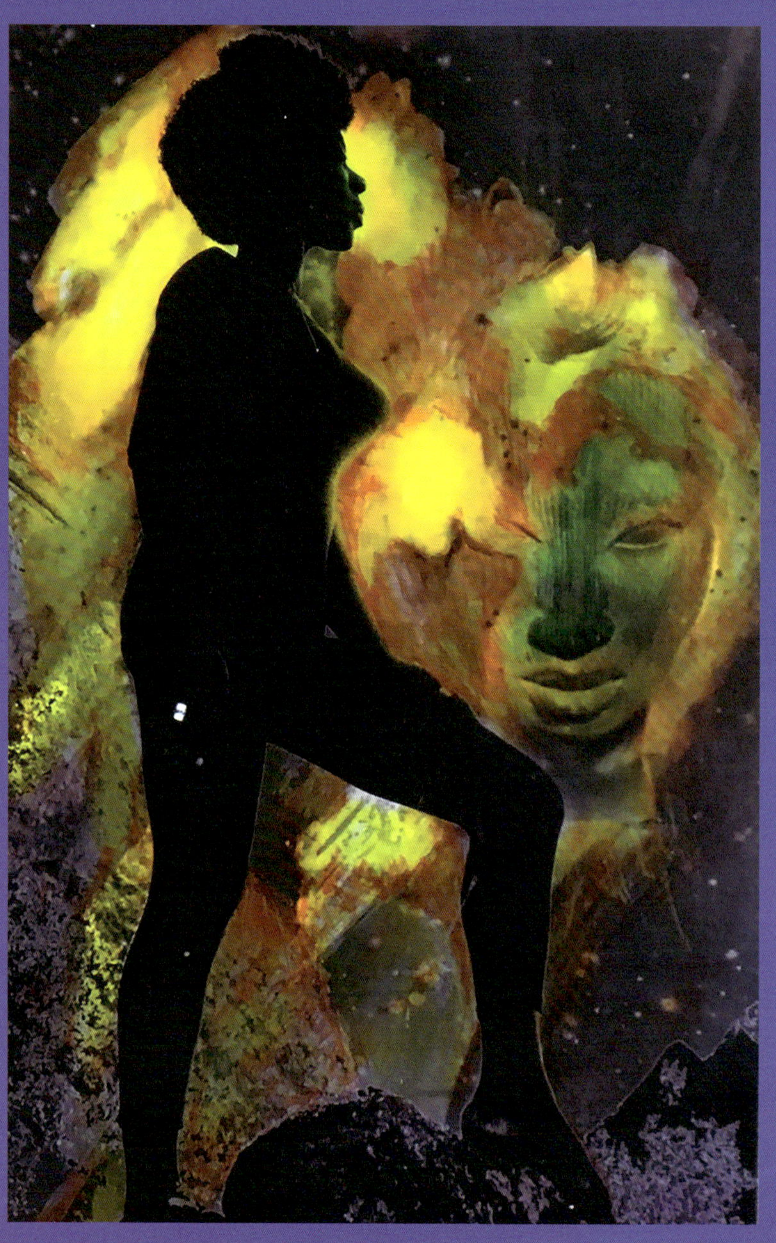

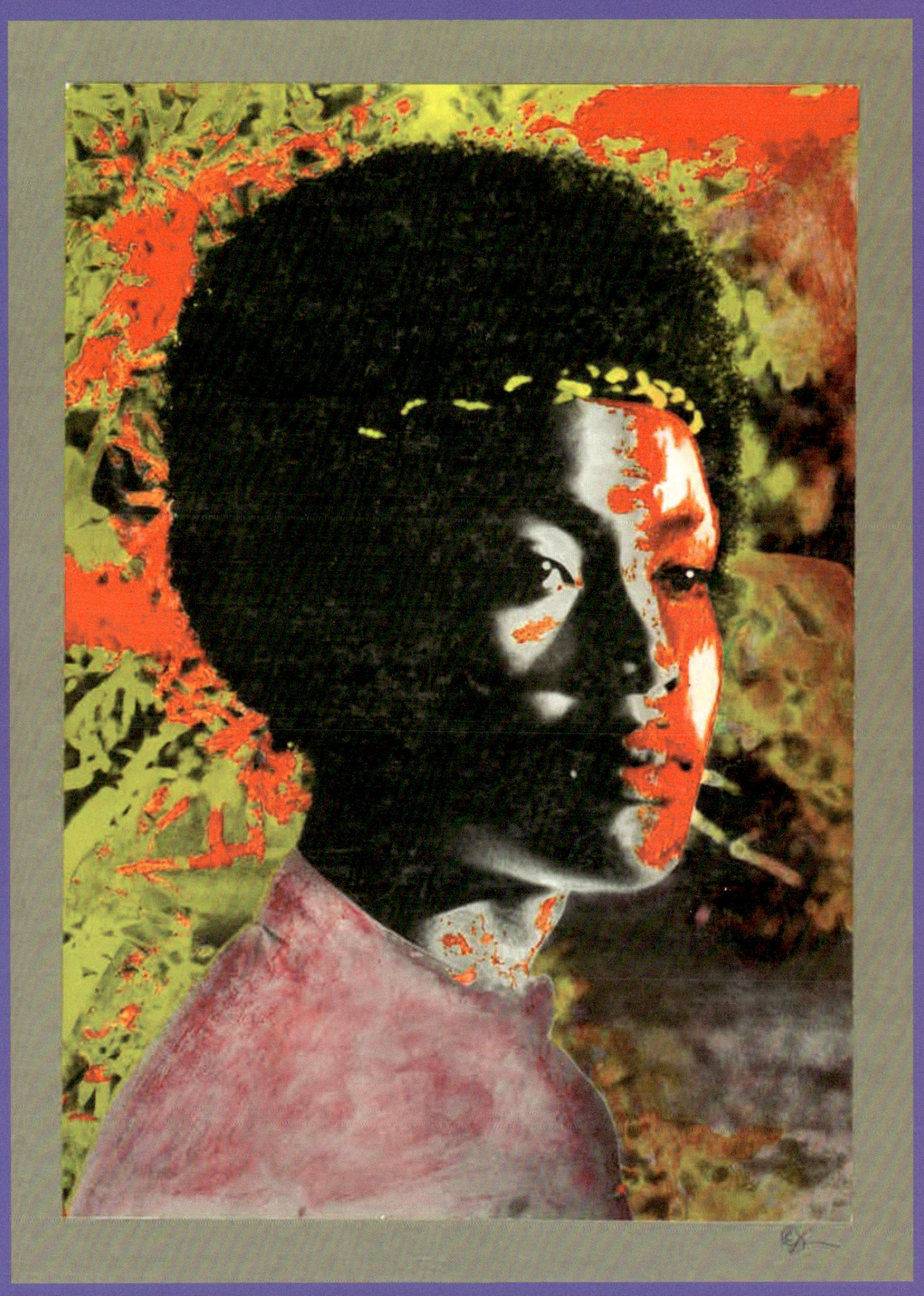

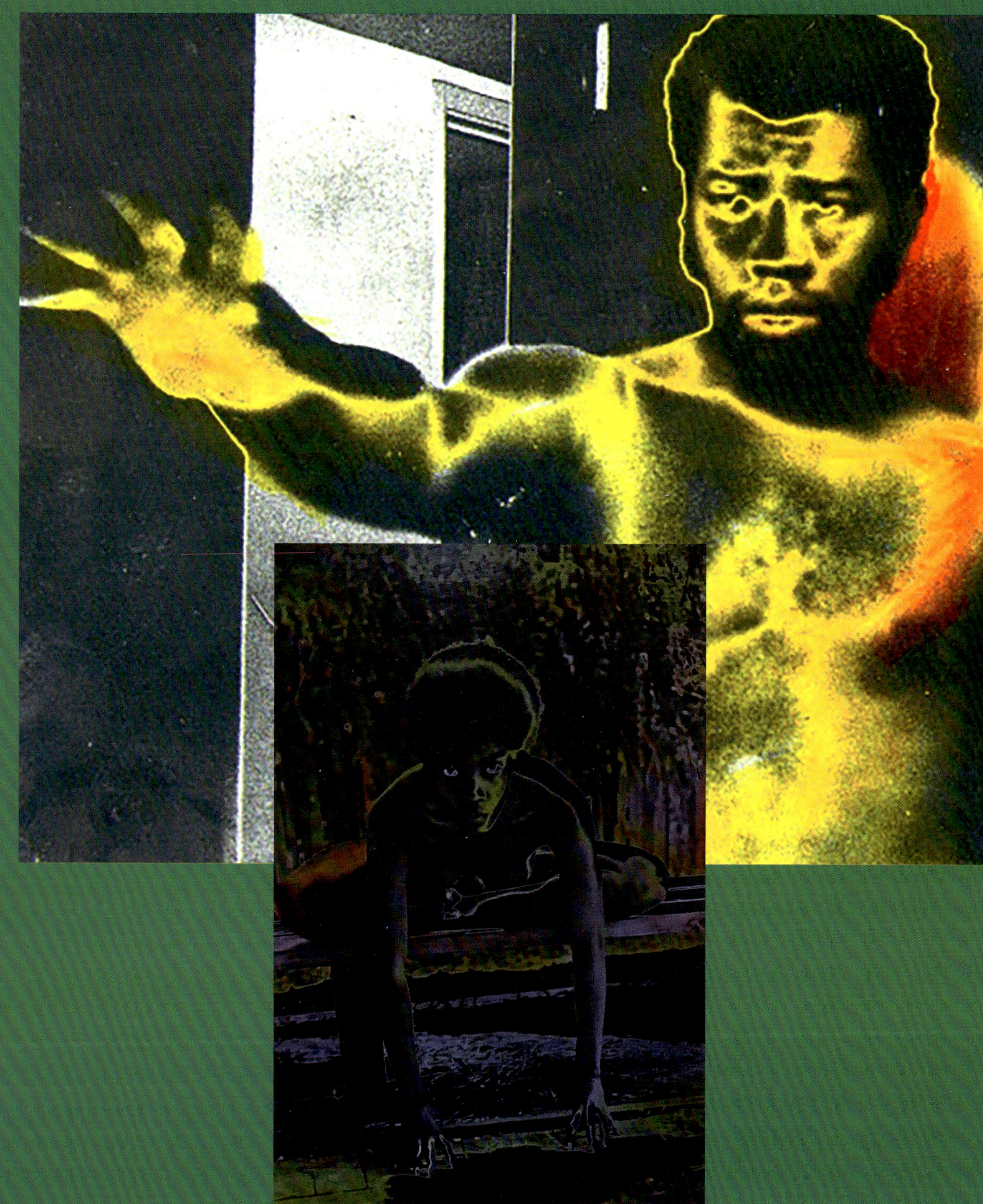

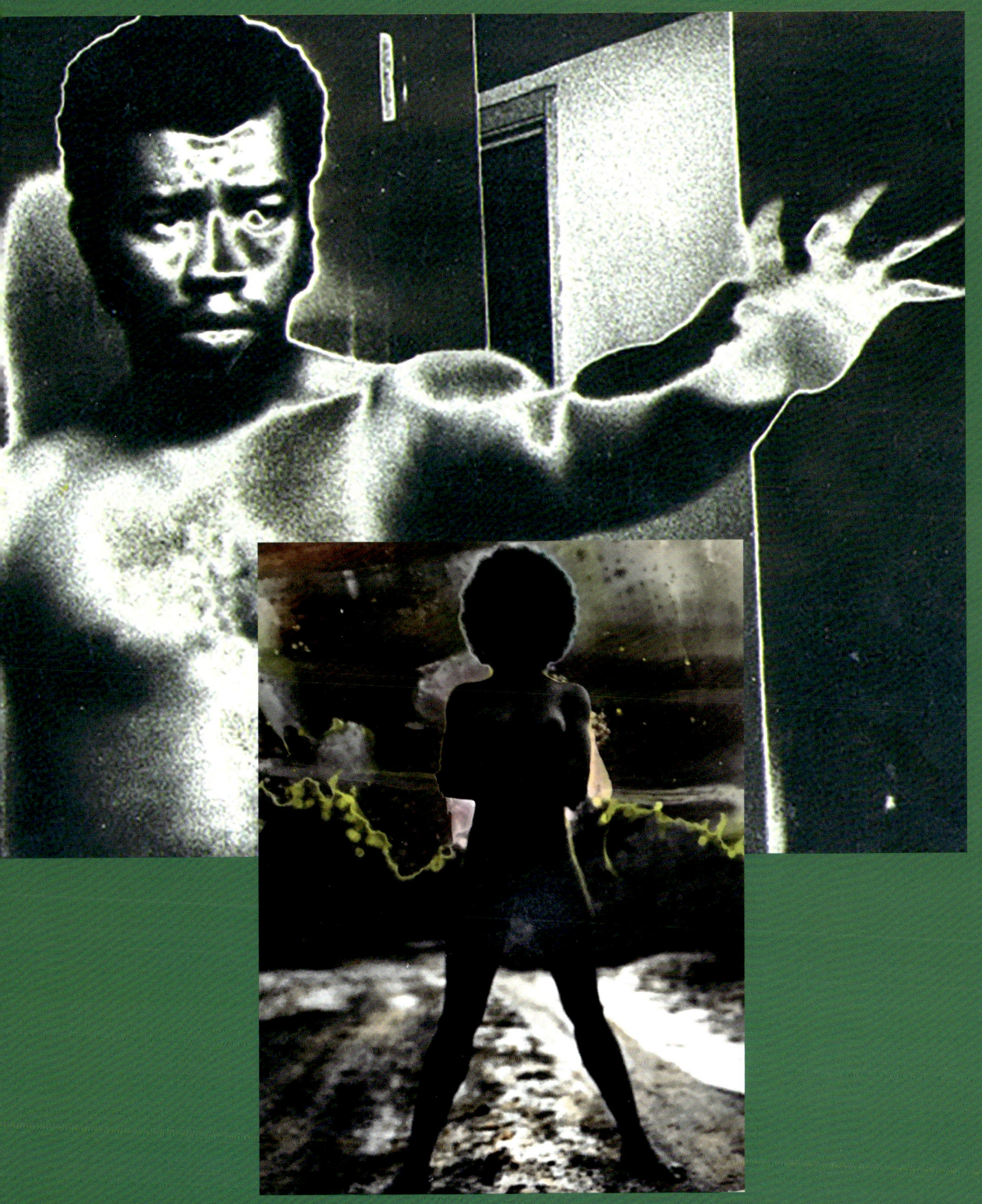

It was an experimental project, in which Ben incorporated multiple-exposure images and paint on black-and-white photographs of nude Black women in the Arizona desert. Adaybe, a friend and one of the models Ben photographed, helped him conceptualize the series. In their life drawing class, he shared with her his idea of creating images that represented the Southwestern desert as a cosmic entity connected to Black people and non-European cosmologies. She suggested he take pictures of Black women's bodies posed against the desert landscape. "There is a resemblance," she explained, "between the forms that the desert takes—its earthiness, curves, shapes, and color palette—and that of Black women's bodies, skin tones, and presence. Why not photograph that?"

The subjects of *AMKA* are photographed in different desert settings: on top of rocks with mountains in the background; in the middle of empty roads with trees and clouds in the distance; in front of bushes and plants. The women's faces and torsos are darkened by shadow and low lighting. Some subjects appear anonymous whereas others' faces are shown, their expressions either serious or nonchalant. The desert's different phenomena and environments are also brightened and darkened. This contrast of darkness and light on the photographs' subjects and settings enables the images to take on an X-ray-like quality; the images seem to depict both the desert's and models' internal composition and electromagnetic structure.

This is further enhanced by Ben's use of multiple exposures and paint. For example, one photo is overlaid with the image of an African mask, which appears to exist in the sky as if it is the sun. The mask and the trees are hand-painted with a mixture of reds, yellows, oranges, and greens—colors from shoe polishes that Ben got from his job at Bakers Shoes. The colors encircle the woman who stands at the center, silhouetted against her surroundings. In other photos, stars and clouds are outlined in neon yellow; women's bodies are accented with a violet hue and charge; rocks blend and transform into bushes. The exposures and paint are subtle additions. Yet they heighten the photographs' surrealist quality, their dream-like character.

Ben's use of paint on the photographs grew out of his dissatisfaction with photography's techniques of gradation. Paint, unlike gradation, provided Ben with a wider spectrum of colors to explore artmaking and moreover express a different kind of sensibility. Ben also developed his images on fluorescent orange, red, and green paper, unlike his peers who, following convention, used wood pulp-based or cotton rag paper. When combined with the paper, Ben's use of paint created a portal to a broader range of feelings, emotions, rhythms, and vibrations than that articulated in the two-tone minimalism of black-and-white photography.

In any case, by framing the desert as a Black woman, and Black women as symbolizing the desert, *AMKA* reproduced the liberal, humanist depiction of nature, the environment, and land as feminine, á la discourses about "mother nature" and "the motherland." Yet the series is not grounded in patriarchal narratives of the need for humans (read here, men) to protect and care for the earth (read here, women). Nor does it hinge on colonialist and sexualized notions of the desert as "virgin land" that is "ripe" for development and taming. In *AMKA*, Black women and the desert are not depicted as consumable and controlled by the camera or the gaze of the photographer and viewer. Instead, Black women and the desert are indicative of somewhere else, as revealing an *elsewhere*: a different plane of being, existence, and interconnectedness. Or to put it another way, Black women and the desert embody terrestrial and extra-terrestrial dimensions that are beyond the scope of Euro-American forms of knowledge, belief, representation, and being. They are symbolized as the vibrant, electric, and interstellar charge that animates everything.

The result was a psychedelic Afro-diasporic interpretation of the U.S. Southwest, the photographic counterpart to the music and iconography of Miles Davis's *Bitches Brew* (1970), Jimi Hendrix's *Electric Ladyland* (1968) and *Band of Gypsys* (1970), and Parliament's *Maggot Brain* (1971).

All of Ben's professors agreed that the *AMKA* series offered a unique way of seeing, perceiving, and experiencing the Southwest. Several faculty even likened Ben's work to that of Minor White and Alfred Stieglitz, two photographers whose images attempted to free certain subject matter and natural phenomena (like the sky, clouds, rocks, mountains, and rivers) from literal interpretations. Consequently, in his own way, Ben recast a setting that had been captured by numerous other photographers and supplied it with a cosmic, supernatural, darkened feminine ambiance. It offered viewers a different way of perceiving and feeling not just the desert, but everything and everyone around them—everything and everyone as carriers and conjurers of otherworldly possibilities.

AMKA served as the basis for Ben's application to UCLA's film school, one of several programs to which he was later offered admission and a full scholarship. When he landed there, he was part of a small number of nonwhite student filmmakers recruited to the campus, part of a university-wide effort led by Professor Elyseo Taylor (the film school's first Black faculty member) and several others. It was among these students that Ben established long-term friendships and cinematic collaborations. People like Pamela Jones, Haile Gerima, Charles Burnett, Larry Clark, Glen Williams, Majid Mahadi, Teshome Gabriel, Janet and Winston Henderson, Jamaa Fanaka, Beverly Robinson, and, in later years, Barbara McCullough, Billy Woodberry, Grace Ibekwe, Allie Sharon Larkin, Don Amis, Bernard Nichols, Julie Dash, and others.

Ben arrived at UCLA at a tumultuous point in the university's history. The campus was reeling from the murder of two Black Panther Party members during an on-campus meeting in 1969, as well as the university's firing of Professor Angela Davis due to her political activism and membership in the Communist Party. However, the campus's tense political atmosphere was eclipsed by that of greater Los Angeles, most centrally the swell of Black and Brown political and creative fervor that developed after the Watts Uprisings of 1965 and the

Chicano/a student and anti-war movements. Such vibrant grassroots activity and energy, alongside the whirlwind of organizing and resistance efforts taking shape throughout the U.S. and world, inspired Ben and his peers. It, moreover, influenced their evolving collaborative and community-based approach to film-making and screening films.

It was a unique time to be a Black filmmaker. The success of Melvin Van Peebles's independently produced and financed hit, *Sweet Sweetback's Baadasssss Song* (1971), and several other subsequent films underwritten by Black investors, provided Hollywood with a new template to generate revenue and increase its profit margins, while simultaneously tapping into an audience it had historically ignored. Consequently, the 1970s saw a wave of Hollywood-financed films centered around urban Black characters and communities that appealed to Black audiences.

But the films weren't universally celebrated. Their detractors dubbed them as "Blaxploitation" because their storylines were often premised around glorifying the criminal underworld, and because their anti-heroic characters amplified stereotypes of Black criminality and hypersexuality. Furthermore, while the films employed Black actors and enabled a small number of Black filmmakers to gain access to Hollywood resources, they also exploited Black people's desires to see themselves on the silver screen and their willingness to spend their hard-earned dollars at the cinema.

What constitutes a "Black film," and what could Black cinema be?

What subjects should it tackle?

What approaches must it take, reject, smash, generate?

Where could it go and what could it do in terms of structure, spatial and temporal organization, rhythm, tone, and intonation?

In what ways could it intervene in Black life? Listen to and express the latter's cultural retentions, resonances, innovations, and desires? Showcase Black life as Black people imagine and experience themselves?

These were the questions the UCLA crew discussed and debated in UCLA's Melnitz Hall. And it was inside and just outside the building's closet-like editing rooms, where this contingent and other filmmakers of different races, ethnicities, and backgrounds discussed the structures and ideas they were working on, and cross-fertilized concepts and storytelling methods.

Over the next two decades, the collective made numerous independent films. They took seriously the fact that they were filmmakers in the belly of the Hollywood beast. They maintained that American cinema was a leading culprit in the circulation of racist, stereotypical narratives and depictions of Black people and other non-white groups worldwide. These representations were fundamental

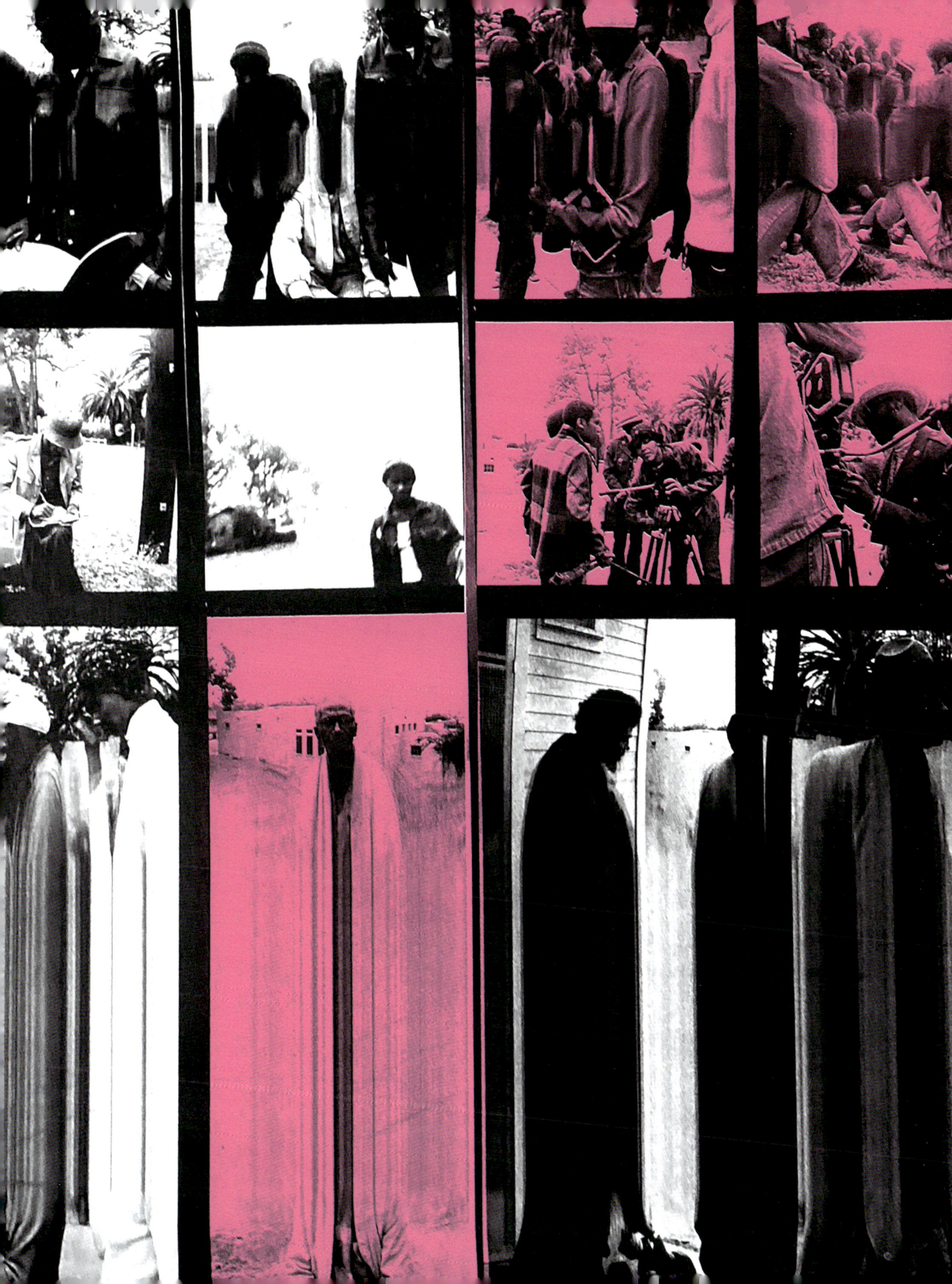

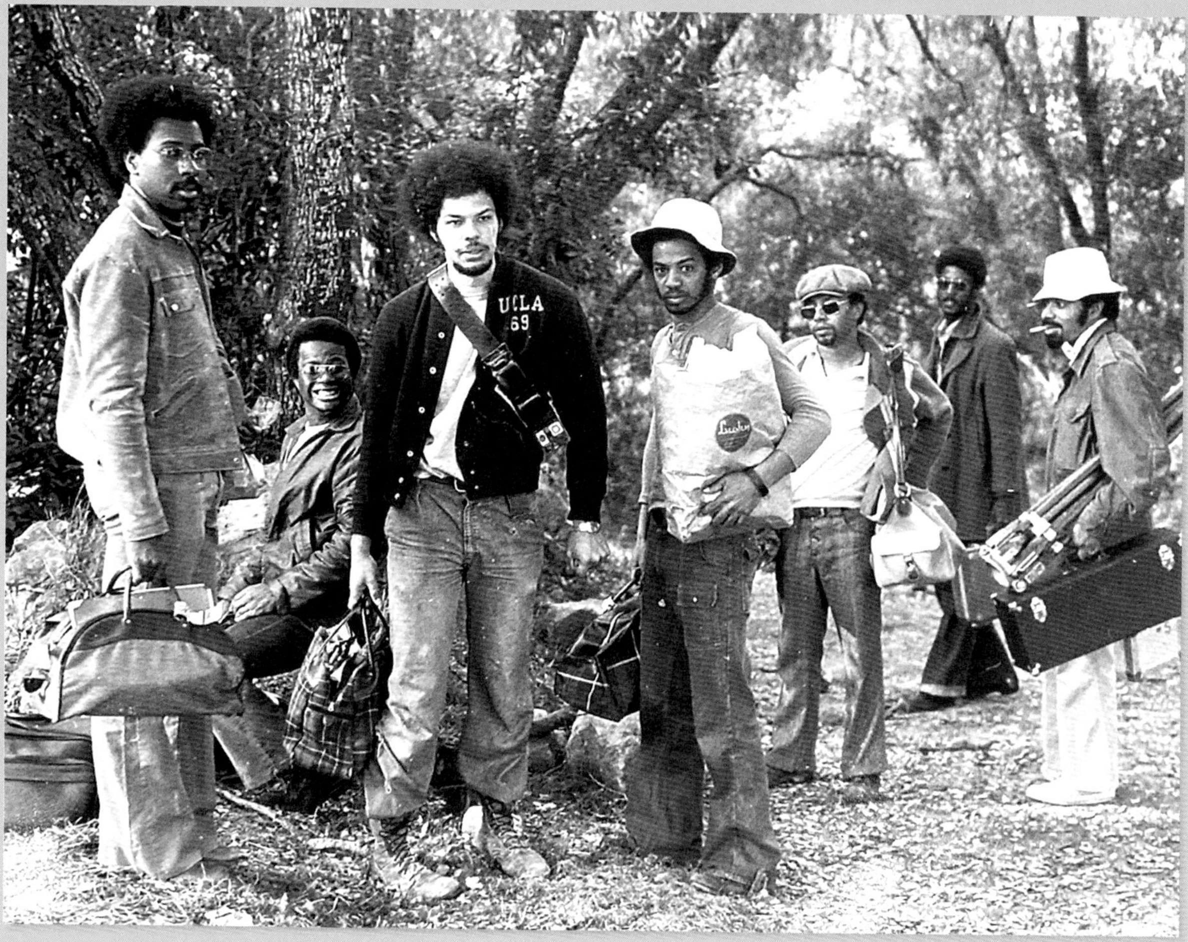

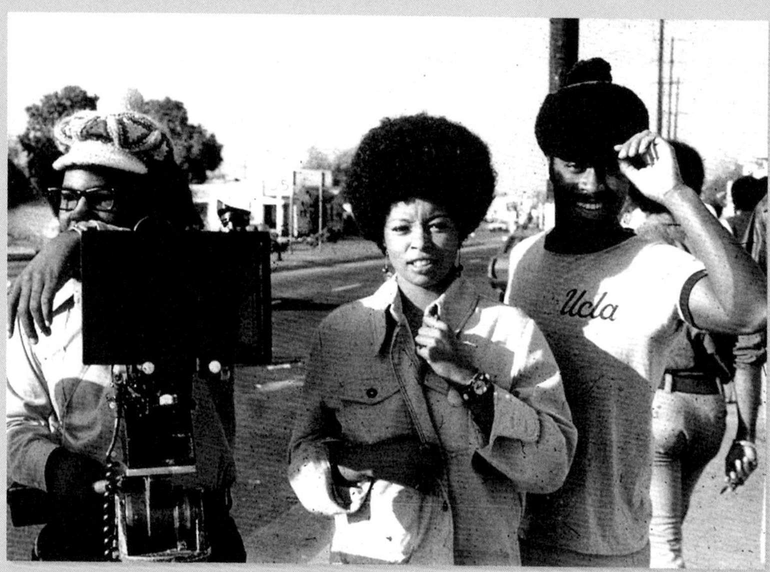

(TOP, LEFT TO RIGHT) FILMMAKERS GLEN DIXON, JACK RADAR, GARY GASTON, AL COWART, PERSON UNKNOWN, JOHN RIER, AND DON AMIS, 1974–1975 (BOTTOM) FILMMAKERS GEORGE GEDDIS, UNIDENTIFIED WOMAN, AND CHARLES BURNETT ON THE SET OF JAMAA FANAKA'S *WELCOME HOME BROTHER CHARLES* 1975

to white supremacy and Euro-American projects of empire, warfare, and resource extraction. Ben and his peers consequently made films that they believed would contribute to Third World anti-colonial struggles, as well as to global upheavals against systemic racism, social injustice, and poverty.

In so doing, their village was part of a citywide, national, and international Black Arts movement—the Westwood branch of a larger global crusade aimed at raising people's consciousness, pride, and sense of self-love. They pushed themselves to create art that directly engaged Black people and other communities, and which prioritized their histories, cosmologies, and the issues and power dynamics that directly impacted them.

Ben's first film, *Medea* (1973), translated these sentiments and his own evolving outlook onto illuminated celluloid. Shot in 8mm film with nonsynchronous sound, *Medea* is an experimental surrealist work that explores Afro-diasporic memory and the histories of violence, resistance, and struggle that a mother (and her ancestors) communicates and passes on to her child in the womb.

The seven-minute film begins with live-action shots of the natural environment (the sky, shifting clouds, tree branches, and leaves) overlaid by wind sounds and a ringing gong that changes into a heartbeat-like rhythm. Three minutes into the film, the main human subject enters—a pregnant woman. She is lying down in a grassy, forested area, her hands caressing her exposed stomach. A female narrator begins to recite Amiri Baraka's poem, "Part of the Doctrine": "Raise the dead. Raise the dead nigger. Raise the covenant. Raise the race. Raise the rays of the Sun's race to raise in the raze of this town and this place for the next, and the next race."

As the poet-narrator speaks, a series of still images flash across the screen: first, of different populations of African descent; and then primarily of Black Americans. The latter include images from the *AMKA* series, as well as photographs of musicians, artists, athletes, and celebrities; adults and children; people attacked and terrorized by police, police dogs, jails, and white civilians; and people marching, protesting, preaching, praying, and communing together. Throughout the sequence of flashing images, the poem continues: "God is who we raise ourselves, who we hover in, and are raised above our bodies and machines," the narrator states. "Those who are without God, who have lost the spiritual principle of their lives, are not raised. And their race is to their natural death."

Toward the film's end, the pregnant woman returns to the frame. Her body is stretched across boulders. Her knees are arched, with her stomach pointed to the sky. The curvature of her torso fuses with the rocks to form a single mountainous terrain, her womb serving as its apex. The screen turns white and a crying baby's scream rings out. The final shot depicts a blue balloon and an infant girl who proceeds to pick it up. The screen goes dark with the sound of the balloon popping. The film closes with a male voice reciting a stanza from Ghanaian writer Ayi Kwei Armah's 1973 novel, *2000 Seasons*. "A culture provides identity, purpose, and direction," the voice says. "If you know who you are, you'll know who your enemy is. You'll know what to do, what is your purpose."

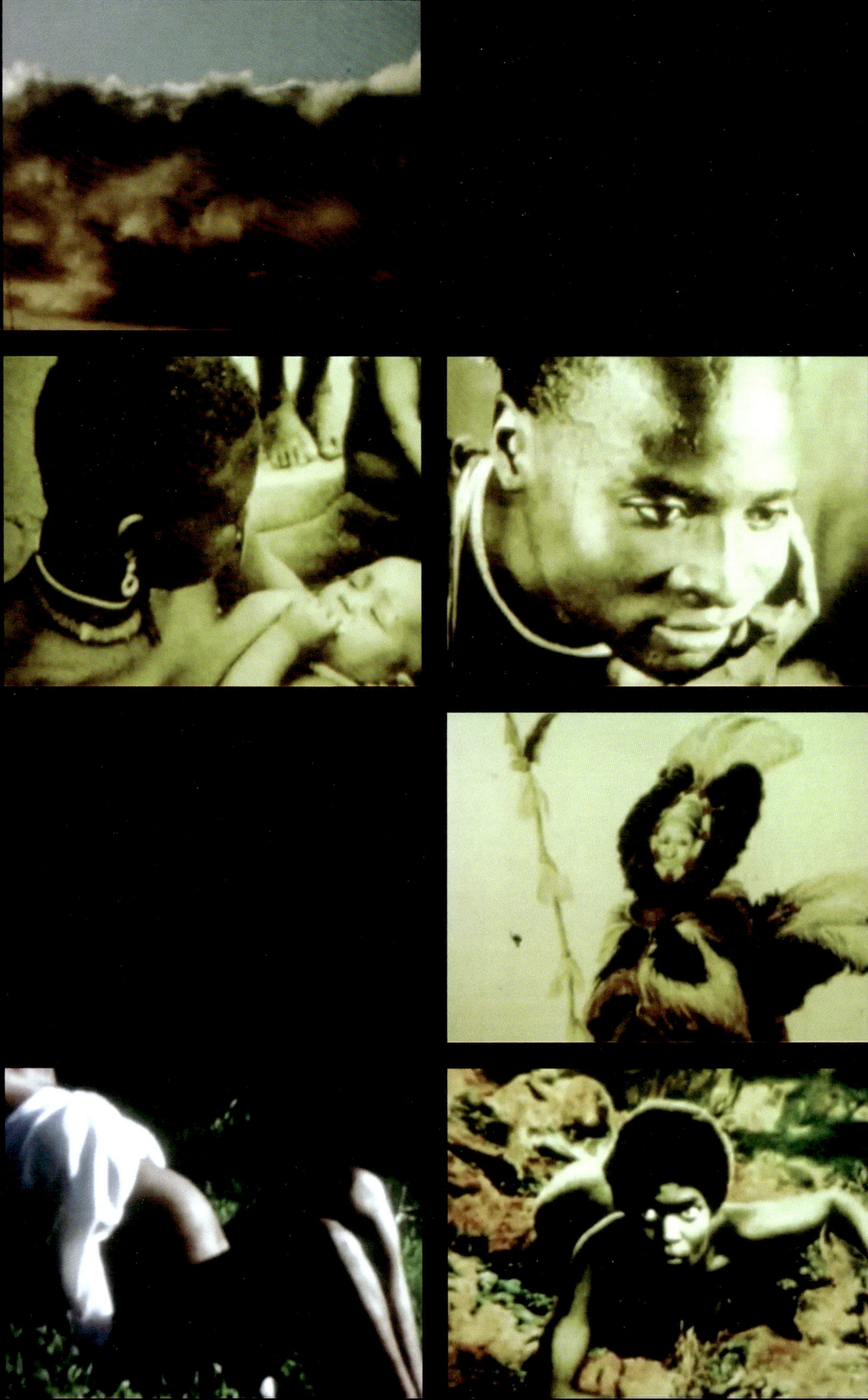

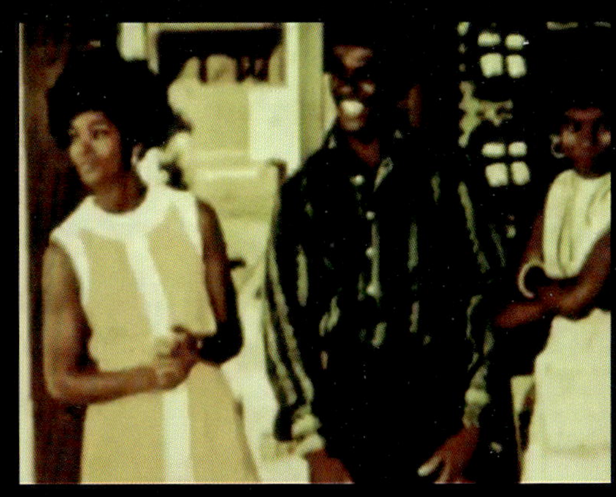
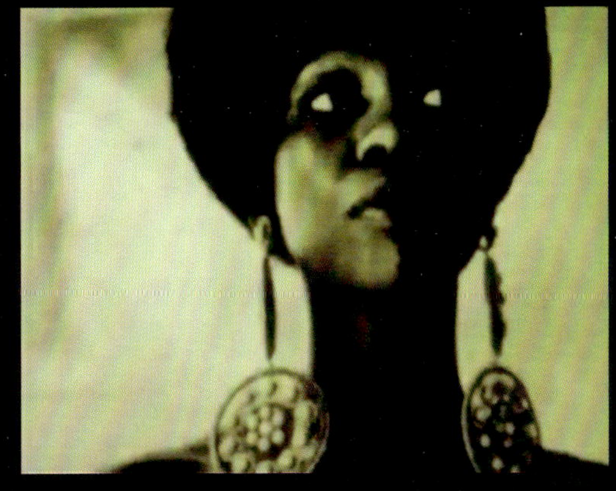
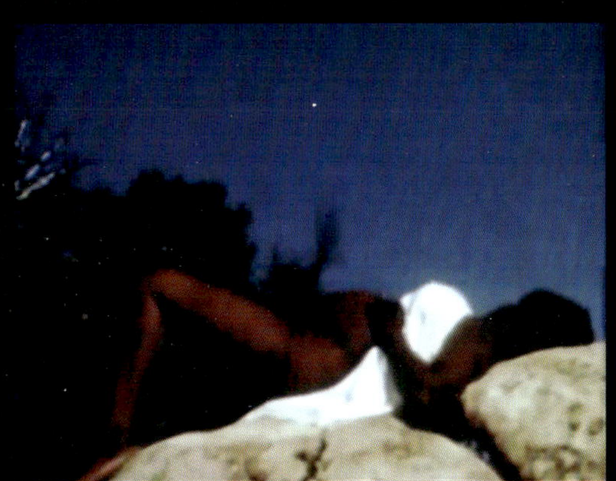
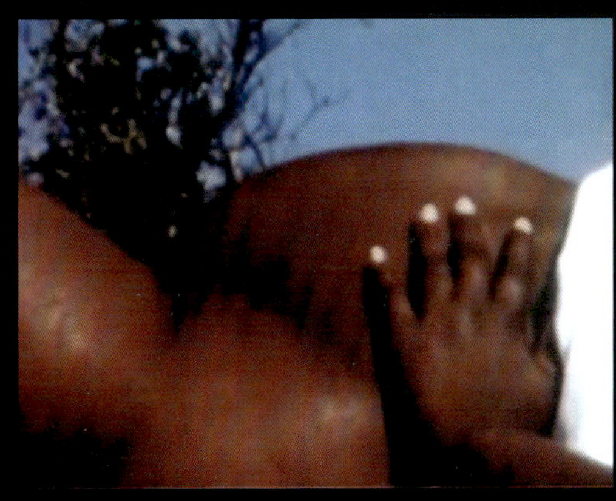
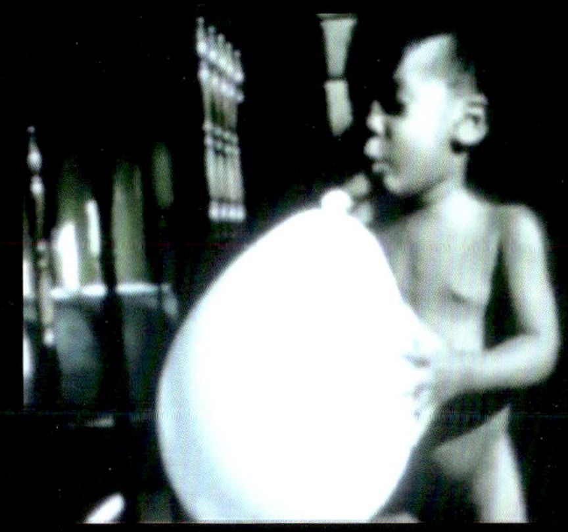

Medea is a proclamation about the rituals and principles of existence and struggle that people of African descent brought with them into the new context of the Americas. The film asserts that it is all this, and more, that Black people have reconfigured and deployed to endure, coexist, resist, and build new worlds. In *Medea*, these multiple histories, traditions, and identities "flash" before viewers' eyes—symbols of the information and cultural inheritance that the unborn child (who stands in as a symbol for Black Americans) carries within them. It is this legacy, the film maintains, that Black people must press on with to survive and liberate themselves and others.

Shifting from photography to film empowered Ben to test out new concepts and practices. For example, he edited *Medea* entirely in the camera and created its flashing visual collage sequence on an animation stand. He got the idea for the flashing image sequence after viewing his animation professor Dan McClaughlin's short film, *God Is Dog Spelled Backwards* (1963). McClaughlin's film features images from 3,000 years of art that flash across the screen over the course of three minutes, with Beethoven's Fifth Symphony playing in the background. This sparked Ben's idea of visually compressing several centuries of African civilization within a montage of images that are then made to represent the DNA that a Black child is born with, which makes them strong, and which they must activate in order to survive and thrive. Ben admired not just the speed and compression of McClaughlin's flashing sequence, but the sonic and musical thinking that inspired it. McClaughlin equated each still and cinematic image to a musical note; he perceived a filmmaker's different visual frames as the different notes and systems of chords they relied on to communicate a feeling, phrase, or message. Ben subsequently began describing his evolving style in a similar manner. In composing *Medea*, he treated every frame, especially the still images for the film's flashing sequence, as more than just a series of visual representations; each image was a note and percussive element of a broader, more elaborate lyrical and visual phrase. As an ensemble, the flashing sequence's images carried and communicated a polyrhythmic, dissonant pulse similar to that of a dance or djembe drum solo.

The other main inspiration for *Medea*'s flashing sequence and Ben's evolving style of filmmaking was the creative experimentalism and polyrhythmic foundations of Black music, poetry, and vernacular speech, especially the lyrical phrasing, rhythms, and freeform play of bebop and experimental jazz musicians and the vernacular spoken word of jazz-influenced poets. Like these musical and oral forms, *Medea* is organized around the juxtaposition and density of various elements (splicing and fragmentation of still-images; live-action footage; variations of sound, music, and verbal narration). And the film's flash sequences are marked by shifts in speed, drive, and intensity—visual swings and film edits that mirror a bebop quintet or soloist's improvisation or a poet's lyrical wordplay.

Ben perceived cinema as an authoritative medium, its power coming from its ritualistic and subliminal processes of address and reception. He often remarked that it had the capacity to put the viewer or The American and European film industries had used cinema's sorcerer-like capacity to inculcate and titillate audiences with a white supremacist system of seeing and imagining the world. It was a system of narratives and images that reinforced the dominant perception of whites as triumphant and complex, and Blacks and other nonwhite groups as inferior and subhuman. Black people's material and psychological oppression was thus deeply connected to the Euro-American film industry's regime of racist archetypes, tropes, figures, and symbols.

Ben wanted to counter the industry's symbology by channeling cinema's ritualistic tendencies toward a different direction and purpose. One organized around giving audiences an experience of heightened perceptual and spiritual ecstasy, healing, and transcendence. Ben determined that his films would create a visual poetics—a cinematic style that enabled the viewer to view, feel, and experience film in a radically different way. He believed that by eliciting a depth of psychological and emotional response among audiences, he might enable them to time-travel through history, memory, and their imaginations into alternative presents and futures. Decades later, he explained it to a researcher as an endeavor "to change the ritual" by "way of emancipating the image."

He spent the next three years fleshing these ideas out, especially his objective of developing a filmmaking and editing style influenced by Black music and poetry, psychology, and African and Afro-Atlantic art and media. Various people, cultural spaces, and businesses nurtured these ideas. This included his filmmaking peers; professors Elyseo Taylor, Mazisi Kunene, Teshome Gabriel, Shirley Clarke, St. Clair Bourne, and Dan McClaughlin; discussions led by Dr. Alfred and Berniece Ligon, owners of the Aquarian Bookshop and Spiritual Center; the anthropological analysis of Zora Neale Hurston; the scholarship and "African Art in Motion" exhibition work of art historian Robert Farris Thompson; the youth arts-training programming led by Vantile Whitfield and the Performing Arts Society of Los Angeles; the community music and poetry events of The Gathering; filmmaker Ivan Dixon and artists including Carlos Cobbs, John Outterbridge, John and Mary Ellen Ray, and others; the artist salons hosted by sisters Ruth Waddy and Gladys Little, as well as those organized by brothers Dale and Alonzo Davis at Brockman Gallery.

Amid all of this, and as Ben made strides in his graduate studies, Ben and Pam adjusted to parenthood, each of them internalizing the truths that *Medea* foretold. For both parents, being attuned to Dara and her development was supreme. They moved into a bigger place in Santa Monica and, to make ends meet, Pam worked first as a receptionist and later as an English teacher at a junior high school in the Valley. Ben, on the other hand, worked as a janitor in Westwood and then with a company where he provided logistical support for families and companies that were moving. Soon thereafter, he got a position as an outreach counselor with the Los Angeles Department of Veteran Affairs (VA) at their Santa Monica office, one of several county agency branches responsible for supporting the needs of veteran military personnel.

At the time, the VA was struggling to support troops returning from tours in Vietnam. Many veterans came back with crippling injuries, severe physical disabilities, psychological trauma, and drug and alcohol addictions. A significant number were unable to secure long-term employment. On top of these challenges, they were experiencing a homecoming unlike that of any other generation of war returnees, frequently encountering a climate of indifference and suspicion. Their traumatic war experiences were often disregarded by a society that appeared to have little interest in understanding their ordeals or the difficulty of their readjustment to life back in the States.

The VA hired Ben to help with its outreach programs, which were established to support veterans in their processes of societal readjustment. Ben was tasked with planning job fairs and job banks, providing job counseling and interview tutorials. It was no big surprise to him that many veterans were plagued by problems associated with basic social, economic, physical, and psychological needs. And he understood that their difficulty securing work and sustaining themselves was compounded that much more if they were poor. Being poor meant living in areas of high unemployment, high crime, poor health, and limited housing options, education facilities, and access to public transportation.

What was surprising, however, was how inadequately resourced, staffed, and placed the VA was to support poor and working-class veterans' different needs. The most glaring example was the disparity of resources dedicated to veterans living in L.A.'s predominantly Black neighborhoods. While the VA's Santa Monica office and other Westside locations were decently staffed, its branches in Los Angeles's South Central and East Side neighborhoods were short-handed and located in small spaces expected to serve veterans from numerous Black and Brown neighborhoods. Ben consequently requested and received a transfer to a branch in South Central L.A.

A year later, the VA promoted Ben to director of a new assistance center located at the intersection of Compton Avenue and Nadeau Street. Although he was still a graduate student, Ben accepted the position and the responsibilities that it entailed. He hired a secretary and five counselors. Together, they transformed the office into a multipurpose community space that provided job training and informationals, legal aid, and assistance with college enrollment and bank loans.

Initially, only a few veterans took advantage of their services. Ben's team realized that some veterans were reluctant to seek assistance. To draw them in required a creative approach—one that positioned the space less as an "assistance center," and more as a source of refuge and community-building. The center began screening films, inviting local artists to perform, and, most importantly, holding events for veterans, their families, and other community members. They cultivated programming where vets led discussions about their struggles reacclimating to life and the challenges they faced. VA administrators queried Ben about the center's various non-assistance-related activities. "What do the arts have to do with assisting veterans?" they asked. Ben explained.

This sentiment was the undercurrent of his next film, *I & I: An African Allegory* (1977), a work that weaves experimental filmmaking with documentary and dramatic narrative. The title was inspired by the Rastafarian principle of `"I and I,"` which denotes the oneness of God and every human—that all humans are connected by a larger celestial power—that is to say, "I" is not "I" but rather "we." The film builds on this theme by exploring Black disconnection (familial, ancestral, and spiritual) and the power of reciprocity and healing in reconnecting Black people to one another, to the paradoxes and power of their history, and to the cosmic forces of nature and the universe.

I & I: An African Allegory opens with an image of water. This shot is then overlaid by a written statement explaining the film's sources of narrative and stylistic inspiration: African history and lyric arts, Black music, and Yoruba mythology. The film then follows its main character, Alefi (Pamela Jones), who is the incarnation of the Yoruba orisha and wind spirit, Oyá. She serves as the audience's eyes, whereby she travels and casts her sight on different scenes of American life. This includes a dramatic scene of enslaved Africans enduring the Middle Passage ship journey to the Americas; a flashing sequence of photographer Diane Arbus's images, which overlay photographs of a group of protestors; a scene where a Black man confesses his rage to his dead white father; an elderly Black woman recounting her family's experience of enslavement and white violence; and the final scene, where Alefi impresses upon her young son `the power of reciprocity,` which she defines as the overarching force that connects all beings and things.

The different sequences symbolize the psychosocial traumas, histories, and internal conflicts of being Black in the United States. They also reemphasize ideas put forth by Ben's first film, *Medea*, regarding the power of Black cultural retention. Like *Medea*, *I & I: An African Allegory* portrays the abundance of information, philosophy, mores, and ways of living and being that circulate within people of African descent's minds, spirits, and bodies. The film maintains that it is these ways of being, belief, and becoming that must be transmitted to and reconfigured by each new generation. These themes serve as the film's closing motif, the character of Alefi summing up this message through the word "love." Love, she explains, represents the greatest cosmic and terrestrial force. It is the source that all humans must reconnect with to maintain their coexistence with one another, with other species of life, and with the Earth. "What's going to happen on this planet is really up to us," the character of Alefi says to the child. "We have to submit to each other, look after each other, respect each other, and love each other … You see, the energy behind everything that is, and the shape that everything takes, and what makes up everything that is, all there is, is just love."

When Ben screened *I & I: An African Allegory*, it was received well. The film opened first at the 1977 Third World Film Festival in downtown L.A. and then months later at the Philadelphia Film Festival. In the discussions that followed the film, audience members expressed admiration for the film's Afrocentric and cultural nationalist message. The response at the film's screenings at UCLA, however, was mixed. While several faculty members likened its form to that of filmmaker Stan Brakhage, there were grumblings among some white attendees that the film was "semi-racist" in its treatment of its lone white character. Still, at this event and subsequent screenings, viewers described the film as beautiful and avant-garde in its style and tone and sang praises for its ambitious modes of storytelling and structure.

People frequently asked about the film's inspiration. Ben gave different answers: A poem on the back of a Wayne Shorter album. Carl Jung's essays on synchronicity and the collective unconscious. Ayi Kwei Armah's novels. And occasionally, Ben said "war. War and its manifestations—colonialism, racism, poverty, genocide." He would explain that the film's title was inspired not just by Rastafarianism, but also by ancient belief systems. "'I and I' is a word that goes back as far as Sanskrit, as far as Egyptian mythology," he explained in a televised interview with a UCLA cable program. "It's a concept that basically deals with a lack of division of people. It's saying that we're both the same. I and I." To create systems organized around division, segregation, and injustice, he maintained, was counter to that. These systems were premised on a "you and I" distinction—one that transformed people into objects and things and which encouraged people to perceive and treat one another as such. The framework of "you and I" was the organizing principle for empires, enslavement, and the modern age. "Wars, killings, hangings, lynchings," Ben remarked in the interview. "The stuff that we call 'modern-age man' split us from each other; split us from being who we really are."

There were people who didn't appreciate Ben's film. Some said it was confusing and abstract. Others maintained that it needed a more transparent critique of class, and that this could have been achieved if the character of Alefi had been depicted as a working-class woman rather than an ethereal being. Most of the criticism, however, revolved around the film's structure; several viewers stated that Ben had utilized a film language, methodology, and structure that was drastically different from that of his predecessors, and which they found to be difficult to translate and comprehend. "The structure that we know of now is basically the structure of the inventors of this particular medium known as film," Ben commented. "It was born in a Western world. And it's very similar to Beethoven, and that's all we're hearing right now. I'm trying to get into African languages like Zulu, Yoruba . . . and checking out the syntax, checking out the structure to see if there's similarities that I can transfer into film visually.

At the 1977 Flaherty Film Seminar, a week-long series devoted to film and media, this debate about cinematic structure and film language was a hot topic. In the discussion that followed the screening of *I & I: An African Allegory*, several attendees questioned Ben's cinematic point of view.

AUDIENCE MEMBER 1: You said you're trying to find your own language and form to speak to your own people . . . I wonder what emotional responses you're hoping to achieve, and to what end . . . it's unclear to me exactly what kind of inspiration you're hoping to create. I'm afraid I missed it.

BEN: It's something that I think most people here in this country have, with the possible exception of the Black people here. Here in this country, it's just a cut umbilical cord. It's a cut to your source. And what I was trying to do was hook up that bridge, to show what *Roots* [the film] in a profane way tried to do. I don't know. Once you understand who you are and your history behind you, then there's no problem as to when situations hit you, then you know how to deal with it. But if you don't understand who you are and your heritage behind you, then you wander around and end up doing things over and over and over again.

AUDIENCE MEMBER (AM-2): Many places in the film, I felt really touched by the depth and mystery of the imagery. But I kept finding myself coming back to a heavier feeling that somehow there was a problem with grammar in the specific sense of sequence of ideas. We're dealing here with the mass media, and every form of communication has its grammar. In the grammar of the film, you're reaching out to a general audience and touching cords of responses, and there has got to be some sort of commonality in your vocabulary and our vocabulary. And you have to work with that common vocabulary. Or else you have to build a vocabulary in us so that you can communicate . . . You're using your own private vocabulary and your own private imagery and, for at least some of the audience, I know for me, I feel that that's not my vocabulary. And you haven't built in me a vocabulary that you can use . . . you have to work on it in me so that it becomes something that you can use . . . That's the real problem I had with the film.

MODERATOR: [to AM-2] You're talking not only about English words, but film language also.
And even there, he's [Ben] not really inventing a new language. He's trying to use it to
say what he's saying. Many other filmmakers are creating new cinematic languages. And I'm
not really sure it's the function of the filmmaker to teach us the language. We have to
work at comprehending that language.

AUDIENCE APPLAUSE

MODERATOR: Communication works both ways.

AM-2: Well, I do certainly agree with what you're saying . . . But he [Ben] has to do a
certain amount of work to tame my mind, or somehow make my mind part of his. It's my
responsibility to make my mind open to him, but he's got to work on it somehow.

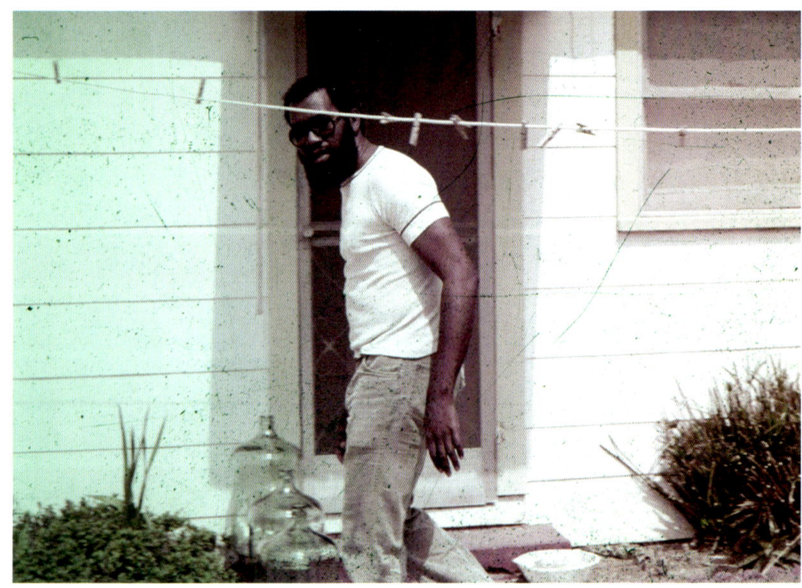

BEN, OUTSIDE SANTA MONICA
HOME (OPPOSITE) *I & I: AN AFRICAN
ALLEGORY*, 1977 BOOKLET

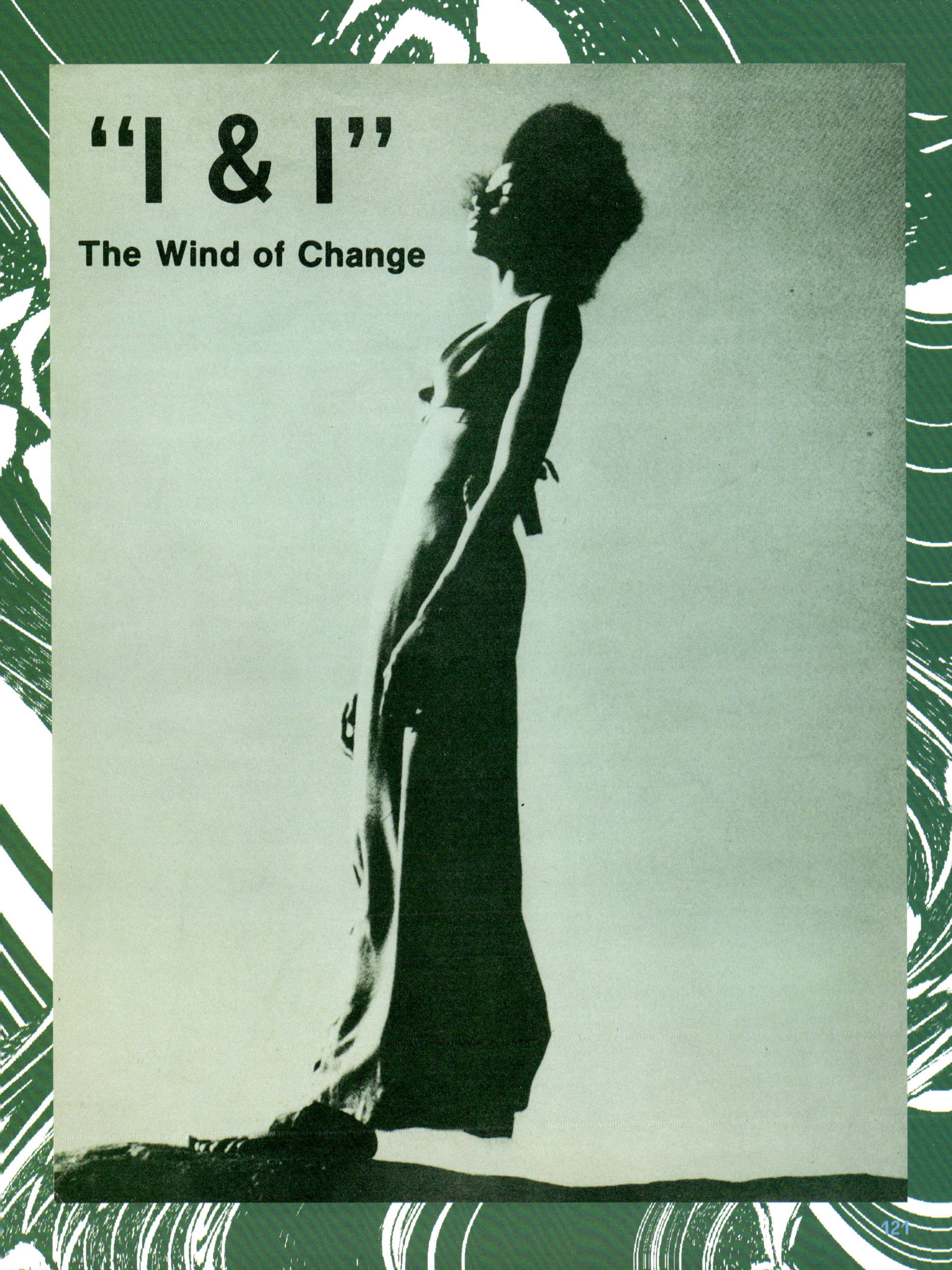

"I & I"
The Wind of Change

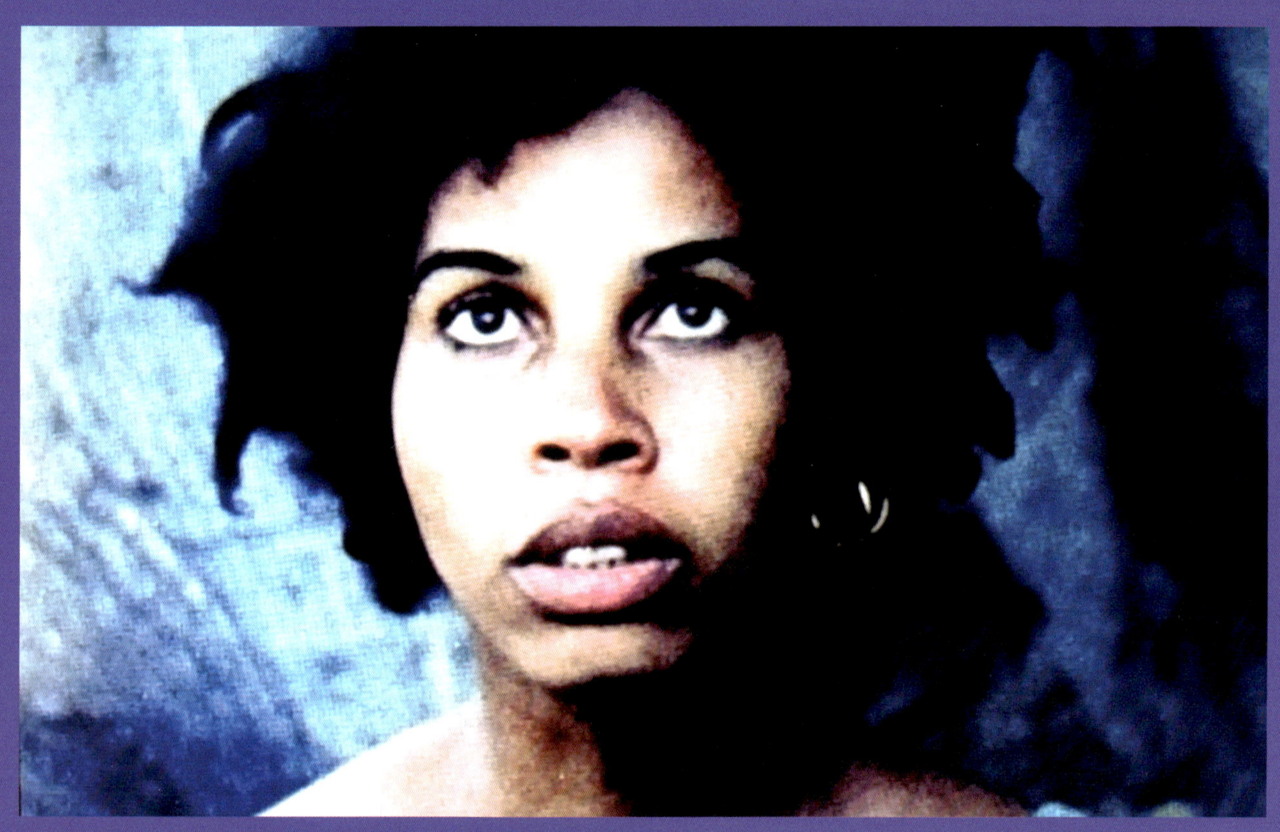

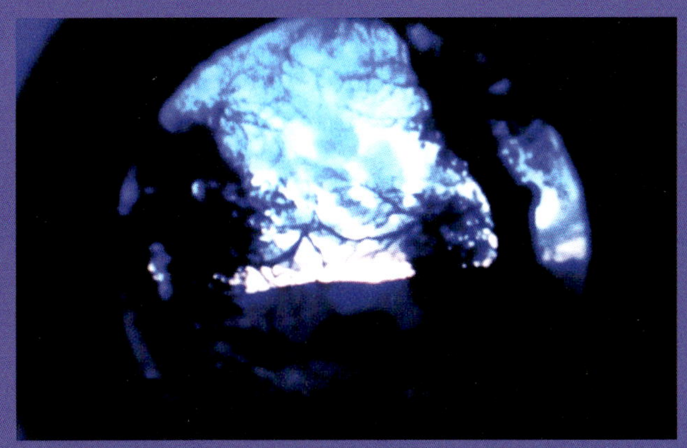
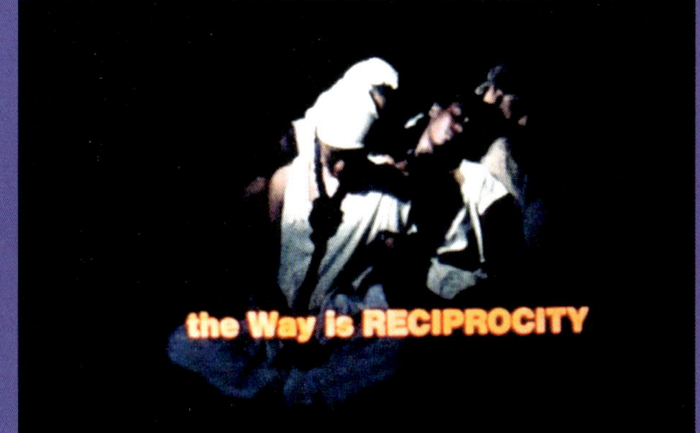
the Way is RECIPROCITY
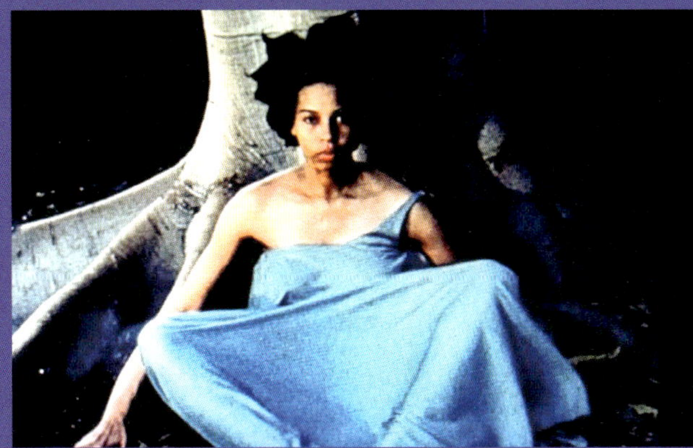
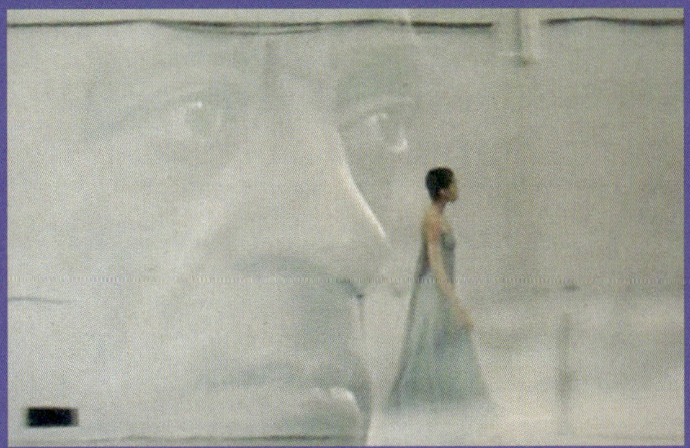
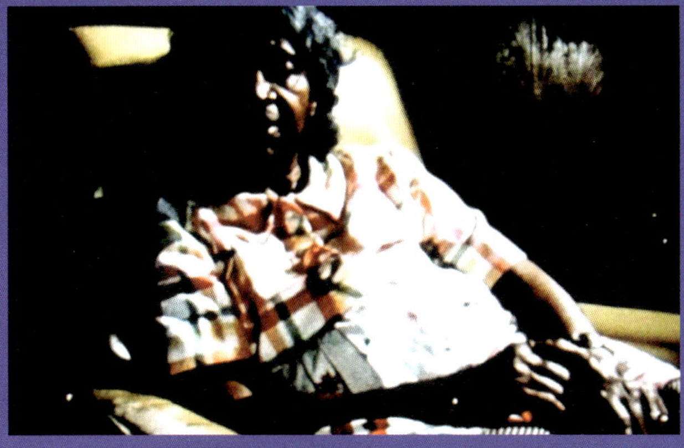
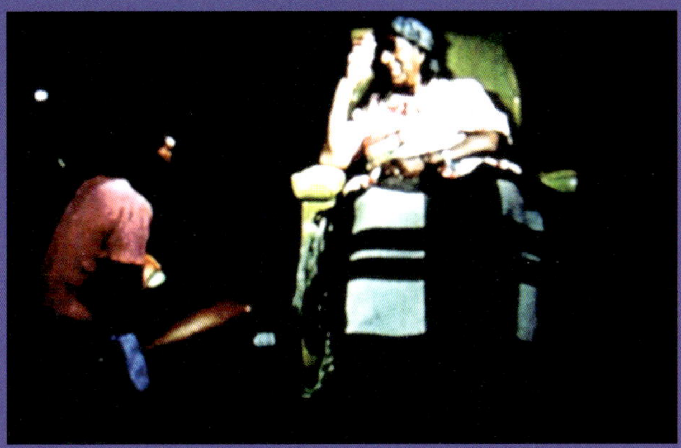
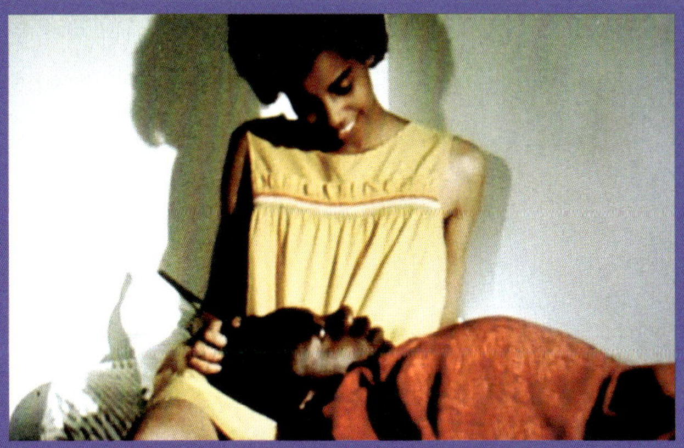
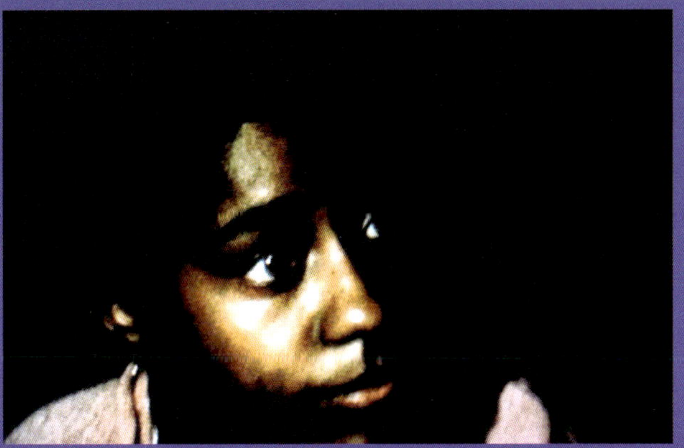

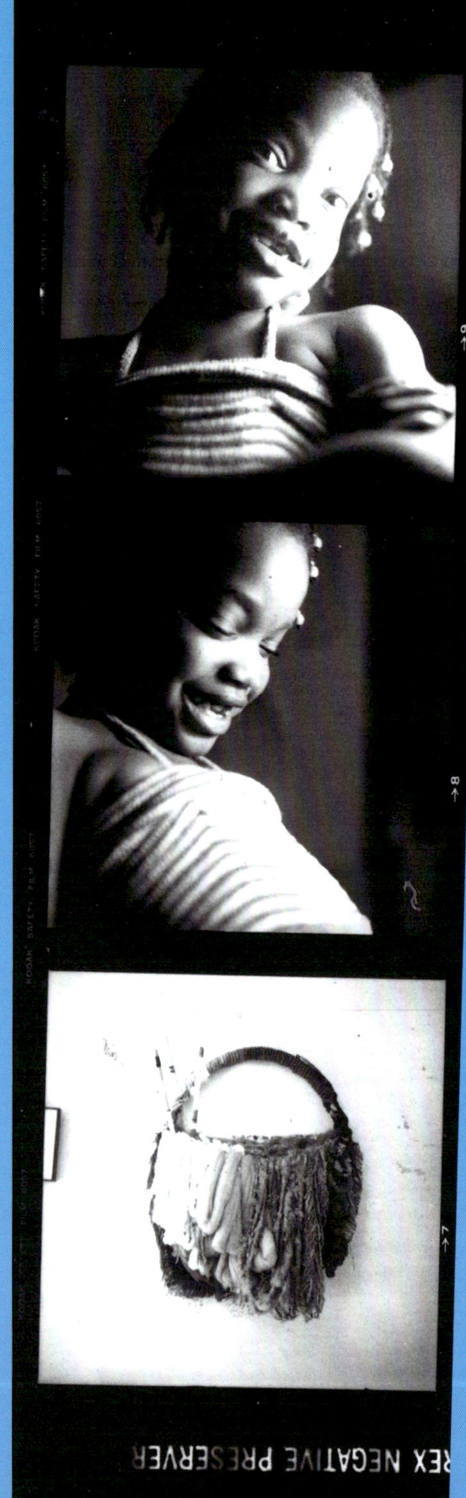

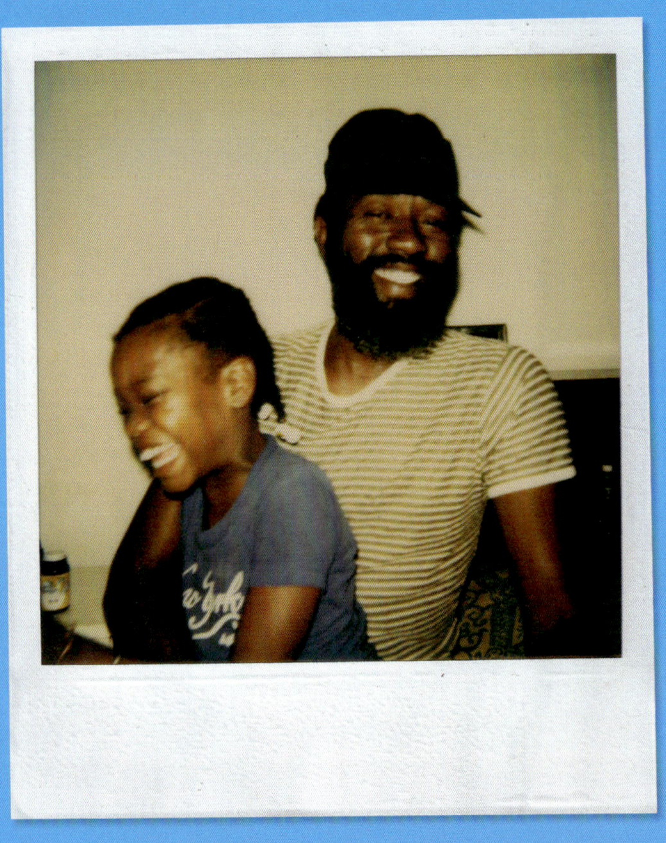

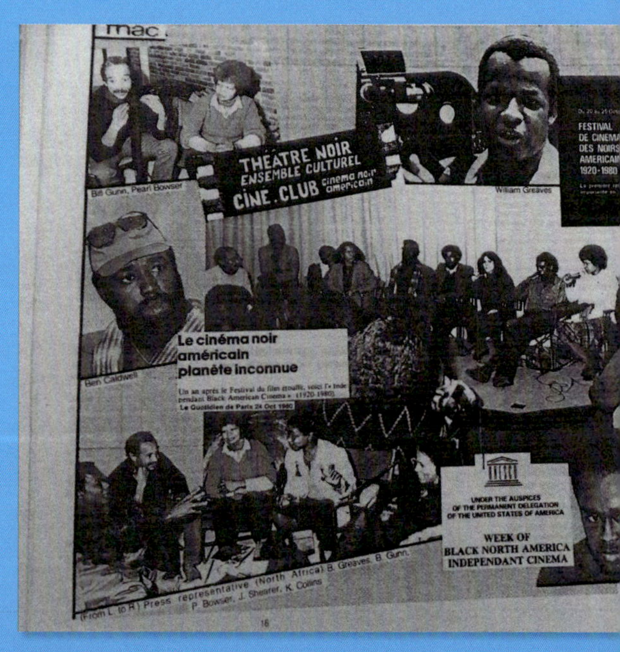

(LEFT & TOP) DARA AND BEN CALDWELL,
LATE 1970S/EARLY 1980S

Mr. Ben R. Caldwell   October 16, 1980
1759 35th Street
Los Angeles, California 90018

Dear Ben:

Please accept this letter on behalf of Brockman Gallery Productions to express a deep appreciation for your unselfish contribution as Program Coordinator of the 7th Annual Film Festival. It is not often that a festival centered around independent filmmakers has brought together so many people from varied cultures of the Los Angeles community. Not only was your entry "I and I" an outstanding example of film artistry in its own right, but your unusual capability to assemble a qualified selection committee exposed the Greater Los Angeles community to truly unique films. These films not only individually point to a new direction in cinematography, but collectively expand the scholarship and artistry of the film industry. In addition, your expertise in facilitating and administrating the activities and open discussions has highlighted the Festival.

So many of the "ups and downs" that we experienced in developing and realizing the Festival has and is culminating with success. An achievement that again warrants us to say thank you for your personal input and wishes for your continued success.

With Deepest Respect,

Beverly J. Robinson
Festival Director

Larry Simpasa
Co-Director - Brockman
Gallery Productions

BJR/LS:gy
cc: African Studies Center
    Univ. of Calif. — Los Angeles

4334 DEGNAN BOULEVARD/LOS ANGELES, CALIFORNIA 90008 / (213) 294-5201

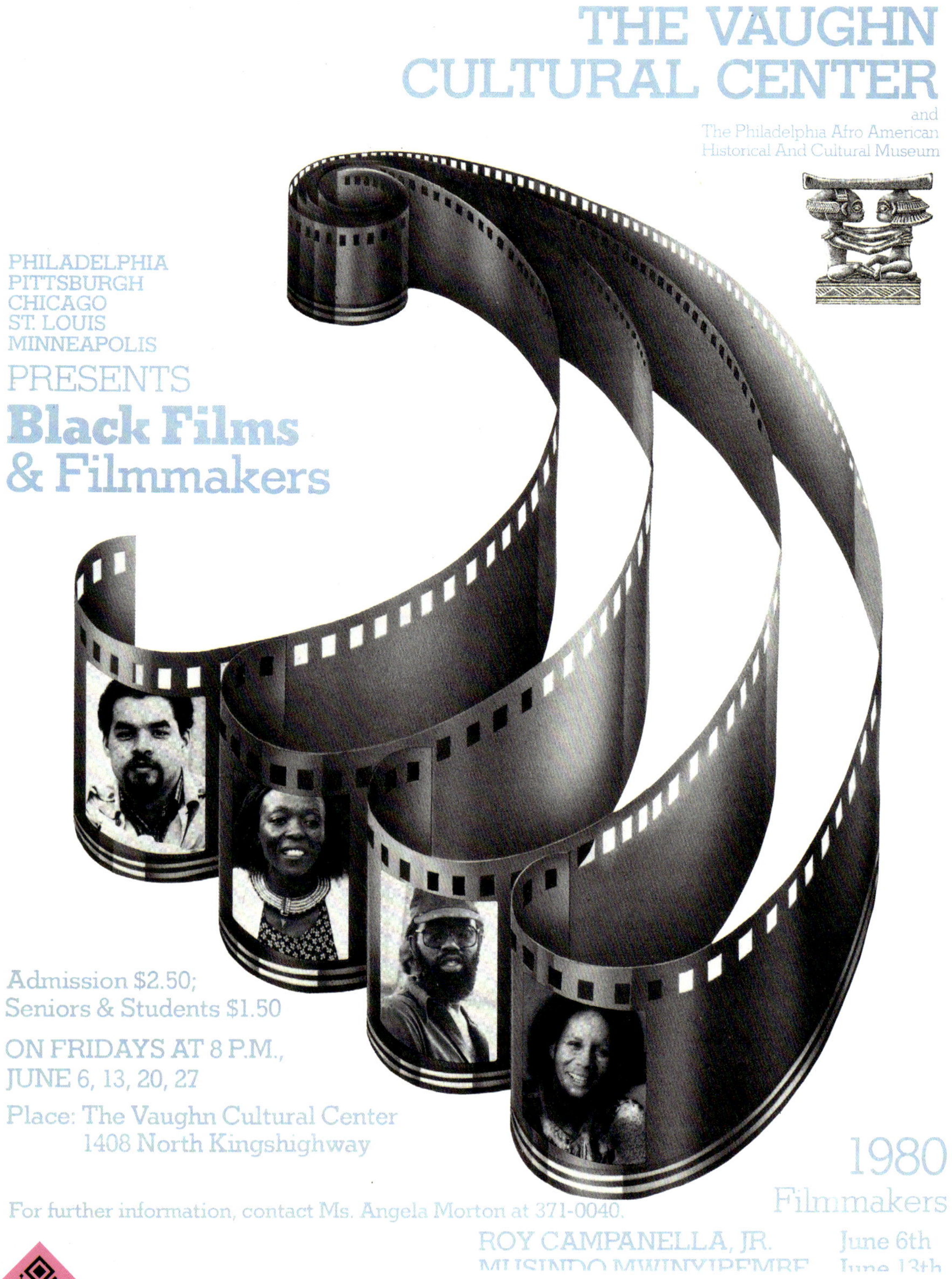

THE VAUGHN
CULTURAL CENTER
and
The Philadelphia Afro American
Historical And Cultural Museum

PHILADELPHIA
PITTSBURGH
CHICAGO
ST. LOUIS
MINNEAPOLIS
PRESENTS
Black Films
& Filmmakers

Admission $2.50;
Seniors & Students $1.50

ON FRIDAYS AT 8 P.M.,
JUNE 6, 13, 20, 27

Place: The Vaughn Cultural Center
1408 North Kingshighway

For further information, contact Ms. Angela Morton at 371-0040.

1980
Filmmakers

ROY CAMPANELLA, JR.   June 6th
MUSINDO MWINYIPEMBE   June 13th

2nd national BLACK FILMS & FILMMAKERS series

AN INTERVIEW:

Ben Caldwell

IN CONVERSATION WITH OLIVER FRANKLIN

Caldwell entered the filmmaking world early in the 1970's from a fine arts background as a painter. His affinity for surrealism was transferred to an avant-garde, experimental film style, and he is one of very few Black filmmakers working in this style.

Ben Coldwell grew up in southern New Mexico and received his Master of Fine Arts degree from UCLA's Film School where he is currently a lecturer, and is also working on an M.A. in African Studies.

The films Coldwell will screen for the 2nd National Black Films and Filmmakers Series are: I and I: An African Allegory (16 mm., 28 min.), an examination of Black images and myths; The Nubian (16 mm., 20 min.) -- a premiere showing; and several short films done by students at UCLA's Film School.

• • •

OF: How did you get the idea for *I and I* ?

BC: *I and I* evolved out of a piece of music and a poem by Wayne Shorter. The album "Voyage of Isha" had a poem of Shorter's on the back that went like this:
   "Imagine a wind so vast in scope,
   so boundless as to suggest,
   unifying taking past, present and future,
   once in a lifetime odyssey..."
   So, I took off from there.

OF: Is this film about the Egyptian Sun God myth?

BC: Yes, I'm trying to say that, but not only in the sense of Egyptian because all African people are from the sun area. Also, it's not necessarily dealing with African people because Native Americans are people of the Sun, too. People of the Sun are those who deal with life in naturalistic ways, identifying with nature more than the atom. Our atomic bomb is the sun -- the naturalistic atom -- that's the kind of entity we praise instead of an atomic bomb and all of the things that come out of it. And "The Way of Reciprocity" [statement at the beginning of *I and I*] deals with the circular aspect of what Mother Nature is all about, too. Everything has a circular perspective to it.

OF: You are a person who makes the kind of films not stylistically associated with Black filmmaking, as we know. The many film techniques of combining still and moving footage, and the use of Diane Arbus' photographs, and other filmic techniques are unique. Why did you juxtapose the Spanish images which have a western feeling with the pictures of the Civil Rights Movement, which has a southern feeling?

BC: That's the same way of dealing with reciprocity...circular sun people. All of us are the same universal peole, and being brought up in the Southwest, I can see it more than most. For instance, the Chicanos were under more pressure than I was as a Black person, because I was less of a threat to the establishment. So when they wanted to call me something ugly, they'd call me a Mexican. They didn't call me nigger because there weren't enough of us, but the Mexicans were right there. My partners were Mexican and they'd say we had more in common. So, it was that on-going feeling that I was brought up with. That's part of the reason I use those photographs. And, in juxtaposing pictures, I was expressing with that particular sequence what Dr. Karl Jung, the psychologist, says that a repetition of images in pictures is similar to casting a spell. I was certainly conjuring a spell, by juxtaposing those pictures to show the incongruity of feelings with our existence in Los Angeles the concrete and cement city. By juxtaposing the Black people's pictures with white people's pictures, we see the effects of the environment physically on their faces. That's the reason I used Diane Arbus. She was the only person who has really dealt in a seeing fashion; she saw artistically the hurt that people were going through in the cities in this country. And when the film was shown at the Flaherty Seminar [held every August in New England to showcase new independent films] the filmmakers there questioned my use of her photographs because they thought she projected negativity of white people. Now, I didn't do it that way at all! I saw what she was doing as capturing an interpre-

tation of a particular life, and the way the people showed it on their faces. I didn't think it was negative. It's a perspective of life that she sought and was able to encapsulate. And, operating in film, I do feel that I have to use images that mean more than one picture, because each picture is a symbol of an overall feeling.

OF: You move forward and backward in time, yet one of the most powerful scenes was on the old woman.

BC: Yes, I wanted to deal with an older woman because one of my friend's grandmother had just died with a similar leg problem that the woman [Mrs. Collins] in the film has. So, for me, the woman was full of images and symbolism. I searched for a woman who was politically astute in a common everyday sense. I didn't want her to be telling me about "Only God...and so forth." Unfortunately, the sound for Mrs. Collins doesn't come across as well as I'd like. She is an 87-year-old woman. But the things she says; for instance, her uncle was the son of a slave owner. And he left because his father, the slave master, was going to whip him. He said, "I'm not going to let my father whip me!" and left. That was interesting because it showed an understanding of how she thought of life too. One of the things that was a surprise to me was the way Mrs. Collins dealt with the Native American. She is telling the story to the girl of leaving her home to go to South Carolina by wagon, and she told about being attacked...and the girl said, "You were attacked! .. by Indians?" And, Mrs. Collins says, "No, not by Indians, by some crazy white men." And the girl remarked that it didn't happen like that in history books, and Mrs. Collins responded by saying, "Well, they'll just have to rewrite the books then." I really like that capsule, but unfortunately many people miss it.

OF: Why did you use the Middle Passage sequence in the beginning?

BC: I wasn't really using it as the beginning. I started with water, then an icon of Africa, to show that's the place she was from. And then the transition was the Middle Passage -- where the feeling of whole masses of people coming across the Atlantic -- millions upon millions of people -- is one of suffering. There is no way one can understand the African-American until one understands the horrors of the Middle Passage. So horrifying, that one event can't capture it. It was the worse atrocity to ever happen to a people. The Middle Passage made her an African-American! That was the spiritual/blood bath she had to go through. I dealt with it in a sound sense rather than a physical sense of whips and chains. I feel that there is more than one way to get the information across... I wanted her to feel the spirit of all those folks who had died in the manner that they did.

OF: That is what unites us, no doubt.

BC: When I talk with people about this film, they don't remember a lot of what specifically happens. It ends up being blocked off into a sense of feelings. The film deals with a lot of feelings.

OF: Why don't you go out and make a documentary?

BC: I question the structure of the way films are made and put together. Even the documentary piece that I did was an exercise in passing on information in ways that are usual and would be interesting to me. Because I felt that those were the things that we have to question, I worked in a way that made me feel right, more so than some preconceived structure that someone says you must do because things are done in order to make money. Only in the film art form does this notion exist. If they did that in music, it would be dead! And they would have very few Blacks in it!

OF: What are you doing artistically in film?

BC: Well, I want to be a person who deals with film as an artist, and I ally myself with musicians and the manner in which they attack the musical form. I want to attack the film form in the same way -- because they are questioning, dealing, and artistically probing for different ways of stretching sound, and stretching pictures, and playing with colors. Film is still being helped by other art

▶ ▶ ▶ ▶

/

Say go! GO!

Say go! GO, GO!

/

This is the I-Fresh Party Patrol

/

GO, GO, GO!

GO, GO!

/

Give it up!

Give it up for 'em!

/

Get Down Brothers Sisters

/

GO AHEAD!

GO AHEAD!

/

Let's show them what partying is about

/

Give it up for 'em!

/

It's about a reason

/

GO AHEAD!

GO AHEAD!

/

And sometimes our reason is love

Love of one another

Having fun with one another

/

Scream!

HOOOO!

Now Scream!

HOOOO!

/

Ah-yeah!

AH-YEAH!

Say ah-yeah!

AH-YEAH!

/

/

Say get it boy!

GET IT BOY!

Say get it boy!

GET IT BOY!

/

It's all about dancing in a circle

/

GO AHEAD!

GO AHEAD!

/

We dance for a reason

/

FIRE IT UP!

FIRE IT UP!

/

Dance with roots

/

FIRE IT UP!

Fire it up!

FIRE IT UP!

Fire it up!

/

In the House!

/

And in the House

/

FIRE IT UP!

FIRE IT UP!/

/

I can't hear you!

/

What we always did was we brought the Spirit

/

A W W W W W

W W W W W W

W W !

/

Our ancestral spirit

/

LOUDER!

LOUDER!

/

That's what dancing is about

/

LOUDER!

LOUDER!

/

Possession

/

LOUDER!

LOUDER!

/

The birth of Possession

/

Put your hands in the Air! FRESH!

FRESH!

/

—Ben Caldwell
"VO I-Fresh
Extracted Audio"

CHAPTER 5

GEORGIA AVE × LEIMERT PARK

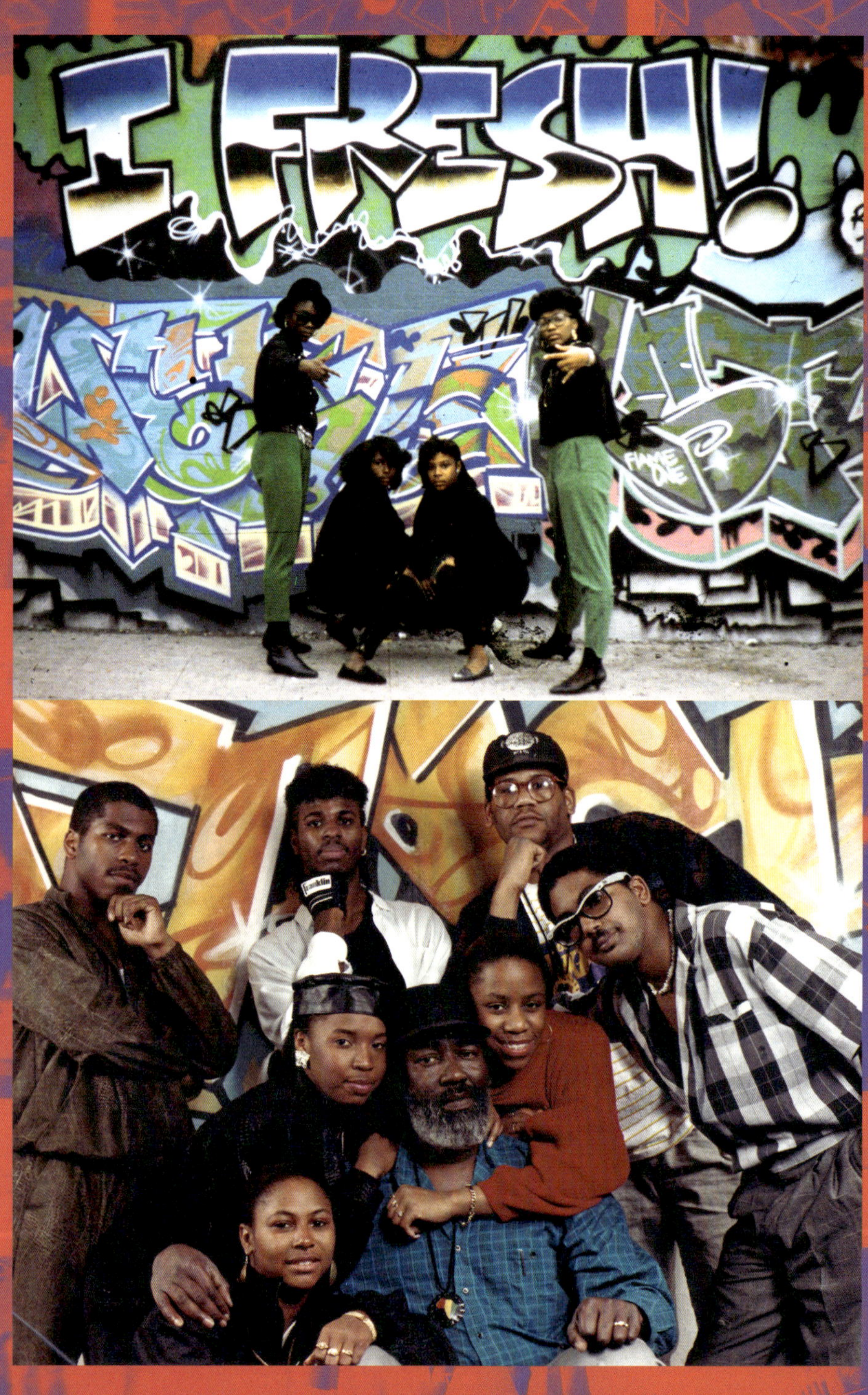

What is a village? Is it a group of houses and buildings, larger than a hamlet yet smaller than a town?

Is it the formations—familial and communal—into which we are born and reared? Those we choose and those that choose us? The people among whom we age, labor, struggle, play, love, reproduce, wither, decay?

Is it the spaces where we congregate, commemorate, grieve, and anchor ourselves? Is it the bodies and life-forces that orbit such spaces? The spirits that energize and **FLASH** in our communion with the living and the dead? The feet that shuffle and hips that gyrate to the earth's irregular rhythms and the spirit-world's frenzied pulse?

Is a village the presumed whole of its parts, the resolution of a complex equation involving humans, rituals, worldly and otherworldly forces, and the sites where life is made? The naming of a disorderly ensemble of elements that each generation form unique compounds and bonds that activate and generate ancient and new reactions? Or the hubs of activity—the nuclei that emit warmth and connection and whose gravitational pull induces motion, direction, purpose?

Perhaps it is all this, and more.

TEACHER · TEACHER

Charletta Johnson was ready to head home. From the morning's first period bell, the day had felt long. Yet here she was. Sitting in the main office even though the school day had ended.

She had always loved teaching. She had taught her younger brother to read in their Vallejo living room and had earned good grades through high school in Sacramento and college at Berkeley. So when she moved to Los Angeles in 1976, she pursued a teaching credential.

Her first assignment was as a language arts instructor at Van Nuys High School. She lasted there for four years. It was a good experience. But it wasn't affirming. She wanted to be leading classrooms composed of Black and Brown teens, young people in whom she could see herself and her family—everything that the predominantly white San Fernando Valley just wasn't. She was therefore excited when she got transferred to George Washington Preparatory High School.

Located in the Westmont section of South Central L.A., right at 108th Street and Denker Avenue, Washington Prep served teens from low-income neighborhoods including Westmont, West Athens, Athens, and Hawthorne. By the early to mid-1980s, it was one of hundreds of L.A. schools hit hard by cuts in education and social services, deindustrialization, youth unemployment, gang and police violence, drug addiction, and the LAPD's criminalization of Black and Brown youth. Struggling with poverty and unemployment, increasing numbers of these young people picked up work in shadow economies. This included black-market consumer retail, vehicle theft and grand larceny, sex work and pimping, and—most significantly—narcotics and gun trafficking.

The influx of cocaine into the city's poorest communities prompted an expansion and reorganization of these neighborhoods' street organizations. Struggles over turf were now business-driven armed conflicts over the illegal drug trade. The battles were fought out by the poor, young, and unemployed, numbers of whom were armed with imported AK-47s, M-16s, Uzis, and MAC-10s with thirty-round clips—arsenals befitting the Green Berets or a highly trained special forces military unit, not that of the city's most underserved, vulnerable inhabitants.

City leadership's response to the chaos can be best described as community dismemberment by design. Grassroots organizers, educators, and activists demanded jobs, higher wages, school funding, better social services, and a regional and national response to systemic poverty. What they got was a militarized city manned by the LAPD and headed by LAPD chief Daryl Gates. The police had at their disposal a military-grade arsenal of battering ram tanks, helicopters, and other weaponry, and anti-gang tactical divisions like the CRASH (Community Resources Against Street Hoodlums) unit that operated with impunity. Local and national media compounded the problem. On nightly newscasts, they circulated and profited from sensationalist representations that framed L.A.'s epidemic of violence and drug addiction as a crisis of "street terrorism" that could only be quelled through the court system, incarceration, and better parenting.

No South or East L.A. community was left untouched by this carnage. This included Washington Prep. A visitor couldn't miss the list in the school's lobby. It contained the names of more than five hundred students—former students and their friends and relatives who had died violently over the past decade.

However, the school's administrators, led by Principal George McKenna, were set upon transforming Washington Prep. They needed teachers who were up to the challenge. Charletta joined McKenna's brigade and never looked back.

Her love for her students knew no bounds. She would do just about anything for them. Let them stay at her home if they needed a place to crash. Advocated for them and defended them in discussions with other teachers. But she wasn't a pushover. She had no problem calling them out and demanding their best.

If you asked any of her students, they would tell you that Charletta was an unconventional instructor. Unlike other teachers, she never referred to her language arts classes as "English class." To her, this just reinforced the U.S. education system's legacy as a Euro-American colonial project—non-white students reading Anglo-European and Anglo-American authors' writings. So, Charletta flipped

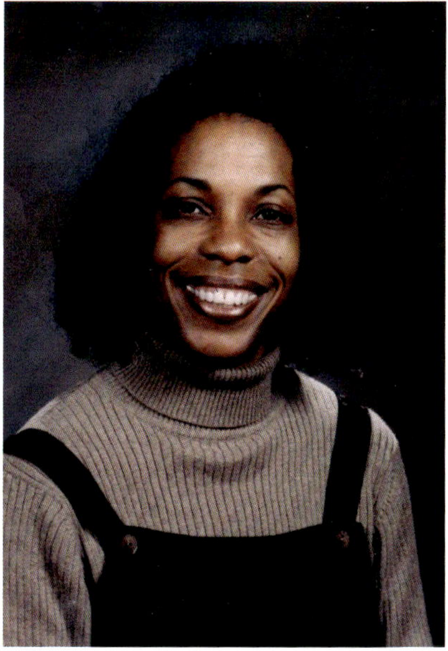

the script. Students read the works of James Baldwin, Walter Dean Myers, Zora Neale Hurston, John Henrik Clarke, and others.

Charletta therefore couldn't hold it against the students when they turned literature and poetry lessons into rap battles. A student would recite Paul Laurence Dunbar, Langston Hughes, or Gwendolyn Brooks's work, and then someone would start banging on their desk, someone else would start beatboxing, and the poem would inevitably take on a four-beat rhythmic cadence. How they could turn Nikki Giovanni into Kurtis Blow was a mystery to her. But she never shut it down. She encouraged it.

At the end of another long day, long after the last bell rang, Charletta should have been heading to her car. But where was she? Leaning on a desk, captivated by Yolanda Whitaker, a short, caramel-complexioned sixteen-year-old whom everyone called "Yo Yo," a beauty with hazel eyes and sharp, clever rhymes to match:

> *. . . Oh, and not to mention*
> *That I am controlling*
> *And maybe you could even say*
> *I'm high rolling*
> *Cuz my mic is the game*
> *And the rhymes is what I slang*
> *The way I do it*
> *Hell, I know you can hang*
> *With my gift, my gift*
> *Check me out*
> *Without a doubt*
> *I'll turn you fake emcees right out*

There was no question. The teen was talented! Witty wordplay, confidence, an easy ability to connect with the listener, a distinctive voice, and captivating presence.

Let's be clear. Charletta was not a fan of rap music. It sounded like noise to her. Plus, too much of it was about sneakers, cars, gold chains, and killing folks. But for better or worse, these were her kids. And oddly enough, she knew where and with whom Yolanda could enhance her abilities.

As Yolanda was rocking the mic, Wesley Michael Groves Jr. was in the Venice neighborhood of Los Angeles, pulling his car over to the road's shoulder. He kept his hands steady as he handed his driver's license and vehicle registration to the police officer. The paperwork was in order, but he had been speeding. And he was a Black man. Or, more precisely, he was a Black man with two boisterous elementary-aged, blonde-haired white children in the backseat. How was he going to explain this?

They were his boss's kids. Wesley was head of technology at On Time Offline, a Los Angeles-based company that handled film and television post production (footage storage, picture and sound editing, sound mixing, dubbing, sound and visual effects, and color correction and grading) for music videos by the likes of Madonna, Paula Abdul, Nirvana, Prince, and others. His road to working at On Time Offline began nearly thirty years earlier in 1958, just months after his birth, when his family relocated to Los Angeles from Kansas City, Missouri.

They made a home first in Baldwin Hills and later in View Park, two adjacent upper-middle-class communities at the top of South Central L.A.'s hills. The neighborhoods had opened to Black homeowners in the 1950s when racially restrictive covenants were declared unconstitutional. As a child, Wesley loved messing around with technology. It started when he took his aunt's transistor radio apart. She freaked out when she discovered him with all the parts laid out on the floor. Yet within the day, Wesley had reconstructed the machine and, go figure, it turned on and played! From that point on, he was stuck. At the elite Harvard School for Boys, Wesley was introduced to the workings of an ohm and a spectrum analyzer and the differences between series circuits and parallel circuits, and he helped build, wire, and run the school's television station.

However, it was as a transfer student at Howard University in Washington, D.C. that Wesley's world got rocked. The historically Black college and university (HBCU) was the perfect environment for Wesley to come into his own, enhancing his understanding of himself and his identity as part of a larger, global, multidimensional body of dispersed African peoples and cultures. It was never hard to spot Wesley, clad in gym shorts and a Bison t-shirt, roller-skating at a leisurely speed around the Yard (the grassy quadrangle and open space on campus, one of the primary student gathering spots). In addition, attending Howard enabled Wesley to study broadcast production and learn the ins and outs of media at WHMM, the university's state-of-the-art television station. It was there, in Studio A, located on Fourth and Bryant Streets NW, that Wesley met the person who revolutionized his thinking about media and culture.

Wesley initially underestimated Professor Ben Caldwell, the faculty member who taught the video production courses. Professor Caldwell was less interested in the nitty-gritty technical aspects of video. Instead, he explored its conceptual dimensions and constantly approached the subject matter from the perspective of film, art, and aesthetics. He would ask the students to consider composition, pacing, and the artistic merit of what they were creating. One time, Wesley finished editing a video only to discover that the edited footage had a glitch (an unstable signal or a disruption of a signal). The distortion of the footage irritated the technically savvy Wesley. But Professor Caldwell loved its look. There was something about it aesthetically, he said, that made it stand out from other students' work.

What ultimately transformed Wesley's view of Professor Caldwell was when he recruited Wesley and a few other students to assist with several off-campus video productions. The professor was documenting and interviewing blues musicians and other music artists who had come to perform at local venues. Over the next three years, this group filmed performances and interviews with musicians Willie Dixon, Sonny Terry, Ester Phillips, Brownie McGhee, John Lee Hooker, Memphis Slim, B.B. King, Billy Eckstein, Ron Carter, Grady Tate, Oliver Lake, Steve Coleman, David Murray, Bob Marley, Peter Tosh, and many others. The group was also hired to document the 20th Anniversary March on Washington, an event that honored the 1963 March for Jobs, Peace, and Freedom, and which drew 250,000 people to the nation's capital to condemn racism, Reaganism, and nuclear arms proliferation.

Their team was usually composed of at least five people: one who carried the camera, another who carried the Portapak (a battery-powered, self-contained video tape analog recording system), and then three or more people who handled the boom and lighting and managed the sound and visual gauges on the camera. Listening to the musicians discuss their lives and craft was a history lesson like no other. In addition, Wesley and his peers gained valuable hands-on production experience by working on their feet and trouble-shooting problems. The team's success helped them draw more students into their collective. This group would go on to produce the *Bison Information Network*, a student television program, as well as the video magazine *Studio 32*, all of which aired on WHMM.

These experiences inspired Wesley to pursue a career in media. Upon graduating from Howard in 1983, he returned to L.A. and bounced around for several years as a production assistant and associate. Once Wesley got his feet wet in the industry, it was Professor Caldwell who helped Wesley get the gig at On Time Offline. Wesley loved working there. But he could not get over one aspect of the job. By the mid-1980s, everyone producing a music video wanted the video's editors to manufacture glitches into the final cut to give the video a distorted, static-like look. "MTV is requesting a few more glitches," Wesley's boss would relay. Go figure. The glitches that had bothered Wesley were now the trend.

B R A N D • N U B I A N

Thinking about the glitch always made Ben smile. From his first encounters with Wesley at Howard University's WHMM, Ben was impressed by the young man. Wesley had deep knowledge and zeal for anything technology-related. It was a no-brainer for Ben to include Wesley in the professor's off-campus video productions. In time, Wesley became Ben's go-to tech expert.

But Ben also discovered something else about Wesley: his technical perfectionism sometimes got in the way of his willingness to experiment. The glitch in Wesley's Studio A video project was a prime example.

Wesley perceived the glitch as ruining the edit. Yet Ben interpreted it as a **"spark"** or **"flash"** in the video's form. It was as if a spirit or ghost entered the frame, and the camera's technology couldn't fully capture the life force's shape. It was like an analogue for the hidden worlds of Black life and the dissonance that results from attempting to translate and transfer one form of expression or data into another, especially within a chaotic and disruptive environment. Ben likened the glitch's aesthetics to that of the homemade one-string diddley bow or jitterbug instruments played by Black families in the rural South, or when blues musicians played slide guitar. These were devices and practices that originated in West Africa and had been transported to and transformed in the Americas by people of African descent, and which took on a ghostly presence when played by Black Americans.

Such insights became more common after Ben accepted an offer to teach in **Howard University's Department of Radio, Television, and Film.** In the fall of 1980, he quietly packed up his Los Angeles studio and moved across the country to Washington, D.C. As the only HBCU with plans to create a top-tier graduate film program (later established in 1983), Howard University provided Ben with a unique opportunity. There, he could help sculpt future generations of Black media-makers.

By the time Ben arrived at Howard, faculty members like Alonzo Crawford, Abiyi Ford, Arthur France, Haile Gerima (Ben's former UCLA teaching instructor and an accomplished independent filmmaker with his own distribution arm), and the school's dean, Lionel C. Barrow Jr., were spearheading a shift in the department's culture. As a faculty ensemble, they positioned media-making as essential to the raising of people's political and social consciousness. In a university publication dedicated to exploring the department's new vanguard of faculty, Ford summarized the collective's evolving approach:

It is naive to believe that the viewing of a single movie, regardless of how progressive it may be, can liberate anyone. . . . No movie ever liberated anyone. It is the involvement in the process from conceptualization to critical analysis which liberates both filmmaker and "audience." It is the perception of the process of filmmaking—the conceptualization, production, distribution, exhibition, and criticism—as an organic whole through which the participants dialogically interact which is liberating. The power of cinema as a tool of authentic pedagogy is grounded in trust between the community and the filmmaker, for the filmmaker, too, is an oppressed member of the community struggling toward liberation as a person and as an artist. This pedagogy brings the traditionally isolated artist face to face with the raw contradictions of society.

This commitment to process as a pedagogical model and means of raising social consciousness among artists and audiences aligned with Ben's previous experiences at UCLA. It therefore took him little to no time to acclimate to the department and find other faculty with whom to share ideas.

One of the first people he gelled with was William "Bill" Barlow, a white professor from California who taught courses on radio. Bill was a blues and R&B enthusiast who grew up listening to Black radio and moonlighted as a radio host and music programmer for WPFW-FM, a local D.C. alternative station. Alongside his reputation for spinning the hottest jazz, blues, and soul records, Bill wrote extensively about blues cultures and used his radio show as a space to interview musicians. At Bill's invitation, Ben started filming these interviews. This eventually grew into a bigger operation that included Bill and Ben's students.

While the experience immersed Ben in blues music and culture, it also enlightened him to the magic of the compact handheld video camera, which at that time was a new technology. Prior to the 1970s, video cameras were large, heavy, and often separated into multiple parts; the technology's bulkiness alone made it more frequently used in television studios and broadcast trucks than among filmmakers who, for the most part, preferred to use 16mm and 35mm film. Yet film was expensive, whereas video was more affordable and enabled a much faster turnaround time for editing and completing projects. Still, despite the utility and lower expense of video, throughout the 1970s and early 1980s, most film-school-educated filmmakers continued to revere film, perceiving video as film's substandard substitute. For less dogmatic filmmakers like Ben, though, the introduction and later commercialization of portable video cameras and reusable videotape was an exciting technological advancement because it democratized who could in fact experiment with filmmaking and cinematic documentation.

Ben's fascination with the video camera as a storytelling instrument and ethnographic tool had been developing since his graduate study at UCLA. There, he had been mentored by Shirley Clarke, a filmmaker and pioneer of video art. Throughout the 1970s and 1980s, Clarke produced experimental videos, video theater, video installations, new video technologies, and video-based workshops. The workshops were all-day and all-night events where ten to twenty or more filmmakers, videographers, and artists from other disciplines created live video-based collaborative works. They would share pre-recorded footage and record live footage, as well as engage in video game-playing, multi-screen video sculpture and portrait painting, tape-making, and other activities—all of which were showcased live on a totem-pole sculpture or mosaic wall-screen composed of black-and-white video monitors, culminating with a multichannel playback of the event's undertakings.

For Clarke, these live collaborations broke down the distinction between creator and audience. First, because the barrier to entry and participation was not high—anyone could participate by using the camera and creating live images. Second, because the live footage was made immediately available via the monitors in the creators' and audiences' shared environment, not on a big screen in a darkened theater. Furthermore, video, unlike film, enabled filmmakers and video artists to share, collaborate, and get feedback on footage in real-time, not in the aftermath of filming and/or editing.

Clarke likened this, what she described as "video as a process art form," to the daily exercises, rehearsals, regiments, and "skills and drills" required of dance companies and musical ensembles. "One unique capability of video is that we are able to put many different images from many different camera and playback sources into many different places . . . and we can see what we are doing as we are doing it," Clarke explained. "We need the skill *to see our own images in our own monitors* and at the same time see what everyone else is doing. We need to acquire the ability to see in much the same way that a jazz musician can hear what he is playing and at the same time hear what the other musicians are doing, and together they make music." There was power, Clarke maintained, in viewing the image while you shot it, especially when working in collaboration with others.

Furthermore, this kind of practice encouraged spontaneity and risk-taking because it invited imperfections—imperfect timelines, transitions, cuts, etc. Imperfections, according to Clarke, were not always errors; they could also be sources for aesthetic and conceptual breakthroughs, creative openings that produced unique collisions and pathways for invention and exploring the unfamiliar. Imperfections were also useful because they were reminders that what was couched, sometimes, in arguments for technical perfection and expertise was the authoritative push for standardization and a disdain for experimentalism. Clarke thus concluded that video represented a visual instrument and weapon of mediation, contestation, and collective action. Via video, she insisted, social change would be transmitted "not only into the streets, but [also] into our homes."

Ben admired Clarke's ambition and guerilla approach. And Clarke encouraged Ben's process of editing on the fly and mining the glitches and imperfections for different modes of expression and feeling. Filmmaking, for Ben, consequently became more like a live music or dance rehearsal and performance set as a result. This was because experimentation, collaboration, and play moved even more to the center of his work. Texture, mood, color, sound, and tone were perceived, not simply as means to articulate a film's narrative and invoke a particular reaction among a film's audience. They were, instead, understood as capable of creating emotional and psychic environments of experience, and moreover sensations and new contexts for self-sufficiency and well-being. Ben no longer wanted to make films *about* liberation, spiritual awakening, and healing. He wanted to make films where making, viewing, and experiencing the cinematic work *was* therapeutic and liberatory in itself. He wanted to create new contexts *for* healing.

These were the ideas and concepts that Ben experimented with in his radio and video production courses at Howard University. Students were given the freedom to test out concepts and techniques and encouraged to collaborate and take their video cameras beyond the campus's walls, beyond the Yard. They were empowered to perceive themselves as media-makers with unique stories to tell. They were told to stress little about aesthetic perfection and focus more on working with their peers in a manner where everyone's ideas were given consideration, and everyone's contributions were valued.

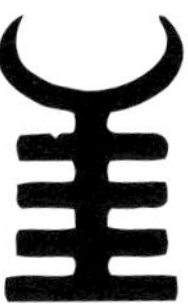

Ben's decision to teach at Howard was prompted by several significant life changes. After completing his degrees at UCLA, he had spent the end of the 1970s touring with *I & I: An African Allegory*. The film won second place at San Francisco's Poetry Film Festival and was included in "Black Independent American Cinema 1920–1980," a traveling multi-city retrospective that took Ben and other Black independent filmmakers to Paris, Rotterdam, London, and Berlin.

Yet as *I & I* received accolades, Ben's personal life was coming apart. After months of being in and out of the hospital, John Waits, his grandfather, died in June 1977. Then in 1979, Pam and Ben ended their marriage.

The split had been slowly developing. After Dara's birth, Pam and Ben argued more and more over different things—finances, their careers, the future. Pam wanted to write children's stories, study music, and develop her talent as a singer. Yet she was apprehensive about forgoing her steady income as a teacher and making such a big leap. The idea of prioritizing her artistry scared her. Ben vocalized his support for her desires, but sometimes felt that Pam didn't reciprocate this same sentiment for his films. This tension and their frequent disagreements increased the emotional distance between the couple.

They tried to patch things up over the summer of 1977. They organized a cross-country road trip. Their main objective was to reconnect through travel, conversation, and art. For two months, their family of three traversed the country in their Honda Civic. They visited family in the Southwest and friends throughout the South and East Coast. Ben screened his films and took photographs while Pam read and wrote in her notepad. Ben called the undertaking "Dark Shadows Moving Under Broken Glass."

Still, their emotional divide was too wide. By the fall of 1979, Pam and Dara were living in the couple's Pasadena home and Ben was operating primarily from his studio in Jefferson Park. In December, they decided to divorce.

To steady himself, Ben busied himself with art, which had always been his salvation. Even as a child, it was art that allowed him to persevere and wend a way through the trials and tribulations. It helped quiet the noise of his parents and siblings, the nonstop energy of eleven people occupying a four-bedroom house. It was the dark and mysterious portal hidden in the Deming library and the Southwestern desert and the Central Highland mountains and UCLA's Melnitz Hall. It was the underground source that grounded him, that enabled him to see and feel more, cool his spirit, and make space amid the solitude.

He divided his time between providing camera support for his peers' projects (most notably Barbara McCollough's *Water Ritual #1: An Urban Rite of Purification* (1979) and Bernard Nicolas's *Gidget Meets Hondo* (1980), helping plan and facilitate Brockman Gallery's yearly international film festival, and holding down an internship with Columbia Pictures. But at the center of his professional life was his passion and commitment to making films.

For Whose Entertainment (1979) was an investigative study and educational documentary that explored the image of Black people in American film, the economic impact of Blaxploitation and Black film consumption, and the new directions being forged by Black independent cinema. Produced with screenwriter and journalist Ardie Ivie and filmed over the course of one night at a UCLA studio, the film is a collage work. It fuses clips from popular American films with pre-recorded content from Ardie Ivie's public access television show, lectures from both Ivie and educator and poet Majid Mahadi, and a roundtable discussion with UCLA professor Teshome Gabriel and filmmakers St. Clair Bourne, Pamela Douglas, Grace Ibagwe, and Larry Clark.

The Nubian (1980) was a meditative short film about an anonymous man at a crossroads in his life who spends his days walking through an airport terminal. There is no dialogue in the film and no resolution; the protagonist never gets on a plane, speaks to anyone, or leaves the terminal. He just wanders slowly and somberly, ascending escalators and moving steadily amid the airport's moderately busy atmosphere. The imagery is an allegory for the necessity of being physically still and mentally present yet allowing your imagination to drift—even amid chaos, even when everything around you is moving and changing. This footage is also fused with shots of bright, vibrant, interspersed colors. Ben's objective was for the images and colors to influence and, with any luck, coincide with the audience's emotional and psychological state, providing them with a feeling of serenity and peace.

Tenor saxophonist Rahsaan Roland Kirk's "Theme for the Eulipions" (1976) serves as the film's score and inspiration. The song fuses spoken word poetry and jazz musicianship, and shifts from a slow, somber pace to upbeat rhythms backed by a singing choir. It is a melancholic ode to the desolate state of the "journey agent" and "eulipion," an undefined term that Kirk concocted, what the song's poet describes as those creative travelers which include poets, artists, and musicians. Yet the song does not lament loss, heartbreak, or an artist's sense of loneliness. Instead, it tries to generate healing for these emotional and psychological states. The lyrics from "Theme for the Eulipions" illuminate this point:

> **if there were no song**
> **you would have this song**
> **to give warmth at night**
> **and to keep you strong**
> **it would make love a guess**
> **spinning round and round**
> **and when meteors fall**
> **love would reach the ground**
> **if there were no moon**
> **to control the tides**
> **there would be these notes**
> **as the sail goes by . . .**

The Nubian makes a similar offering. Footage, colors, and sound are used to induce catharsis for the viewer, film becoming a vessel for therapy, restoration, and sustenance. Its purpose was not to entertain, but to evoke a mood and engender introspection and most importantly healing.

The film was a good preface for the subsequent three years that Ben spent teaching at Howard University and living in Washington, D.C. Leaving L.A. and immersing himself in Howard's and D.C.'s cultural life contributed to Ben's own healing process. It also transformed his understanding of what it meant to be an artist. More and more, Ben found purpose and joy in artistic collaboration and in the mentoring and instructing of other aspiring artists.

Amid his and Pam's divorce, the couple remained steadfast in their commitment to the best possible parenting for Dara. Consequently, even after Ben moved across the country, six-year-old Dara came to visit often and eventually moved to D.C. to live with Ben for a year. With Dara by his side, Ben soaked in the city's vibrant life and culture.

They moved into a three-bedroom, two-story brownstone on the corner of 14th and F Streets that they shared with Bill Barlow, Ben's colleague and

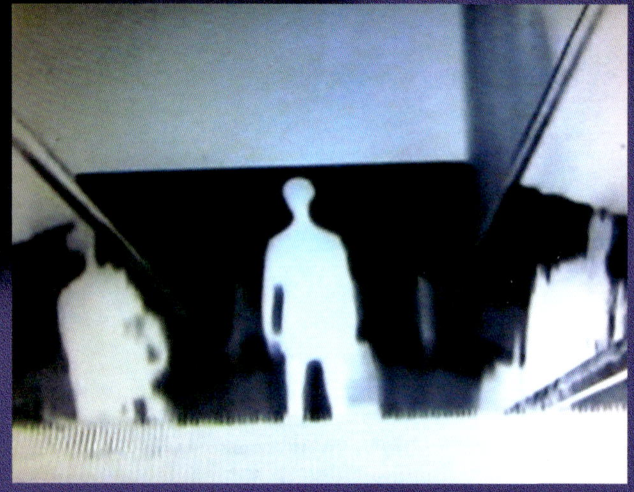

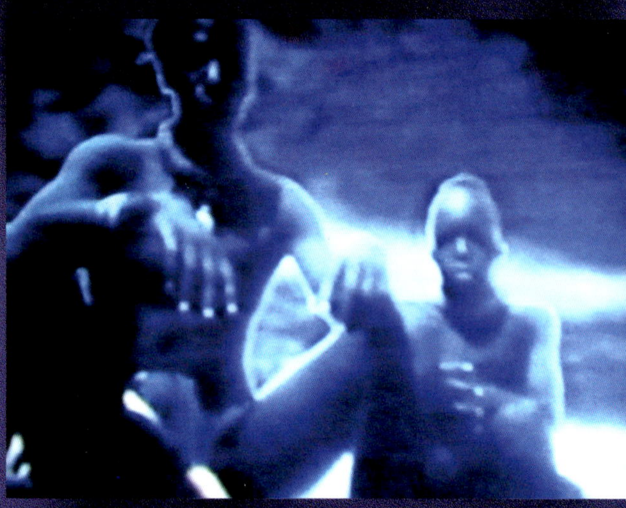

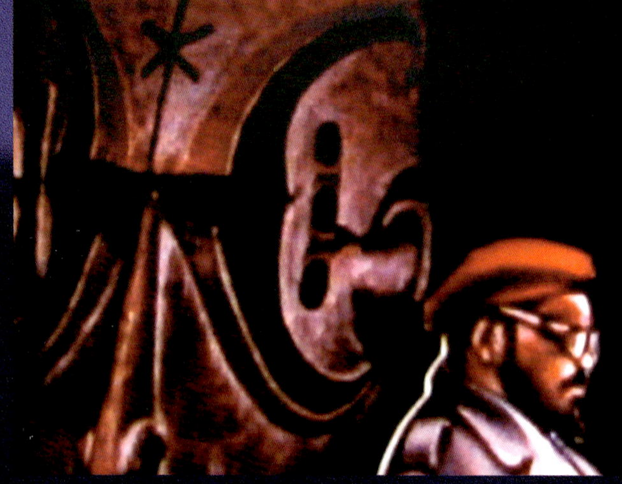

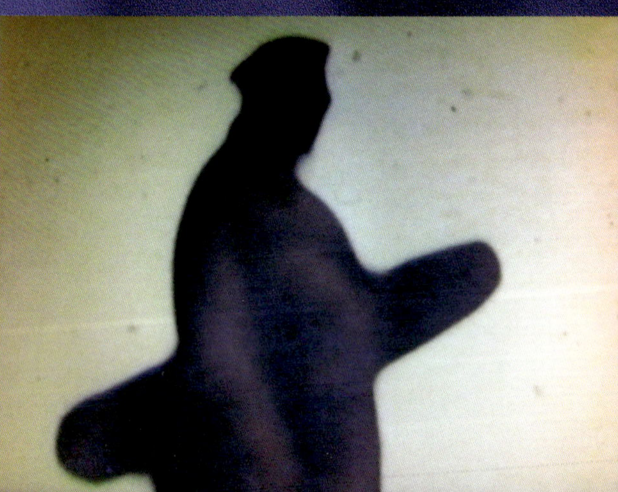

video-series partner. Ben would screen his films on the brownstone's walls for a growing community of friends and collaborators. Ben and Dara's village included his Howard colleagues and friends Haile Gerima, Abbie Kendricks, and Janette Dates, as well as film and integrated media students Wesley Groves, Don Q. Hannah, and Arthur Jafa Fielder; Nandi Bowe, Brandon Bates, and the rest of the Bison Information Network production team; writer/critic Greg "Iron Man" Tate; actor Bob Wisdom; Sweet Honey in the Rock members Berniece Reagon and Arnae Batson; and numerous educators, filmmakers, artists, musicians, organizers, and city professionals.

There was nothing like living in America's proverbial "Chocolate City." For Ben, the District was a portal to different galaxies of Blackness. All around him were identities, sounds, rhythms, smells, vibrations, and colors to learn from, explore, and be inspired by.

Best of all were the go-go parties—the city's own percussion-heavy, call-and-response-saturated, highly improvisatory subgenre of funk and hip-hop music and celebration. Among the bodies that danced, sang, chanted, and jammed to go-go's syncopated rhythms, callouts, and cadences, Ben discovered a late-twentieth-century analogue to the blues. He felt a similar way about reggae music and especially about hip-hop, the emerging subculture of music, visual art, and dance that he encountered during his visits to New York City. Both seemed to be part of the same continuum of expression as that of the blues and other African diasporic arts. But in D.C., Ben got to experience go-go in an intimate way where he wasn't simply an observer but a participant. And what was clear was that it was not simply music. It was a city and region-wide expression of Blackness.

Go-go represented and generated neighborhood pride and joy. Black Washingtonians felt affirmation and jubilation in go-go parties' celebratory atmosphere and the music's hyper-localized slang and references. This was especially so for the city's young people. For D.C.'s young, poor, and Black, go-go provided a bountiful forum for merriment, pleasure, and carnival. And such catharsis was necessary, considering that it was this group who most intensely experienced the sting of the city's inequalities. They were constantly misrepresented and disparaged in the media and encumbered by racist policing, under-resourced schools and social services, unemployment, gangs, and youth strife. Yet while this contingent felt empowered by go-go culture, upper-class elites and elements of the city's leadership vilified go-go. They deemed it a "public nuisance," instituting strict curfews on concerts and clubs, and harassing and raiding go-go parties and performances.

Go-go supplied Ben with a sonic portal into the economic and social conditions that divided the city, and even more importantly, the city's own brand of Black youth and young adult consciousness. With video cameras in hand, he and his students documented the raw and organic energy rocking clubs like Cheriy's in Southwest, the 9:30 Club in Northwest, and Celebrity Hall on Georgia Avenue, and blasting out of car stereos and speakers at picnics at Hain's Point.

When Ben moved back to Los Angeles in the final months of 1983, one thing was clear: he had been bitten by the go-go bug. Go-go was a specific phenomenon which grew out of D.C.'s expressive and vernacular cultures. Yet what was obvious to Ben was that a similar experience of alienation and angst was fueling youth nationwide. And in L.A., signs of its presence were all around him: spray-painted and tagged on building walls, freeway signs, and public bus windows; blaring from low-riders, boomboxes, and Walkman headphones; and manifested through language, dance, and music on the beach boardwalk, in street corner ciphers, and in after-hour lounges and dance clubs across the city.

V I D E O • 3 3 3 3

DonKingski was late. Real late. But the party couldn't start without chief rocker DonKingski, aka Donald Funk, on the 1 and 2's.

Every week, Don, born Donald Thomas, mistimed the journey from Carthay Circle to the Village in South Central L.A. He had spent his life shuttling back and forth on public transportation from his family's Mid-City home to his grandmother's residence in the Crenshaw District. And you never knew what might transpire on any given day on SoCal RTD (Rapid Transit District). Teens didn't rename the bus "rough, tough, and dangerous" for nothing! In any case, Don should have known better than to think it would be a quick ride during the middle of rush hour. But here he was, hustling to get to VIDEO 3333.

The crew was supposed to leave at 4:00 p.m. for their television shoot in Inglewood. Several of them were still nervous about it. But not Don. He had been in the limelight since he was a kid.

At ten years old, he and his brother made a name as competitive bowlers. They crushed opponents at the city's annual youth championships and hustled folks their parents' age at the plush thirty-two-lane Rodeo Bowl on Rodeo and La Cienega, and at the bowling alley beneath the World on Wheels roller-skating rink. In his teenage years, he traded in the bowling ball to compete with skateboards, BMX bikes, and dirt bikes. When he wasn't doing that, he was playing trumpet in the marching band and goofing off at Fairfax High School. At each age of transition, he picked up a new hobby, a new passion project. But nothing prepared Don for hip-hop.

He was a student at Santa Monica College when he became transfixed with rap music and dance, and later, DJing and beat production. He and his homeboys jammed to the Treacherous Three's "Body Rock" (1980), Kurtis Blow's "The Breaks" (1980), and the Funky 4 + 1's "That's the Joint" (1982). But it was Afrika Bambaataa and the Soulsonic Force's "Planet Rock" (1982) that made Don want to produce records and get on the wheels of steel. Thereafter, all his hard-earned dollars were shelled out on an ever-growing collection of records and maintaining his prized Technics SL-1200 turntable deck.

By 1984, he had his own crew. They wreaked havoc and wrecked shop throughout Los Angeles. At house parties and in their apartments, they danced, sang along, and practiced their own lyrics over a budding catalog of music. This included L.A. jams like Egyptian Lover's "Egypt, Egypt" (1984), World Class Wreckin' Cru's "Slice" (1984) and "Surgery" (1985), and Toddy Tee's anti-police anthem "The Batteram" (1985). Don's crew was part of a city-wide multitude that kept their ears tuned both to the street and to the jams blasting from radio programmer Greg Mack and the Mix Masters' shows on KDAY 1580 AM. Across L.A., this mass of bodies popped, locked, and body-rocked at clubs like Radio (later Radiotron) and Eve's After Dark, roller-skating rinks like World on Wheels and Skateland, and park and convention-jams thrown by Uncle Jamm's Army, as well as Ultra Wave parties hosted at Kingston 12 and Maverick's Flat, in public spaces like the Venice boardwalk, and among the city's stucco-covered garages, front lawns, and public housing courtyards.

Add to this legion of hotspots **VIDEO 3333**, a media arts studio in Leimert Park Village. Don was introduced to it after his crew performed at a pool party thrown by a filmmaker up in Baldwin Hills. After their performance, the filmmaker explained that he was looking for rappers, dancers, DJs, and artists to star in a film he was making. All rehearsals would be held in his studio, which was located just down the hill in the Village, Leimert Park's business district.

Ben, the filmmaker, seemed very serious and well-intentioned. Still, Don took it with a grain of salt. It seemed like every few months, a new hip-hop movie was being released. The first films were instant classics—*Wildstyle* (1983), *Breakin' N Enterin'* (1983), and *Style Wars* (1983). But Hollywood's take? *Beat Street* (1984), *Breakin'* (1984), *Krush Kroove* (1985)? Yeah, it was cool seeing hip-hop on the screen, but it was starting to feel overdone, like Hollywood was trying to squeeze as much as it could from hip-hop culture before the bubble burst. And bigger than all that, what could Ben, this forty-year-old dude, even know about hip-hop?

Don ultimately ate those words. When he dropped by Ben's studio, he was blown away. As Don approached the building, he heard Bobby Byrd and the J.B.'s classic "I Know You Got Soul" (1971) blasting from inside. The music's energy was easily matched by the teenagers who sweated working on dance sequences and who spat rhymes into a microphone. In the room's back corner, Ben filmed the performers, with the video's live feed shown on a nearby television screen. He occasionally rewound the tape and let the performers review and discuss the footage. Ben and the other participants would give the performer a few pointers. Then the emcee would go at it again, this time working to implement the group's suggestions into their performance.

Don hung around that day. He even hopped on the mic and got some love for his rhymes. He also received feedback about how to hold the microphone to generate clearer sound and how to perform when in front of a camera. Eager to improve, Don returned the following week, and then the week after that.

He soon discovered that VIDEO 3333 was less a site for kids to audition and rehearse for a film, and more a place for them to hang out and strengthen their abilities as performers (rappers, singers, dancers, DJs, actors, hosts) and learn the basics of video production. Don dug the space's educational, art-first focus. Yet it was VIDEO 3333's positive and funky vibe that encouraged Don to keep coming back. His younger sister even started tagging along.

Don quickly became one of VIDEO 3333's anchors. He was responsible for the DJing and music production. He would spin records on the space's turntable decks (which were encased and protected in a coffin case that Don and Ben constructed with wood and carpet material) and track out beats on his Roland TR-808 drum machine for kids to rhyme over. And as one of the workshop's elder members, Don often provided feedback and mentored other attendees.

One of his favorites was thirteen-year-old Lance Patrick Caldwell, aka Chill. Chill was from Vermont Knolls, a neighborhood just southeast of the Village that spanned the blocks south of Florence Avenue down to Manchester Boulevard, and in-between Normandie Avenue and the 110 Freeway. Chill had grown up around music. Each month, his father faithfully spent portions of the money he made from repairing roofs on boxes of jazz, soul, and R&B vinyl from Cadet Records' distribution warehouse on Normandie and Slauson. Chill's dad would audiorecord his favorite cuts from the records onto cassette tapes that he would mix with songs from local radio; he would then mail the mixtapes to his cousins in Louisiana. This was Chill's introduction to the art of selecting and mixing vinyl records old and new. But it was years later, as a middle schooler being bussed to the Valley, that he really got his nose wide open on this, and more centrally on its significance within hip-hop culture. At Woodland Hills's Hale Charter Academy, Chill and his posse traded freestyle and written rap verses daily at "the flats" (the landing area in the middle of the school's staircase).

It was through this group of friends that Chill was introduced to Darryl Jackson, aka Mixmaster Wolf, a teenage DJ who had a four-track recorder and mini-studio in his bedroom. There, he taught Chill the basic ins and outs of handling studio equipment and how to create a pause-mix/pause-tape. Even better, Wolf's dad, Mr. Jackson, had a full studio in the back of the family's Leimert Park home, the room equipped with an "electronic arsenal" of samplers, digital drums, drum machines, and computers. But "Mr. Jackson" was Darryl Munyungo Jackson—the master percussionist who performed with Stevie Wonder, Miles Davis, and numerous others. And he wasn't for the teens messing around with his equipment! After catching Wolf and Chill in his space for the umpteenth time, Mr. Jackson ordered the boys to get in his car. He drove them around the corner to the Village. This was how Wolf and Chill were introduced to Ben, DonKingski, and the rest of the VIDEO 3333 crew.

The VIDEO 3333 collective was a fun and dynamic group. Besides DonKingski, Chill, and DJ Mixmaster Wolf, there was DJ Mike, Darryl with the Curl, Stacie, Pee Wee Jam, Candyman, Bam-Bass, Beatbox Josh, Yolanda (aka Yo Yo), Tonya, Kool Chill, FBI (Freak Body Inspectors), Idle King, the Wash House Crew, Poetic Style, and many others. And they came from different high schools and sections of the city. Kids reppin' Crenshaw High, Dorsey, Manual Arts, Loyola, Bishop Conaty, Jefferson, Westchester, Washington Prep, Gardena, Centennial, Compton, and Dominquez.

Sometimes elementary and middle school kids visited the workshop, too. They would come with their older siblings or be drawn in from the street by the music. The one child who was always there was Dara, Ben's daughter. When she wasn't posted at the building's entrance greeting people, she was up front watching the performances or finishing her homework in her bedroom, which was in the back room behind the rehearsal space.

Adults also frequented VIDEO 3333. There was Wesley Groves, who oversaw the technology. You could find him wheeling around a speaker, handling cable wires or a video camera, and strategizing camera angles and choices with Ben. Joyce Hart and her family helped with managing the studio's day-to-day operations, while Lena and Lauran helped coordinate the after-school workshop.

Most integral of all was Charletta Johnson, the high school teacher who helped recruit teens for the program. It was Charletta who hipped teens from her school to the workshop, and who helped Ben with his outreach to other neighboring schools. But even more, Charletta helped to create a nurturing, loving environment inside VIDEO 3333. She was always there showing love, offering encouraging words, and even letting Ben and crew use her home to rehearse and film.

Some teens came to VIDEO 3333 to enhance their emceeing and rapping skills. But there were others who attended simply to have fun, to feel like they were part of something bigger than themselves. Dancing was a key practice that connected all of them. Some would bop, others would pop, a few would lock, and a small contingent would break. They would uprock, kick step, blender, and finish with their torsos and legs upended in a windmill. Everybody did the wop. Trendy dancing, the poser, the cabbage patch, the robot. These were their dance moves. Bugging out and moving flamboyantly to Egyptian Lover's "Computer Love (Sweet Dreams)" (1984) and Channel One's "Technicolor" (1986). Dance crews would perform routines, and several of them had as many as eight routines ready just in case a dance battle proved to be competitive. It was a space where individuals could shine, but where great teamwork and collaboration stole the show. Where dance, fashion, style, and embodied self-expression was what really got the party rocking. You could even discern specific crews and their preferred dance styles based on the dancers' apparel. B-boys and B-girls in T-shirts, sweatpants, and tracksuits, rocking Puma Clydes and Adidas Superstars or Campuses. Other dancers kept it simple and clean in Dickies jeans and black Converse Chuck Taylor 70s. They saved their most beloved garments for VIDEO 3333's parties and weekend events. Some young women wore outfits mirroring that of

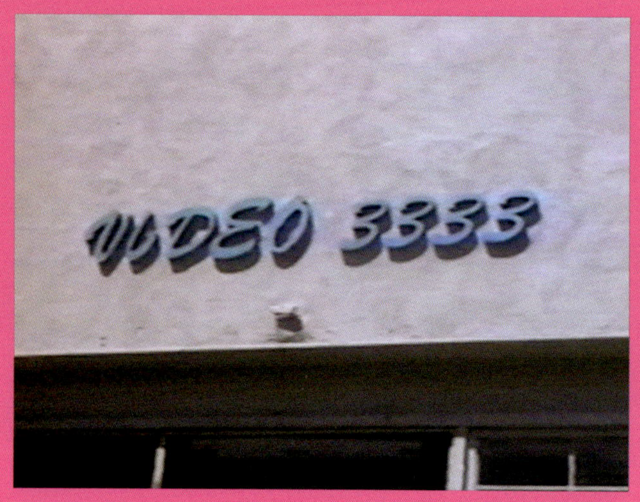
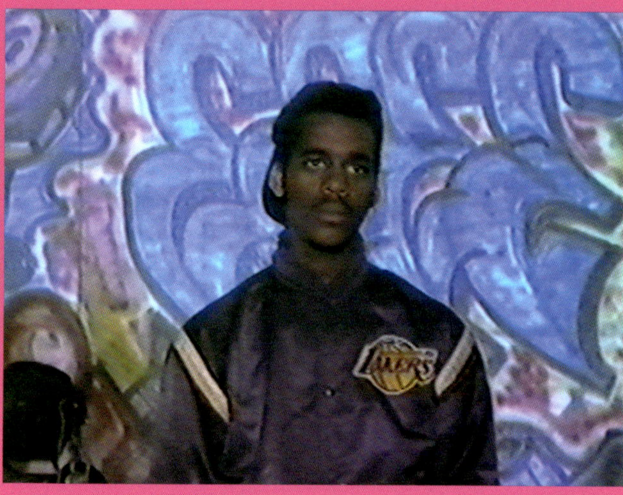
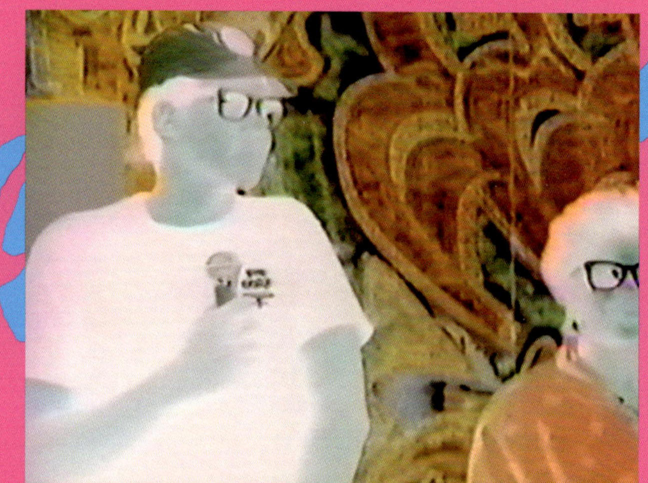
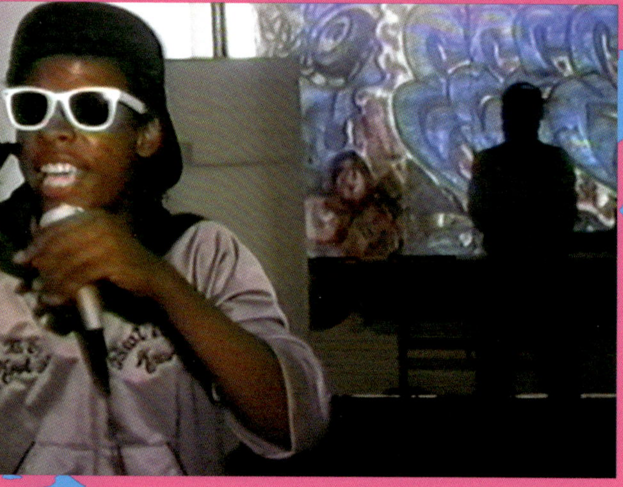
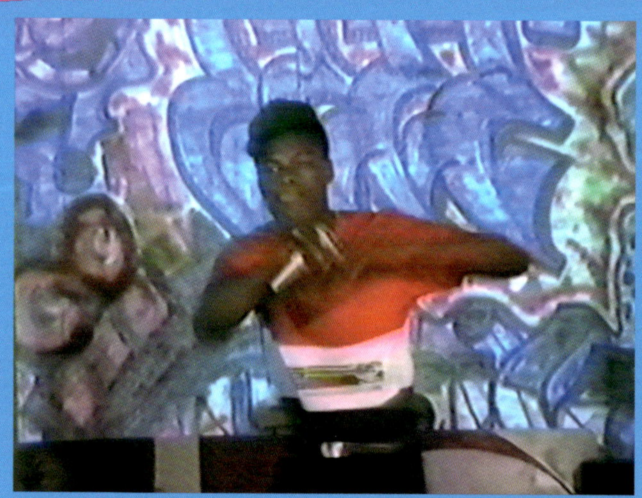

VIDEO 3333 REHEARSAL, 1987

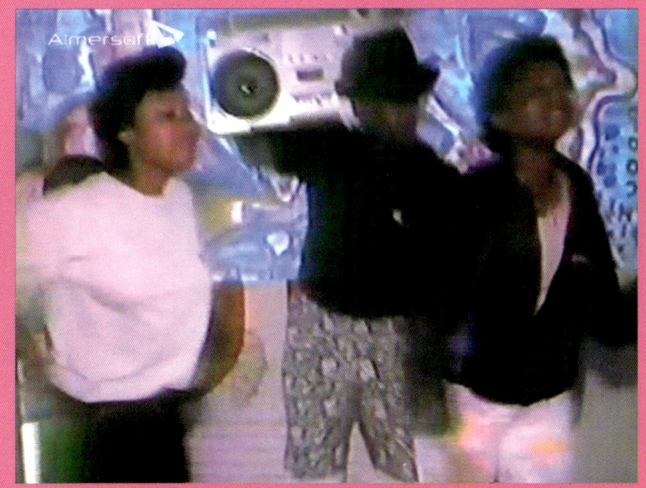
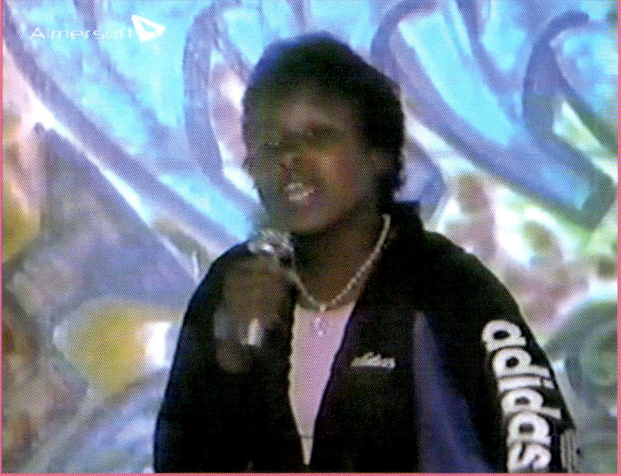
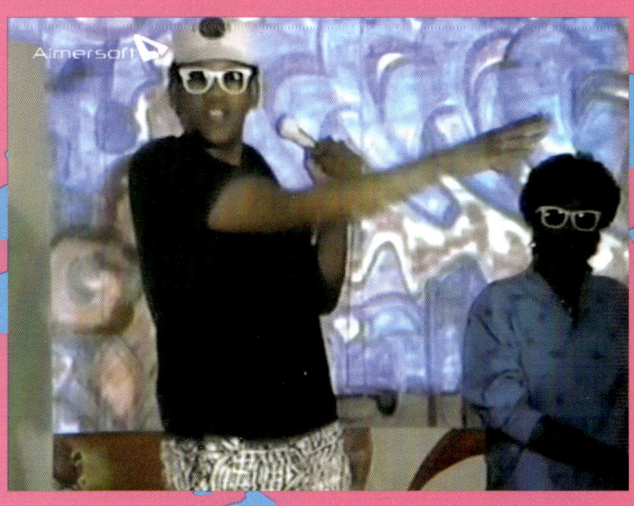
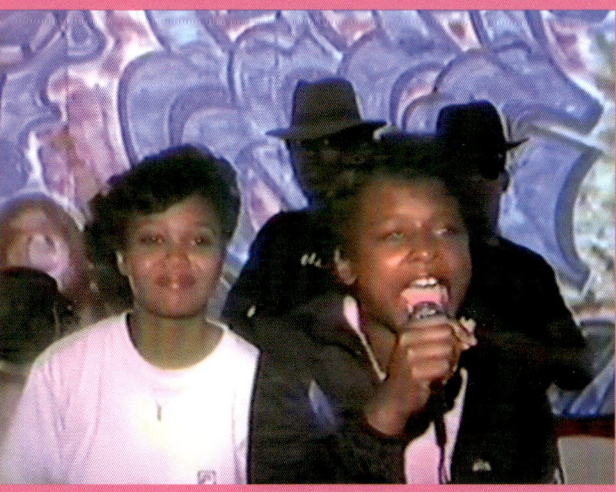
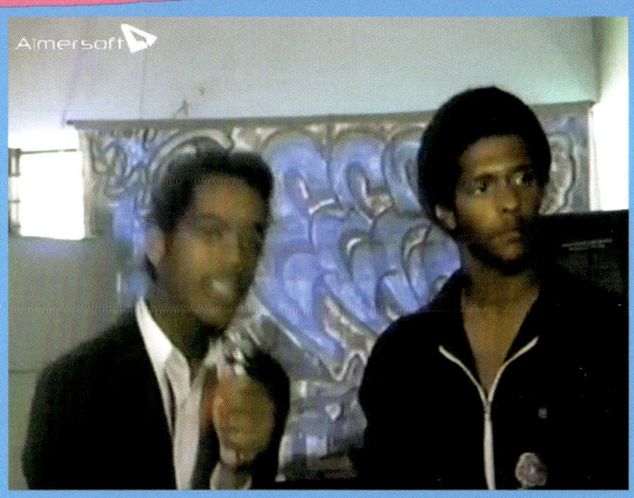

singer Lisa Lisa—fuschia and metallic bodysuits and spandex dancewear with matching headbands, rooster bangs, and dangling earrings. Other teens wore the same colors and shirts or jackets with their crew name stitched on the back or on the sleeve.

What was so cool about VIDEO 3333 was that it wasn't your neighborhood or the money in your pocket that got you respect (although it didn't hurt). It was your skills. Your enthusiasm. Your love for the culture. Your devotion to getting better at getting down. But you had to come with respect—for yourself, everyone else, and the space.

One time this short, charming dude from Compton hopped on the mic. His name was Eric, but everybody called him "Eazy." His flow was simple yet relaxed. He rhymed about money, cars, and women—not the kind of content preferred by Ben, Charletta, and some of the other adults, but still nothing to cry home about. But when Eazy kept cursing, Ben shut the mike off. There were two main rules in VIDEO 3333. No fighting. No cursing. And Eazy crossed the line.

Still, there was a lot of promising talent at VIDEO 3333. Yolanda, aka Yo Yo, the teenaged Washington Prep student who Charletta introduced to the space, had this one song, "The Nissan," that everyone loved. In the song, Yo Yo showed love for her ride and her neighborhood:

Crenshaw Strip that's where I trip
Hanging out and chilling out
And feeling the groove
Well, I turn on my sounds
And I bust the move
I do the Nissan . . .

Pee Wee Jam and Darryl with the Curl's song "Extensions" was another VIDEO 3333 favorite. In the song, the duo poked fun at women who wore wigs, weaves, and hair extensions. That a brother with a Jheri curl would clown women for processing their hair added to the song's irony and ridiculous hook:

DARRYL:
Ladies in the house
Please don't get offended
We want to talk about your damn, uuuh!!

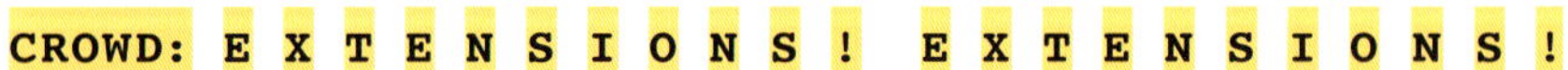

PEE WEE:
She had no hair and her name was Fay
Came back with a lot of hair the very next day
Plain imitating in the place don't leave

But I really do know about your weave
Because we were having cold rocking the bed

PEE WEE/DARRYL:
She starts pulling that stuff right out of her head, Now Fay!

PEE WEE:
I don't mean to kick it
But that's what happens when you have those . . .

CROWD: E X T E N S I O N S ! E X T E N S I O N S !

The song was boyish and crude. Yet it was catchy. And it was rapped in a back-and-forth cadence that imitated the rhyming style of Run-DMC, the Fats Boys, UTFO, and Whodini (Pee Wee and Darryl even remade Whodini's "One Love" (1986) into a religious-themed song called "One Lord"), as well as that of earlier crews like the Cold Crush Brothers and the Treacherous Three.

Still, the majority of the kids' lyrics had more breadth and depth. Take Pee Wee and Darryl's song, "Moses." This song used the well-known Biblical narrative about the Hebrew prophet who helped the Israelites escape oppression in Egypt as an analogy for the struggles waged by Black Americans. Or rapper Candyman's "Hard Life/Smart Life," a song he performed with a buddy that was co-written with one of Candyman's Washington Prep teachers. The song explored the impact of drugs, violence, and poverty on teens in South Central L.A. It was one of several songs where the VIDEO 3333 teens gave voice to the unjust conditions of their neighborhoods and the struggles impacting their families and communities.

The inequities described in the songs were the impetus for Ben's decision to establish VIDEO 3333's after-school hip-hop program. Ben had left Howard University, first and foremost, to be with Dara. He wanted her to grow up in one place with both parents. But a second priority for Ben was creating projects that engaged youth and which built on the foundations that he had established at Howard.

When he arrived back in L.A. in 1983, he initially showed his films at events run by his friend, video artist Ulysses Jenkins. Jenkins also got Ben involved in the Electronic Café project led by multimedia artists Kit Galloway and Sherrie Rabinowitz, where, as part of the 1984 Summer Olympics Art Festival in Los Angeles, they linked five different L.A. locations and communities in real time using emerging video teleconferencing technology. But Ben's primary work was at Brockman Gallery and the Watts Tower Arts Center, two arts institutions located in Leimert Park and Watts, respectively. He helped with their educational and community outreach. This entailed video-interviewing and documenting artists, musicians, and community events, especially the center's annual Drum Festival. It also consisted of leading media classes at Watts's

Grape Street Elementary and Markham Middle School, as well as at Mid-City's Alternative High School.

The schools' students and administrators were an inspiring, spirited group. Yet Ben left each visit disturbed by the conditions of poverty, urban divestment, ghettoization, violence, and police repression that they were forced to endure. The schools were also reeling from the Reagan administration's massive cuts to the federal education budget, and California's 1978 passing of Proposition 13, which slashed the property tax rate and subsequent property tax revenue. This latter bill effectively decimated the funds available to local schools and was part of a series of policies that eroded local school districts' power and funding. In schools like Markham and Grape Street, this meant fewer teachers and staff, more overpopulated classrooms, fewer resources to meets students' needs, and the elimination of summer schools, adult education, school libraries and librarians, counseling, maintenance services, school-funded field trips, art/dance/music education, and extracurricular after-school programs.

Ben's experience in the schools hammered into him two lessons. First, there was a glaring need for arts and media education and opportunities for creative expression for low- and middle-income Black and Brown kids. Most essentially, it must be relevant to their lives and everyday realities. Second, with the proliferation of gang sets throughout the city and, more significantly, the LAPD's criminalization and violent crackdown on poor Black and Brown communities, teens needed safe neutral zones—public spaces not occupied or claimed by gangs and not intensely policed and surveilled by LAPD—to interact and develop ideas freely.

The life forces revealed the idea to him. The teens deserved a healing facility. It couldn't look or feel like a classroom. No, it had to be a space they could easily identify with and make their own. A space where they could feel comfortable being vulnerable and open to fully unearthing and activating themselves. And it had to be the kids who helped facilitate this process for themselves and for one another. They had to be the leaders of their own "process art form," their own creative practice of collaboration, risk-taking, and mediation.

Assisted by fundraiser Judith Bowman, who helped run the Friends of Watts Towers Arts Center, Ben applied for and was awarded a California Arts Council "Artist in Community" grant. He proposed to create an after-school arts and media workshop that served inner-city teens and young adult creatives from different L.A. neighborhoods.

Ben's decision to run the workshop in Leimert Park Village was a product of strategy and chance. Several months prior to receiving the grant, he had signed a rental agreement for a two-story building at 3333 West 43rd Place that he intended to use as a studio and living space for himself and Dara. It was in the southeast corner of the Village, sandwiched between the Watchtower movie theater/assembly hall and Jewel's Hair Conspiracy beauty shop.

Ben couldn't believe it when he moved into the space. Middle-class Leimert

Park had always felt like it was beyond his reach. But it was an ideal location for a media-arts studio and education program.

The neighborhood was in the center of the city, along major thoroughfares with widespread access to public transportation. This made it a good destination for young people of modest means lacking car transportation. Furthermore, the neighborhood was a junction that connected the city's Black economic elite and middle class with poor and working-class residents. This made it the kind of "neutral zone" Ben was looking for. A centralized, non-gang-oriented site for relatively safe interactions among the city's different socioeconomic communities of color.

Plus, the village of Leimert Park had an interesting history. The neighborhood had been built after Walter H. Leimert, a German-American real estate developer, purchased the land in 1927 from Clara Baldwin Stocker, the eldest daughter of prominent real estate speculator and developer Elias Jackson "Lucky" Baldwin. The Leimert family advertised its new development project as a neighborhood composed of "workplace dwelling(s)" and "homes, not houses" for middle-class and economically mobile Anglo residents and migrants to Los Angeles. Leimert Park, they maintained, was a community for whites who desired a "home, income, investment, and convenience." The 1948 lifting of racial covenants and the prospect of having non-white neighbors, however, led many of these residents to abandon the area for the suburbs. With their departure came an influx of Japanese Americans into the area, as well as smaller numbers of other groups of Asian descent, alongside a growing number of middle-class Blacks. By the late 1960s, the neighborhood had become a hub for L.A. Black cultural life and community, home to several celebrities and musicians, and numerous shops and cultural spaces.

For Ben, the most important of these cultural spaces was Brockman Gallery, located in the center of the neighborhood's business district. Founded by brothers Alonzo and Dale Davis in 1967, it was one of only a few spaces in L.A. dedicated to exhibiting the work of fine artists of color. Through exhibitions, street fairs, outdoor open exhibits, and film festivals, the gallery helped transform Leimert Park Village into a hub for fellowship around Black arts and culture.

When Ben received the grant to develop the after-school media arts workshop, he leaned on Brockman's past work as well as his own experiences. Teaching at Howard and coordinating the off-campus video productions, running ASU's Black House, managing the VA's outreach office, and organizing film festivals at Brockman, as well as the collaborative environment he experienced during his UCLA studies and thereafter, had prepared him for what was to come.

And such was clear and evident to Don and the rest of the VIDEO 3333 collective. From their purview, Ben ran the program with ease, always demonstrating a calm and level head, always encouraging the teens to listen to one another, cooperate, and embrace their imperfections and uniqueness. Ben would maintain that by mining their glitches, the teens could cultivate pathways of expression

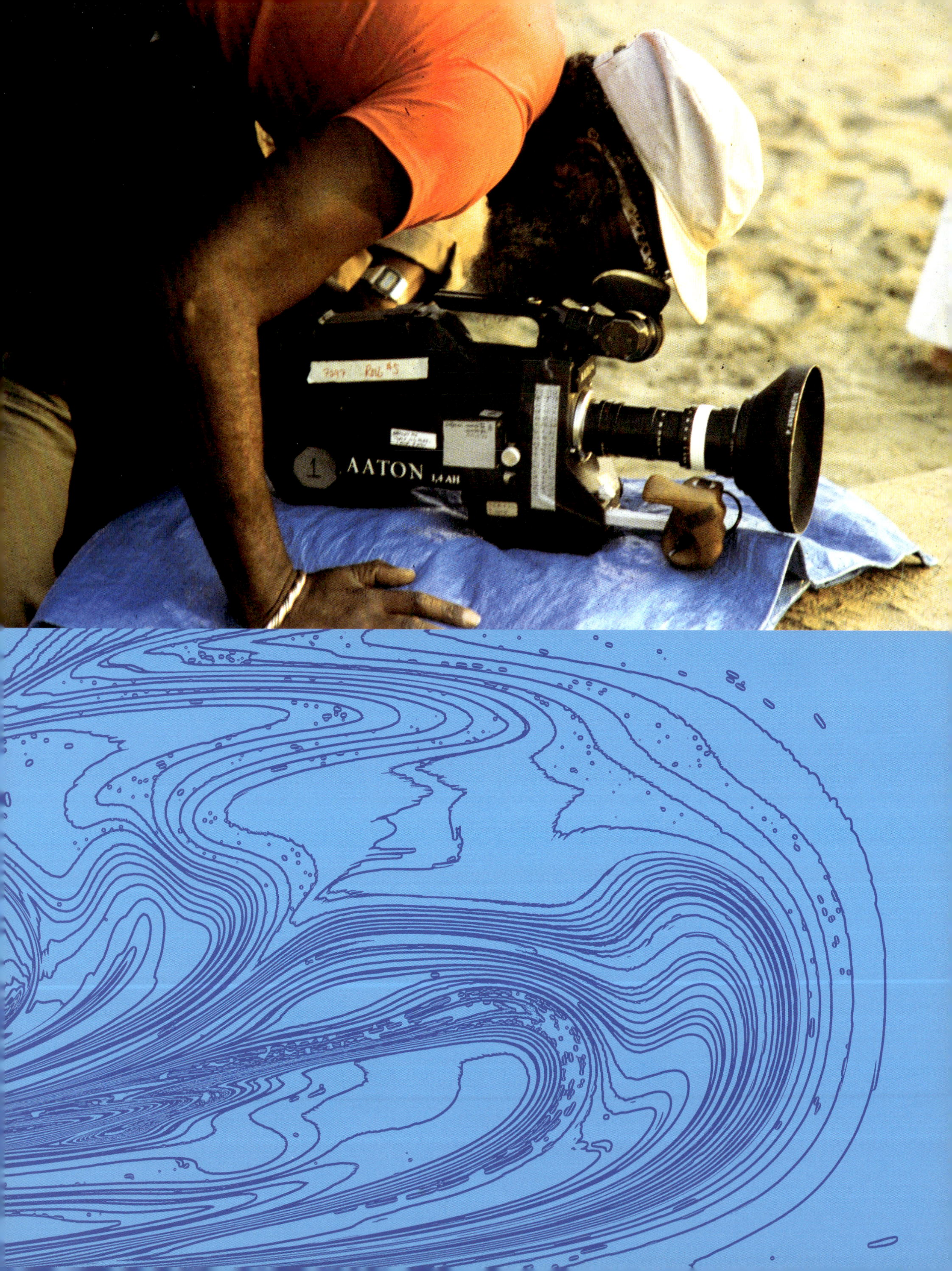

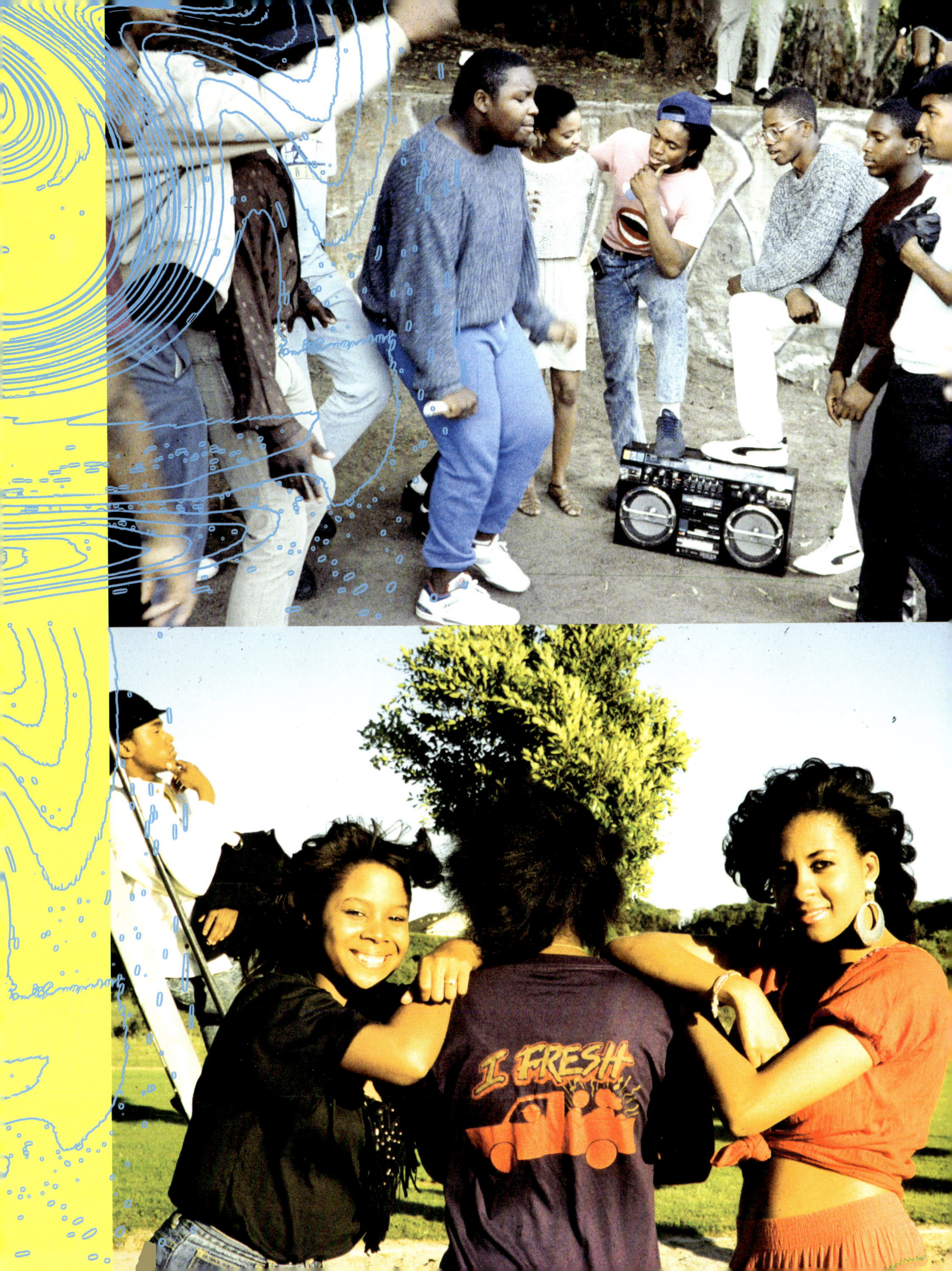
I FRESH

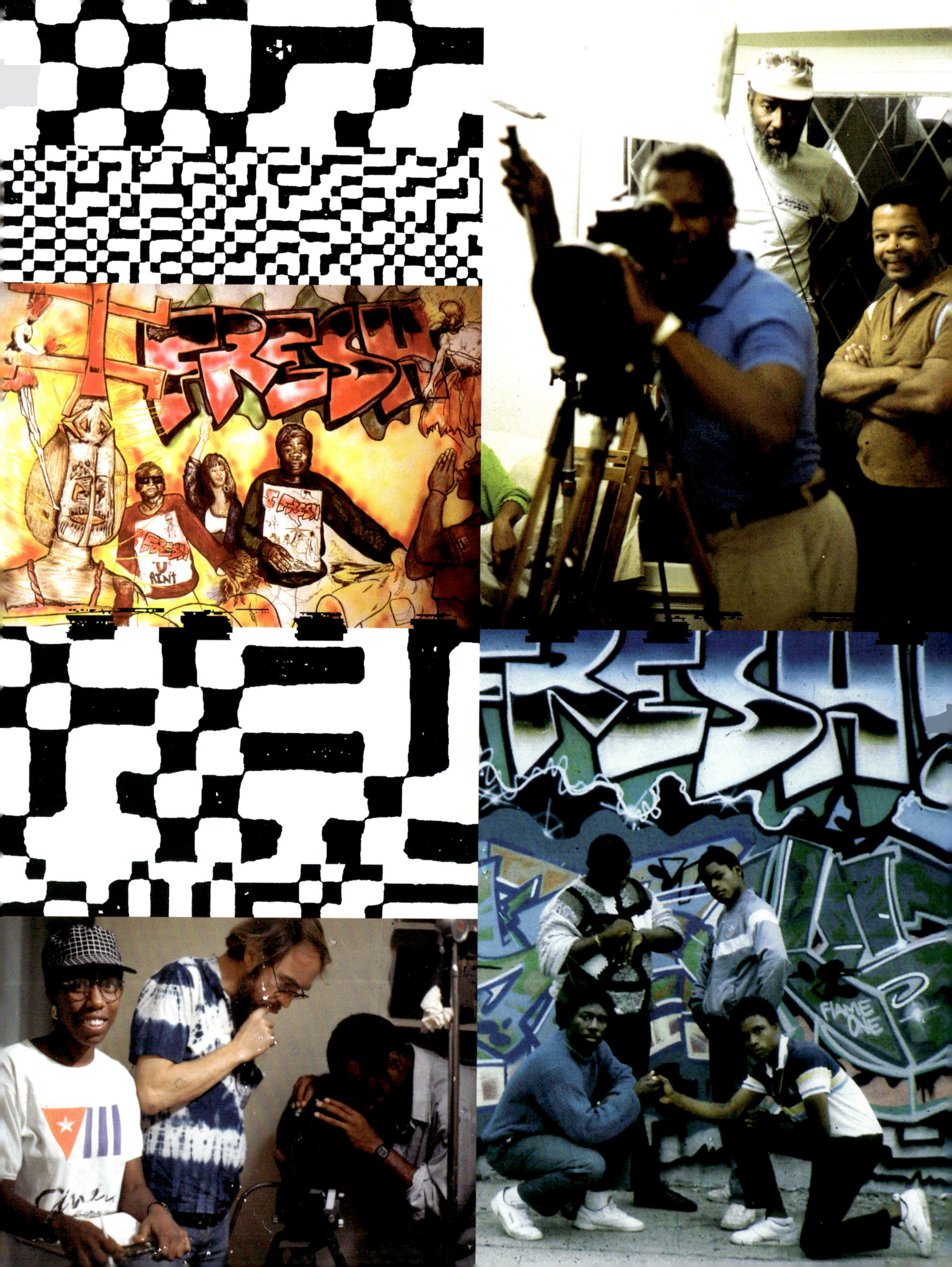

and creativity that could help lift their spirits as well as those of other people, and which might resonate with communities beyond their own. Ben insisted to the teens, "did not have to belong to just the elites, the news media, and corporate conglomerates." It was their birthright, too—their instrument to be played in ways specific to their daily realities and cultural inheritance, and to help liberate themselves and others.

Most importantly, VIDEO 3333 supplied the teens and young adults with a supportive community and a feeling of safety and empowerment. Every day the group, to varying degrees, was compelled to stand their ground against the inequities, injustice, and violence that surrounded them. When they turned on their televisions or listened to politicians and news media, their generation was blamed for society's problems. But when they came to VIDEO 3333 and listened to one another's poetry, beat-making, and DJing, and when they danced and partied, they experienced something else. News reporting from the streets. Condemnation of the system. Pleasure. Joy. Ascension.

For most of the teens, hip-hop wasn't a trend or a hobby to be indulged in after school. It was their community, their village. Their sustenance, their fuel. It was what got them through the day and what helped them imagine different possibilities for tomorrow. It was a life-saving outlet of expression   a time-traveling and space-shifting portal capable of quieting, amplifying, and constructively organizing the noise, turmoil, and trauma of their lives. Inside VIDEO 3333, they knew that their lives mattered and that each of them had important gifts to share with the world.

And that's why they loved rocking with the **I-Fresh Express**. This was the name Ben came up with for their community. Its origins lay in the title of a film, *I-Fresh*, that Ben was making about hip-hop. He had written it with his UCLA comrade, filmmaker Charles Burnett, and comedic writer Mel Preston, and had gotten his friend Roderick Kwaku Young to shoot the film. Its story was centered around a group of teens, one of whom was in his final months of high school and preparing for college. Navigating love and intergenerational tension with parents and elders, this crew of friends found purpose in their music, dance, and performance.

The VIDEO 3333 crew had a blast making the movie. Local funk and R&B band the Brothers Johnson even contributed the film's title track, "I-Fresh," a song they later released on their 1988 album *Kickin'*. Yet what earned the VIDEO 3333 teens the most cred in their different neighborhoods was their television show. Ben originally pitched the idea of a hip-hop dance-party show to several public access television stations. It would be akin to *American Bandstand* and *Soul Train*, but it would feature local teens performing original works. Consequently, during the late 1980s, and especially during Black History Month, Southern California television viewers could catch five episodes of *I-Fresh Express*. Filmed by a three-camera set-up, with a fourth camera that provided titles and roll-in, the one-hour program was composed of rap and dance performances, DJ sets,

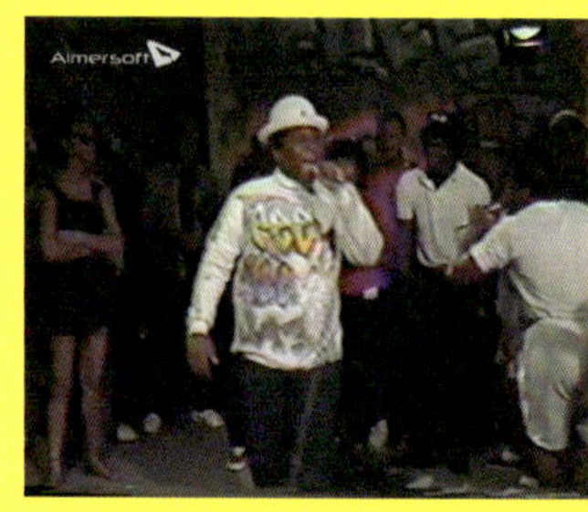
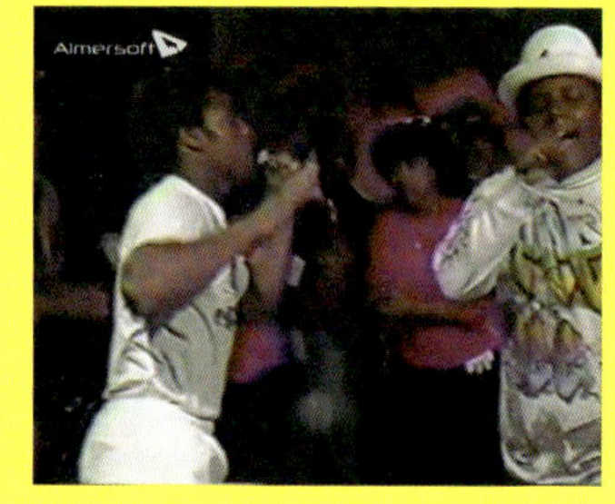
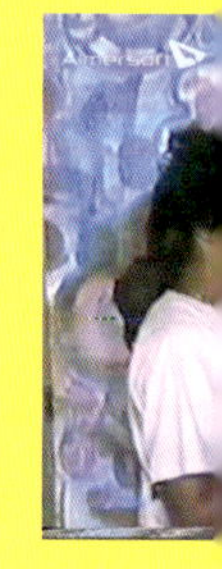
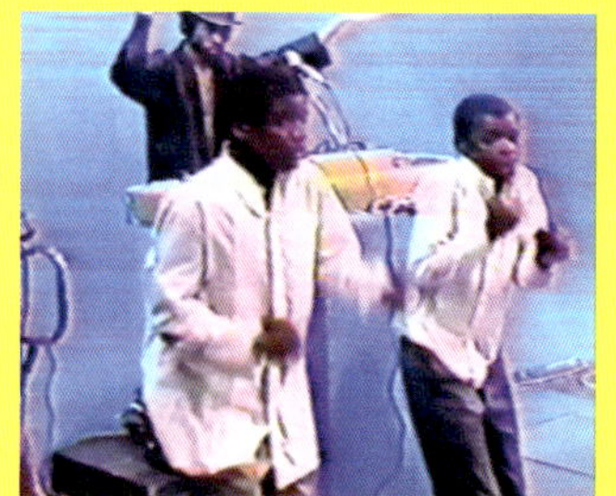
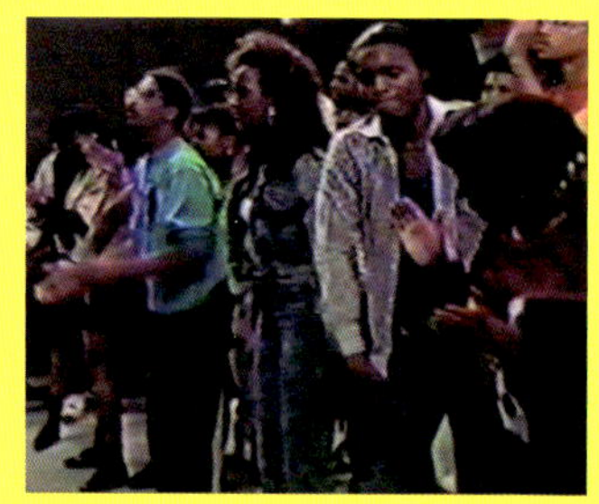
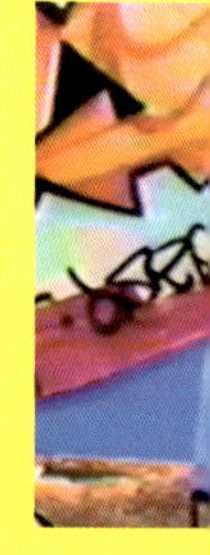
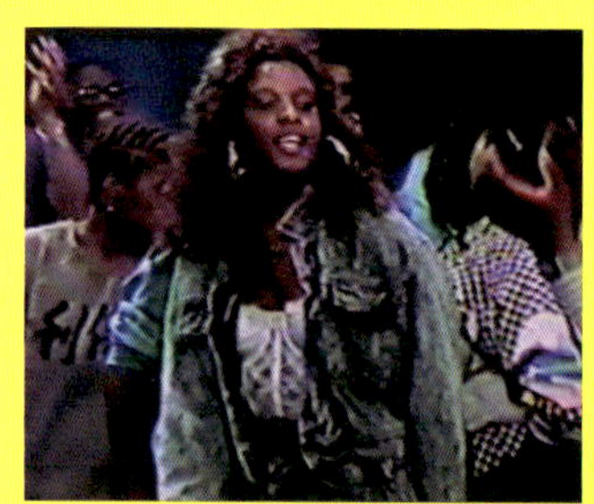
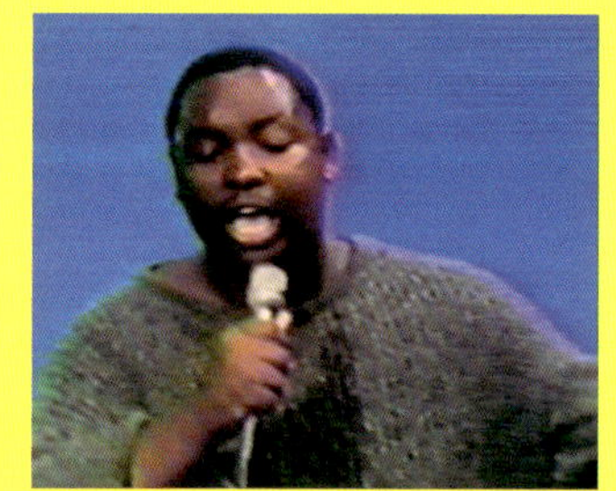
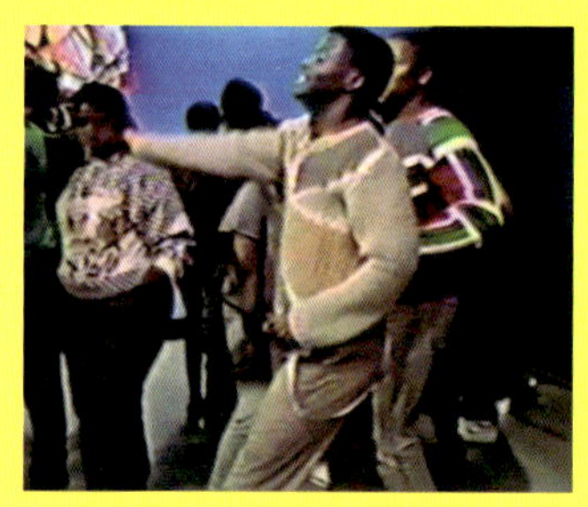
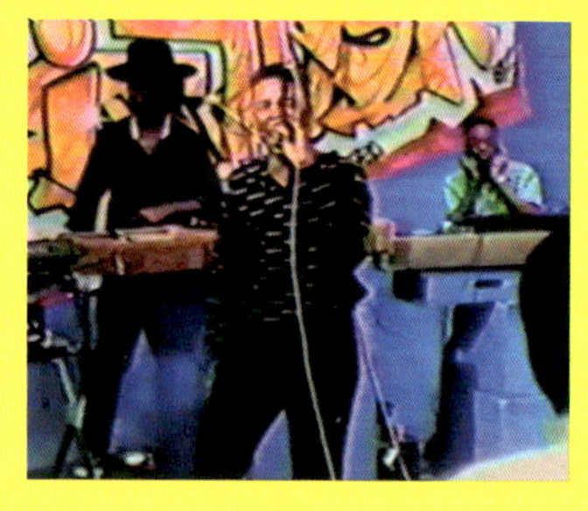
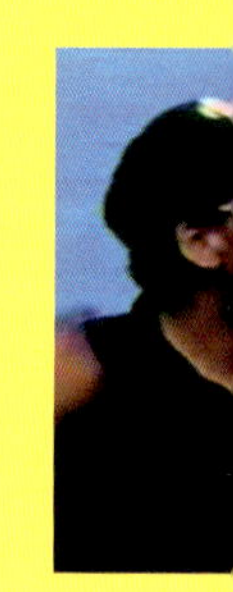
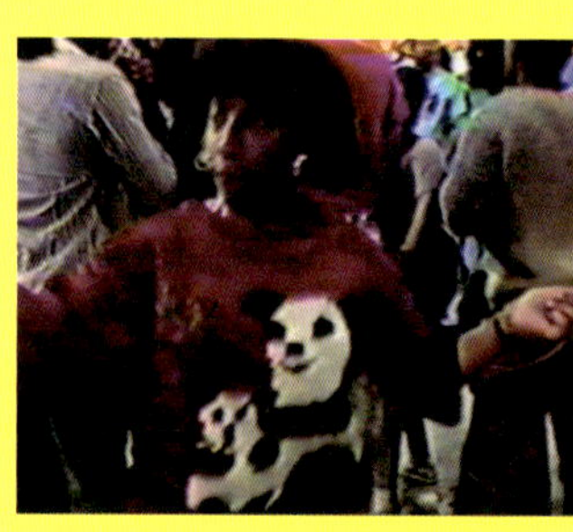
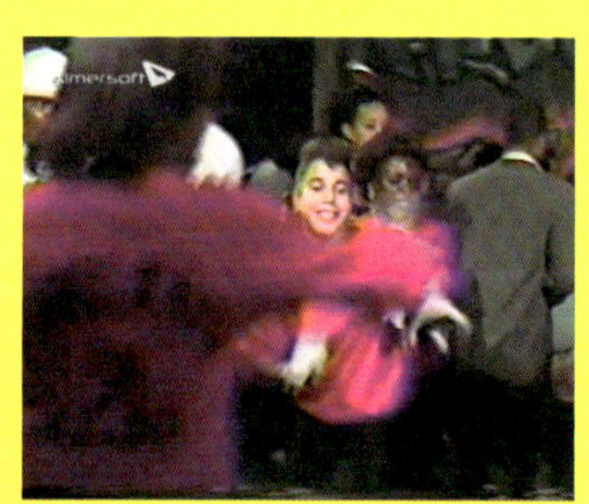
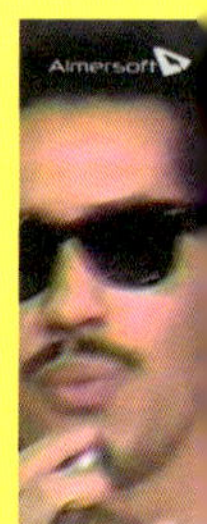

I-FRESH EXPRESS TELEVISION
SHOW, 1988/89

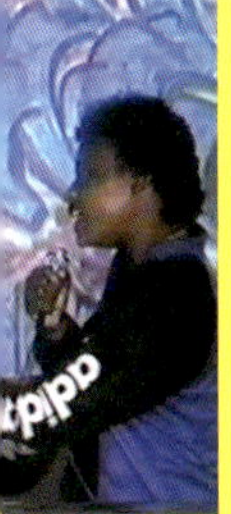
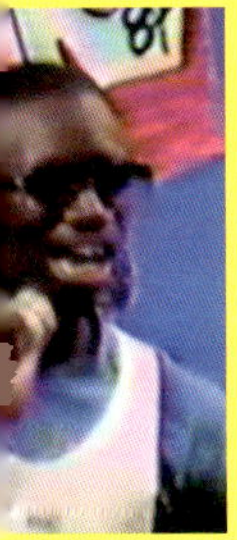
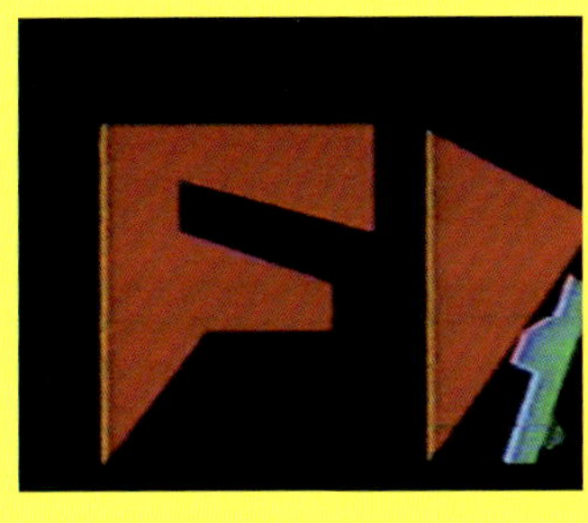
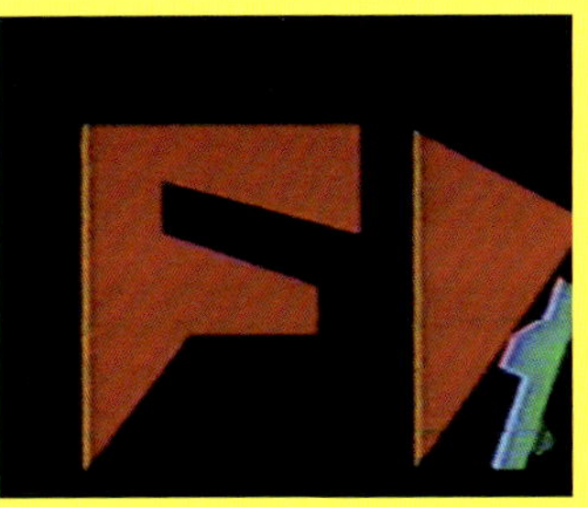
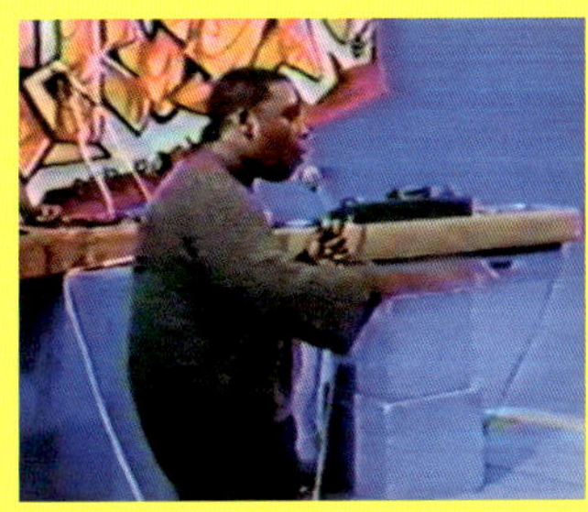
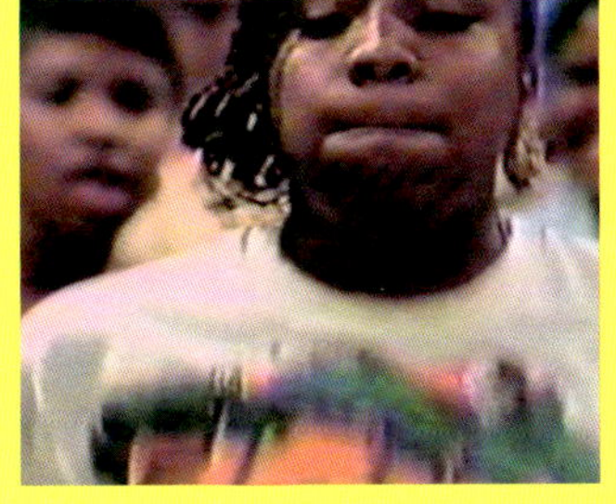
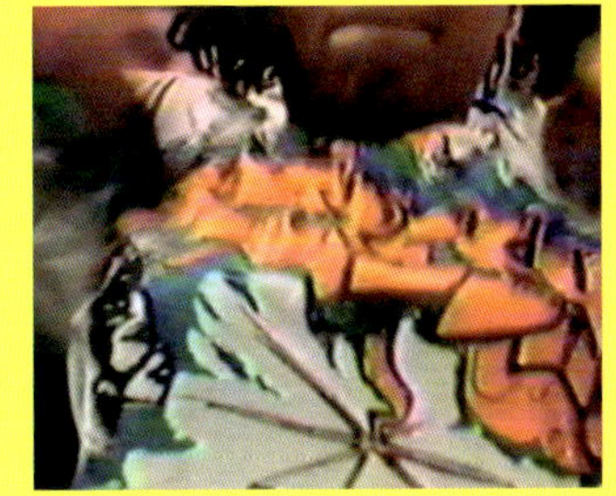
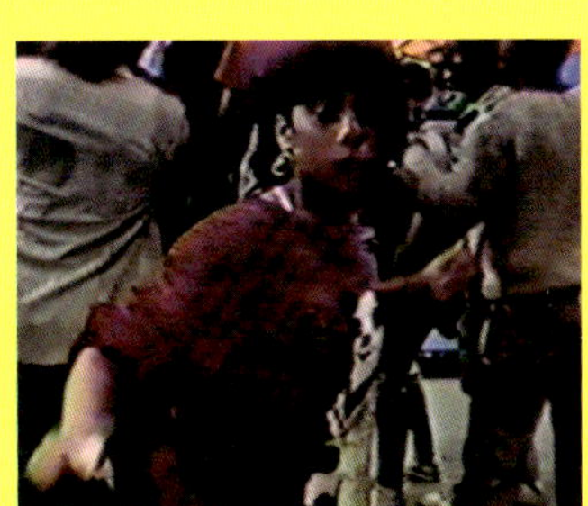
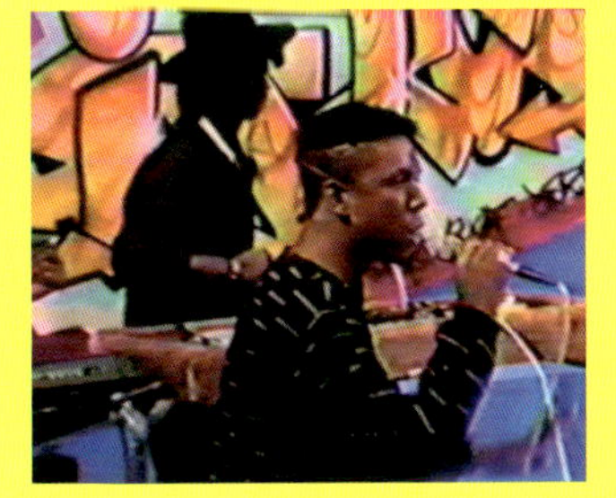
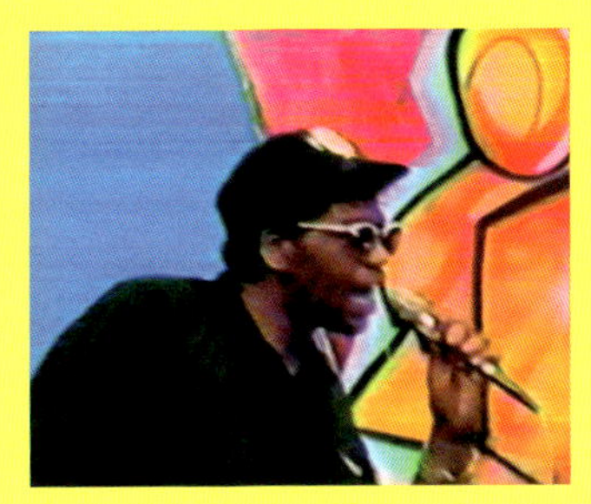
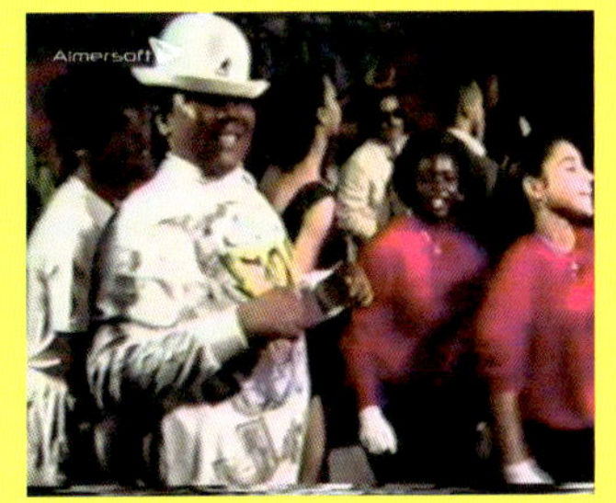
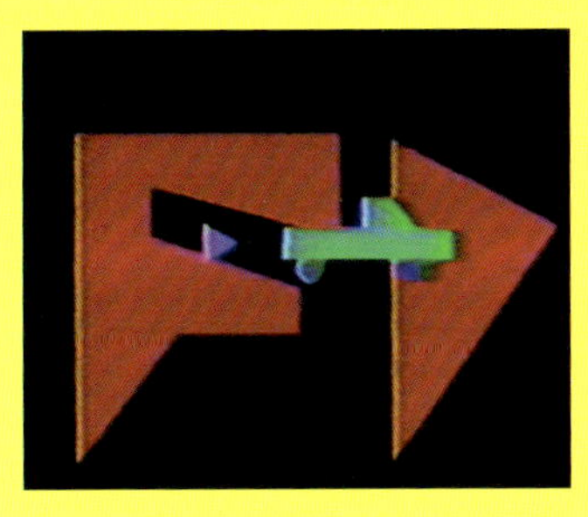
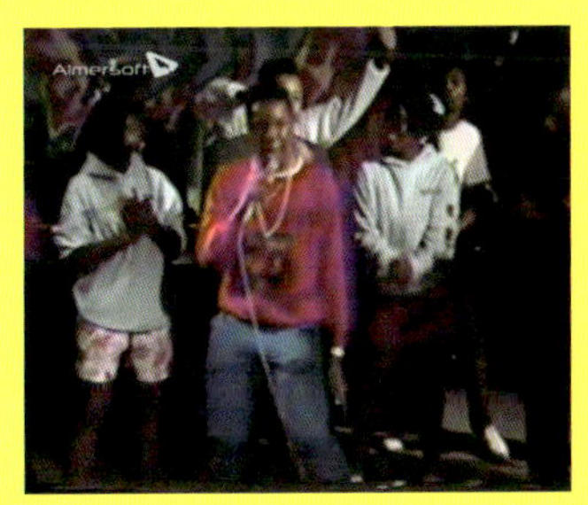

and periodic commentary about Black history and the arts. This was all back-dropped by a graffiti-adorned set and a smiling and dancing twenty-plus group of Black teenagers dressed in Adidas T-shirts and suede sneakers, faux Gucci shirts, matching Raider hats and black track jackets, Kangol bucket hats, self-made crew-themed dance outfits, and skinny gold chains.

Even after Don linked with tastemaker-personality-emcee Gerry "Skatemaster Tate" Hurtado and became a member of Hurtado's Concrete Crew, he continued to be a regular at VIDEO 3333's sessions. And when Island Records signed Skatemaster Tate and the Concrete Crew to a record deal, Don still used his connections to bring superstar rapper Kurtis Blow to hang out at VIDEO 3333.

Yet for all the joy, education, mentorship, and safety that VIDEO 3333 provided, what it couldn't suspend was the war going on outside its doors. Month after month, there was another Black or Brown person killed by the LAPD, or caught in the crossfire of a gang dispute, or murdered over little to nothing.

This truly hit home when Daniel Lawrence Bonner, aka CLEVER, a graffiti writer who was part of the D.E.F. (Doing Everything Fresh) crew and a periodic VIDEO 3333 attendee, was killed on a Wednesday night in April 1987. He was driving home in his Nissan pickup truck after spending the day with friends at an amusement park. As he waited at a stop signal at the corner of Crenshaw Boulevard and Imperial Highway, a bullet burst through the truck, striking the eighteen-year-old high school senior in the chest.

The I-Fresh members took his death very hard. Like so many of the killings, CLEVER's death made no sense. He was not involved or affiliated with any gangs and didn't have beef with anyone. He was a good student and had a great reputation as an artist. Why would somebody just kill him? For the I-Fresh Express and others, it was a reminder of their own extreme vulnerability, of the precarious and violent state of life for the city's Black and Brown communities.

The D.E.F. crew painted several murals to honor CLEVER. The first one was on a garage door at Van Ness Avenue and Imperial Highway, just blocks away from where CLEVER took his last breath. The second mural was painted nearby, on a stretch of Imperial Highway wall just east of Normandie Avenue. The last mural, however, was painted just down the block from VIDEO 3333, on a wall that ran along Crenshaw Boulevard just south of West 50th Street. The image depicted CLEVER as an angel with graffiti spray-paint cans in both hands. Alongside the phrase "DRIFTING ON A MEMORY" was a rap dedicated to him and all the other bronze, chestnut, and ebony-hued angels whose lives had been stolen and would be taken in the years to come:

Thinking of all the friends from past to present
Sometimes of good, sometimes unpleasant
Friends I've known who've become deceased
May memories live, and they Rest in Peace

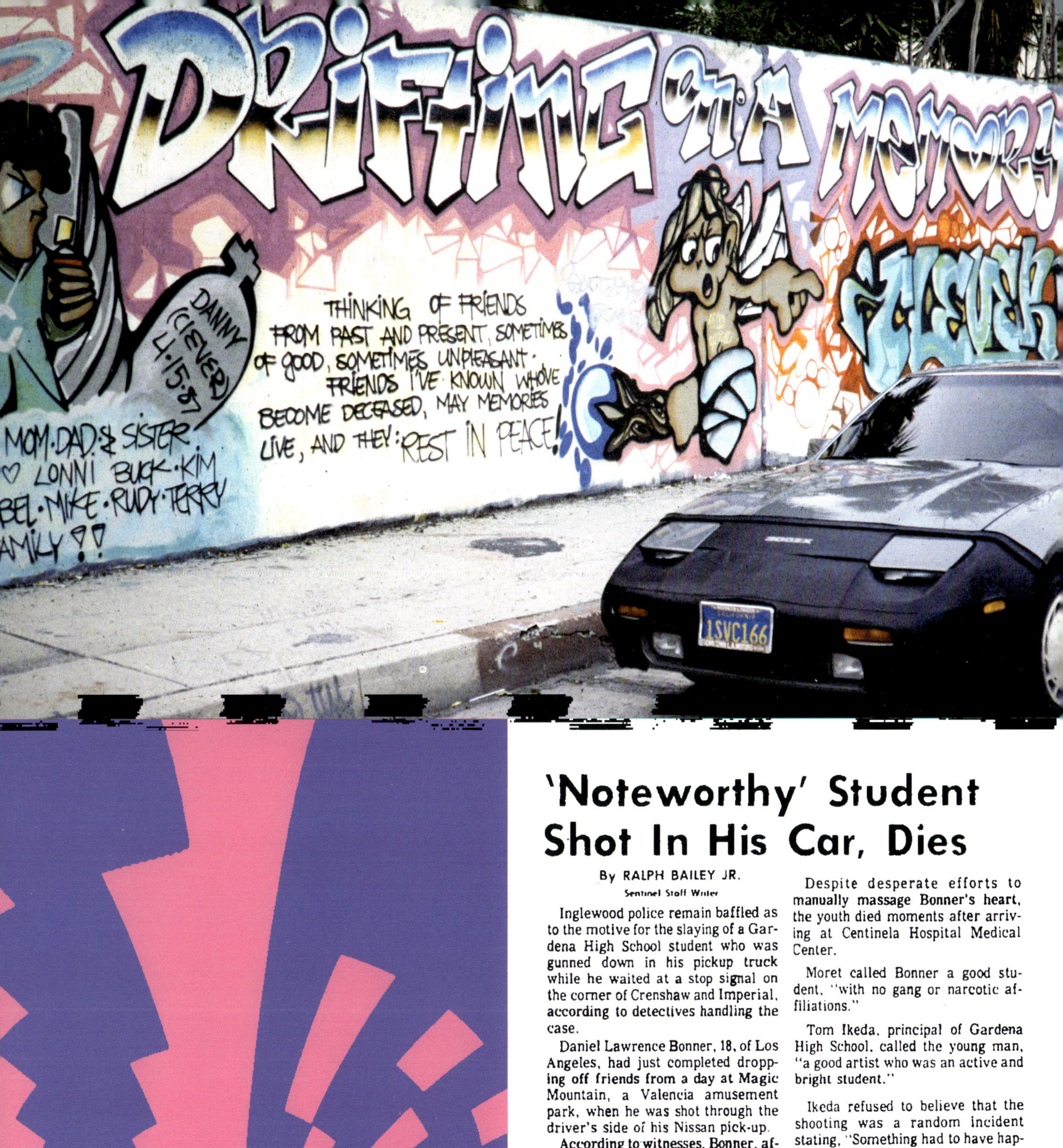

'Noteworthy' Student Shot In His Car, Dies

By RALPH BAILEY JR.
Sentinel Staff Writer

Inglewood police remain baffled as to the motive for the slaying of a Gardena High School student who was gunned down in his pickup truck while he waited at a stop signal on the corner of Crenshaw and Imperial, according to detectives handling the case.

Daniel Lawrence Bonner, 18, of Los Angeles, had just completed dropping off friends from a day at Magic Mountain, a Valencia amusement park, when he was shot through the driver's side of his Nissan pick-up.

According to witnesses, Bonner, after sustaining the bullet wound to the chest, staggered to an ambulance requesting assistance.

The teen-ager's last words were, "Can you help me? I've been shot." according to Police Sgt. Harold Moret.

Despite desperate efforts to manually massage Bonner's heart, the youth died moments after arriving at Centinela Hospital Medical Center.

Moret called Bonner a good student, "with no gang or narcotic affiliations."

Tom Ikeda, principal of Gardena High School, called the young man, "a good artist who was an active and bright student."

Ikeda refused to believe that the shooting was a random incident stating, "Something had to have happened, people just don't get shot."

Yet detectives assigned to the investigation concur with Moret and state that they can find no link between Bonner and any gang or gang activity

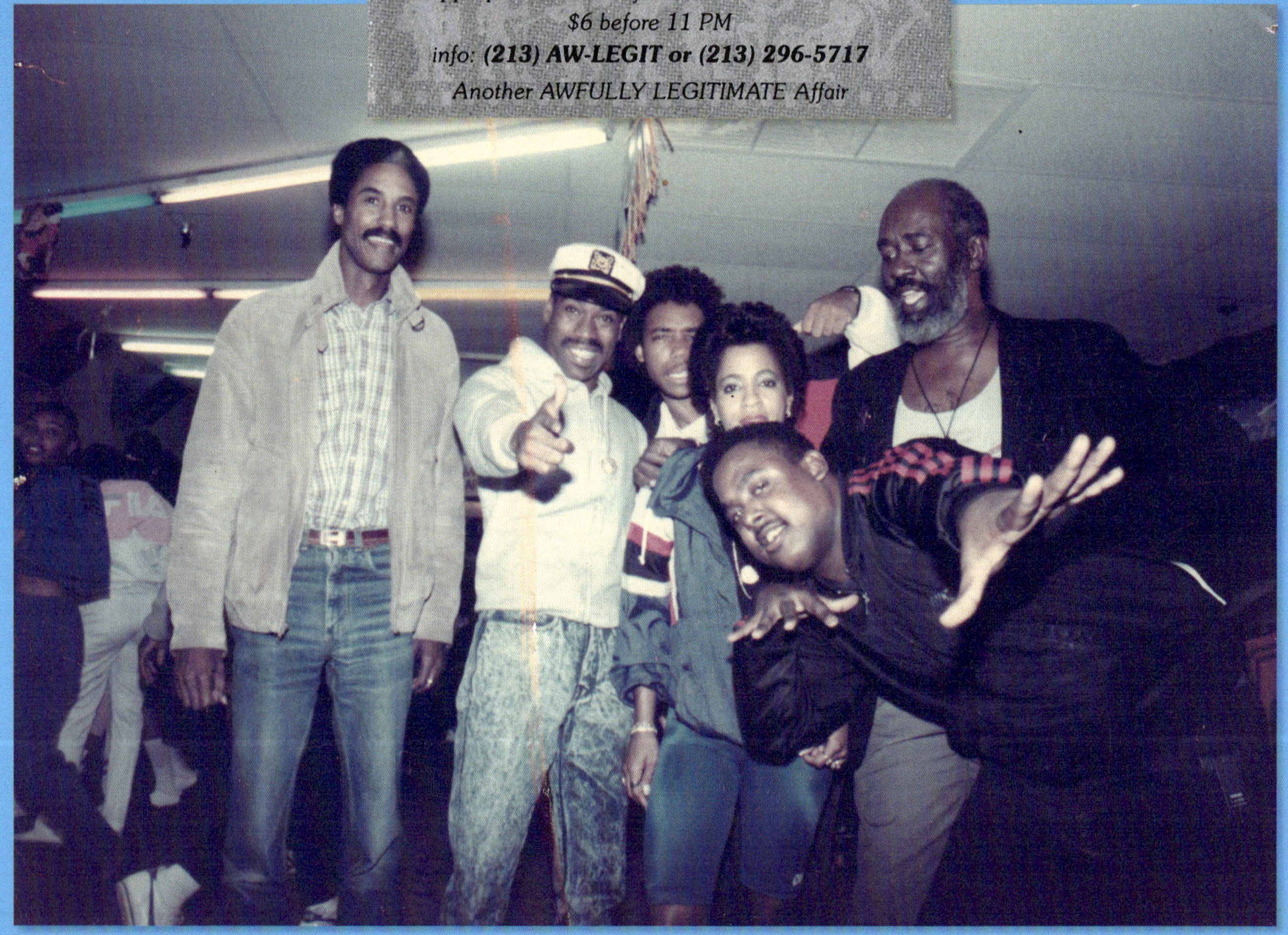

RAPPER KURTIS BLOW, SECOND FROM LEFT, AND THE I-FRESH CREW, WORLD ON WHEELS ROLLER RINK, 1988

COVER STORY

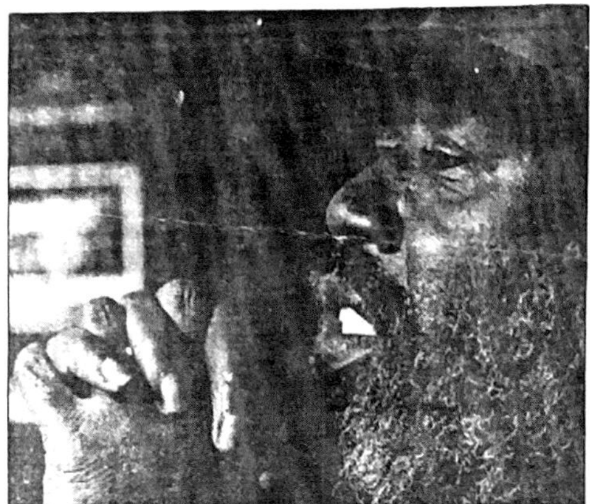

*"**T**oo much of the media concentrates on the gangbanging, the Uzis, the drug wars. But 95 percent of (black teens) are cool, and they live regular lives."*

— Ben Caldwell, right
Director of I-Fresh Express

I-Fresh approach to hip-hop culture

By LEWIS BEALE
Daily News Staff Writer

Take a university-trained artist and filmmaker. Give him a social conscience and a yearning to create positive images for black youngsters. Stick him in a Crenshaw storefront and have him become involved with the local hip-hop culture, that combination of rap music, graffiti art and clothing styles that has become the way of life for many youthful black Americans.

The result is the I-Fresh Express, a combination rehearsal hall, video studio, film training course and rapper's paradise, run by 43-year-old Los Angeles native Ben Caldwell.

"What I'm trying to do here," said the tall, gray-bearded Caldwell, "is something that's uptempo, to make a media image for these kids to show the way they really live. Too much of the media concentrates on the gangbanging, the Uzis, the drug wars. But 95 percent of them (black teens) are cool, and they live regular lives."

Caldwell said this while seated in his funkily eclectic storefront offices in the heart of the Crenshaw business district. The room is filled with a mixture of video equipment, graffiti-art banners, posters relating to Afro-American culture and history and pictures of friends and local teens who are appearing in I-Fresh's long-term, feature-length work-in-progress, "The Nubian."

Enough talk

A cheery man with a background in avant-garde filmmaking who has a master's degree in film and TV from UCLA, Caldwell has been working with local teens since he returned from a three-year stint teaching film and TV at Howard University in Washington, D.C.

"I came here to stop talking (about filmmaking) and do it," he said, "and then to go back to talking about it when I'm old."

I-Fresh has its origins in some work Caldwell did at the Watts Towers Arts Center in 1984, involving teen-agers and interact-

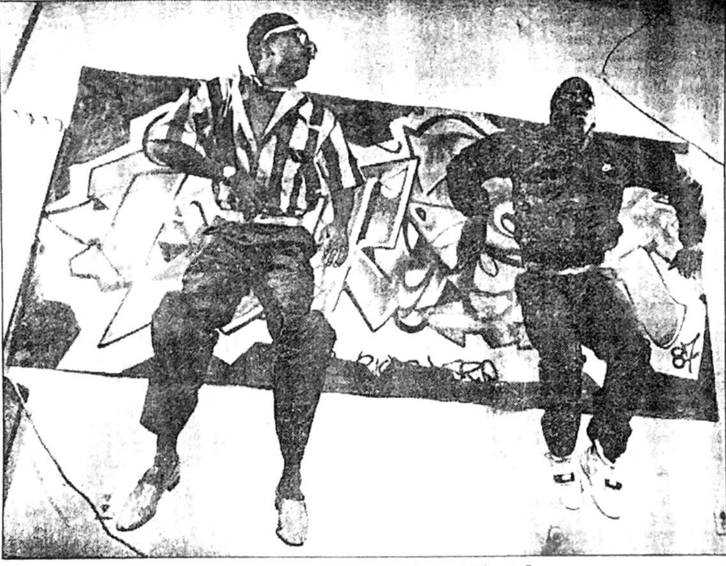

Hip-hoppers Robert Tivis, left, and Jay Utterbach are members of I-Fresh Express

ive videos. He became interested in the world of interactive video years earlier, when he studied at UCLA under the well-known independent filmmaker Shirley Clarke ("The Connection," "The Cool World"). He saw the process not only as a way to introduce teens to the medium but as a means to help them express themselves.

"Media is just like a language," Caldwell said. "The first thing people do is copy what's out there, what's on TV, instead of what they feel. But after a while, the kids decided they wanted to make a tape about hip-hop language, and one explaining their hand signals. They were happy I was interested in their culture, because I'm their parents' age; I'm an older man."

That same year, Caldwell moved into his present digs and began outreach work in the com-

munity. He first hooked up with filmmaker Charles Burnett ("Killer of Sheep"), then worked with a local actor who was holding workshops involving kids, film and video. Next, Brockman Productions, an art gallery around the corner from his office, put him in touch with more locals, and he made more connections at Washington High School. From there, "it was all word-of-mouth. I had kids coming in from Compton and Gardena and other areas. I've probably had 5,000 kids pass through here since 1984."

"When we first started out," said Don Thomas, a 25-year-old rapper who is a graduate of the I-Fresh program, "he stressed that we are the good kids, the 90 percent of the kids in the black community that are positive, that you don't hear about, and he wanted to make a statement. It's

been great, people have learned and become better people."

Caldwell's efforts became institutionalized in 1986, when he received a California Arts Council artist-in-community grant. He has received several grants since, and also works for Venice-based SPARC (Social and Public Arts Resource Center), as a community coordinator for an areawide mural project.

"He works very well with the kids," said Andrea Temkin, program administrator in the artist-in-residence program for the California Arts Council, "and the kids are dedicated to him. He's helping them to look at things that they look at all the time in a different way. By putting the creative process in the hands of these kids, it's very empowering for them. You give them a medium on film, and they take what they interact with and manipu-

late it, process it. They put their creative energies into something positive."

Despite his other projects, I-Fresh is Caldwell's most cherished baby. The name, he said, helps explain the philosophical concept. "'I' means everybody's the same," he said. "'Fresh' is a new way of dealing with it (teen-age black culture), and 'express' is just the expression. I want my work to have a real Afrocentric feel to it, and a proud one."

About 150 kids involved

Caldwell estimates that he now has a core group of about 150 kids who dance, rap, sing and attempt to learn video- and film-production techniques. Meetings are held at the I-Fresh offices on Thursdays and Saturdays, where the teens rehearse their various specialties.

I-Fresh has its own touring show of video artists, rappers, dancers and singers that appears at local cultural centers, nursing homes and places like World on Wheels, a midtown L.A. roller rink that has a weekly rap night. The I-Fresh crew also appeared recently at the Bayview Opera House in San Francisco, and I-Fresh produces a program for public-access cable stations in Compton and Long Beach.

"Ben gave us all the opportunity to merge video with music," Don Thomas said, "to use it as a tool. It was a good tool and helped us develop our skills. He kind of goes for the left-field kind of thing, how he mixes the video and rap. He'll put in images that kind of play with your mind. It's kind of like performance art."

Although I-Fresh attempts to channel teen-agers' energies into positive and creative work, Caldwell admits that the struggle hasn't always been an easy one. Some kids, weaned on confrontation and fighting, have created trouble, mostly of the verbal kind. And Caldwell also admits that the process of defining where the group is headed is ongoing.

See I-FRESH / Pg. 5

cha· os the· o· ry
/ kā äs THirē /
noun
1.   an interdisciplinary theory and branch of mathematics that
deals with complex and dynamical systems whose behavior is highly
sensitive to slight changes in conditions, so that small alterations can
give rise to strikingly great consequences.
2.   a scientific theory that states that within the apparent
randomness of chaotic complex systems, there are underlying patterns,
interconnectedness, constant feedback loops, and repetition.

KAOS

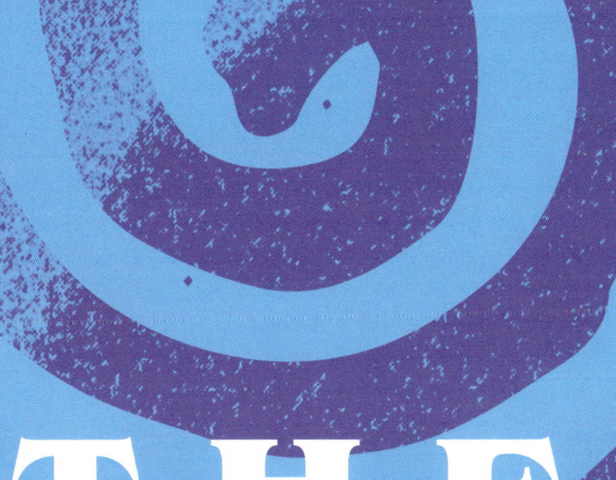

The Blues Aesthetic is the struggle culturally, psychically, and spiritually to survive.
It manifests in the way we walk and talk, the way I comb my hair or don't comb my hair.
It is hard. The blues is self-referential, an attempt for the consolidation of flavors . . .
Only recently has this aesthetic reached mainstream audiences.
Before it worked only in a completely Black cosmos and that was its appeal to the Black
population. This entire Black cosmos could be experienced uncensored.

—Roger Guenveur Smith

THEORY

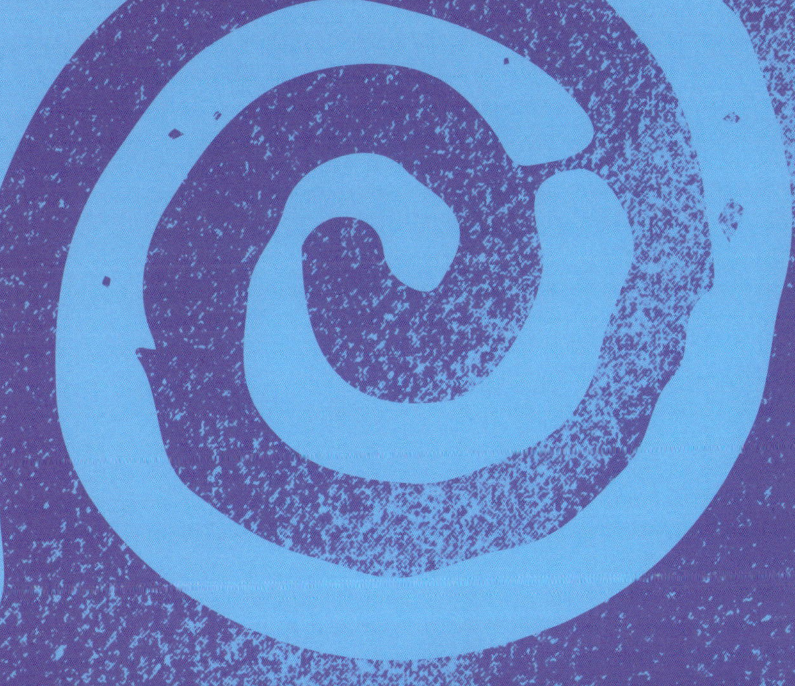

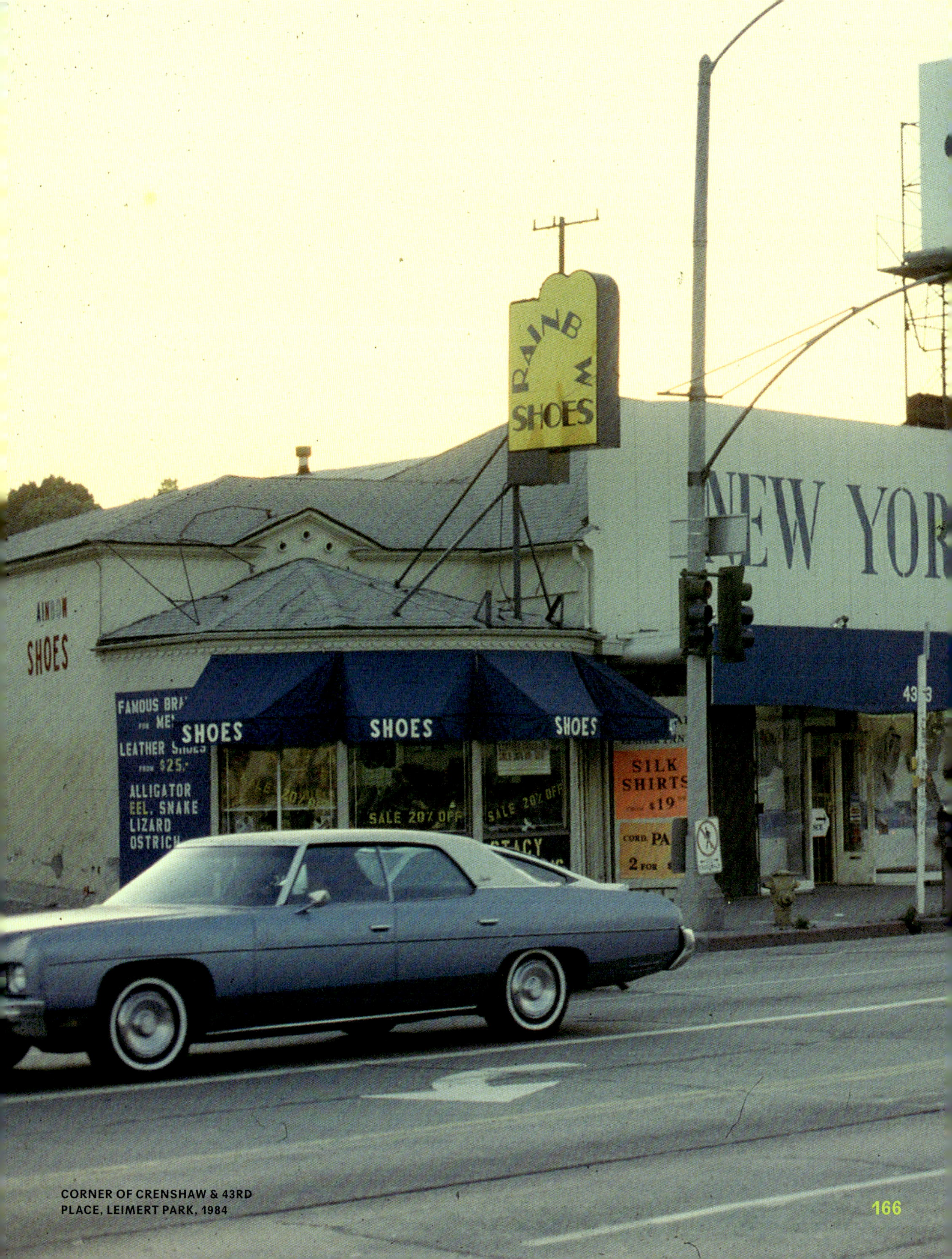

CORNER OF CRENSHAW & 43RD
PLACE, LEIMERT PARK, 1984

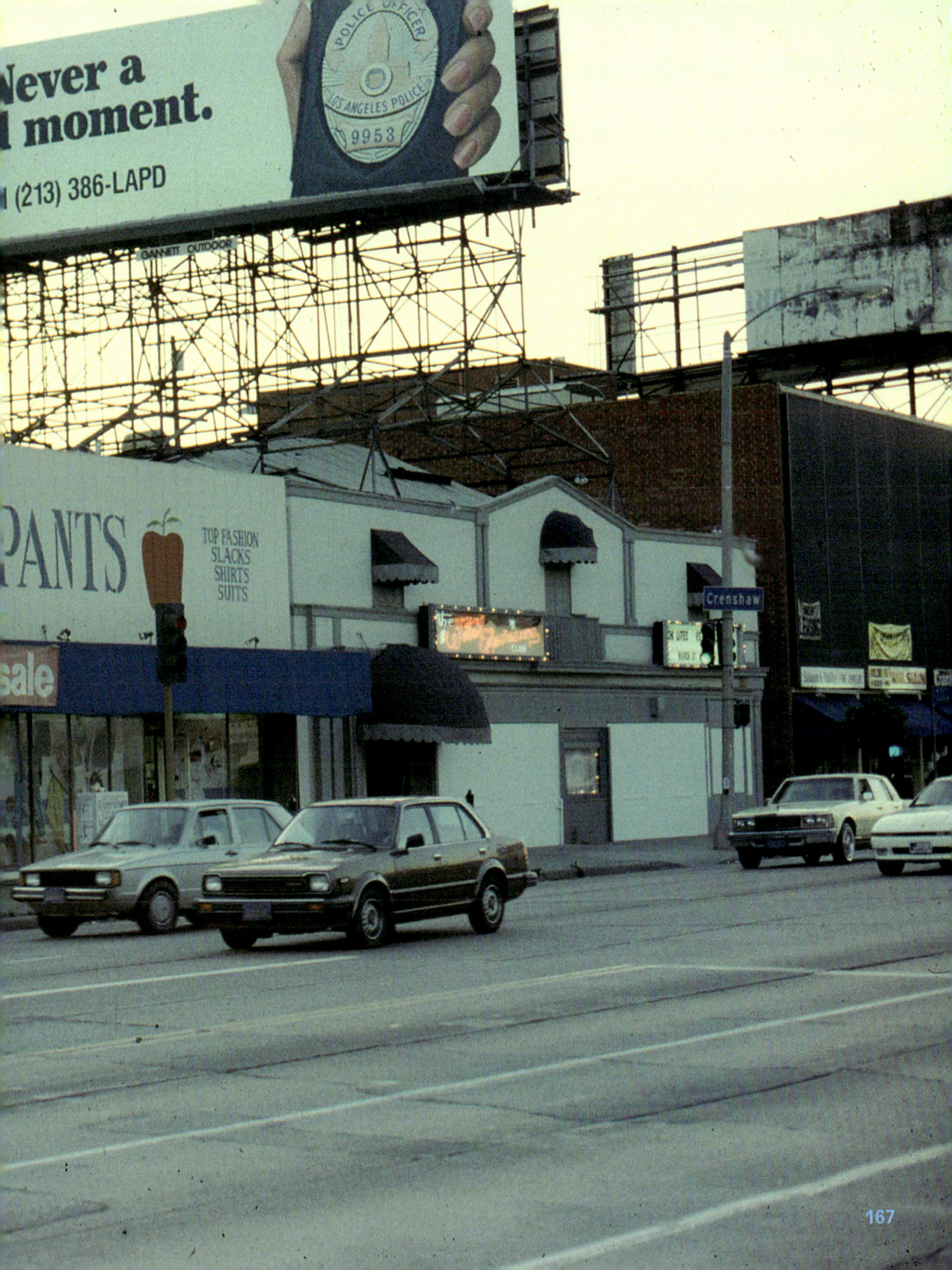

Never a
moment.
(213) 386-LAPD
POLICE OFFICER
LOS ANGELES POLICE
9953
GANNETT OUTDOOR
PANTS
TOP FASHION
SLACKS
SHIRTS
SUITS
sale
Crenshaw

When I fall asleep
In my dreams
It seems real
I always thought THAT was the real world too

A lot of people have been to that other side
It's a realm that we call synchronicity
Which means there's no such thing as an accident,
or a mishap.

—Ben Caldwell
"Input 7.STE-072"

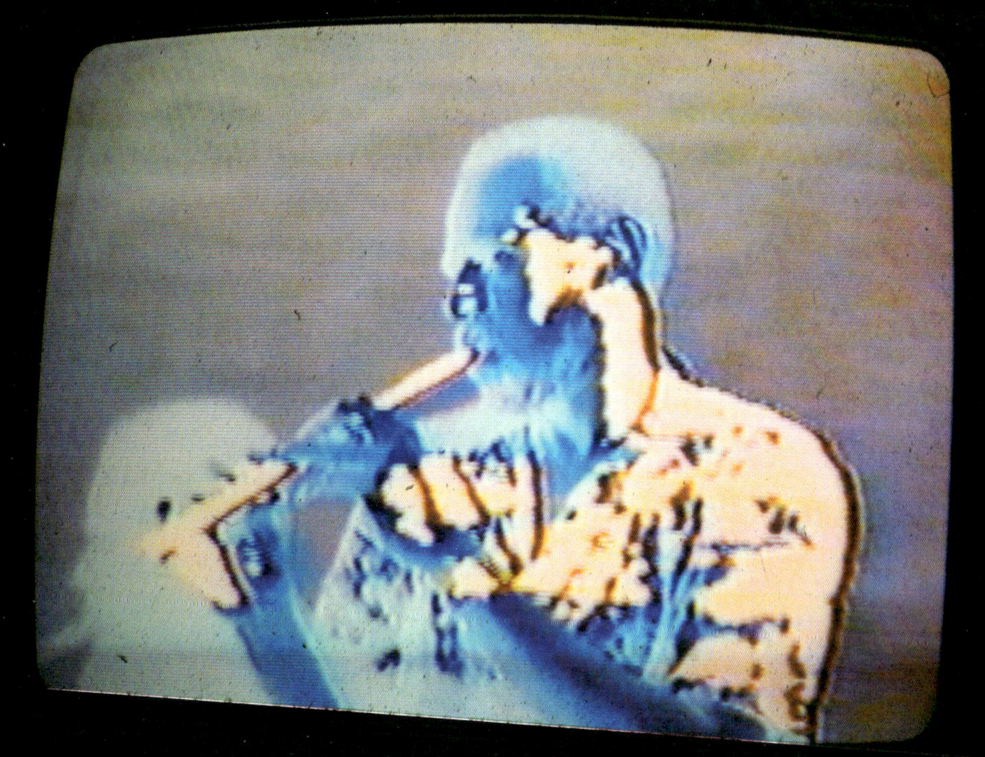

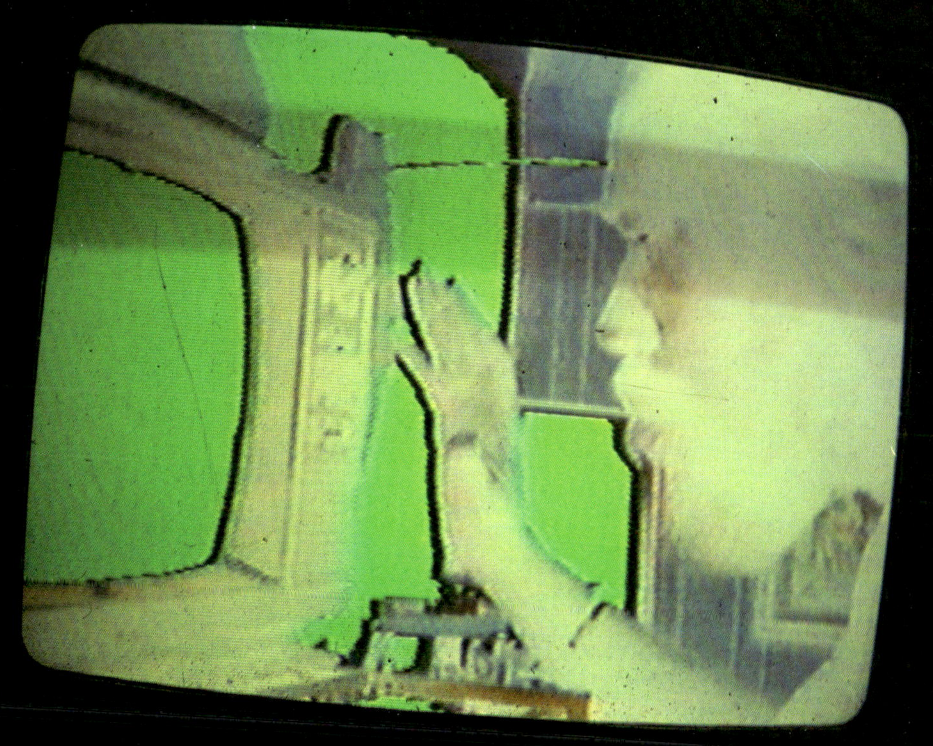

STILLS FROM *SPACES LOOKING OUT
LOOKING IN*, 1984 AND *LOVING LIGHTS*, 1984

Artistry in Beauty
Leimert Park
BEAUTY COLLEGE
SPRING CURLS 19.
Roger Guenveur Smith is
FREDERICK
DOUGLASS NOW
Low Cost Preview
Wed. Nov. 28 8pm
Video Design Ben R Caldwell &
Wesley M Groves Jr
Sound Design
Vinsula Kara
Bob L. Johnson
Associate Producer
INNER CITY CULTURAL CENTER
1308 S. New Hampshire Ave.
Valet Parking Available
OPENS NOV. 29
1 WEEK ONLY!
Thu.-Sun. 8pm
Sun. Mat. 2pm
Reservations
213 413-1103

HOLLYWATTS

The creator has a master plan. Or so thought singer-performer-poet Mark Broyard on a windy Leimert Park night.

It was the summer of 1985. Eddie Murphy's *Beverly Hills Cop* was a box office hit. Prince's "Raspberry Beret" topped the Billboard charts. And the Los Angeles Lakers were kings again, having bounced back from heartbreaking defeat during the previous year to win their ninth NBA championship and cement their position as America's most entertaining sports franchise.

Earlier that evening, Mark embarked on his customary walk. Turning off Degnan Boulevard, he saw a small crowd forming outside the building next to the old Leimert Theater. Mark was curious. So, he walked toward the group to see what the fuss was about.

At the building's entrance, he was greeted by a bright-eyed chocolate girl with twists in her hair. She politely requested a donation. He gave her a few dollars and then entered.

Inside, a lean, long-armed, six-foot-eight dreadlocked fella gently pounded a djembe. There were televisions atop VCR players. And on the wall, projected images illuminated the space. Some of the images were from anthropology books and magazines such as *Life, Time, National Geographic*. But others were familiar...*too familiar*. Pictures of the Village from Mark's childhood. Photographs of Transfiguration, the church where Mark and his siblings attended mass and elementary school, and of school-aged children—people who Mark grew up with. And the wildest image of all: a photograph of Kippy, Mark's older brother, as a child posing with his buddies Roland, Tony, and Roger.

This wasn't even the kicker. At the center of the room was a mustached, fair-skinned man who sweated and rhythmically voiced prose. At one point the man glared at the crowd, his brown eyes penetrating the audience's flesh. He rapped directly to them, encouraging them to feel their power as a community. Mark knew this cat. Knew him well.

Forty years earlier, Grace Broyard, Mark's aunt, met Helen Guenveur, this man's mother, at Xavier University. Grace invited Helen over for dinner at the Broyard family's home on Tonti Street in New Orleans's Seventh Ward. Decades later, they described this first meal together as a "family reunion" of sorts. It was an allusion to the instant connection the women made, as well as to the bond that united their families for subsequent decades. Several things tied them: love of food and community, Catholic faith, and the experience of being Black Americans of African, French, and Indigenous descent. And while the Broyards were Louisiana Creoles of color, the Guenveurs were of Haitian descent and hailed from Charleston, South Carolina.

(OPPOSITE, TOP) LEIMERT PARK BEAUTY COLLEGE ON 43RD PLACE, 1984 (OPPOSITE, BOTTOM) *FREDERICK DOUGLASS NOW* FLYER, CIRCA LATE 1980S

In 1960, the Broyards and Guenveurs reconnected after members of both families moved to Los Angeles. There was Grace and her husband Dr. Arthur Johnson; Grace's brother, Emile, a building contractor with his educator wife Beverly Barth Broyard; and Helen and her husband, Sherman Smith, an attorney and future judge. All three families purchased houses in Leimert Park. Their homes were located between 39th Street and MLK Boulevard, within a six-block radius that spread from the Broyards' on Hubert Avenue to the Guenveur Smiths' around the corner on Olmstead Avenue to the Johnsons' home on Sutro Avenue. Just down Santa Barbara Avenue off Roxton Avenue, Helen's dental practice shared space with Arthur's medical office.

Together, their families and others formed a village. But it was Roger (Helen and Sherman's middle child), and Emile the third (Emile and Beverly's eldest child), whom everyone called "Kippy," that forged the tightest bond. Throughout the 1960s and 1970s, Roger and Kippy were always together—playing pick-up basketball and football, achieving merit badges as Cub Scouts, growing Afros, wearing leisure suits and platform shoes, attending parties, chasing after girls. And always somewhere nearby was Kippy's younger brother, Mark.

FAST—FORWARD TO 1985—Mark standing inside VIDEO 3333, watching his brother's homeboy wax poetic, images of their childhood canvassed by light over the walls. Thirty years' worth of memories flashing before Mark's eyes! When the show ended, Mark couldn't find Roger to tell him how incredible his performance was. So, he did the next best thing. He left a note at the door.

This began the third reunion of the Broyard and Guenveur clans. By the end of 1985, Mark was contributing to Roger's performances at VIDEO 3333.

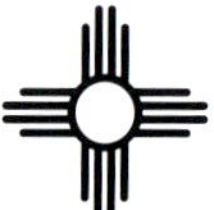

Over the course of the 1980s and early 1990s, the **Hollywatts Posse** was at the forefront of Los Angeles's experimental performing arts scene. This band of artists, which included Mark, Roger, Ben, and others, achieved recognition and acclaim for its multimedia theatrical performances. Their art pushed the bounds of multidisciplinary dramatic arts and was radically Black in tone and subject. But more than that, their performances fused various genres of art, media, music, and performance, and moreover connected different segments of the city: visual artists with actors with performance artists with activists with rappers and so on. It was part of a citywide ecosphere where performance art enabled people to transgress the city's cultural divisions and borders of geography, class, and art.

At the point of Mark's unplanned drop-in, VIDEO 3333 was just hitting its stride. It had been a wild first year of operations for Ben and eleven-year-old Dara.

During the afternoon hours, the father-daughter duo used their new studio-home to launch the I-Fresh workshops, whereas in the evenings and on the weekends, they hosted film screenings and art-related events and parties. Within a short period, VIDEO 3333 was becoming ground zero for linking different pockets of the city. But it was Ben's evolving relationship with actor Roger Guenveur Smith that helped pave the creative road Ben would tread over the next decade.

They may never have met if it hadn't been for Ben's stint at Howard University. The vibrant enthusiasm and diversity of Howard's collegiate life, alongside Ben's visual explorations of blues and go-go music, widened his perspective and deepened his hunger to be more innovative. He left Chocolate City desiring to find more ways to manifest the organic vernacular Black expression he had witnessed in D.C. within his film and video work. He was especially fascinated with the portability and musicality of the handheld video camera, what he perceived as its capacity for more than just live documentation and recording. Ben yearned to transform it into a performance instrument, capable of call-and-response and the syncopated rhythms of Black traditions.

Ben's D.C. comrade, actor-writer Bob Wisdom, helped connect the dots. Ben mentioned to Bob his desire to collaborate with a poet or rapper to develop a vaudeville show that combined theatrical performance, pre-recorded video, and live video work. Weeks later, during his visit to Los Angeles, Bob introduced Ben to Roger. Over drinks and chatter (with a group that included Bob, writer Greg Tate, and artist-filmmaker Arthur Jafa), the two men gelled quickly.

On most days, Roger was hustling in his Ford Pinto from one job to the next: teaching English at Hollywood High School; auditioning for film and television gigs; performing Chekhov, Shakespeare, and Berkhoff on the stage; and hanging at nightclubs, versing himself in the young and emerging hip-hop scene. His life was a daily shuffle between Hollywood and South Central, the entertainment industry and the dramatic arts, the superficial and the concrete. This required a vast capacity for constant culture-and-code-switching—psychological and geographical boundary-crossings that would drive many people berserk.

But not Roger. It provided him with a creative opening. The name and persona came to him in a flash: **HOLLYWATTS**.

Hollywatts was a rap performance artist who explored the complexities of identity, racism, Blackness, popular culture, global injustice, and other topics. His satirical rhymes, introspective storytelling, and use of periodic Caribbean patois and cadence took listeners on a journey across the Black diaspora, both in terms of his sound and his message. According to Hollywatts, there was an urgent connection to be made between the conditions and struggles on Crenshaw and Rosecrans Boulevards to those waged in Tivoli Gardens's and Soweto's shantytowns, between the roots reggae of Augustus Pablo and the disco rap of Sugar Hill Gang and the jùjú Nigerian pop of King Sunny Adé.

United States of Emergency (1984), Roger and Ben's first collaboration, provided Roger with an opportunity to workshop the character alongside Ben's

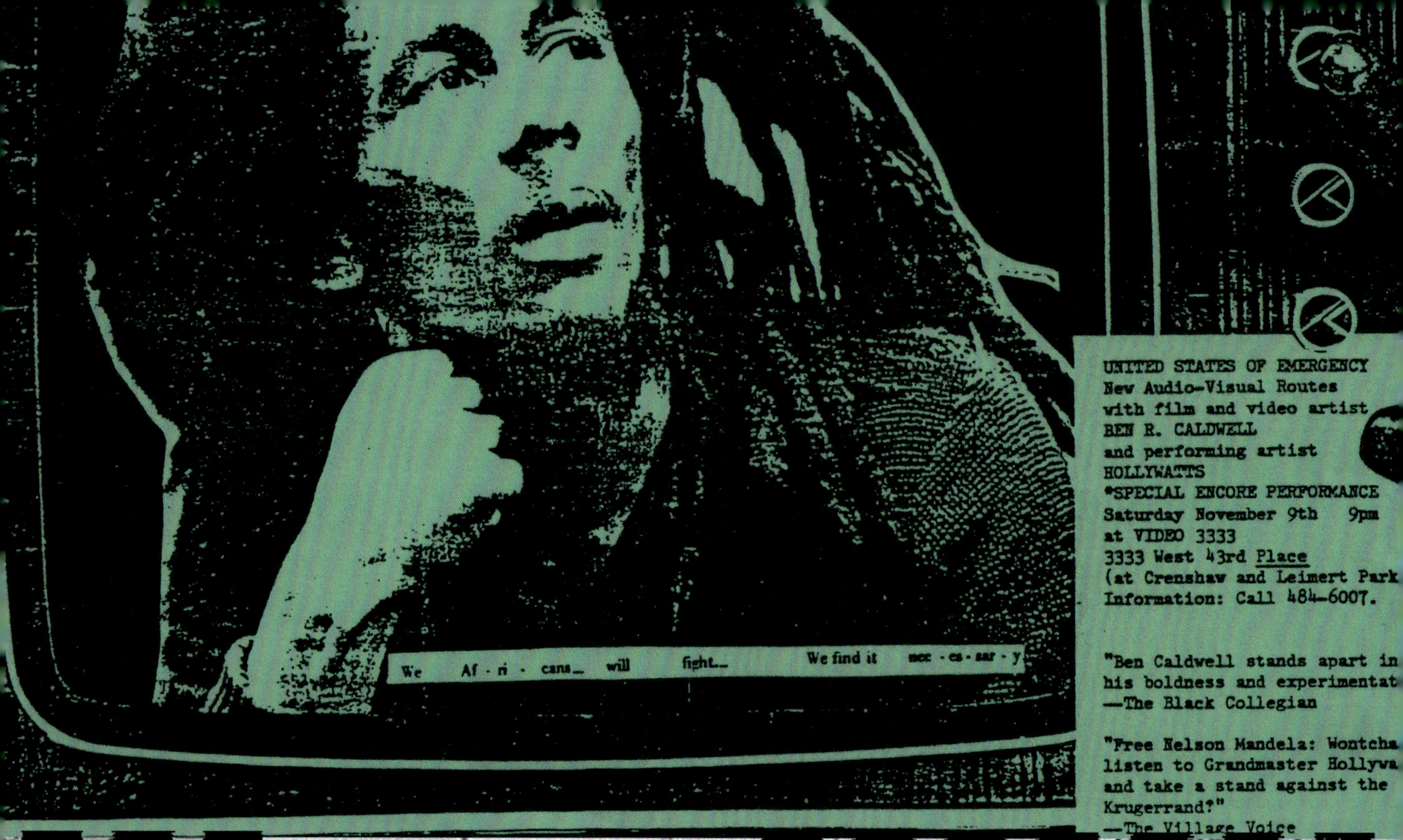

We Af · ri · cans_ will   fight_   We find it nec · es · sar · y

UNITED STATES OF EMERGENCY
New Audio-Visual Routes
with film and video artist
BEN R. CALDWELL
and performing artist
HOLLYWATTS
*SPECIAL ENCORE PERFORMANCE
Saturday November 9th   9pm
at VIDEO 3333
3333 West 43rd Place
(at Crenshaw and Leimert Park
Information: Call 484-6007.

"Ben Caldwell stands apart in
his boldness and experimentat
—The Black Collegian

"Free Nelson Mandela: Wontcha
listen to Grandmaster Hollywa
and take a stand against the
Krugerrand?"
—The Village Voice

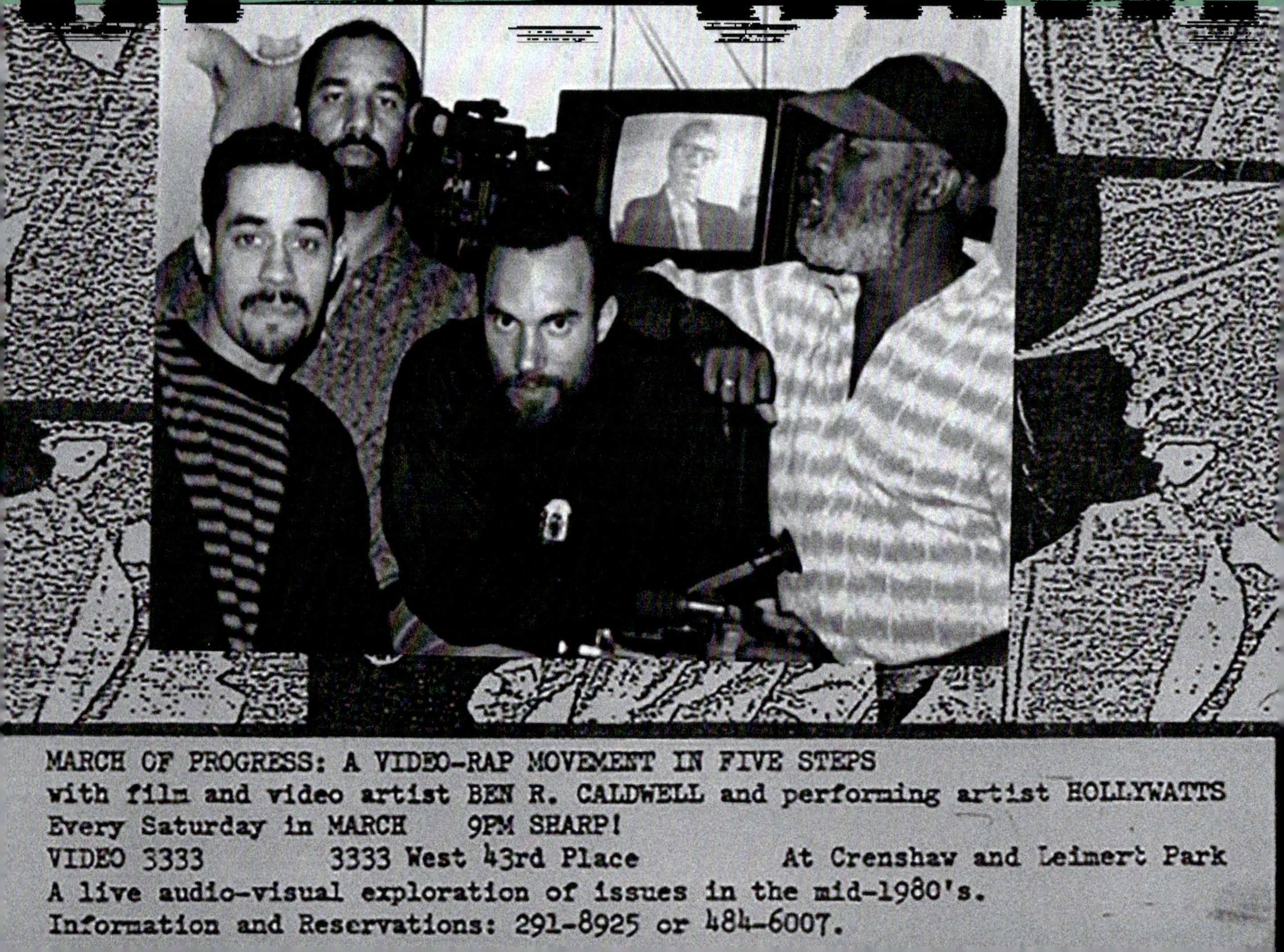

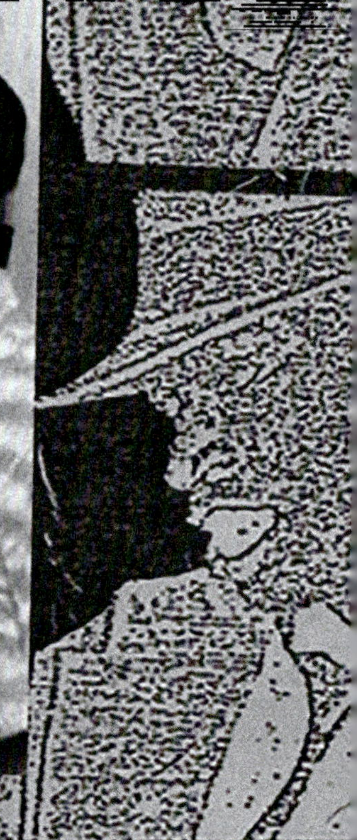

MARCH OF PROGRESS: A VIDEO-RAP MOVEMENT IN FIVE STEPS
with film and video artist BEN R. CALDWELL and performing artist HOLLYWATTS
Every Saturday in MARCH   9PM SHARP!
VIDEO 3333   3333 West 43rd Place   At Crenshaw and Leimert Park
A live audio-visual exploration of issues in the mid-1980's.
Information and Reservations: 291-8925 or 484-6007.

video collage work. The show opened with Hollywatts introducing himself to the crowd:

In the name of the Father,
The Son and the Holy Ghost
I'm the only Soul-brother
Who can rap and toast
To the beat, yeah to the beat
First you say Hollywood,
And then you say Watts,
You put them both together
Then what do you got?
You got Hollywatts
Yo baby that's me . . .

The novelty of the show—fusing thought-provoking social commentary and theatrical storytelling with stimulating and multidimensional video design—wasn't lost on Ben and Roger. They knew they were onto something. So, they began working on several productions at once—a multiple-projection performance piece for *Spaces: Looking In/Looking Out, Installation and Video Art by Seven California Artists* (1985) (an exhibition at the Museum of African American Art), and a multimedia performance work titled *March of Progress: A Video Rap-Movement in Five Steps* (1986).

In the span of these works, Ben and Roger's two-man operation grew to a five-person-plus ensemble. The band included Mark Broyard, tenor vocalist, poet, and slide-projection performance artist; Vernon "King Oji" Vanoy, ex-football defensive tackle, Rastafarian priest, percussionist, and sideman/hype-man; Wesley Groves, tech-wizard cameraman and video design specialist; Ben, visual artist and video design director; and Roger, thespian and performance-art-troubadour. Their first performances were staged at VIDEO 3333 in Leimert Park, as well as at **Cityspace**, Roger's performance and exhibition spot located in a MacArthur Park warehouse.

Like VIDEO 3333, Roger's spot at 712 S. Grand View St. was home to a cross section from the experimental performance, video, film, and theater worlds. A January 1986 installation included video art from Ben, Ulysses Jenkins, and John Cannaday that was played inside the building's freight elevators; slide show art by Rika Ohara; and Mark's performance piece "Four Corners Equals" that featured a trumpet player, bass player, a painting, and Mark sitting behind a keyboard reading a copy of the local newspaper.

But at the heart of these exhibitions was the Hollywatts Posse's performances. The productions centered around Hollywatts's storytelling fused with Oji's drumming and multimedia visual projections from the rest of the crew. Roger's pieces were a mixture of singing, rapping, guitar-playing, dramatic monologue,

(OPPOSITE, TOP) *UNITED STATES OF EMERGENCY* FLYER, 1984
(OPPOSITE, BOTTOM) *MARCH OF PROGRESS*, 1985 FLYER FEATURING HOLLYWATTS POSSE MEMBERS MARK BROYARD, WESLEY GROVES, ROGER G. SMITH, AND BEN CALDWELL

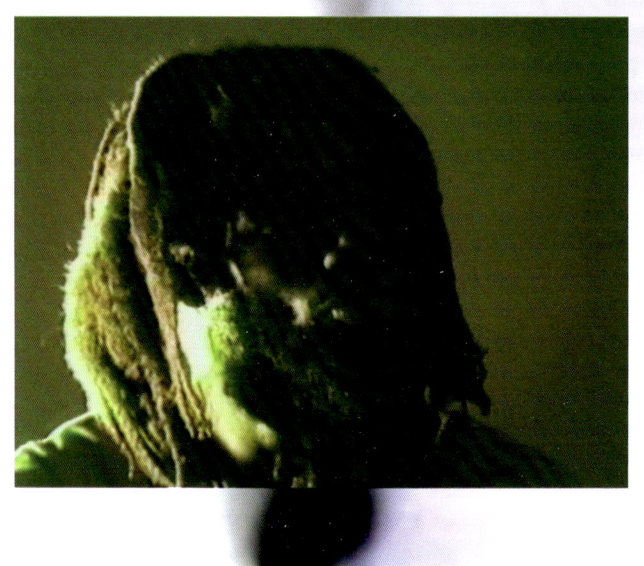
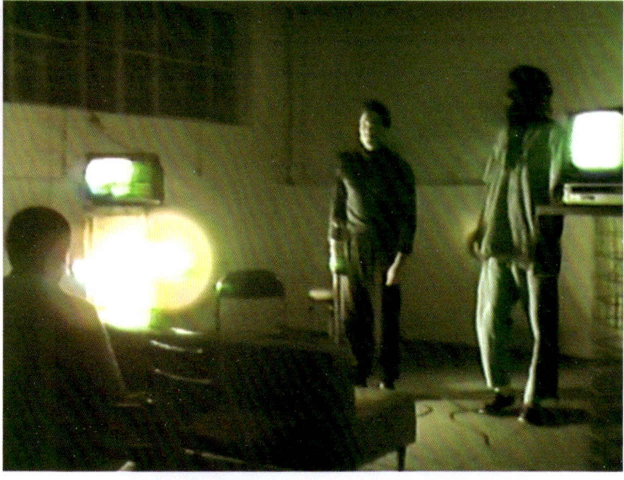
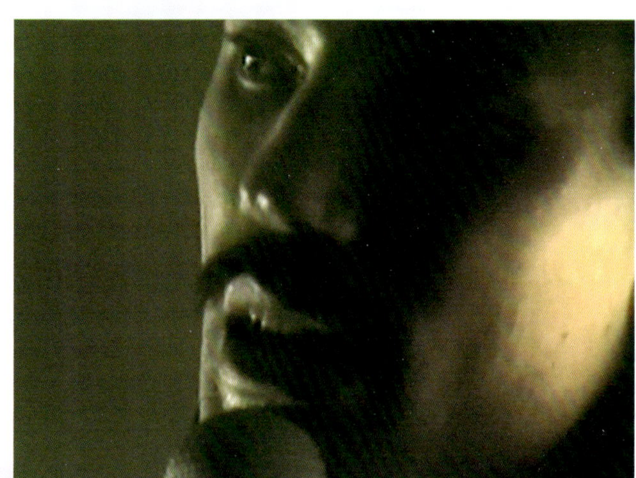
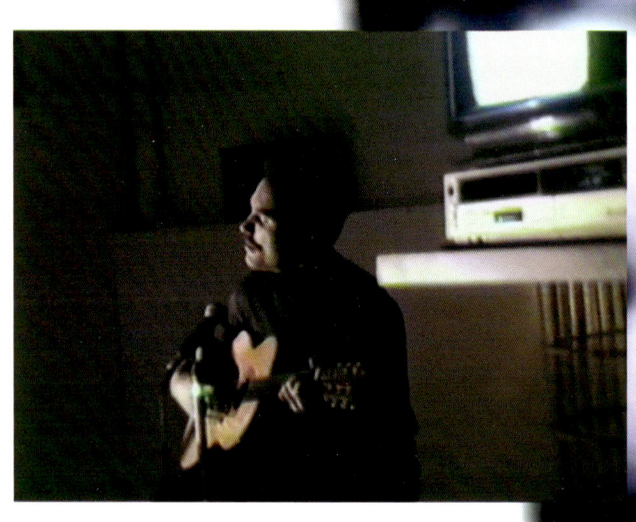
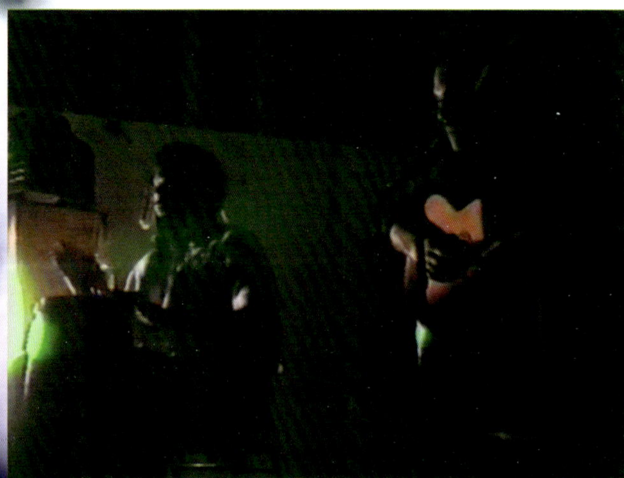

HOLLYWATTS PERFORMANCE
FEATURING ROGER G. SMITH AND
VERNON "KING OJI" VANOY

and confessional truth-telling. He blended the Black American art of folktales and testifyin' with Jamaican rituals of boasting and toasting, taking listeners on an introspective exploration of history and memory. Elaborate stories about his family and upbringing provided him a forum to ruminate on broader topics like death, manhood, the psychological violence rendered by white supremacy, international affairs and injustice, Black political movements in the aftermath of the 1960s, and U.S. popular culture's increasing appropriation of Black creativity. Through narrative, song, and humor, Roger pushed audiences to think deeply about the interior life and psychosocial implications of anti-Black racism and Black resistance.

In *Endurance* (1986), he described the pitfalls of integration and American pop culture's exploitation of Black creative expression:

> *The race is not given unto the swift*
> *Endurance (4x)*
> *They're doing a new dance (2x)*
> *It's called Endurance . . .*
> *They used to call you brotherman*
> *But now you're cakewalking for Uncle Sam*
> *And isn't it strange*
> *Hairstyles have changed*
> *Priorities rearranged . . .*
> *This is not MTVvvvvvv . . .*
> *We're trying to deal with history*
> *We're trying to deal with reality . . .*
> *It's the rap blues . . .*

Later in the same work, he condemned the state violence of South African apartheid:

> *First you say "apart," then you say hate*
> *Put them both together, what do they make?*
> *They make "apart-hate," or apartheid*
> *Whichever way you pronounce it, it still means genocide.*

Throughout, Oji played djembe and provided verbal ad-libs and improvisational commentary that amplified Roger's message. In certain sections, Oji chanted: "RASTAFARI! . . . FREE MANDELA! . . . MAN OVERBOARD! . . . HARAMBE!" Even his voice had a percussive texture, its intensity echoing throughout the space.

Mark handled the slide projection. He would move the slides back and forth—two back, four ahead, three back, four ahead, and so on. It was all in conjunction with what Roger was saying, how he was moving, and the general pacing

of his storytelling. Mark's manipulation of the slide projector also provided the performance with another rhythmic overlay, the machine's motor making a clicking sound akin to "*A-gi-chi-ti-di-du . . . A-gi-chi-ti-di-du . . . A-gi-chi-ti-di-du . . . A-gi-chi-ti-di-du.*" The crew called this *slide scratchin'*. They likened it to how hip-hop DJs transformed record players into percussive instruments by sliding records back and forth, the sound making a scratching sound when amplified.

Wesley would film Roger's performance. Wesley's live video feed was then displayed on television monitors, which were usually placed on either side of Roger and Oji. Ben would chop up and juxtapose these feeds of Roger with cinematic montages that Ben had composed before the event. These montages fused Ben's own pre-recorded footage with an assortment of photographs and scenes from television and cinema including Ben's film *Babylon Is Falling* (1983). As one reviewer pointed out, Ben's visual images "suppl[ied] a third rhythmic force" to the performance.

The rhythmic force of Ben's videos was a product of his editing techniques. The images displayed in the videos periodically rewound back and forth—he had manipulated the images' timing in the editing phase, prior to the performance. This manipulation and play with the footage gave Ben's videos their own percussive feel. It was as if they mimicked and responded to the repetitive nature of Oji's drumming and Roger's wordplay. Moreover, by showing the image and then rewinding it and returning to it several times, the crew was able to prioritize certain images as integral to the performance's overall message. It also enabled Roger to engage in a call-and-response with the videos; he would ask the screen a question, and Ben's edited videos answered with an image or cinematic sequence. Then the image was rewound and reshown when Roger repeated the question or made a statement, he and the screen engaging in a back-and-forth chant.

Their performance included predetermined "constants"—pre-recorded film/video or click-track audio cues and, in later years, scripted parts of Roger's performance. These constants served as the group's collective metronome, supplying them with the foundational indicators, cues, and steady pulse to perform and "play in time." It was within the gaps and breaks between these cues that they experimented, improvised, and cultivated new interpretations. Such improvisational shifts were often rhythmic; it could be Oji altering a drum pattern, Roger redirecting his commentary or rhyme pattern to instigate something among the audience, Mark or Ben shifting the pacing of the slide and video projection to be in tandem with the intensity of Roger's fluctuating wordplay. Their layering of rhythms of sound, visual culture, language, and movement was also intended as a provocation towards the audience meant to encourage their rhythmic involvement.

An essential component of these productions was what the men described as "the scratch effect"—planned and improvisational practices of instantaneous distortion, revision, and remixing of video, still image, and sound. Mark's DJ-like approach to slide projection was one example. Ben's edited video clips utilized a similar aesthetic. The images within his visual collages jumped around, forgoing a linear, smooth arc for one which was choppy, glitchy, grainy, and uneven. Mark and Ben's play with slides and video gave the images a bit of "swing"; the videos seemed to dance from one clip to the next and rub against one another like bodies on a dance floor.

This was further enhanced by the crew's manipulation of live video images (or what Ben referred to as "scratching the video") and spirited use of multiple monitors. Here's how this worked: Wesley would have his video camera on Roger, and Ben would have a video camera on Wesley's live video feed of Roger (that was playing on one monitor). Ben's feed would then play on one or several other monitors and, at certain points in the show, Wesley would simultaneously freeze-frame the live recording of Roger. When the viewer looked at a monitor, they could be viewing either Wesley's altered recording of Roger, or Ben's recording of that feed. They would split the signal between the video camera recorder and the monitors and sometimes even split the signal between the monitors. The resulting live footage was therefore often out of sync with the performance; it was blurred and distorted with squiggles and crazy stuff, imperfections that became part of the look of the posse's productions. In the eyes of the crew, the warped and scratched version of the video on the monitor suggested that they were channeling and communicating at an unconventional, ever-changing high frequency.

The posse situated their productions within numerous strands of fine art and multimedia arts. Roger described it as a performance corollary to the work of his friend, painter Jean-Michel Basquiat. Roger likened his ensemble's scratch effect to the way Basquiat scratched out words and images on his canvases. Ben and Wesley, on the other hand, understood their playful distortion of video and use of multiple monitors as building upon video artist Nam June Paik's work. Ben explained that one objective was to transform Paik's innovative approach of using sculpture-like TV monitors by "making it Black . . . [to] do what [Parliament] Funkadelic did, adding some funk to it," in particular Paik's installations *TV Cello* (1971), *TV Buddha* (1974), and *Video Fish* (1975). The crew's ongoing experiments with technology and innovative set and video design were also influenced by Mabou Mines, a New York City-based experimental theater company that Roger performed with, as well as the productions of Steven Berkhoff, whom Roger also worked with during this period.

The most important inspiration came from Los Angeles's tradition of Black assemblage art and freeform jazz and funk musicianship. Just as assemblage artists Betye Saar and Noah Purifoy composed visual art from found material (most notably, discarded mass cultural objects and consumptive goods from Black homes and communities), the Hollywatts Posse repurposed Black vernacular speech, music, rhythmic patterns, images, and iconography. They maintained that their different technological devices and performative elements communicated *with* Roger, not *behind* him. "We are working with cameras and language in the same way that musicians are working with saxes and drums," Roger insisted. "Stuff would happen, and we would respond to it … different venues shaped the dynamics of each performance work … what we were doing was *performative assemblage*." Chief among all the members was their commitment to improvisation. "This is something more akin to a jazz piece," Roger explained years later. "There's a foundation we refer to, but we leave room for improvisation— riffing. No two shows will ever be the same. It's something that came to us as a reaction to theater by some element of the performing community that tired of the staid, text-based expression that theater represents. It seems to be more persona, more responsive to the artist who isn't necessarily performing something for posterity, but more for himself."

Conflict (1987), Hollywatts Posse's production at Occidental University, allowed them to experiment with the scale and scope of their multimedia performance. Set in 1999 on the set of "the last late-night television show in human history," *Conflict* opens near the end of human life; humanity has been decimated by environmental disaster and political warfare. The television show is broadcast live from a sandy, barren Mojave Desert oasis, and features the live music of Babalade Olamina (Sherman McKinney III), alongside two hosts (played by Mark and Bob Wisdom) who interview several guests. Their guests for that night's episode included former-showgirl-turned-guerrilla-militant "Sophie" (played by Suzanne Ashley-Trimble) and comedian "Murphey Blast" (played by Daryl Sivad). But their main attraction was an interview with soap opera actor "Shecky Smith" (played by Roger), who mused about his career, popular culture's infiltration of political life, and the passive nature of humanity's last stand. Two camera personnel (Wesley and Ben) create the show's live telecast quality, their live-feed playing on television monitors on the stage. The monitors also play televised scenes from Shecky's soap opera (pre-recorded footage filmed at Roger's apartment). Audience members at Occidental were also incorporated into the production; they were treated by the late-night host characters as if they were a live studio audience.

The posse's avant-garde ideas and approach gained national attention with their next production, *Frederick Douglass Now* (1990). When the show opened at New York City's La MaMa Experimental Theatre, Roger was already riding high from his acclaimed performance in Spike Lee's film, *Do The Right Thing* (1989). But *Frederick Douglass Now* was something else, most certainly not the celebratory tribute or theatrical paean that many attendees presumed it would be. The one-man improvisational stage show consisted of Roger reinterpreting and translating the nineteenth-century abolitionist's life and legacy across the arc of modern history and the global struggles of the late twentieth century.

The show's contemporary feel was revealed via the fact that Roger was not made to resemble Douglass with make-up, costume, Afro, and postiche; instead,

Roger appeared as himself and was garbed in black jeans and a black leather jacket, clothing that conjured images of the Black Panther Party for Self-Defense. Furthermore, throughout the show, his performance was superimposed with slide projection images and video that ranged from historical to current-day: burning cities and uprisings in the 1960s; schoolchildren and civil rights activists blasted with water cannons; police violence from Watts 1965 to Virginia Beach 1989; a white mob's murder of teen Yusuf Hawkins in Bensonhurst; Marvin Gaye's soulful performance of "The Star-Spangled Banner" to introduce Roger's enactment of Douglass's "What to the Slave is the Fourth of July?" address. At one point in the show, Roger even called Harriet Tubman on a cellular telephone and praised her for "labor[ing] in the night."

It was a show that challenged the conventions of biographical one-man productions. Rather than commemorate Douglass, the show situated his message within the context and urgency of current-day life. With video monitors surrounding him and over a hip-hop-reggae soundtrack, Roger rhymed and lectured about a variety of topics: the plight and struggles of unemployed military veterans; the global movement to free Nelson Mandela and end South African apartheid; police brutality and state violence against poor people; society's silence about injustice against Black women and the importance of the Black women's liberation movement; the power and cosmic force of Black music, art, and aesthetics; and the value of family and community. And the methods the show used to articulate these ideas—Black music, multimedia, witty and provocative lyricism, humor, audience engagement—enabled the production to resonate with different audiences. Roger fittingly closed the show by turning Douglass's most recognized declaration into a rap:

> *If there is no struggle, there is no progress.*
> *This was the rap of brother Frederick Douglass . . .*
> *Frederick Douglass will never run out of breath:*
> *If there is no struggle, there is no progress.*

Critics praised the production, describing it as "an intimate portrait . . . that spoke to those who will inhabit the 21st century, tailored for the soul video generation." Another reviewer wrote that it was "an evocative portrait drawn from the orator's insightful, beautifully articulated observations . . . [Smith's delivery] suggests how Douglass might appear as a charismatic commentator of the 1990s." *Newsday* featured the production and an image of the Hollywatts Posse on the cover of its Black History Month weekend edition. The *New York Times* published Roger's rap that ends the show on its editorial page. On any given night, celebrities like Russell Simmons, Branford Marsalis, LL Cool J, Jeff Goldblum, Laurence Fishburne, and Spike Lee were in the audience. Even *Yo! MTV Raps* covered the production, showing excerpts from Roger's performance and having host Fab 5 Freddy and rap group Gang Starr interview Roger at the end of the episode.

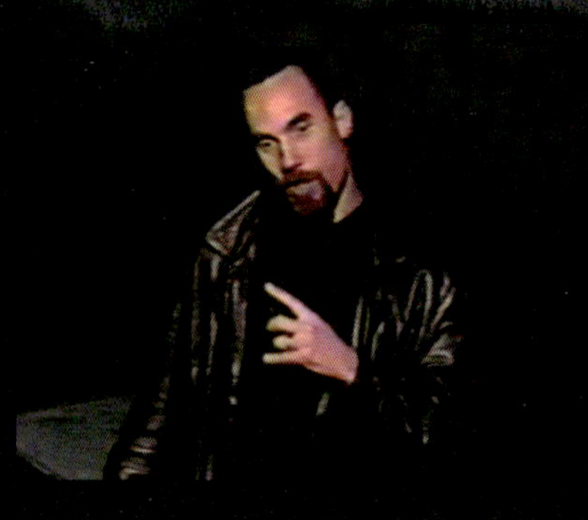
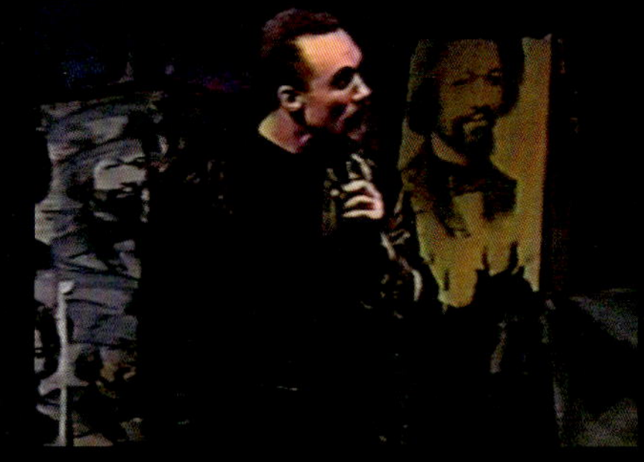
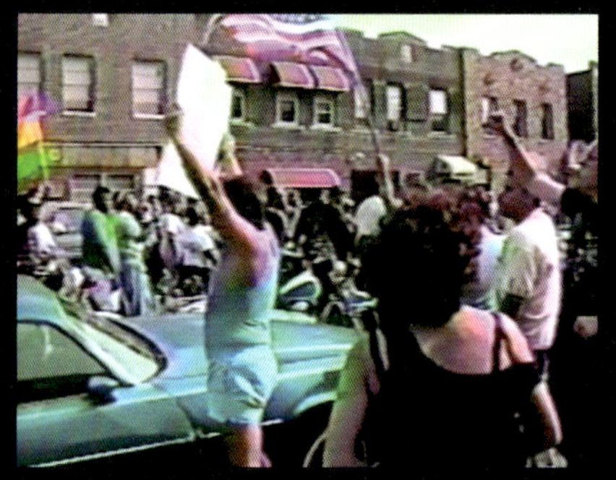
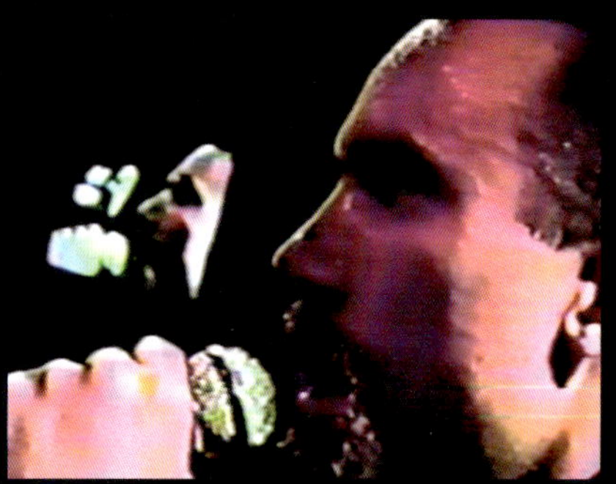
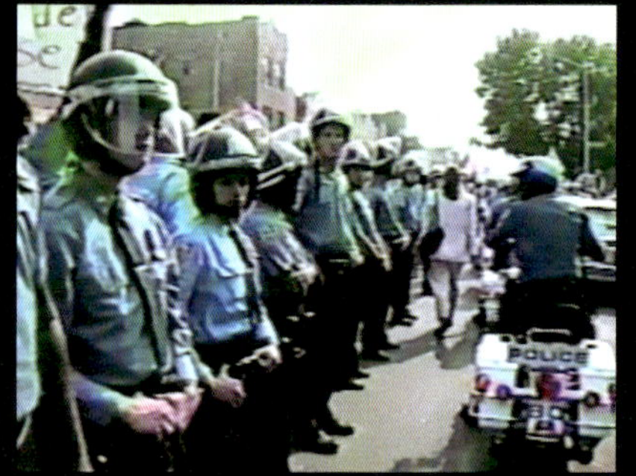

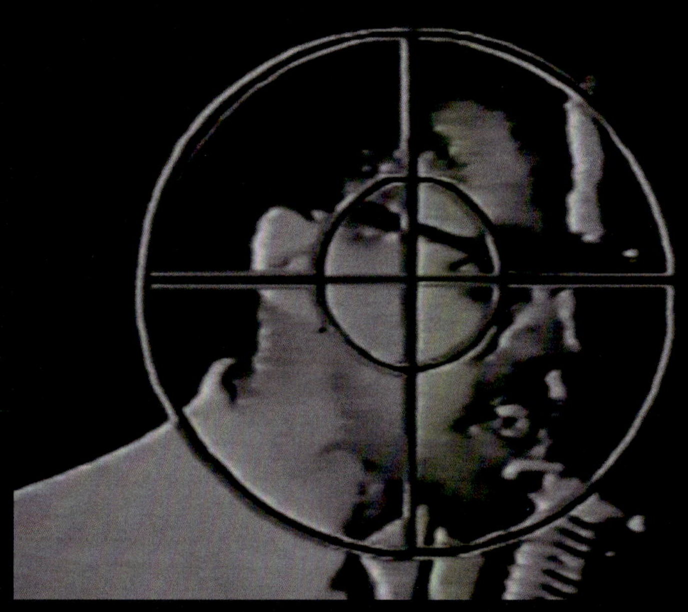

FREDERICK DOUGLASS NOW, 1990

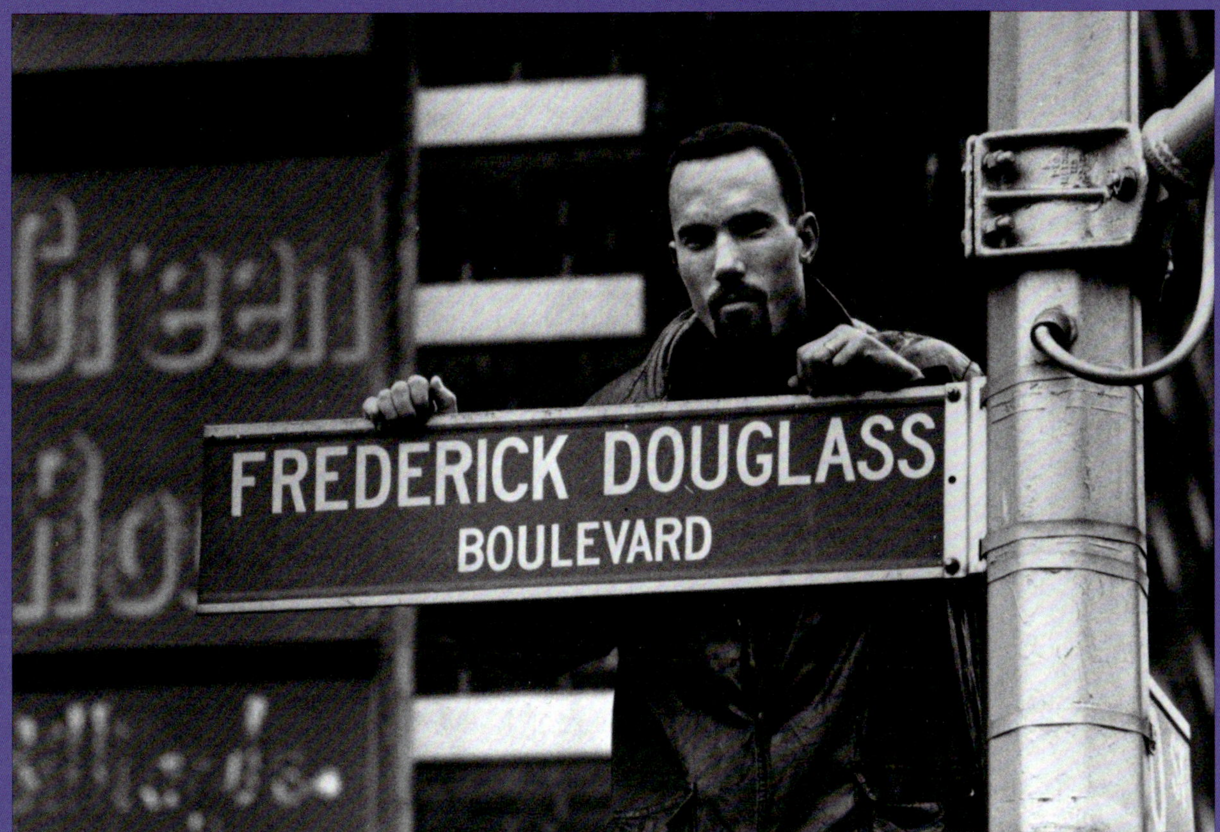

La MaMa E.T.C

presents

FREDERICK DOUGLASS NOW

Conceived and Performed by
Roger Guenveur Smith

Cinematography • Ben Caldwell
Associate Producer • J.N. Productions
Set Design • Tom Moore
Photographer • Carl Brunn
Production Manager • Lapacazo Sandoval

Jan. 25 thru Feb. 11, 1990 at 8:00 PM
Weds. matinee on Jan. 24 at 2:00 PM

La MaMa E.T.C• 74A E. 4th St. • NYC
Box Office: (212) 475-7710
Student/Group Discounts: (212) 254-6468

TDF accepted weekends

With this momentum, Roger and Mark got to work on *Inside the Creole Mafia* (1991). This satirical sketch-comedy, co-written and co-starring the two men, had a very personal meaning to them. It returned them to the traditions and shared history that linked their two families—the cultural imaginary and complex identities of New Orleans's Creole of color communities and their descendants. Over the course of ninety minutes, Mark and Roger centered the experiences of Creole people as a lens to unravel the intricacies of race and racism in the United States. They played Creole dandies who belabor over who is the most "Creole" and use different tools to resolve this: brown paper bags to determine whether or not they are of right shade of complexion; fine-tooth hair-combs suspended from the ceiling, which the characters use to decipher if they have "good hair or bad hair"; attending a "Creoles Anonymous" meeting; and quizzing the audience about their knowledge of Creole terminology and which racial category they think other audience members fit into ("Quadroons, octoroons, mulattos, or passé blanc?"). Humor and self-deprecating banter, skits, songs, and audience spoofs allow Mark and Roger to interrogate the multifaceted dynamics of racialized identity, colorism, classism, intra-racial conflict, internalized racism, and many other subjects.

Every night, the audience left with food for thought, as well as the experience of tasting real-deal Louisiana Creole cuisine (a pre-show buffet was included with the ticket price). "[It is] a mesmerizing production," one critic wrote. "These young men are clever writers; they play off each other's antics, reminiscent of the vaudeville era," another reviewer added. "No one is safe … [this] is a hard-hitting, straightforward approach to the delicate topic of race which divides and subdivides groups in America." "[The show gives] a subtle satirical jab at the theater of multicultural identity," a journalist commented, while another championed it as an "intelligent piece" that finds a way to be "enormously entertaining" amid its serious, dark subject matter. The highest praise was offered by another critic, who wrote, "[*Inside the Creole Mafia*] is an important theatrical triumph with an enormous potential for telling impact to provoke audience thought . . . It illuminated commonality, facilitated communication, and made possible a bond across the entrenched divide of intraracial prejudice … Productions like *Inside the Creole Mafia* are invaluable statements for having vitalized the dialogue of Black theater."

In the years that followed, Mark and Roger continued to perform the show and frequently updated their performance. *Inside the Creole Mafia* won awards from *LA Weekly* and the *Los Angeles Times*. The show was so good that the New Orleans City Council even made a proclamation recognizing Mark and Roger as honorary citizens.

Yet as the 1990s progressed, the Hollywatts Posse performed less often as a full ensemble. Family life and responsibilities, as well as new projects and passions, drew them in other creative directions. Mark expanded his interdisciplinary arts practice to include sculpture and fine arts. He apprenticed with assemblage artists Betye and Alison Saar and went on to develop his own catalog of assemblage works. After returning from the New York run of *Frederick Douglass Now*, Ben revitalized the open-mic hip-hop workshop at his studio. **Project Blowed,** this new iteration of the workshop, built off the I-Fresh Express legacy. But it also pulled from Hollywatts's radical, improvisatory approach to performance, and in time became the most important gathering spot for underground L.A. hip-hop. As Project Blowed picked up steam, Roger was revolutionizing the one-man stage show. With singer-composer Marc Anthony Thompson handling the sound design, Roger has created productions where he has performed as a legion of characters. The most notable, perhaps, is Black Panther Party leader Huey P. Newton, a performance for which Roger earned an Obie Award.

FAST-FORWARD TO APRIL 25th, 2015—Several posse members are at London's Tate Modern museum. Dub-poet Lindon Kwesi Johnson and actor/theater director Steven Berkhoff are in the audience. There's a small, white, rectangular-shaped stage with a wall-length glass panel behind it revealing the River Thames and the sun as it slowly sets.

Hollywatts jumps back into action. The posse performs a piece that mixes several of their older works with a more recent production Roger created that explores the life and tragic death of Rodney G. King—the Black motorist whose vicious assault by the LAPD was video-recorded by an onlooker, the assaulting officers' 1992 trial subsequently propelling a citywide uprising that transformed Los Angeles and the world. In this Hollywatts production's concluding sequence, Ben manipulates the video camera's image of Rodney (played by Roger) as he completes his final monologue. If you stare hard enough at these images projected on both sides of the stage, it appears as if Rodney is drowning in the River Thames. "Quite appropriate," Roger remarks after the show. "For Rodney to drown in the Thames is politically appropriate." The river's history of trafficking enslaved Africans isn't lost on Roger. He dryly points out, "It's the river that brought us here."

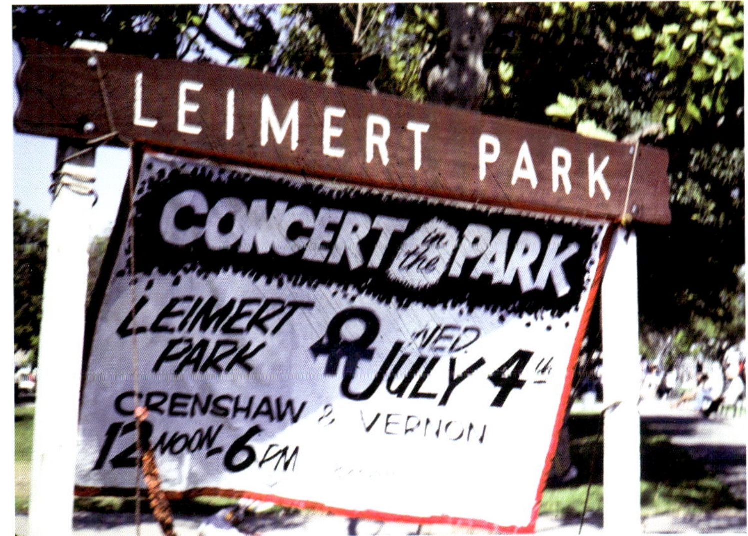

4TH OF JULY CONCERT IN
LEIMERT PARK, 1984

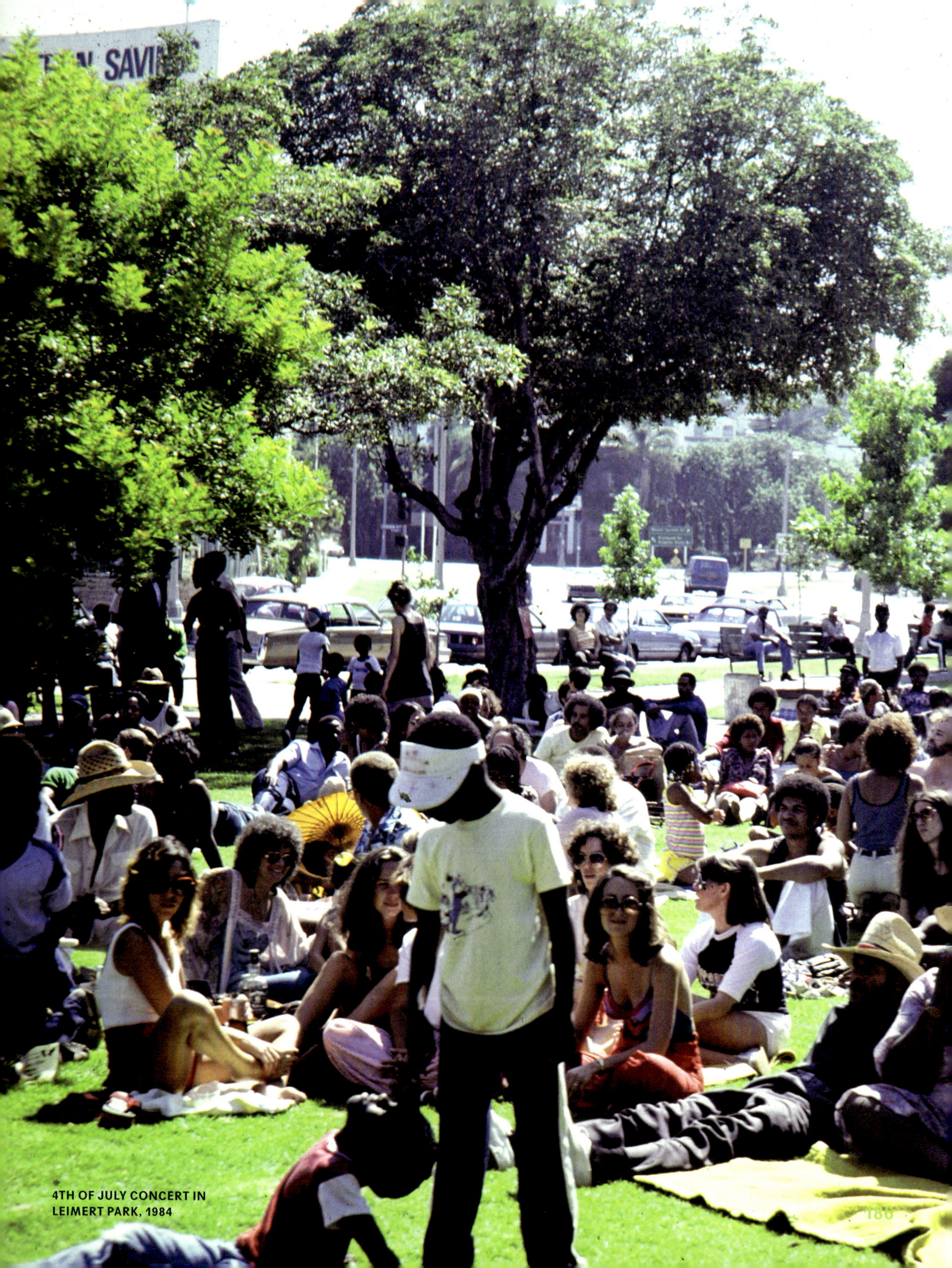

4TH OF JULY CONCERT IN
LEIMERT PARK, 1984

186

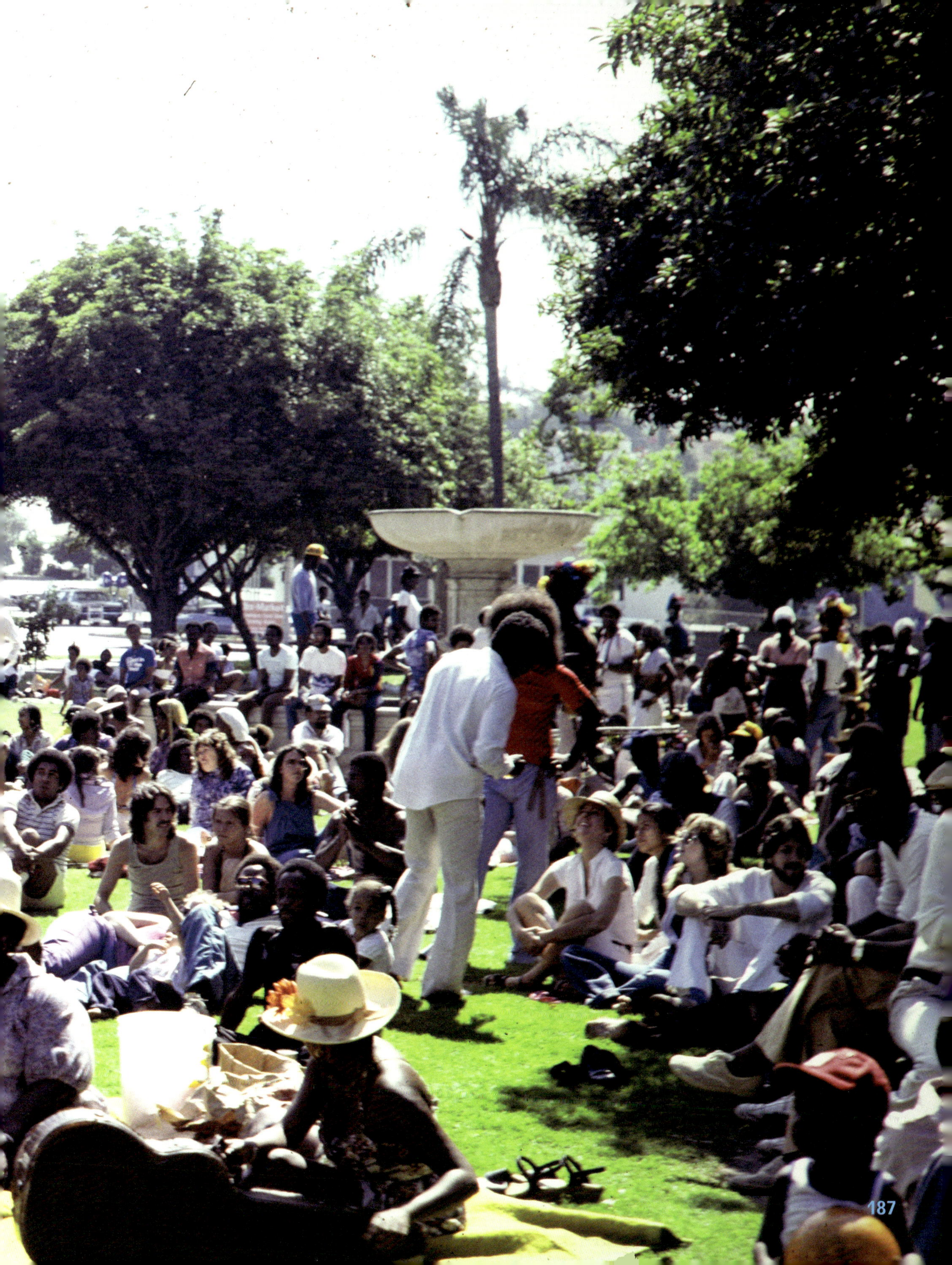

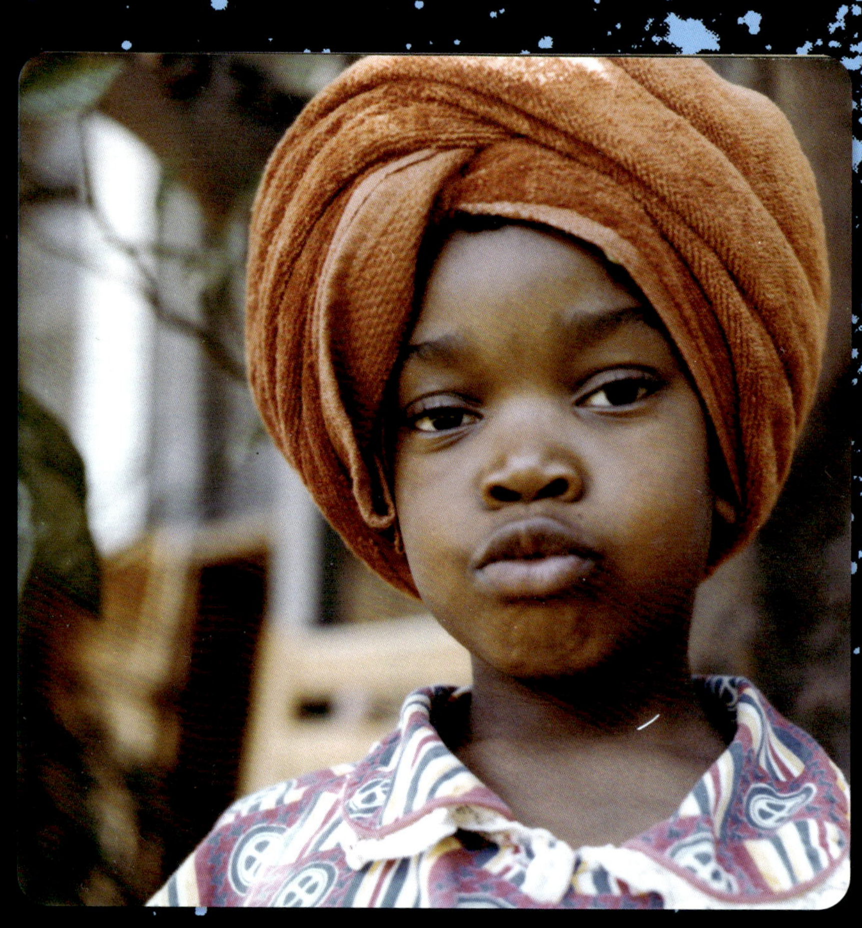

DARA CALDWELL, CIRCA 1980

love is supreme
it's an extraterrestrial feeling
an alchemy
                the magical mixture of cultural tonics
                        within the soup of the cosmos
                                guided by light
like the celestial movements of the skies
that peer down at us
and enter our bodies

—Ben Caldwell

"MOMYSTERY15 — LOVE"

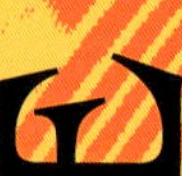
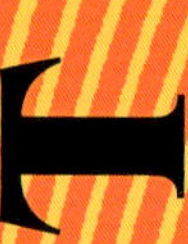
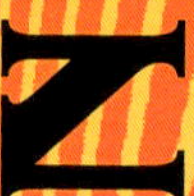
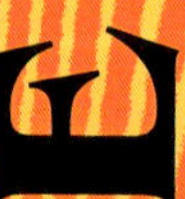

ENTER

THE KAOS

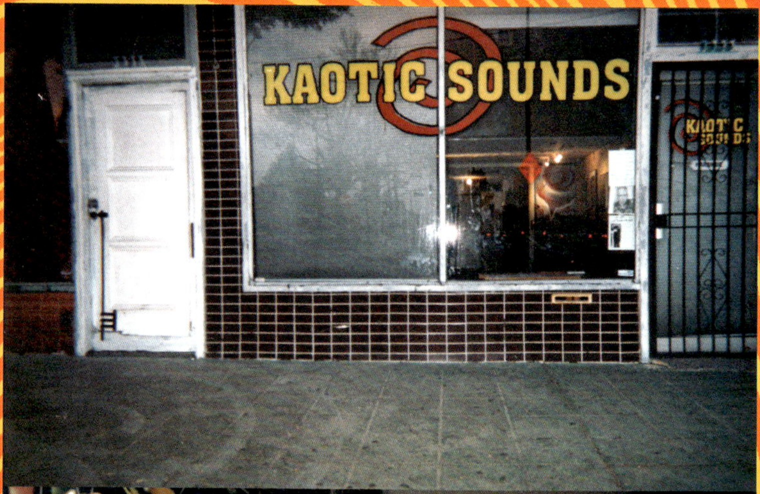

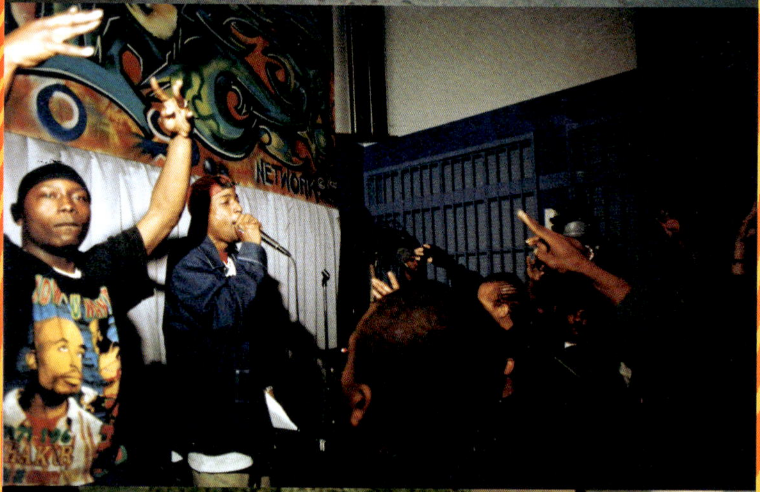

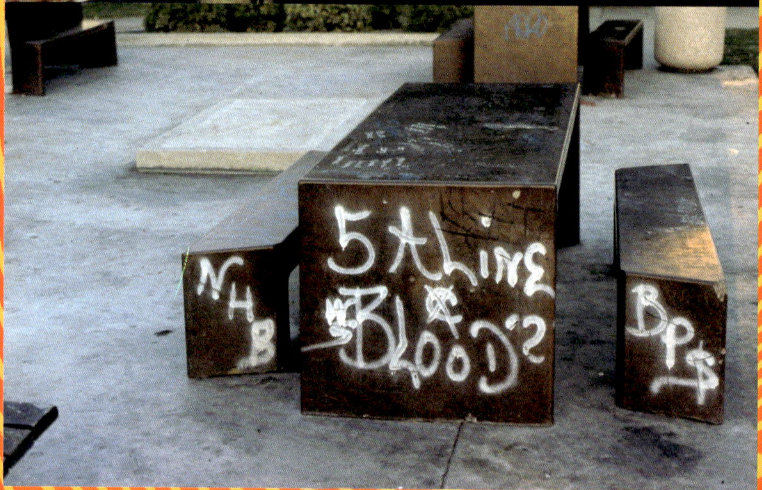

Before she saw the cops, she felt their presence. The floors and walls trembled. The windows rattled.

From up high, the ghetto-bird's wings emitted an unending series of vibrations. Two floors below, there were murmurs and whispers of what to expect next. Outside stood more than sixty police officers.

It was Thursday, January 4, 1996, around 11:30 p.m.

Dara was in the office, just behind the stage. She and her homegirl Ruthie were operating the video toaster for the open-mic workshop. Each week they would use this video-editing software and hardware in conjunction with several VHS recorders and VCRs to televise the night's list of performers. The list would be displayed alongside visual designs and animation, all of which aired on television screens inside the performance space. The toaster also enabled Dara and Ruthie to switch between certain images on the fly.

Running the machine was the centerpiece of their Thursday routine. It usually began with Dara leaving work at Tower Records or classes at Pasadena Community College. Hopping into her Mazda Rx7. Heading to the Valley to scoop Ruthie. Then south to her father Ben's studio/multimedia lab.

Dara had grown up there. As a youngster, her bedroom was in the back section of the building. For years she had worked the door for her dad and Roger's multimedia performances. For years she had a front row seat for the I-Fresh Express's rehearsals and parties, watching as many of the kids transitioned from teens to adulthood. To put it simply, as VIDEO 3333 had matured and been transformed, so too had she. So it made sense that Dara was part of Thursday's night action. It wasn't *just* her father's studio-lab. It was hers, too.

She and Ruthie would arrive to find folks setting up. Cheatham on sound and tech. Ngafsh coordinating the performers' list. Ben moving tables and chairs, giving directions. And then, before start-time, others straggling in. Chu Chu, Riddlore, then Ab, J-Smoov, Acey, TrenSeta.

By dark, the spot was packed. Medusa hosting. Emcees of the likes of Aceyalone, Abstract Rude, Myka 9, Ellay Khule, 2 Mex, Ganjah K, Self Jupiter, Figures of Speech, Pigeon John, P.E.A.C.E., Busdriver, C.V.E. (Chillin Villain Empire), and others. Outside, others formed ciphers and battle-rapped while some just smoked bud, joked, and broke bread.

Just another Thursday night at ==Project Blowed==. Telebeamed from Leimert Park, Los Angeles, the underground source, to the world.

Blowed was an echo of the "Good Life," an open-mic rap event that used to be held at the ==Good Life Café==, a health food market just up the Crenshaw

Strip. Launched in 1989, the Good Life's weekly gathering quickly became a community showcase for the city's best emcees and a platform for Los Angeles's rising independent rap scene. Out-of-town rappers with record deals of the likes of Biz Markie and Fat Joe even dropped by the Good Life to spit rhymes and experience its electric vibe. In 1994, Good Life organizers B. Hall, R/Kain Blaze, and Janie Mae Scott-Goodkin (aka IfaSade), reached out to Ben about opening his space to a group of Good Life rappers interested in holding an after-hours open-mic event. With Ben's permission, the group (led by emcees Aceyalone and Abstract Rude) began holding an event that they initially called the "After-Life." By the end of that year, this had transformed into Project Blowed.

Blowed's open-mic workshop had just reached its one-year anniversary when shit hit the fan.

That night's acts had been all the way live. Or at least Dara thought so. There had been only a few instances of the crowd chanting "PLEASE PASS THE MIC!" during someone's performance. Everyone else who had hit the stage had killed it.

Then word spread that the police were outside. And not just a few. Southwest Division, plus Newton and Mid-City's squads, many of whom were in riot gear.

At the command of the police, Project Blowed's members and attendees began filing outside into the streets. They were angry and just wanted to go home. But when the police surrounded several Blowedians and prevented them from walking toward their vehicles and homes, things exploded. In the process of steering the Blowedians out of the area, the cops became more aggressive. They began to push and pressure the crowd. Then officers assaulted Medusa, struck another woman to the ground, and, in the process, pulled another woman's dreads out.

The Blowedians rose up. They threw bottles, desks, chairs—anything they could get their hands on.

After the arrival of more cops, a dozen police cars, and another helicopter, Ben and two others were arrested. Dara and Ngafsh rushed to the Southwest Division to bail him out. Ben was charged with running an overcrowded establishment and several other building-and-compliance-related charges.

It was all bullshit. A product of complaints from a subset of the Village's residents and business owners, anxious over more than just the energy and sounds emanating from 43rd Place and Leimert Boulevard. Their objections grew out of longstanding class and intergenerational tensions within the Leimert Park community. Concern over gang violence and young people whom the elders claimed lacked respect and good morals. All of which was further stoked in the years following the 1992 L.A. Uprisings.

Nearly four years before the raid at Project Blowed, Los Angeles had erupted in the aftermath of the 1992 Rodney King trial. Black Angelenos perceived the jury's acquittal of the four LAPD officers who viciously beat King as part of a long arc of state-sanctioned terror, violence, and injustice. The jury's "not guilty" ruling echoed the 1991 trial of Soon Ja Du, the convenience store owner who was given a mere suspended sentence, a five-hundred-dollar fine, community service, and probation for shooting fifteen-year-old Latasha Harlins in the back of the head after accusing the teen of theft in Du's store. It was an echo of 1979, when the court exonerated the police officers who killed Eula Mae Love, a thirty-nine-year-old mother and widow who they shot eight times in front of her Watts home after a dispute over a gas bill. It was an echo of countless court cases and countless accounts of police and denizen violence against Black and Brown people.

So, when Black and Brown folk and others swarmed into the streets on the evening of April 29, 1992, it was this loop of abuse, brutality, and subjugation that drew them out. It was the underlying patterns of colonialism and cruelty that spawned five days of protests, violence, death, arson, vandalism, looting, and property damage. The system's willingness to, yet again, release the greater society from accountability for the violence committed against Black and Brown people was simply too much to take.

FAST–FORWARD TO THE EVENING OF JANUARY 4, 1996. This too was an echo, a tremor, an aftershock of 1992, a reverberation in the bend.

When the Blowedians were instructed by the police to file out and leave the premises, Dara grabbed her father's video camera. She pressed "record." With the Village's streetlamps and the police's flashing light providing intermittent background lighting, the camera recorded the melee: helicopter lights shining down, almost blinding the crowd, blurring the camera's focus; police rushing a group of Blowedians, forcing them in the direction of Crenshaw Boulevard; several police holding a person down on the ground. Like the videotape recording of Rodney King's assault, Dara's video recording was an instrument of witnessing. It offered visual documentation and another damning example of the LAPD's brutality and systematic abuse.

In the week that followed, Ben and others circulated the videotape among the news media. Their intention was to shift the narrative. The police maintained that they had received calls from several residents and business owners. The people had alleged that Ben was running a nightclub, and that his events were drawing "the wrong elements" into the Village.

Ben and the Blowedians refuted this characterization of Ben's space. ***This is not a nightclub. It's an educational space. A classroom. And we're running a workshop which just happens to take place in the hours when our participants are not at work or at school.*** They weren't saying anything new. It was an argument Ben had been making for years. Long before the raid, long before the advent of Project Blowed. ***This is a classroom. We're creating a space for our kids, our teens, our young people.***

Other people came out in their defense. One of the first was Michael Zinzun, coordinator of the **Coalition Against Police Abuse** (CAPA). Since 1976, Zinzun and CAPA had been at the forefront of L.A.'s grassroots community organizing movement against police abuse and violence. Ramona Ribston, director

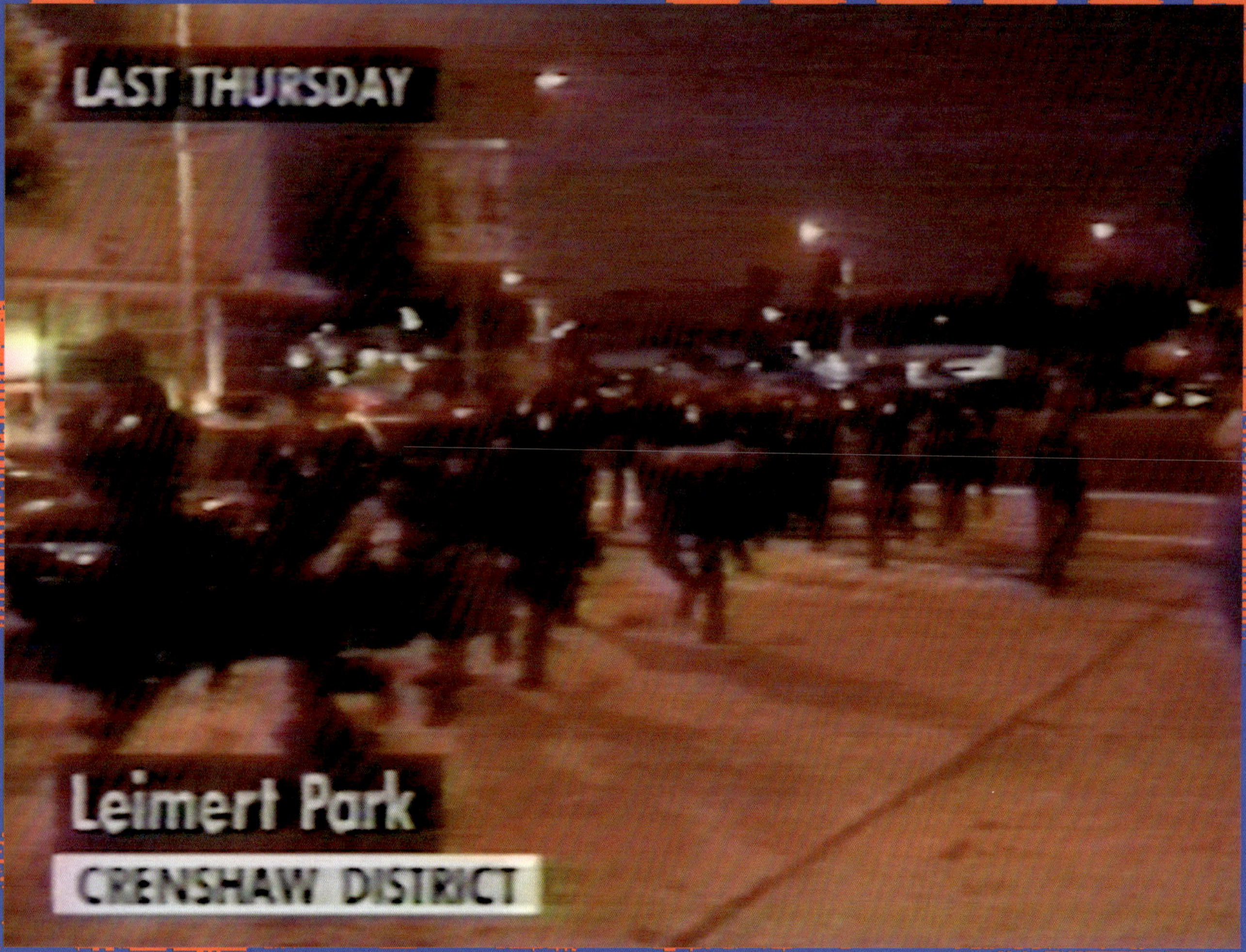

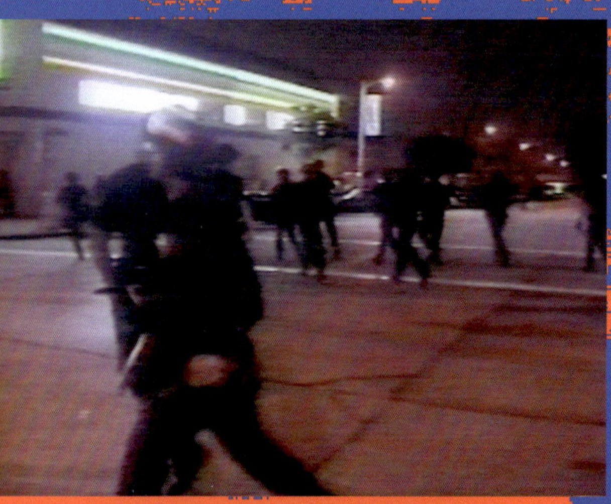

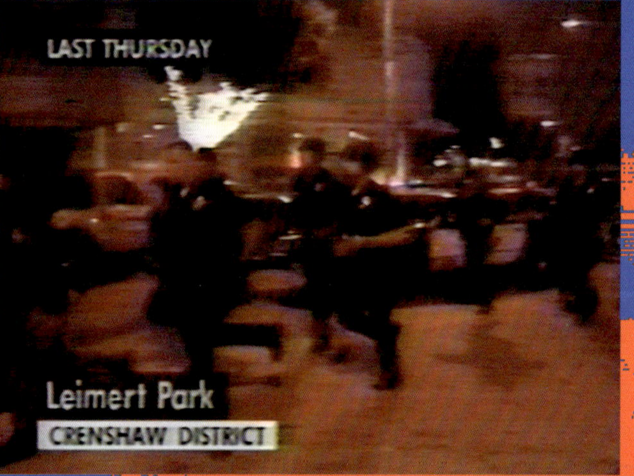

NEWS COVERAGE OF THE POLICE
RAID OF KAOS NETWORK, 1996

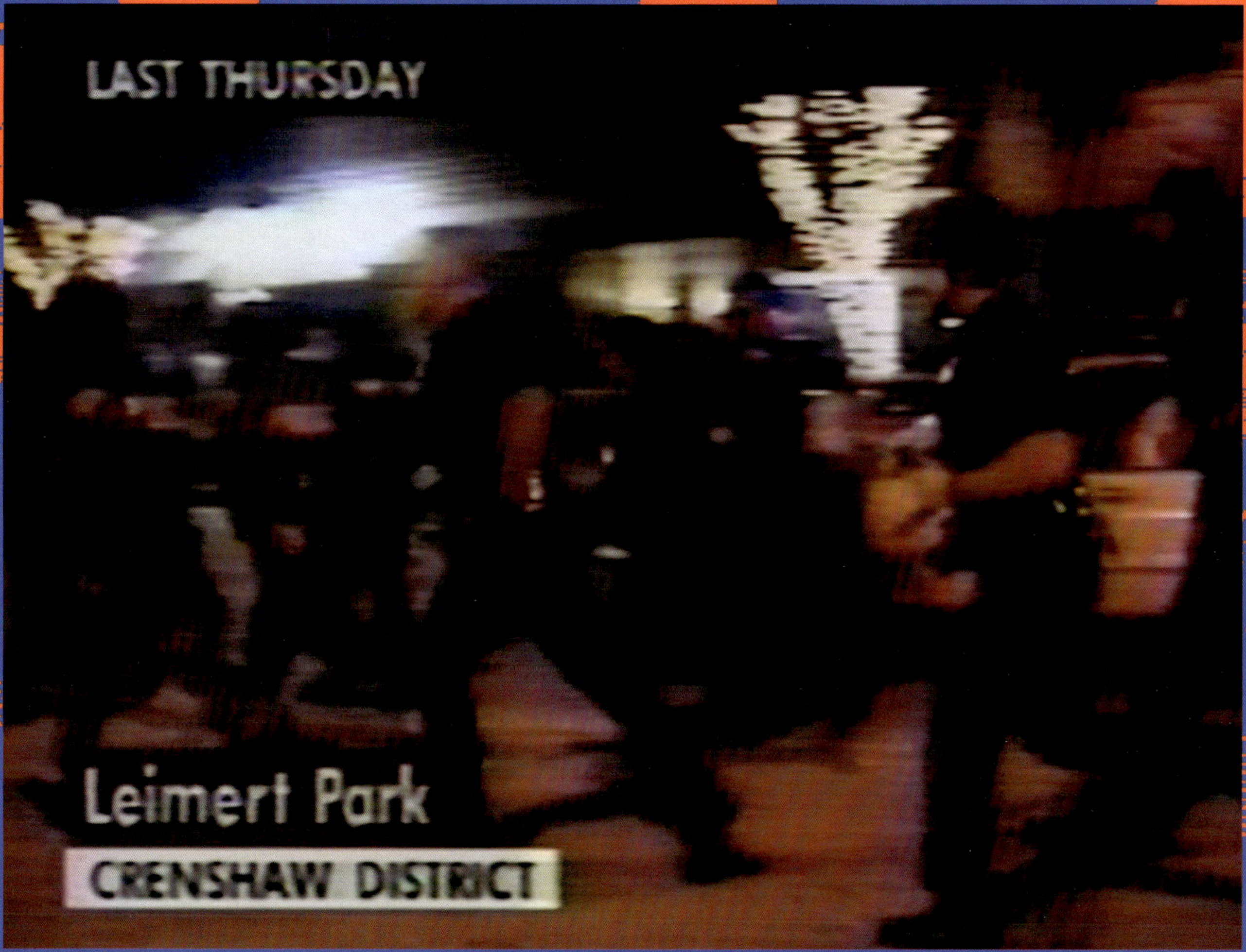

LAST THURSDAY
Leimert Park
CRENSHAW DISTRICT

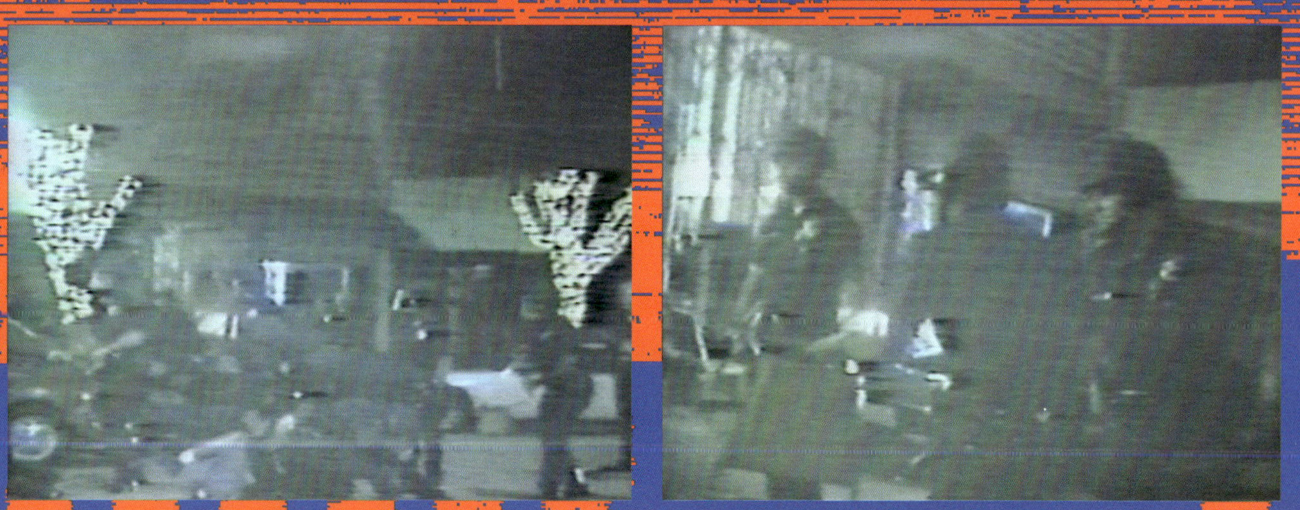

of Southern California's ACLU (American Civil Liberties Union), also voiced support and offered the ACLU's legal services to help Ben fight the charges. Several of the Village's business owners also came forward to condemn the raid and offer praise for Ben's space.

It was Black women, though, who stepped up the most. *Rap Pages* magazine editor Sheena Lester helped coordinate a press conference and rally. There, as the videotaped footage of the raid was shown to the news media, segments of the Project Blowed collective and other community members voiced their frustration with the LAPD and with Leimert Park's residents and business owners.

Newspaper coverage by Black women journalists was also essential. For years, writers Lynell George and Erin Aubry Kaplan had been publishing articles about Ben's studio and the various workshops held there. Their coverage had been instrumental in helping him legitimize his work as a community educator and in helping circulate VIDEO 3333's mission. Thus, in the aftermath of the raid, George, Kaplan, and several other journalists deployed the power of their pens to again highlight the importance of Ben's space.

All in all, the public relations campaign was effective. The charges against Ben were eventually dropped. Just as important, the rally and media coverage prompted long-overdue dialogue and reflection among some members of the Village. Elders, business owners, and elements of the community's middle class were pushed to reconsider their perceptions about hip-hop and their fraught relations with the city's young people of color. Several admitted that seeing groups of young Black and Brown people concentrated in one place during late hours stirred up their anxieties over street gangs and of a repeat of the 1992 uprisings. That their unease and fear of young Black and Brown people was reflective of a broader citywide and national cultural outlook, one that led to the criminalization and mass incarceration of these young people.

During these discussions, the community's young people spoke passionately about how it felt to live with a target on their backs. Every day, they had to navigate being watched and surveilled by the police, educators, media, business owners, their parents, and one another. Every day, they had to be smart on their feet. They had to know how to move through different neighborhoods with different gang sets, where wearing the wrong colors or being presumed to be gang-affiliated or waving the wrong hand signals could get you stomped out, arrested, placed into the police's gang database, shot, or killed.

Throughout these dialogues, one question lingered: ***Where can our children go to be themselves, to become themselves, if not here?***

A few years before the raid, Ben had changed the name of VIDEO 3333. This decision was prompted by several shifts. For one thing, with the rise of music video channels like MTV and BET, as well as video chain stores like Blockbuster and Hollywood Video, video was everywhere. Ben felt that, while it was great that video cameras were becoming more affordable and available to the everyday consumer, video was losing its luster as a disruptive, rebellious instrument and medium of visual representation and art. There were also indications that it would soon be obsolete, replaced by new digital media and computing technologies of communication and representation. And the most striking sign of this was the emergence and growing importance of a global system of interconnected computer networks (which in subsequent years came to be more popularly known as "the Internet").

Ben had witnessed the power of this evolving "network of networks" in 1984 as a member of the **Electronic Café**, a project that virtually linked five disparate L.A. community spaces/businesses and culturally diverse communities in real time. Over the course of seven weeks, café-goers at four restaurants and visitors at L.A.'s Museum of Contemporary Art communicated with one another via computer screens and video equipment; they talked and shared and exchanged drawings, photos, personal stories, poems, and messages—interactions that linked them and their different locations. The project's objective was to create an informal, localized, and participatory telecom network and information commons. One that connected communities and which raised social consciousness—an alternative model for the evolving "globally networked cultures" of the future, especially in lieu of the rise of corporate controlled telecommunication and information services. In their manifesto, the Electronic Café explained that this "Network Project" was their "creative response to the arrival of the Orwellian year" and an artistic alternative to "the dark side of the new world information order." With it, they desired to "humanize emerging technological environments" and cultivate "multimedia creative solutions networks" that were non-hierarchical, anti-imperialist, multicultural, multidisciplinary, and community-centered. "We must create at the same scale as we can destroy," the group explained. "The counterforce to the scale of destruction is the scale of communication."

Even into the early 1990s, the Electronic Café experience loomed large in Ben's mind. People needed informal physical spaces and community settings where they could prioritize learning and experimenting with new media communication technologies, in particular technologies that would enable them to obtain information and connect and communicate with people over new digital platforms. It was also integral that these settings and technologies activate people to build solidarity within their own communities and with communities elsewhere, most especially groups enduring the extremity of global capitalism and white supremacy's systematic violence, poverty, and terror.

These were some of the ideas shaping VIDEO 3333's name change. Still, the biggest impetus was Ben's expansion of his studio. As the 1980s became the 1990s, VIDEO 3333's two-story storefront operation grew to include the two buildings adjacent to it.

Both changes—VIDEO 3333's name change and the studio's expansion into the adjacent buildings—would not have happened without Lori Harris, Ben's wife.

They had met in 1984 after Ben screened his film, *Babylon Is Falling* (1983), for a United Nations-sponsored series of events organized to commemorate the

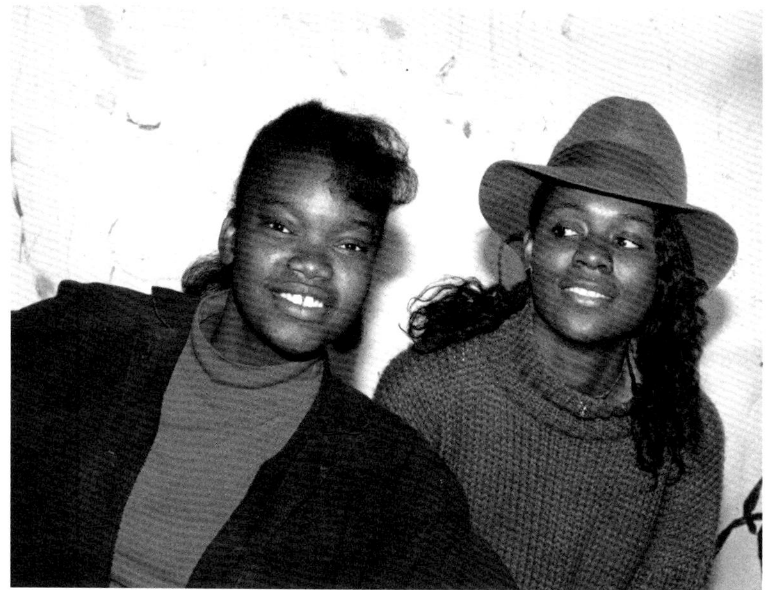

1976 Soweto uprising in South Africa and the multitude of South Africans that had been killed in the struggle to end apartheid. Lori was working at Inner City Cultural Center and had been tasked with planning and coordinating the event.

When Ben met her, he thought she was attractive, spirited, and smart. But she was sixteen years his junior, and he didn't want to rob the cradle. So, he kept his distance. Lori, in contrast, was persistent. She would query him about what he thought of certain artists, hoping that her knowledge of Black art and interest in collecting it might make a positive impression on him, or at least convey her level of maturity. She flirted, and would randomly lock eyes with Ben, eager to hold his attention.

Her effort was not for naught. In the spring of 1986, after a Hollywatts performance, a group of folks went out to party at the nightclub inside the Ambassador Hotel. There, on the parquet floor at the Cocoanut Grove, Ben and Lori slow-danced. By the evening's end, the two were holding hands at the afterparty at Cityspace, Roger's studio in MacArthur Park.

Lori and Ben were married in front of their friends and families on April 29, 1989, in Lori's father's church in Riverside, California. Nearly three years later, in the morning hours of Sunday, February 23, 1992, their daughter Elizabeth Nozwe was born.

One of the first major decisions of their marriage was expanding Ben's studio and workspace. For years, he had queried his building's landlord about purchasing the property occupied by VIDEO 3333 (3333 West 43rd Place). When the landlord finally connected him to the building's owner, Ben and Lori learned that the property owner also owned the adjacent lots (4343 Leimert Boulevard and 3335 West 43rd Place) and would consider an offer for all three. Ben and Lori decided to take the big leap. They negotiated a lease-to-own agreement for all three properties.

They initially imagined the corner property, 4343 Leimert, as a café. They tried this out for several months. But it didn't bring in enough revenue. So, they decided to pivot. Ben would continue to use the center property as his studio. They would rent out 3335 West 43rd Place to Richard Fulton, owner of a nearby storefront jazz coffeehouse and chess-playing gathering spot called 5th Street Dick's, to run an independent art gallery. And Ben and Lori would rent out the corner lot for events.

Reset. The days of VIDEO 3333 were over. Ben's studio and their community event space would now be known as **"KAOS Network."**

The name grew out of Lori and Ben's fascination with chaos theory, especially the philosophical arguments of mathematician Robert Abraham. Chaos theory is an interdisciplinary field of study in mathematics, with applications in several other disciplines. Its main gist is that within dynamical systems (like, say, the human process, processes of nature, or that of the universe) small differences can yield widely diverging outcomes, rendering long-term prediction impossible.

Abraham's arguments about chaos and the mathematics of complex dynamical systems, specifically, rejected the idea of linear systems, linear histories, and the idea of knowing a system through its parts. He asserted that the universe and human history should not be presumed to be rigid, straight, unidirectional systems with fixed rules or an end-oriented design. No, they were complex, curved systems; wavy, chaotic arrangements that were unpredictable and could take on new shapes and directions. "Chaos is everywhere," he maintained.

Yet Abraham also insisted that when observed *in relation*, what could be distinguished about a system's different parts were the vibrations and resonances that forced them to collide, and which therefore linked them. These sudden splits or "bifurcations"—what Abraham liked to refer to as "strange attractors"—were indications of the "harmonious resonance [that exists] between all the components, parts, sub-systems, and so involved in the life process." Chaos, he insisted, represented "a kind of mathematical, sacred guidance" to the turbulence of dynamic systems and processes of change.

Ben and Lori drew connections between these ideas and the principles put forth among various Native, West African, and Eastern cosmological systems. Chaos theory seemed to echo axioms made within many non-Western accounts of the universe and its workings. That to fully know and understand the universe was impossible. That what was more vital was to work and struggle to be in alignment with the universe, and moreover stay attuned to its ebb and flow and its hidden and mysterious networks of exchange.

Chaos theory also seemed to pinpoint something that Ben had felt all his life—an intelligence and intimacy between all phenomena, even those that appeared to be most random. If you looked/listened/felt/sensed/tasted closely enough, you might discern aspects of these relations and come to better understand their patterns and convergence. With this awareness and an unceasing inventive and imaginative approach, an artist could create new connections, new collisions, new arcs/arches.

Sharing. Giving. Collaborating. Improvising. Imagining. Dreaming. Pushing the limits. Building. Creating. Loving. These were colors in the spectrum of human vibrations. The bifurcations, the strange attractors, the crossroads that created new reactions, pathways, bends in the curve, and points of contact and intersection between different curves.

Another part of Abraham's analysis that resonated with Ben was the mathematician's criticisms of the American education system. Education and the evolving socioeconomic system of capitalism, according to Abraham, were "destroying the native intelligence that children have, the capability they have to understand the world around them in its complexity, in its chaos, in its resonance and harmony and love." Abraham thus insisted that there was a need for a "new educational system outside the usual channels of the school system," that is, a "school outside of school" where young people's embryonic, wondrous, and utilitarian capacities to perceive connections could be nurtured. And essential to this, Abraham concluded, was use of new technologies and networks of media, computation, and communication.

KAOS Network, Ben's newly reimagined technology-media-arts lab and community performance space, was conceived in response to this void. One of its first endeavors was *KAOS TV* (1991). This was a series of public access television episodes and vaudeville multimedia performances featuring the Hollywatts Posse and others. One episode, conceived and produced in response to the video of Rodney King's assault, forecasted the uprisings of 1992.

The episode was shot as if it was a CNN news special. Behind a backdrop of a huge map of L.A., the news report hosted by Roger was composed of different segments. Acting as a journalist, Kim Nickerson reported on the numerous missing and kidnapped Black women in L.A. The camera then panned to Mark Broyard, who stood outside KAOS's building. Mark, when cued, demonstrated for viewers "the proper cover-up technique" a person should resort to if stopped and attacked by the police. "Rodney got beat about the head quite a bit," Mark explained in the segment, "so you want to roll yourself on the ground into a ball and protect your head and your balls, because when they beat you with the baton you have to protect the most vital things. Either your head or your balls."

KAOS Network also became a hub for community events and educational programming: West African dance and djembe classes, spoken-word performances, comedy shows, mask-making and arts and crafts classes, bazaars, art exhibitions, film screenings, dance and yoga classes, experimental performance showcases, health and wellness seminars and informationals, and music and theater arts classes. And Ben insisted on keeping the rental fees reasonable, so that all sectors of the community could afford to use the space.

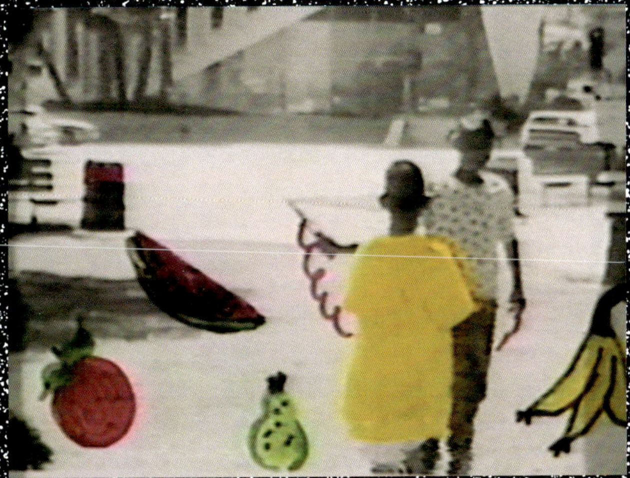

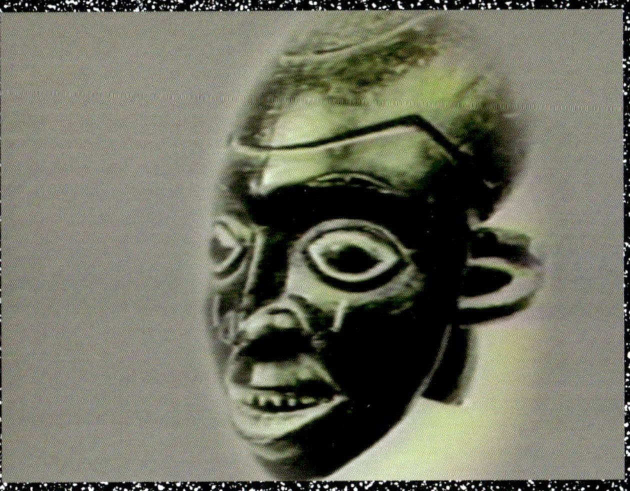

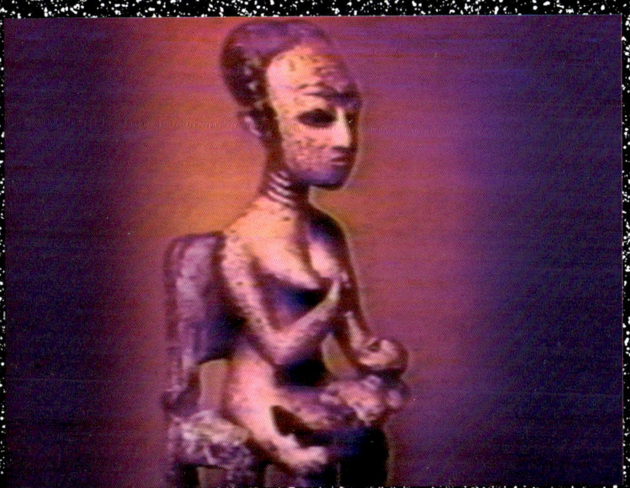

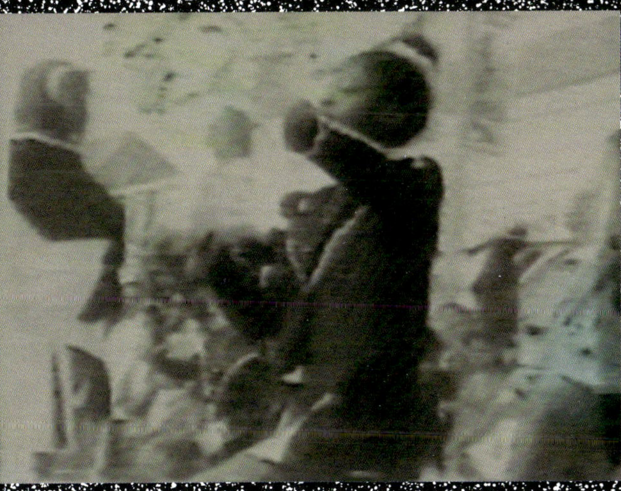

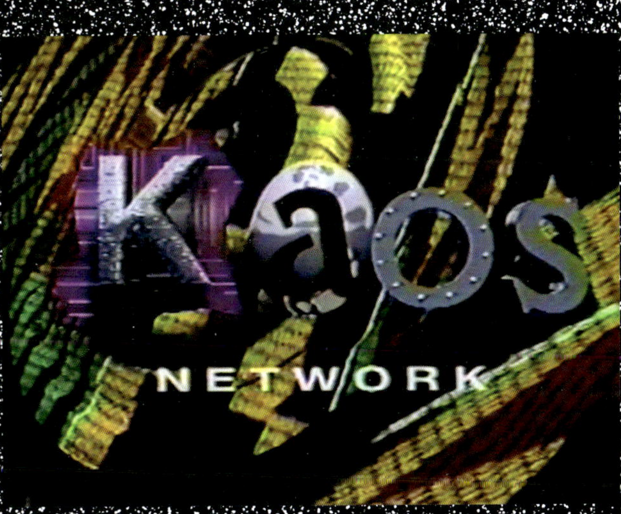

URBAN
YA YA

KAOS
NETWORK

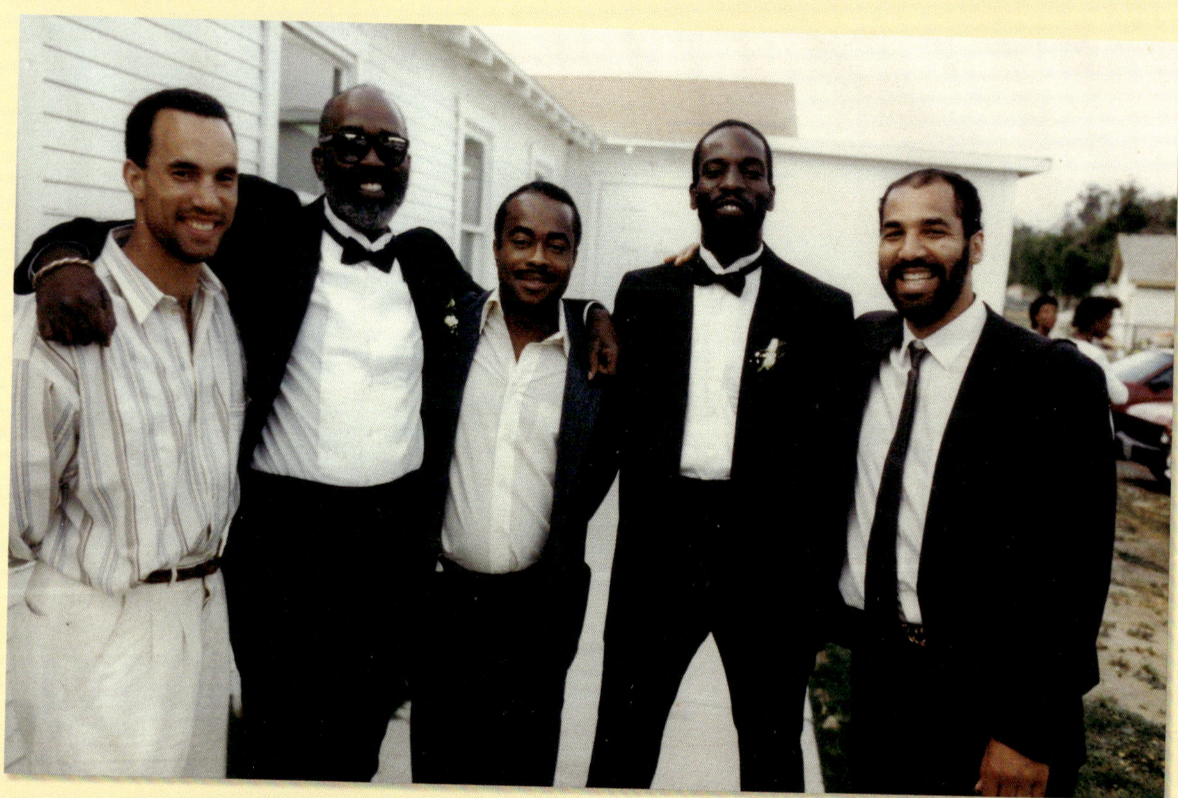

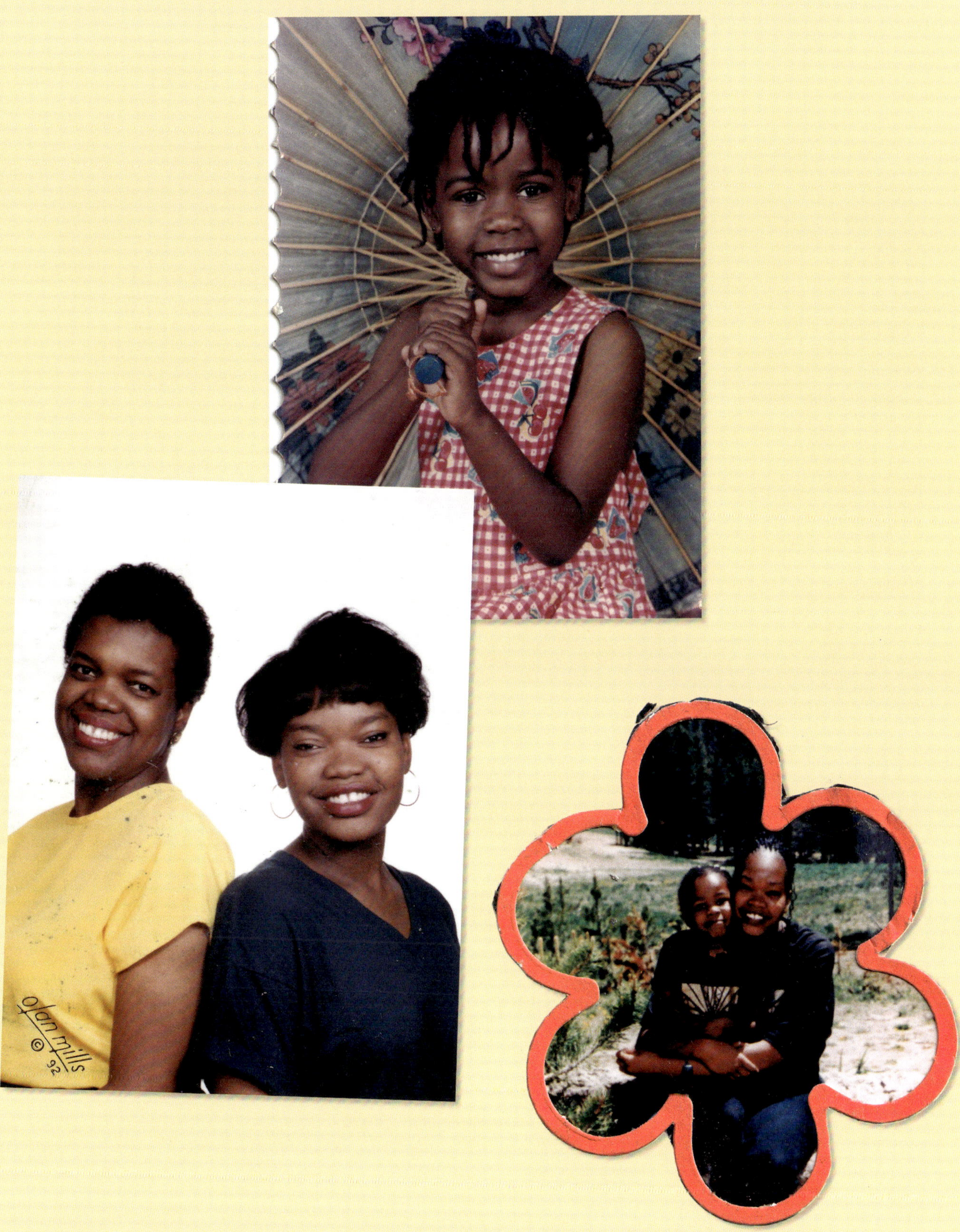

KAOS Network's doors and stage were open to everyone. Gay and queer Black men hosting drag-ball performances and house-ballroom gatherings after being kicked out of the downtown venue where they usually convened. Yoruba Christians seeking to congregate and worship together. And later, aspiring rappers, DJs, graffiti artists, and dancers in search of a space to have fun, make art, and be in fellowship.

It was through these different activities and events that KAOS Network became one of several storefront businesses to help rejuvenate the Village's cultural life. This included spots like the **World Stage Performance Gallery,** the live jazz performance space and writer's workshop created by master-drummer Billy Higgins and poet and community arts activist Kamau Daáood; **5th Street Dick's;** the **Dance Collective,** a dance studio cofounded by Pat Taylor, Nzingha Camara, and Lady Helena Walquer Vereen; **the Museum in Black,** an African American history, artifacts, and memorabilia shop run by Brian Breye; artist Ramses's art gallery; **Final Vinyl** record shop; and later Marla Gibbs' **Crossroads Arts Academy,** as well as the **African Drum Circle** that convened every Sunday in the park.

Running KAOS Network also enabled Ben to lean into VIDEO 3333's initial educational mission. The space frequently facilitated technology and media tutorials, workshops, and discussions. This was given a bigger boost once Ben was hired to teach at California Institute of the Arts (CalArts). There, he taught film editing, still photography, and video production. His favorite class was a jazz visualization course, in which he helped artists of different mediums consider how to employ philosophies, techniques, and strategies from Black music and expressive cultures within their respective mediums.

A key benefit of CalArts's loose and experimental educational culture was that Ben was able to periodically hold class sessions at KAOS Network and include his students in KAOS's different cultural and educational activities. Thus, over time, his educational and creative cultural initiatives came to be composed of CalArts and other university students, as well as young people from the Village and other surrounding neighborhoods.

Numerous young adults and teens made KAOS Network the place to be. Of course, there was Project Blowed's eclectic mix of emcees, artists, and creative rebels. And an important leader among this group was Tasha Wiggins. The Inglewood/Orange County-raised writer had just started working with *Rap Pages* Magazine when she met Ben, right around the time of the first Project Blowed event. They quickly developed a bond. Like Ben, Tasha had a two-year-old daughter, Asia, her baby girl born just a month after Ben and Lori's daughter Elizabeth. And like Ben, Tasha wanted to tell stories, particularly through film. But Tasha didn't know how to make her dream manifest. She was twenty years old with a baby. Her college acceptance offers instantly became less of a priority once Asia was born.

"Go finish school," Ben encouraged her during their first conversation, the two of them sweeping up the area outside of KAOS Network. It was a simple suggestion and discussion. And she listened. In the months that followed, she enrolled in Long Beach City College to pursue an associate's degree in journalism. She also began working at KAOS Network. She managed the door at Project Blowed. She helped sell Blowed members' music and merchandise.

Besides her positive attitude and savvy handling of Blowed's sometimes hyper-masculine atmosphere, what Tasha really brought to KAOS Network was a sharp business sense and skillset as a cultural translator, business manager, and event planner. With Ben and several others, she planned and coordinated a trip that brought Ben, Tasha, and several Blowedians to Havana, Cuba, to participate in cultural and musical exchanges with Cuban hip-hop performers and activists. The trip was sponsored partly by CalArts, leaving Ben and Tasha responsible for raising the rest of the funds. They ran fundraisers and wrote grants. And to ensure that the Blowedians would be permitted to travel to Cuba—a country that the U.S. government restricted American access to, with only a few exceptions (an important one being cultural and educational exchanges)—Tasha transported the crew to the Wilshire Federal Building for their visa appointments and assisted them with their applications.

The two weeks their group spent in Cuba was one for the ages. Each day, they met and interacted with Cuban emcees, educators, and grassroots organizers. Each day, they engaged in serious discussions and debates with these people and one another—exchanges that forced them to reflect and rethink their ideas and outlooks about numerous issues. U.S. consumer culture. The more distinctive African-ness and percussive traits of Cuban rap and culture. The history and living traditions of rhumba, salsa, and Santeria. The commonalities and historic connections between Black, Brown, and Indigenous American peoples. The fact that, even amid the U.S. government's embargo of Cuba and its resultant economic impact on Cuban life, many of the Cubans that the Blowedians met demonstrated a political aptitude and appreciation for life and culture that was shoulders above that of many Americans. The connections between their people's struggles for liberation and self-determination.

The Blowedians and their Cuban *compadres* also performed and recorded music together. With turntables, djembes, microphones, and their bodies, mouths, and voices, they shared and blended styles of sound, rhyme, and movement. Cuban emcees of the likes of rap duo Anónimo Consejo, Hermanos de Causa, and many others. Together, they danced and made music videos. They argued, listened, broke bread, and laughed. And in the end, the Blowedians left Cuba with a different perspective. "We see things here [in Cuba] that we'd like to have—the culture, that people are so alive here," Blowedian member Riddlore remarked in one of the filmed discussions from the trip. "We come here and we see that there's another way. That they have the bare necessities, but still they're strong, their pride, the sense of knowing who they are here, [something] that we don't have."

That was part of the trip's purpose, at least for Ben. He hoped that the experience would intensify the Blowedians' sense of connection to their brothers

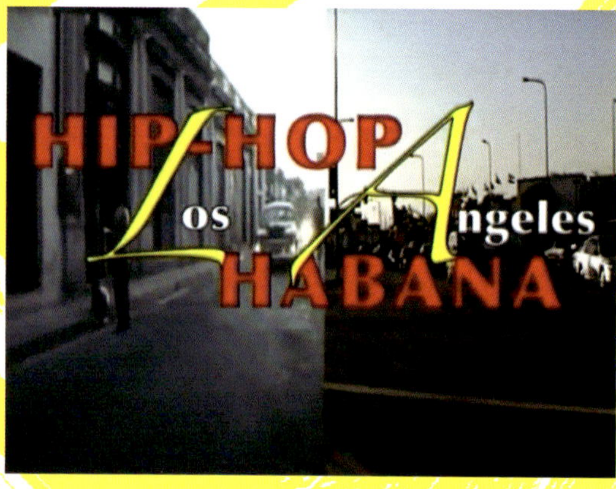
HIP-HOP
Los Angeles
HABANA

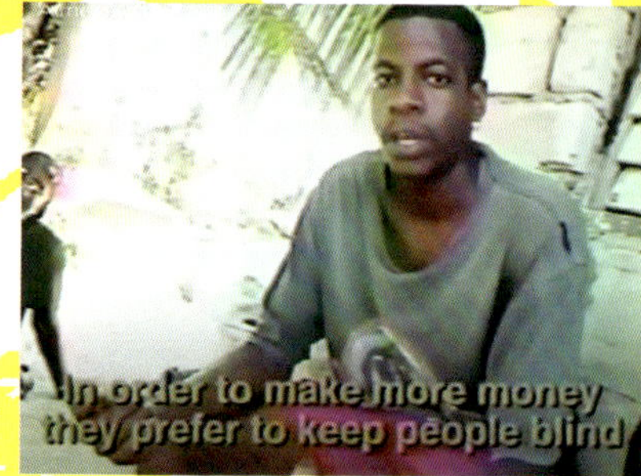
In order to make more money
they prefer to keep people blind

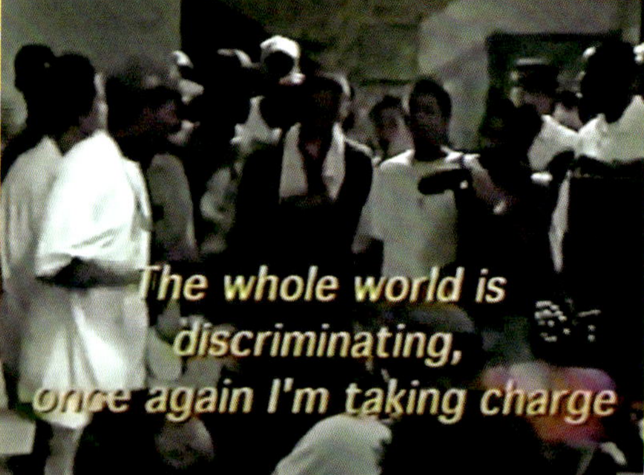
The whole world is
discriminating,
once again I'm taking charge

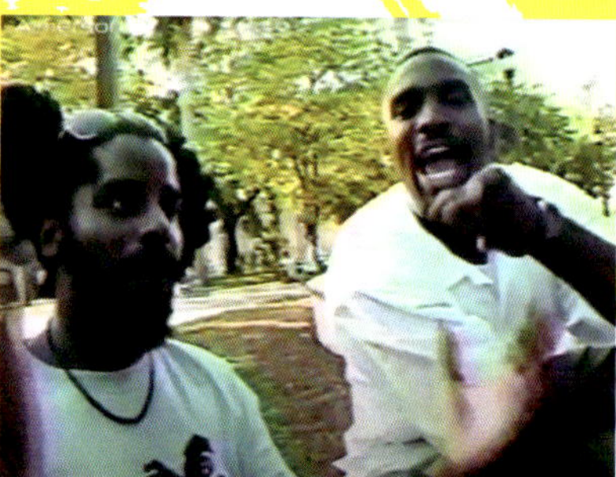

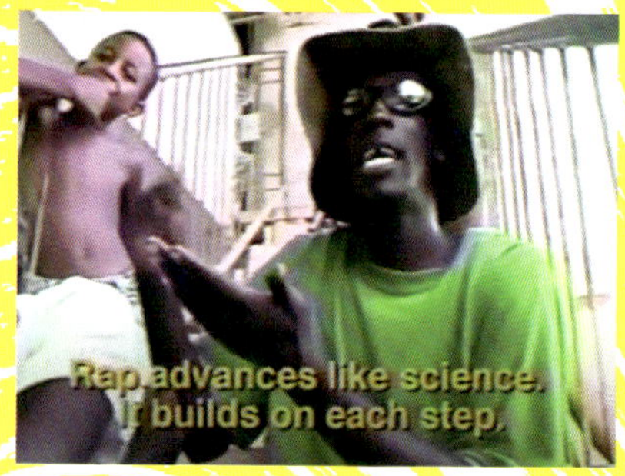
Rap advances like science,
it builds on each step.

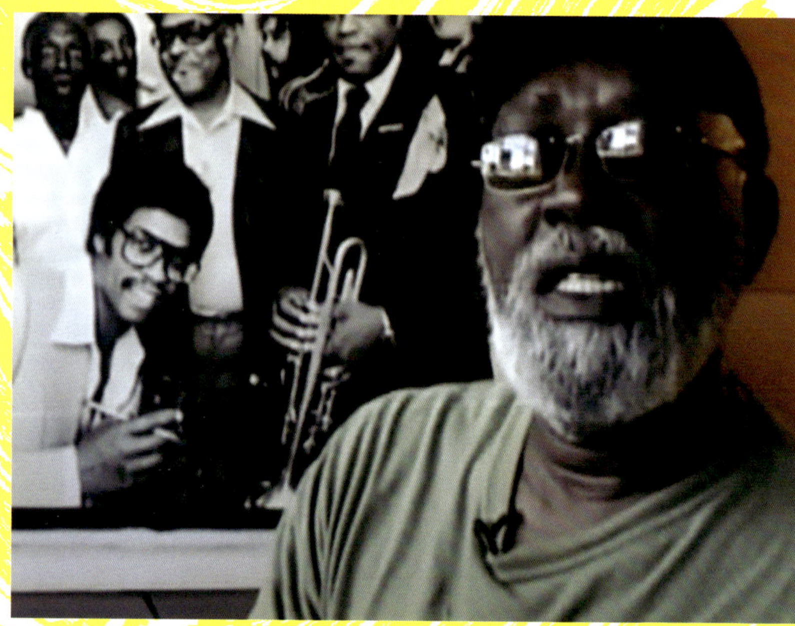

and sisters in Cuba. And that it would serve as a reminder throughout their lives of the power of art, media and culture. Their crew would return to Cuba over subsequent years, and it was these experiences, as well Tasha's work aiding Ben in creating a documentary about these travels, that played a role in her future admission into UCLA's School of Theater, Film, and Television to complete her undergraduate studies.

She wasn't the only person contributing to KAOS Network's ethos of creative community. Alongside Tasha, Glen "Gee Dawg" Williams was another of its more unconventional and extraordinary members. The Compton eleventh grader first visited KAOS Network in the spring of 1994. He was sent there by his Centennial High School instructor and mentor, Ms. Charletta Johnson.

Earlier in the academic year, Charletta had proposed that Centennial High produce a video yearbook. She expected school leadership to reject her suggestion. For years, she had pushed its administration to provide more media- and technology-based classes and opportunities, but often to no avail. Still, Charletta was relentless. She would find media and technology programs and workshops outside the school and then broker spots for her students. And Glen was one of her students who always participated. Hence, when Centennial's leadership surprised Charletta by approving her video yearbook idea, she recommended Glen to produce the project.

Glen spent that academic year video-recording classes, music and arts clubs, pep rallies, sports competitions, and students kicking it in the lunchroom and outside the building. He had a blast documenting the school's culture. But then he hit a roadblock. Filming was one thing. Editing the footage was something else! Glen needed help. So Charletta sent Glen to Ben.

When the seventeen-year-old arrived at KAOS Network, he was taken aback. Though raised in Compton King's Triangle (a redevelopment community in the northern section of Compton, near Martin Luther King Jr. Community Hospital), he had grown up visiting the Village. His family frequently ventured there to attend Jehovah's Witness circuit assembly meetings at the Watchtower theater, located just two doors down from Ben's studio. Yet neither he nor his family ever really knew what was going down inside Ben's space.

KAOS Network contained numerous books, poster-sized photographs of Black political and cultural icons, large works of graffiti, and an abundance of technological equipment. Video cameras, televisions, computers, and film and video editing equipment. Glen's eyes grew wide. Never in his life had he been around so much technology. Glen was also amazed to see that the people using KAOS's technology that day were rappers and producers that he recognized. Crazy! But even crazier was his realization that the middle-aged, hiply dressed man in the middle of the room was the person Glen was there to meet and seek assistance from.

Ben and Wesley Groves ultimately helped Glen edit the yearbook. In the months that followed, Glen periodically returned to KAOS Network. He would

try to appear nonchalant, but he was always excited when he arrived. He was smitten with the creative energy, technological know-how, and innovation brewing inside the space. Without a doubt, it was an extreme contrast to the other space where he dedicated much of his time.

Glen was a member of the Tree Top Pirus, a Blood set also known as the West Side Trees. He joined the gang at fourteen, a few years after his parents split up. The end of their marriage and their long working hours meant Glen was often left to his own devices. It was during this interval of his life that he began to hang out on the block more frequently, usually with the older boys who kicked it on Compton's westside, just south of Rosecrans Avenue, along a group of streets named after trees.

It wasn't like he woke up one day and decided to gangbang. It was the outcome of a long socialization process. Of many days kicking it with the same folks, some of whom might happen to be in the gang or affiliated with it. And of proximity. Where you lived, where you hung out, and where you went to school often shaped who you were cool with. Glen had grown up with homeboys in the set. Several were like extended family members, "brothers from a different mother." And they always had his back, no matter what.

This was crucial. Despite being a village of roughly ten square miles, Compton, like much of Los Angeles, had become engulfed by gangs. Since the late 1970s, L.A. had endured a rapid increase in street gang membership, most centrally among Black and Brown organizations. The number of gangs exploded over the course of the 1980s; by 1993, there were somewhere between 57,000 and 61,000 gang members in L.A., according to police reports. In conjunction with other systemic factors, the rise in gang membership helped to intensify gang strife over territory, identity, and the drug trade. Ultimately this had a cataclysmic effect. There were more than 3,300 gang-related murders in L.A. during this period, what historian Mike Davis described as L.A.'s own "murderous arc." From 1989 to 1993, there were more than 6,327 drive-by shootings and a steady increase in the total number of gang-related homicides each year. These numbers were further compounded by the violent response of the LAPD, which included the massive number of gang sweeps, arrests, and killings by LAPD.

Being young, Black, and from Compton put Glen and thousands of other teens at extreme risk. And although gang-related homicides in L.A. began to decline after the 1992 Uprisings (which some people posited as the result of a citywide cease-fire agreement developed by several Watts gangs), gang culture and violence nonetheless remained an ever-present part of life in the city.

Still, even amid the violence and conflict, the set provided Glen with a community, a village of sorts. And the most important of all was Glen's best friend, Joseph "Joe Boy" Davis. Glen and Joe Boy had been best friends since they were kids, both boys' families worshiping together as Jehovah's Witnesses. Joe Boy was two years older than Glen and looked out for him throughout their time at Dickinson Elementary and Benjamin O. Davis Middle School. Anyone bigger than Glen who stepped to him had to get through Joe Boy first.

It was Joe Boy who convinced Glen to take rap seriously. Glen had grown up around music production, with his uncle running an independent rap label in Compton. Yet, while Glen thought rapping was cool, he felt that making beats and creating songs was even cooler. He and Joe Boy pooled their money to purchase their own equipment and began producing songs for their friends. Over time, it became clear that rather than create songs for others, they would be better off putting out their own music. So the two focused on honing their skills as rappers and producers. In 1994, they released a demo with several songs. They called their group The Low Lifes.

When Glen told Charletta, she initially rolled her eyes. "The LOW LIFES?!" she asked. "That's the name y'all came up with?" But Glen convinced her that he and Joe Boy had talent and were serious about making music. Charletta gave it some thought and decided to support the duo. At first glance, the two young men were an interesting contrast. Lean, medium-brown Glen and the stocky, Black-Mexican Joe Boy. And while their songs' lyrics were dark, the narratives effectively spoke of the grim realities of being young, marginalized, and Black in L.A.'s low-income communities.

So Charletta took a risk. She rented studio time for them to record their first album, Gee Dawg 'N' Joe Boy's *They Don't Understand* (1996). And she helped them negotiate a distribution deal with Solar Records—home to acts such as Shalamar, the Whispers, Lakeside, Midnight Star, and the Deele—whose foray into hip-hop was producing the soundtrack for the film *Deep Cover* (1992). With a completed album and distribution deal in hand, Charletta and the Low Lifes reached out to Ben, seeking help with filming their first music video on a shoe-string budget.

The music video for the album's lead song, "They Don't Understand" (1995), was produced by Charletta and Ben, edited by Glen and Wesley Groves, and directed by Chris Shank, one of Ben's CalArts students. The video opens with the song's hook, a melodically sung four-bar stanza:

> *They complain about my saggin' pants*
> *The way I stand in my gangsta stance*
> *They don't understand*
> *Why I must be that way*

The video features shots of Gee Dawg and Joe Boy dressed in red shirts, rapping in abandoned lots, alleys, and amid barbed wire fences. Sometimes it's just the two of them rapping, and in other shots their homeboys stand around them staring into the camera. The video is also composed of a montage of shots: an attempted drive-by shooting, men scattering to avoid the gunshots; men on the verge of fighting in front of a crowd; a far-off light surrounded by darkness, the light resembling that of a slide projector as well as the helicopters that surveil L.A. at night; and a bottle smashing on the ground. As these images are displayed, Joe Boy raps:

It's like this, it's like that
Always on my back
None of this, none of that
Expecting a youngsta to tap
Into the same frame of mind
In a different period of time
Back in the day bats and chains were used
But now I'm dodging nines
So please
Ease off those stories you be telling me
On how you hanged and banged
Cause man that ain't your history
Realize, open your eyes
I know that it tends to make you cry
Terrorized, mother's eyes
Wondering if I'm going to die
But them the events I gotta go through
It ain't cool
Pondering on the homies
Lost a man, hope it's only a few
Dippin' limos to the funerals in large numerals . . .

As Joe Boy raps these last lines, the video shows someone opening the door of a white limo. A young Black man steps out of the vehicle. This image is then overlaid by a photograph of another young Black man. This sequence is repeated several times, each time displaying a different person stepping out of the limo overlaid by a different photograph. At one point the overlaid image displays a funeral program booklet with a young man's picture on the cover. The sequence is quick but makes a lasting impression. Gee Dawg, Joe Boy, and their crew are forced to constantly attend funeral services for their friends, teenaged and young adult homeboys who continue to be slain in the springtime of their lives.

Joe Boy's rap continues:

Retaliation is the aftermath
I got to blast
On the lame suckers
That left my homies in the bloodbath
Incarceration can be a consequence

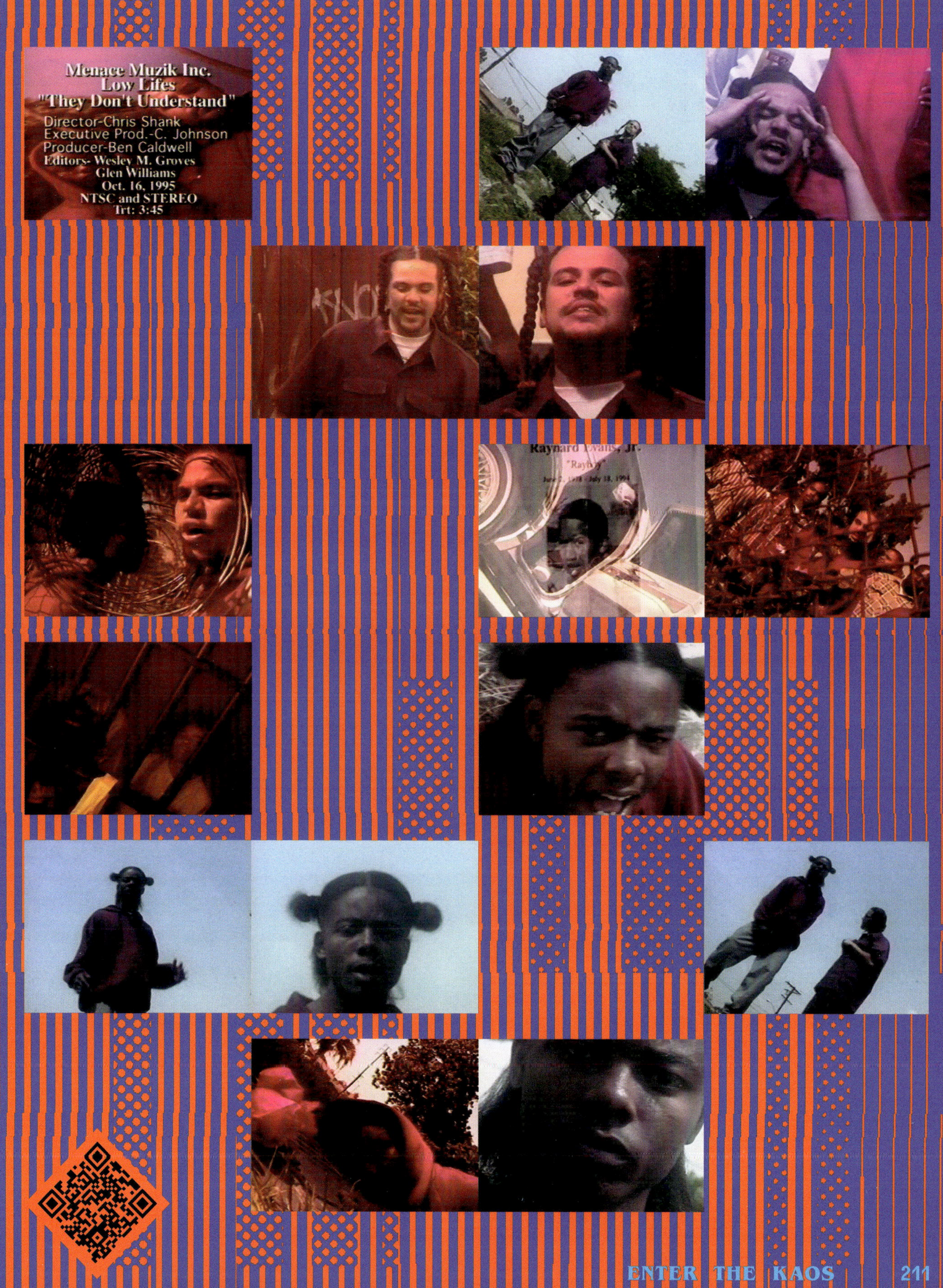
Menace Muzik Inc.
Low Lifes
"They Don't Understand"
Director-Chris Shank
Executive Prod.-C. Johnson
Producer-Ben Caldwell
Editors- Wesley M. Groves
Glen Williams
Oct. 16, 1995
NTSC and STEREO
Trt: 3:45

Joe Boy's opening verse offers startling and heartbreaking commentary. He relays that it is difficult for him and his peers to accept the insights of their elders, even the OGs (original gangsters) who grew up in earlier generations of gang warfare. The gang culture of his generation, he insists, is on a far different level than previous eras. The intensity of the violence and the conditions of poverty and incarceration, he states, are a pressure cooker that produces unavoidable reactions among Compton's young. Why? Because these people have few other means of "easing [their] pain," Joe Boy relays. Violence and death thus become means of negotiating depression and the constant sensation of "feeling drained." Joe Boy concludes that despite what some people might think, he doesn't believe that he and his peers are mentally ill. Moreover, if they are, their psychosis is not of their own doing. No, it's the result of the world they have been forced to exist within. They are the subjects of a bigger system—"the ghetto"—which wants to "can" them, which is organized around them living with/amid death, killing one another, and dying young.

Joe Boy's lyrics were prophetic. He was killed in a shootout at a party just before the release of the album, mere months after Glen's graduation from Centennial High.

Clearly Joe Boy had sensed that death was near. On "Death's Knockin'," the album's third cut, he and Gee Dawg rap about having to live in everyday proximity to death. But there were other omens. In the summer months, just before Joe Boy's murder, someone shot into Glen's house. A bullet tore through his framed high school diploma, its velocity leaving a coin-sized hole in the glass and document.

The symbolism of the bullet hole in the diploma wasn't lost on Glen. He had to get out of Compton. If not, he would end up in jail or dead like Joe Boy.

Academically, he had done well in his final year of high school. He had produced the school's second video yearbook entirely on his own, and with Charletta and Ben's help, he had received a scholarship to study video, technology, and media at CalArts over the summer. In fact, the video yearbooks were the samples of his work that he submitted with his application to CalArts.

Charletta and Ben stepped in. After Glen finished the CalArts program, Charletta opened her Crenshaw district home to him, providing him with a safe space to live and maneuver away from Compton. There, he was able to focus on his studies and complete a music business certificate program at UCLA.

Ben hired Glen as part of his staff on several projects. The first undertaking was called *L.A. Link* (1996). It was an Internet-video-conferencing collaboration conceived by video artist Wendy Clarke (the daughter of filmmaker Shirley Clarke, Ben's UCLA professor) and produced by KAOS Network and Michael Renov and Marita Sturken, two faculty members from the University of Southern California's Annenberg Center for Communication. The project grew out of Clarke's past video work, most centrally *Lovetapes* (1977–2011) and *One on One* (1991–1994), two projects where Clarke video-interviewed people of diverse backgrounds and produced video dialogues between the participants about different topics.

Whereas Clark's previous endeavors relied on video, *L.A. Link* followed the lead of Ben's 1980s Electronic Café work. It fused the then-emerging ISDN (Integrated Services Digital Network) Internet technology to connect teenagers from two geographically and culturally segregated communities: students at the private, elite Santa Monica Crossroads School for Arts & Sciences, and youngsters from South Central Los Angeles participating in KAOS Network's after-school program. The purpose was to see if, and how, the Internet and digital tools might facilitate or prevent cultural exchange, learning, and connection between similarly aged Angelenos from very different communities who might never have come into contact, despite being separated by only a few geographic miles.

Over the course of several months, the two groups communicated via computers in two discrete locations—a Crossroads School classroom and KAOS Network's media lab. At both locations, there was a deck that recorded the computer's digitized footage and audio. Production/tech teams at both locations also used hi-8 cameras to film each group in its respective setting, as well as their conversations with the participants in the other setting.

In these discussions, the groups shared information about themselves, their families, and their communities, and discussed and debated a range of topics. What it was like to be a teenager. What music and films they enjoyed. The complexity of gender dynamics and romantic relationships. Sex. Teen pregnancy. Abortion. Their assumptions about each other. The students also participated in interactive exercises. Back-and-forth freestyle poetry and rapping sessions. Theater and role-playing games. Sharing something deeply personal. Lastly, the students created monthly video diaries. In these segments, each student was filmed by themselves, where they then offered candid reflections about the group discussions and about the differences and intersections between the two groups.

Initially, the teens left the discussions frustrated, angry, and discouraged. "We're just so different from one another," many of them remarked. The technology also made it easy for them to misinterpret one another, and this bred arguments. They would talk over one another and spend more time bickering than listening.

But over time, the groups began to look forward to their sessions. Things became less tense. More fun. They wrote notes that they shared on the screens. They blamed their disagreements on the technology, rather than on one another. And they began to listen closely and emphatically, opening themselves up to one another's humanity, opening themselves up to one another's unique perspectives and insights. They soon began to find humor and connection in similar things and see the uniqueness of the experience that they were sharing. And with this they developed a bond and a camaraderie.

Glen helped manage the technology for the project and was one of its lead participants. Each week, he used the discussions and video diaries to share very personal things about himself. He often did this through improvisatory, stream-of-consciousness spoken-word poems and raps. He would talk about his decision to leave the gang. His desire to change. His craving to find purpose.

For many of the student participants, Glen's diary contributions revealed a world that they only knew through news media and popular culture. His contemplative reflections and thoughtful commentary offered them a stark, sobering counter-narrative to the images glamorized in gangsta rap music and the entertainment industry at large.

L.A. Link concluded with the two groups finally meeting in person at KAOS Network and sharing a meal at M & M Soul Food. In the months that followed, Glen helped Wendy Clarke edit the footage of the project into a one-hour documentary. He also served as its music supervisor.

Thereafter, he continued to work with KAOS Network, most centrally on its collaborations with CalArts' Community Arts Partnership (CAP). CAP was a university-community partnership that offered free university-level arts and technology training and education for preteen, teen, and adult students from under-resourced communities. The classes were held at community arts organizations across Los Angeles: initially KAOS Network in Leimert Park, Plaza de la Raza in East L.A., Inner City Arts in downtown L.A., and Watts Tower Arts Center in Watts. In subsequent years, other organizations were added to the project. This included the Armory Center for the Arts in Pasadena, the L.A. Center for Photographic Studies and Side Street Projects in Altadena, the Santa Clarita

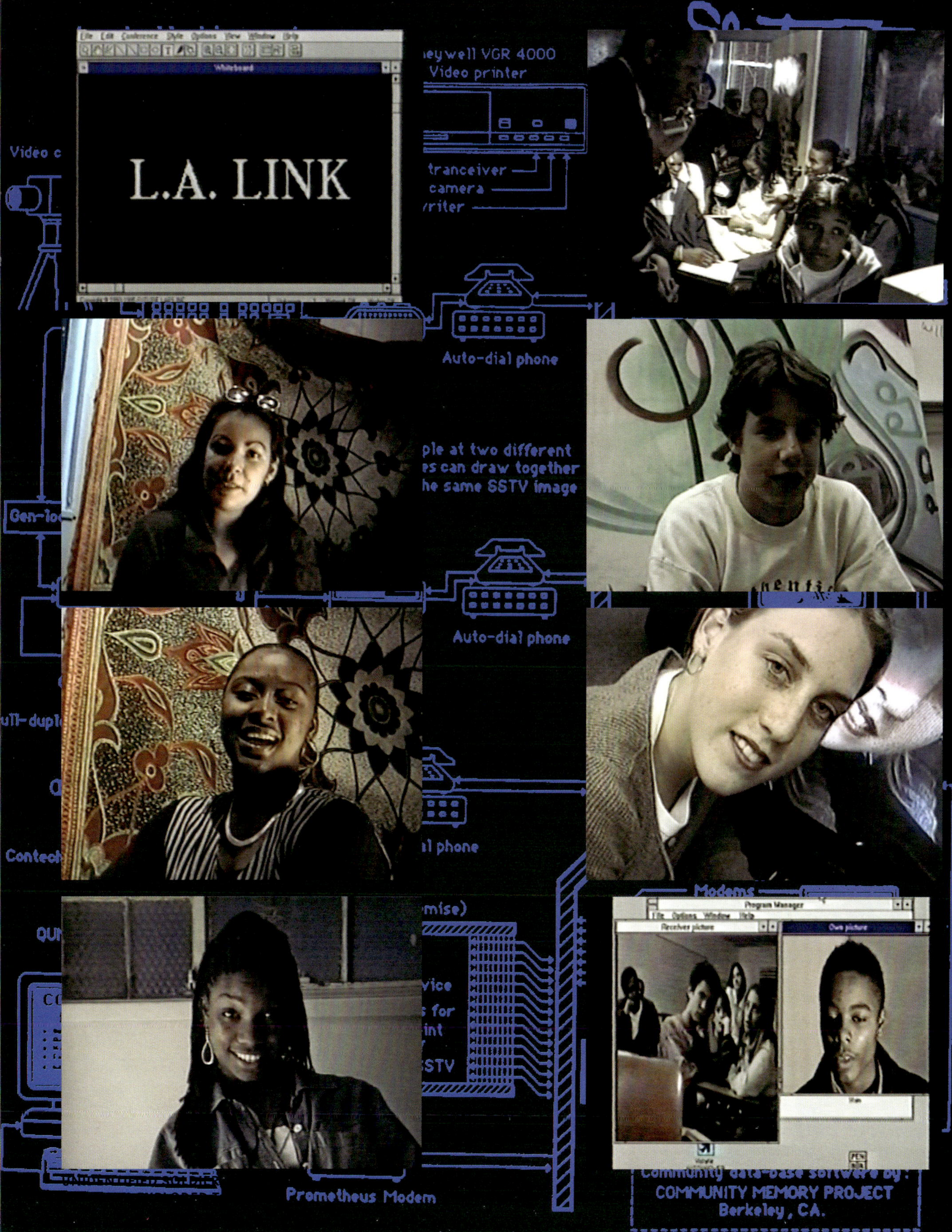
L.A. LINK
Whiteboard
File Edit Conference Style Options View Window Help
Honeywell VGR 4000
Video printer
Video c
tranceiver
camera
writer
Auto-dial phone
ple at two different
es can draw together
he same SSTV image
Auto-dial phone
Gen-lo
ll-dupl
al phone
Conteo
mise)
QU
vice
s for
int
y
SSTV
Modems
Program Manager
File Options Window Help
Receive picture
Own picture
Prometheus Modem
Community data-base software by:
COMMUNITY MEMORY PROJECT
Berkeley, CA.

Valley Boys and Girls Club, Self Help Graphics & Art in East L.A., and Visual Communications in Little Tokyo. At each location, lead teachers and technologists (whose official designation was "Digital Arts Coordinator") instructed students in web development, ISDN video teleconferencing, and digital graphic arts. Students from these different communities also interacted with each other, first via ISDN, and eventually in person. Ultimately, the projects culminated with two CD-Rom-based websites—"Digital Playground" (1997–1998) and "Digiscapes" (2000–2001)—each of which featured the creative work and media produced by these students.

Glen initially served as a class coordinator at KAOS Network and the lead HTML and JavaScript programmer for the "Digital Playground" CD-ROM-based website. But by the point of releasing "Digiscapes," he was the lead Digital Arts coordinator at the Watts Tower Arts Center's CAP location. Working out of a trailer near the Arts Center, Glen taught middle school and high school students, as well as adult residents, the ins and outs of website design, HTML coding, and graphic arts. To his students and mentees, he wasn't Glen or Gee Dawg. Just Mr. G.

One afternoon, he heard music playing from a computer in the trailer. He didn't recognize it. It was raw. An instrumental still lacking lyrics and mixing. But it was distinctive and good. It had a decent balance of bass, drums, synthesizer, and pacing. "Whose music is this?" he asked. "Who made this?" No one knew. Subsequently, over the next few days, Glen periodically played the CD inside the computer, hoping that its creator would pop up.

Glen never found the person who produced the song. The person found him.

Glen was in a daze that day. He had just completed a long web tutorial for a group of middle schoolers and was feeling tired and ready to head home.

"You the one that's been playing my music?!" a sharp tenor voice bellowed from behind. Glen turned around to see who was causing the fuss. In front of him stood a skinny, tall, Eritrean-looking teenager with curly hair and a long face. Beside the teen were two of his homeboys. *He can't be older than sixteen*, Glen thought to himself. But the kid stood straight up, shoulders wide, as if he were a grown man. His squinted eyes locked in on Glen, waiting for him to say the wrong thing.

"Yeah, I'm the one," Glen replied. "I've been waiting to meet you. Your music is really good." The teen looked at Glen long and hard, as if in a state of disbelief. "You serious?" the young man asked. Glen nodded. Then the teen's eyes widened and brightened a bit. He nodded back gingerly, still unsure of what to make of Mr. G's feedback. Then he walked out of the trailer, his homeboys in tow.

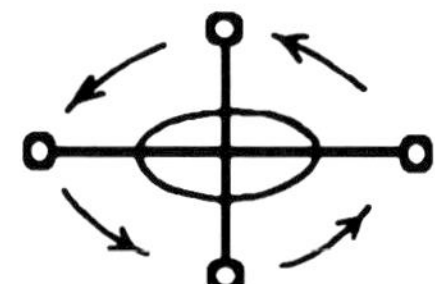

The exchange was an echo of another encounter—one which took place thirty years before, inside a bomb shelter in Vietnam's Central Highlands. Different people, different villages, different moments in time.

What other feedback loops and threads bind these people?

A migrant sharecropper and bluesman-ballplayer turned projectionist-community-leader. His grandson and cultural heir—a filmmaker whose practice is similarly informed by music and nature, who also weaves mentoring with community stewardship. The high school graduate who wants to be a painter and an animator. A young mother in the future who wants to write and make films.

An enslaved North African explorer who became a mystic and a healer. The soldier who cast aside his rifle for a 35mm Yashica camera. The teen who picked up a VHS camera and a microphone.

Brothers, sisters, and childhood friends—their innocence stolen. Generations of downtrodden people. Assaulted, violated, slaughtered in the springtime of their lives. White supremacy, empire, poverty, policing, imprisonment, war.

Wayward people who gift gardens and plots for rumination and imagining. Rebel educators, sages, and life-guides who sow seeds.

The rhythms, repetition, vibrations, and cosmic pull of Black experimentalism, vernacular life, and world-making. The assemblage and improvisation required to build and sustain families and kinship networks and villages.

Reciprocity. Communion with the living, the dead, and the in-between. The power and mystery of sparks, glitches, scratches, flashes. Spirit guides and guardian angels.

Bare feet on muddied soil. Torsos swaying and upended in a storefront after-school program. Body submerged in earth. Healing. Endurance.

Just like Ben, Glen had been at a crossroads. And just like Ben, with art, media, and community, Glen too was discovering his source and otherworlds. It was another split in the bend, a new series of collisions. More stitches in the patterns, echoes, and resonances of Black community and Black love. **KAOS Theory.**

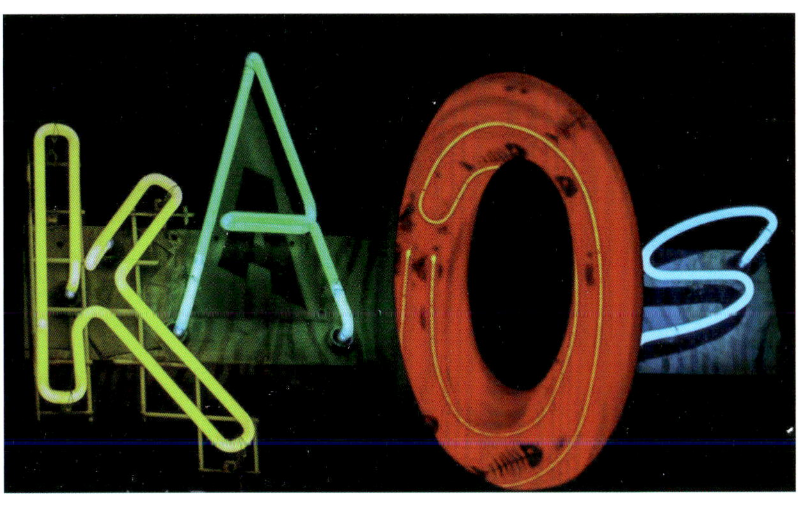

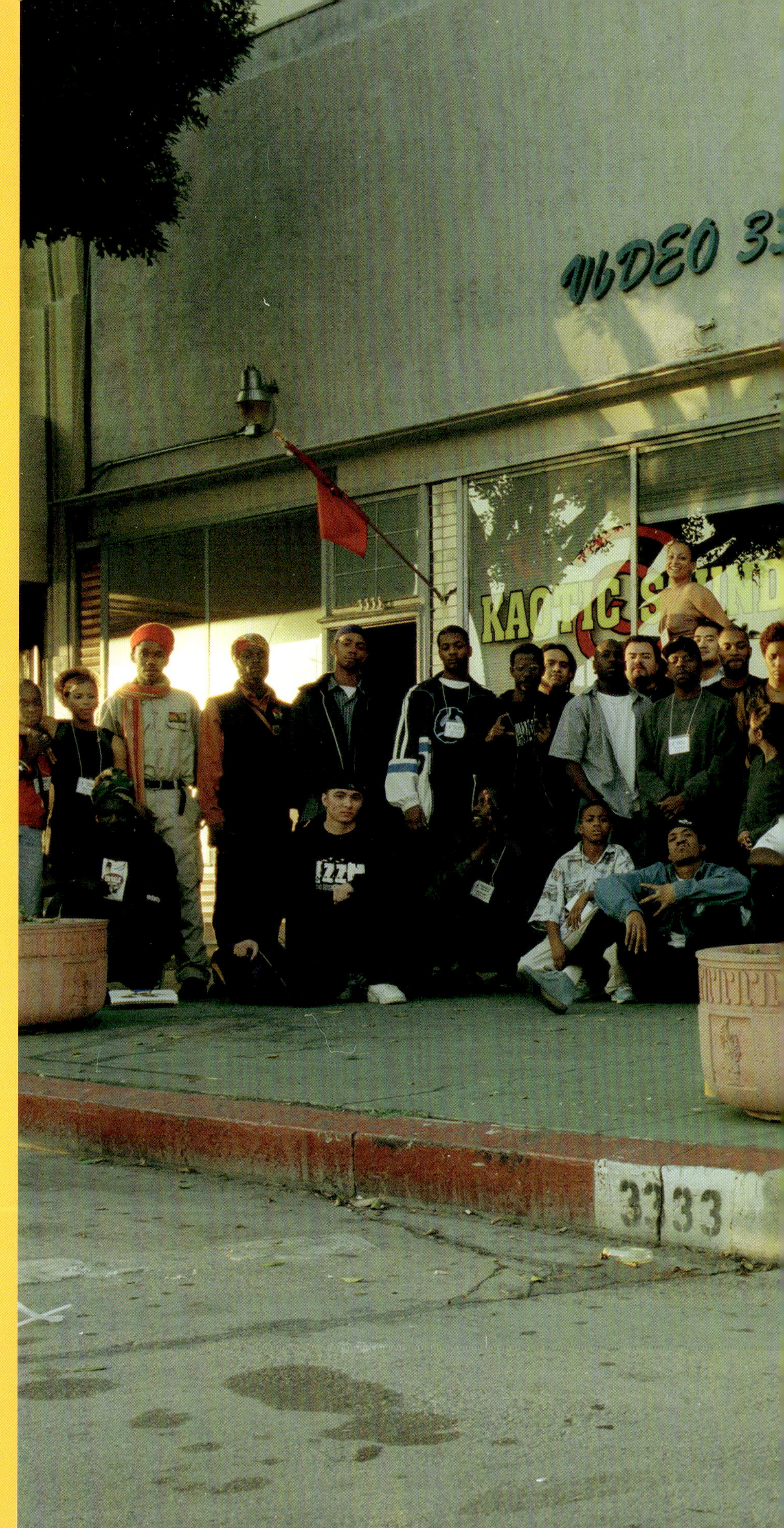

PROJECT BLOWED OUTSIDE
KAOS NETWORK, 1999/2000

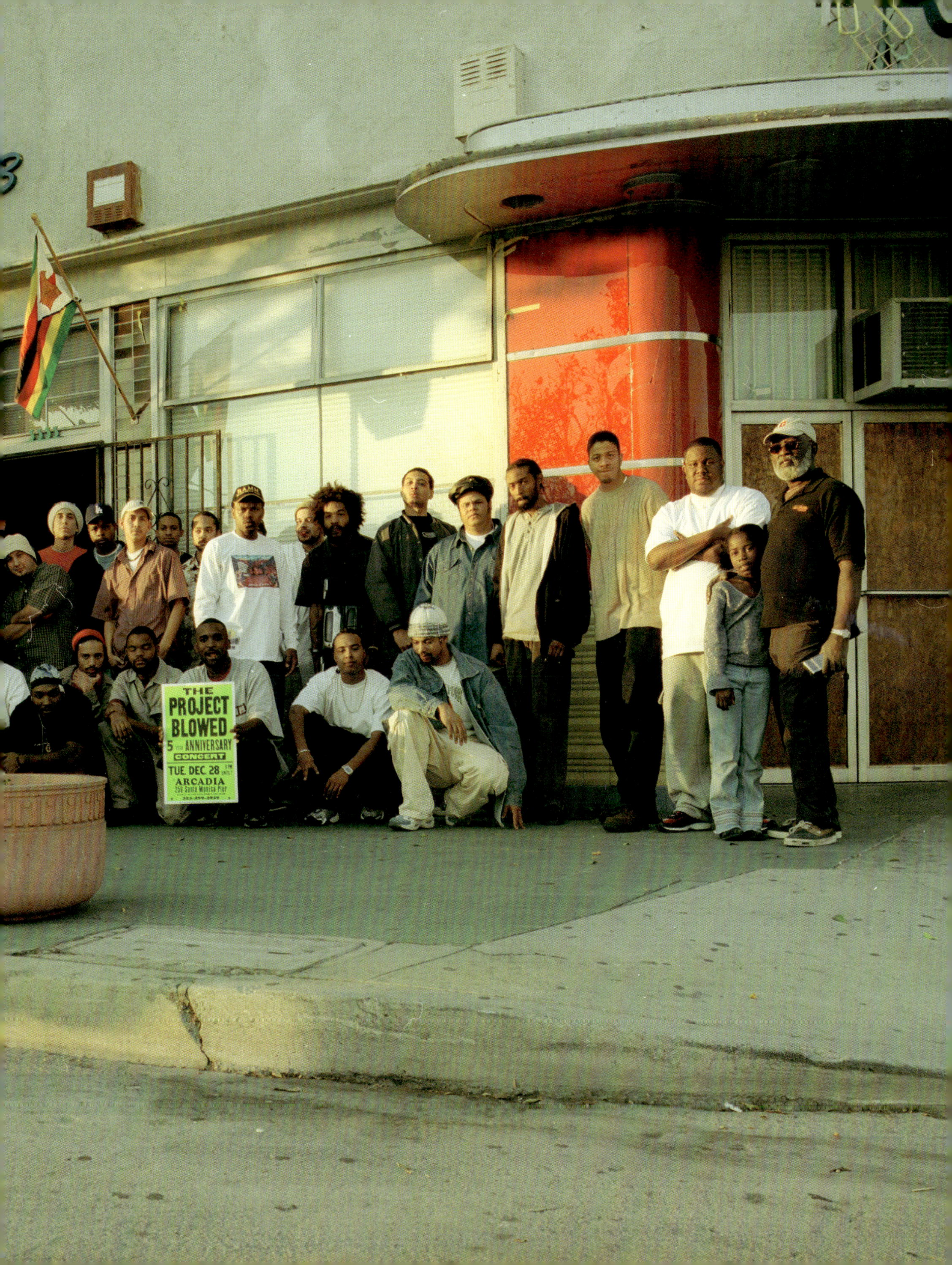

THE
PROJECT
BLOWED
5TH ANNIVERSARY
CONCERT
TUE DEC 28
ARCADIA
250 Santa Monica Pier

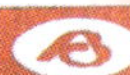

POLICE-STUDENT ENCOUNTER

60 Cops, 150
Students Cla
In Leimert P

By MICHAEL DATCHER
Staff Writer

In a troubling incident last Thursday, police clashed with students who were attending a weekly urban poetry workshop.

Over 60 policemen in riot gear converged on a crowd of about 150 workshop participants and closed it down.

According to several eyewitnesses, when the crowd was slow to disperse and began to verbally protest, the officers responded by prodding the crowd with batons.

Medusa, a rap artist who regularly attends the workshop was involved in the incident that set off the melee.

"My friend and I had just returned from getting tea when [the police] lined up in riot formation and started pushing people," she said.

"There I am, carrying this steaming hot tea, walking and telling the cop he doesn't have to push me."

"Some of the hot tea splatters on the [police officer's] hand and he just loses it. He swings the baton at my

suspicion of assault
weapon on a peace o
said. They were being
$50,000 bail.

Professor Ben C
teaches a class called
Music at prestigious A
Institute said, "The [
Leimert Park] is an ex
Cal Arts class.

See Leimert on p

Lawyer
Pat Mo
Quits C

Ollie Manago, th
ex-Compton City (
Patricia Moore, filed
asking to be remove
stating she is sufferi
and physical illnesse

Manago, Moore'
in her federal extort
sion case, said in her
"now faces the risk o

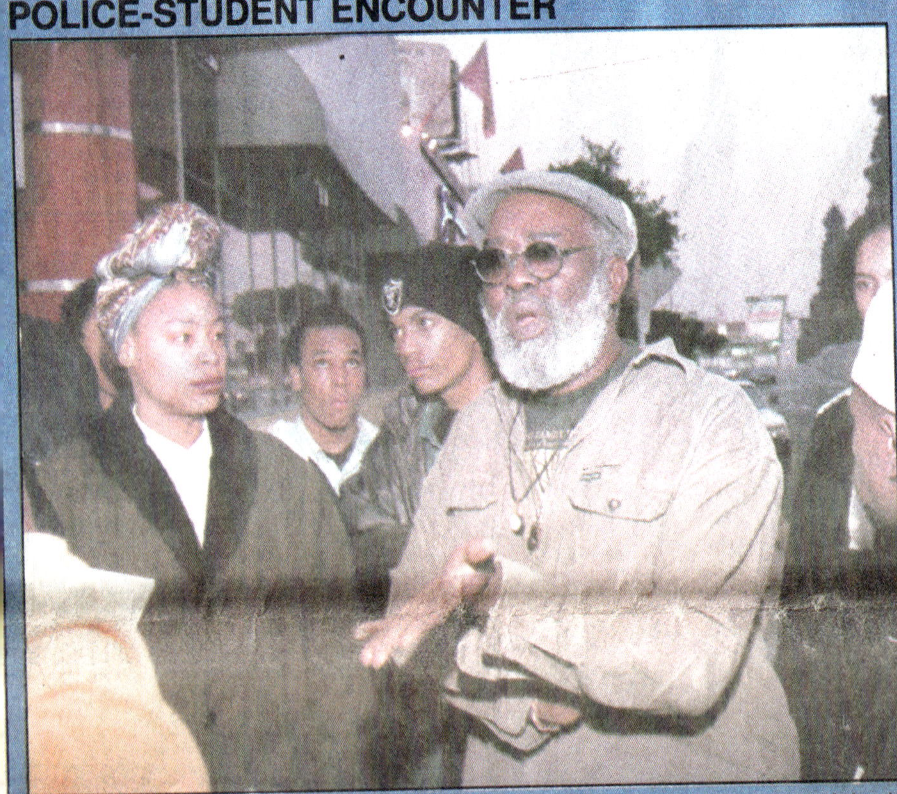

OUTRAGED BUSINESSMAN—Ben Caldwell, center, owner of Kaos Network, an urban poetry workshop in Leimert Park, talks to reporters following last week's encounter between the police and some of his students. A student known as Medusa (in head wrap), was one of the persons involved in the melee. SENTINEL PHOTO COURTESY MICHAEL RIDDICK

You Are Now About To Enter
project blowed
READ THIS FIRST!!!!!

✓ NO **SMOKING** OR **DRINKING ALCOHOL** IN HERE! The owner has "requested" that this be a no-alcohol, no smoking business. Fa' sho'.

✓ THERE IS OPEN MIKE AT THE *BEGINNING* AND AT THE *END*. NO ONE WHO IS NOT CALLED FROM THE LIST BY THE HOST CAN GET ON STAGE *AT ANY OTHER TIME*! REMEMBER THAT!

✓ This is a Hip Hop Educational Seminar, where styles are shown so many can learn and grow. *DO NOT BITE STYLES*, BECAUSE YOU LEARN NOTHING! **DO NOT GET VIOLENT**, BECAUSE THIS IS A BLACK-OWNED, BLACK-OPERATED BUSINESS THAT CAN'T AFFORD TO HEAR THAT! **Take that stuff to WestWood**.

✓ Project Blowed is presented for the love of hip hop entirely by Black people. However, it **can't** get done if everybody's bills don't get paid, so we charge the "participants" TWO DOLLARS to practice their styles, and we charge FOUR DOLLARS to people who want to watch education at work. This pays for using the building, the sound, and keeping it going on - also known as THE CAUSE of keeping hip hop underground.

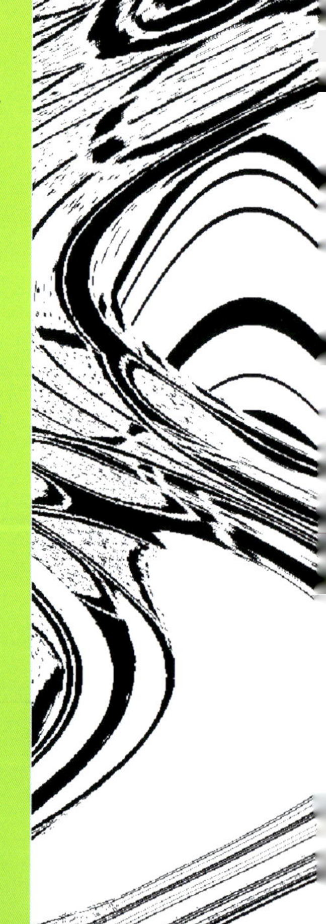

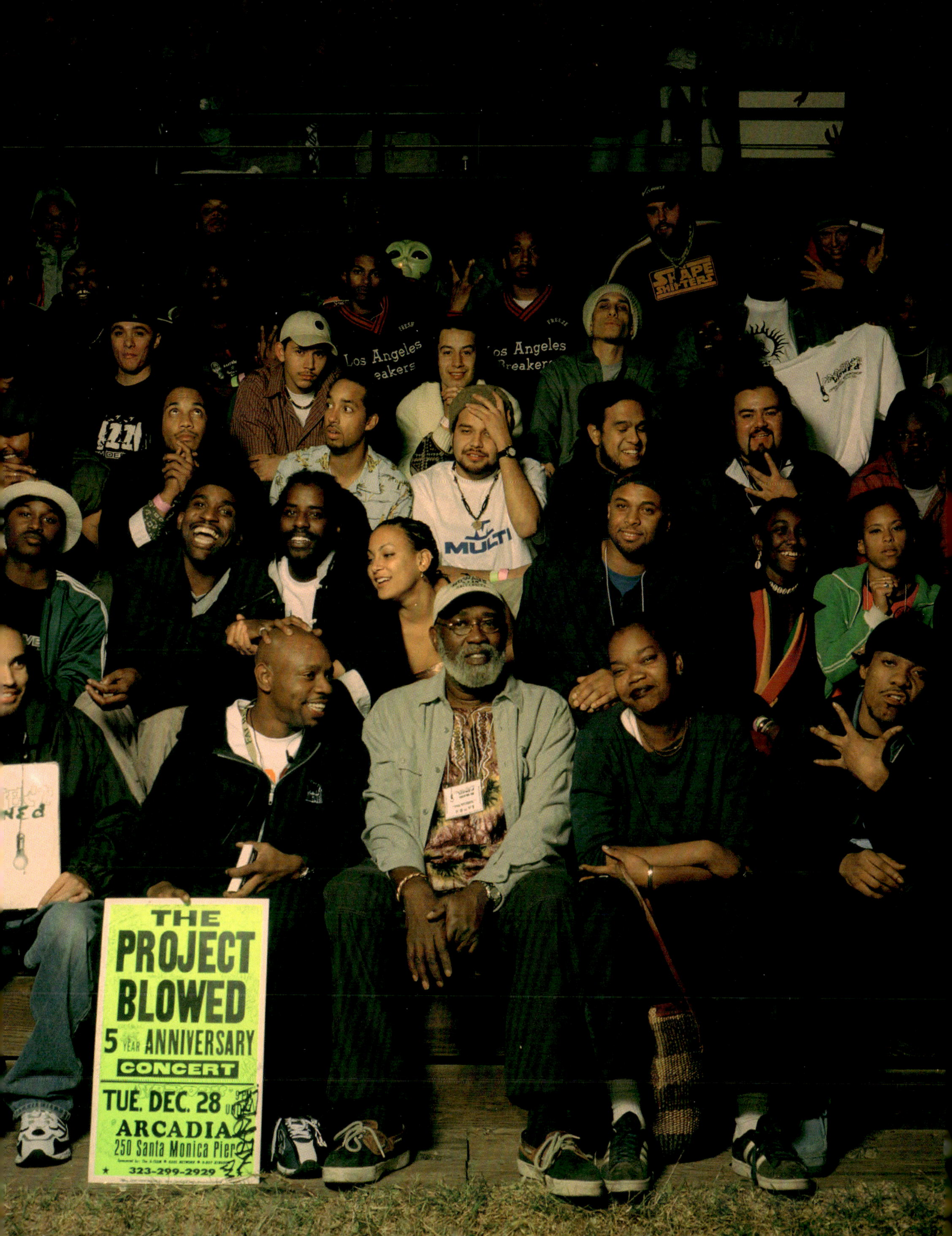
THE
PROJECT
BLOWED
5 YEAR ANNIVERSARY
CONCERT
TUE. DEC. 28
ARCADIA
250 Santa Monica Pier
323-299-2929

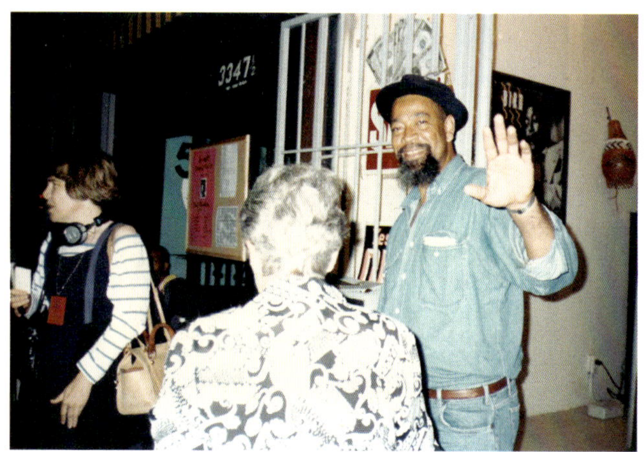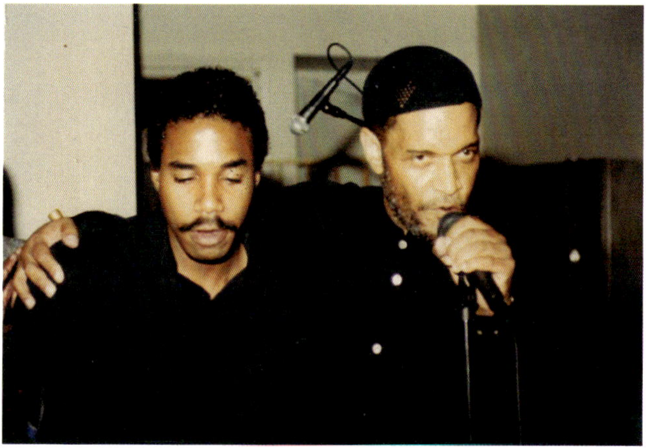

The Leimert Park Village

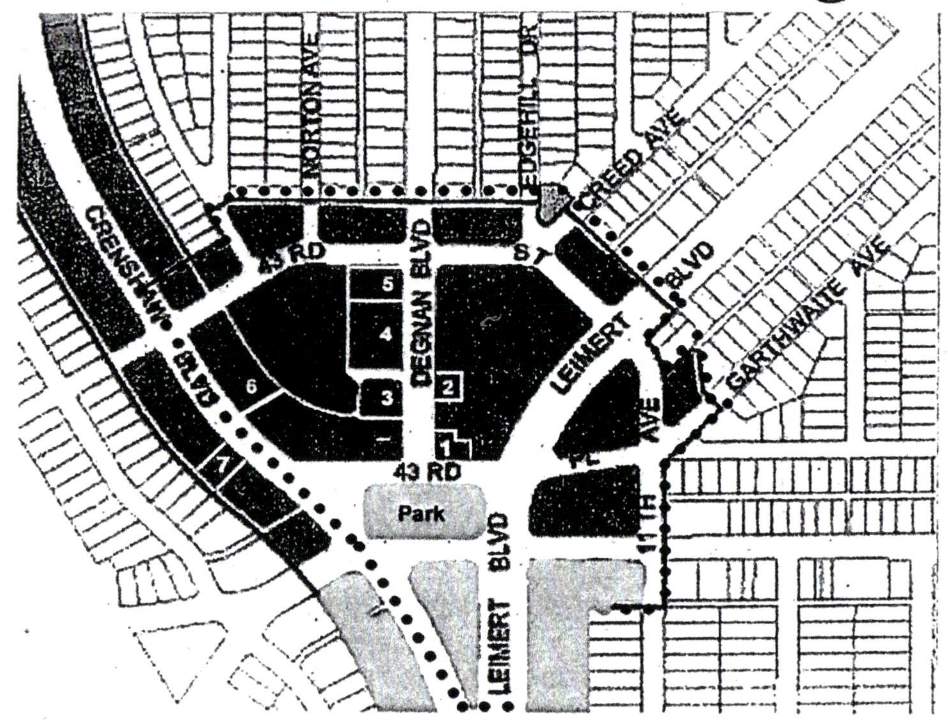

(TOP LEFT) KAMAU DAÁOOD, POET AND AUTHOR, MID-1990S (TOP RIGHT) BILLY HIGGINS, RIGHT, AND RICHARD (LAST NAME UNKNOWN), MID-1990S (BOTTOM) LEIMERT PARK VILLAGE FLYER

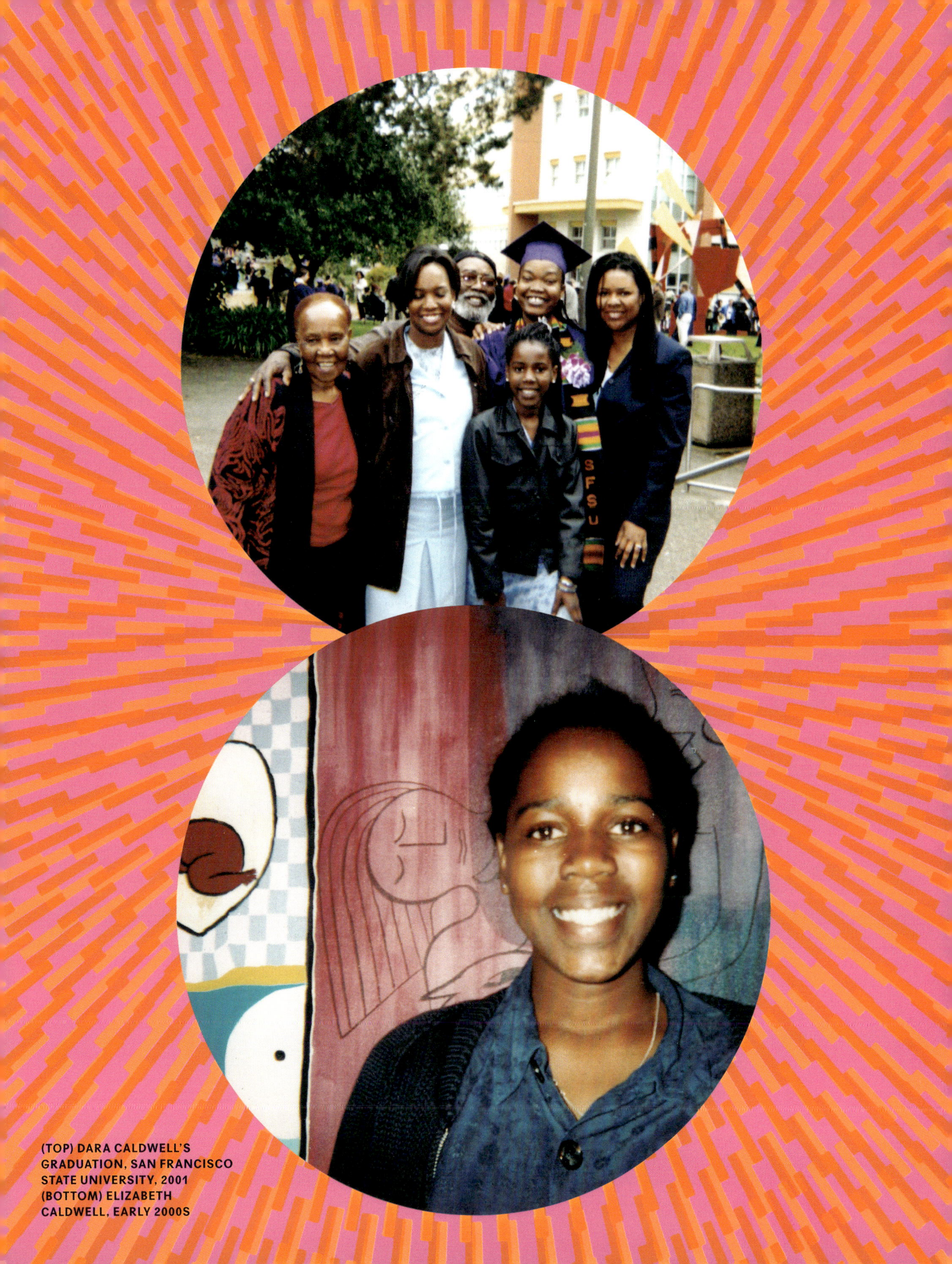

(TOP) DARA CALDWELL'S GRADUATION, SAN FRANCISCO STATE UNIVERSITY, 2001 (BOTTOM) ELIZABETH CALDWELL, EARLY 2000S

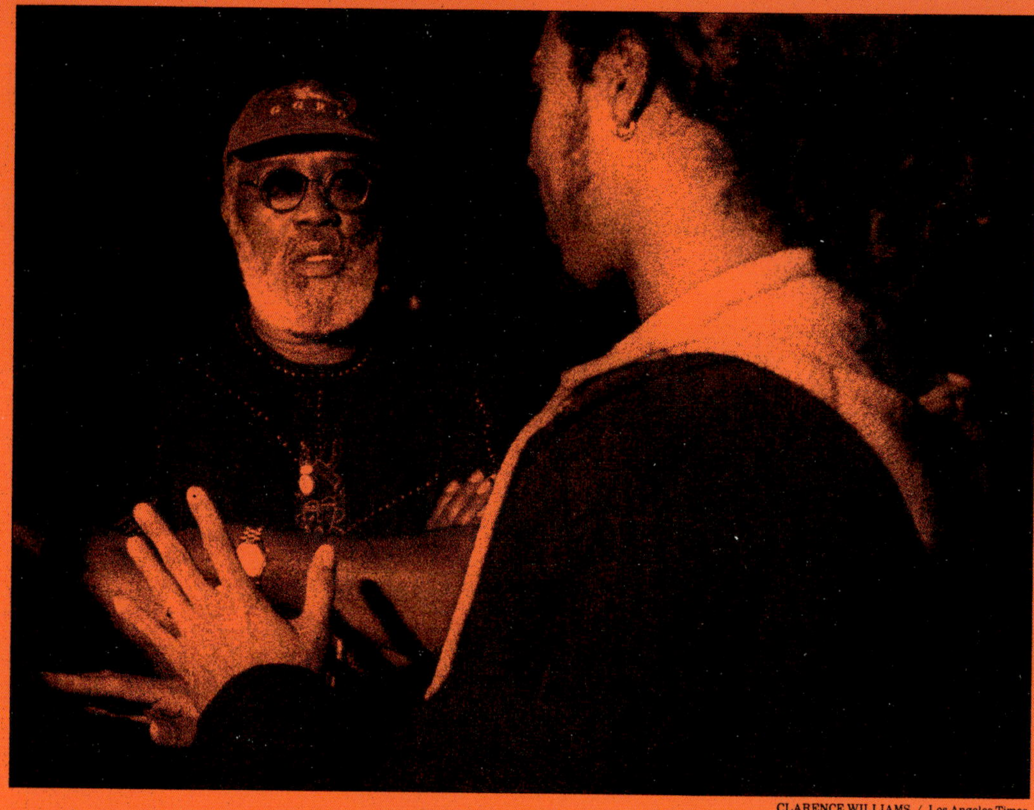

CLARENCE WILLIAMS / Los Angeles Times

Ben Caldwell, left, talks with Saint Mark 9:23 about the police altercation that took place outside of KAOS Network.

The KAOS Theory

Ben Caldwell's Multimedia Sanctuary Provides a Cultural Bridge

By LYNELL GEORGE
TIMES STAFF WRITER

Ben Caldwell can do one better than a scrapbook.

His history and the connecting dots unfold in vivid, video color—cassette after cassette of memory maps.

On a recent afternoon, a little more than a dozen days after a police raid shut down his popular Thursday night hip-hop workshop, Project Blowed, for alleged overcrowding, Caldwell's usually sonorous baritone has a trace of weariness wearing the edges.

He eases another tape in the deck, the black screen shimmers alive as Gee Dawg and the now-late Joe Boy bob their heads to a beat flavored by L.A. street rhythms.

The rap's hook, "They Don't Understand," is a sentiment Caldwell, the director of the KAOS Network, has been pondering since that bad-dream evening of Jan. 4, when police used force to disperse the crowd at the Leimert Park venue.

(Monday, Caldwell was charged with single counts of overcrowding, failing to maintain an unobstructed aisle to required exits and operating without a valid permit from the city Fire

> **'I look at Project Blowed as a real effective connection. A meeting of the minds. . . .'**
>
> Bectemba Barnes
> **A High School Senior**

> **'They tell me that this is church for them. It provides . . . a place for them to release their burdens and stress.'**
>
> Ben Caldwell

reached for comment Monday.)

While the Los Angeles Police Department continues an investigation into allegations that officers used excessive force, Caldwell is wrestling with the suddenly common notion that he operates a rap club. In fact, Project Blowed is just one aspect of Caldwell's multimedia operation.

And for those who have spent any time in the neighborhood, especially community youth, it is quite clear: Caldwell has been a constant when many things were not.

About 12 years ago, he first opened shop with Video 3333, a project he ran out of a smaller storefront just around the corner from where KAOS currently stands, just off Crenshaw Boulevard and 43rd Place. At the outset, the idea was to introduce neighborhood students to the art and power of media, which was important to Caldwell, who is part of the illustrious group of black filmmakers—Jamaa Fanaka, Charles Burnett and Julie Dash—who matriculated at UCLA.

It was at Video 3333 that Caldwell dreamed up a project that captured the spirit of early '80s hip-hop and boasted rapper Yo Yo among its alumni. But it was more than just a place for kids to lip-sync to Madonna or Prince. It was a safe

Out of the chaos/blackness (black-in-us)
or the space of infinite possibility, comes all
variations of the "love thang." Out of Ka/os
Coffee House/Studio comes coffee (which
originated in Ethiopia) to stimulate mental
and conscious associations. From Ka/os
we present this exhibition of various media
to stimulate the "love thang" and het-herutic"
thoughts, dreams, and dialectical associations - like the hypnotic magic of an Afrikan
sistah swaying to a cosmic beat that only
she can hear and you can only see. Like
the magnetic presence of a tall, dark, and
handsome Afrikan man that is so hoochie-
coochie fine that the womens be gettin'
happy before Sunday and don't know why.
It's a Black Love Thang - carbon dating
over here, carbon dating over there. Over
here like Ossie and Ruby, over there like
Rameses II and Queen Nefertari.

Word up, it's a Black Love Thang, when
the het-heratic vibe came down so hard
on the sun (son) God Ra when he left
the womb of the sky goddess Nut in the
morning, he came on back home through
her celestial mouth in the evening. It's a
Black Love Thang, when Iset (Isis) reconstructed her husband Osiris and found all
of his parts except his phallis. Her het-
heruticism came tumbling down and she
created a rise-erection of his phallis from
the earth, which became the obelisk. The
Vatican has an obelisk (Black phallis),
Greece rise-erected one, Paris (the city of
love and romance) rise-erected one, the
Big Apple rise-erected one, even the nation's
capitol, a.k.a. "The Chocolate City," has a
rise erection. Y'all don't know what I'm talking
about. It's a Black Love Thang. You understand?

greg angaza pitts - 1991

san· ko· fa
/sahn-koh-fah/
verb (Twi; Akan)
1.   To retrieve; to "go back and get" (san - to return; ko - to go; fa -
to fetch, to seek and take); to look back while moving forward.
2.   Refers to the Bodo Adinkra symbol represented either with a
stylized heart shape or by a bird with its head turned backwards while
its feet face forward carrying a precious egg in its mouth.
3.   Often linked with the Akan proverb: "Se wo were fi na wosankofa
a yenkyi" ("it is not wrong to go back and fetch what you've forgotten").
4.   Among people of the African diaspora, sankofa connotes the
wisdom to be found in returning to the past to help guide and protect
a people's future.

S A N

You don't realize when you're doing what you love that you're mentoring someone. You really don't. And it's not necessarily humility that makes me this way. It's me doing and moving on to the next…. Throughout my L.A. life, and Project Blowed, if I've touched someone's heart or I've inspired them, I don't know that until later. And it becomes a blessing and one of those Karma points. . . . When you're young, you want to be attached to what is important in the whole picture. Some people just want to be attached to the smallest things and they're okay with that. In life, I see a bigger picture for this world, and if I don't attach myself to enough of it, then I'm not going to make the necessary marks to inspire you or to make you a different person.

—Medusa (Monae Smith)

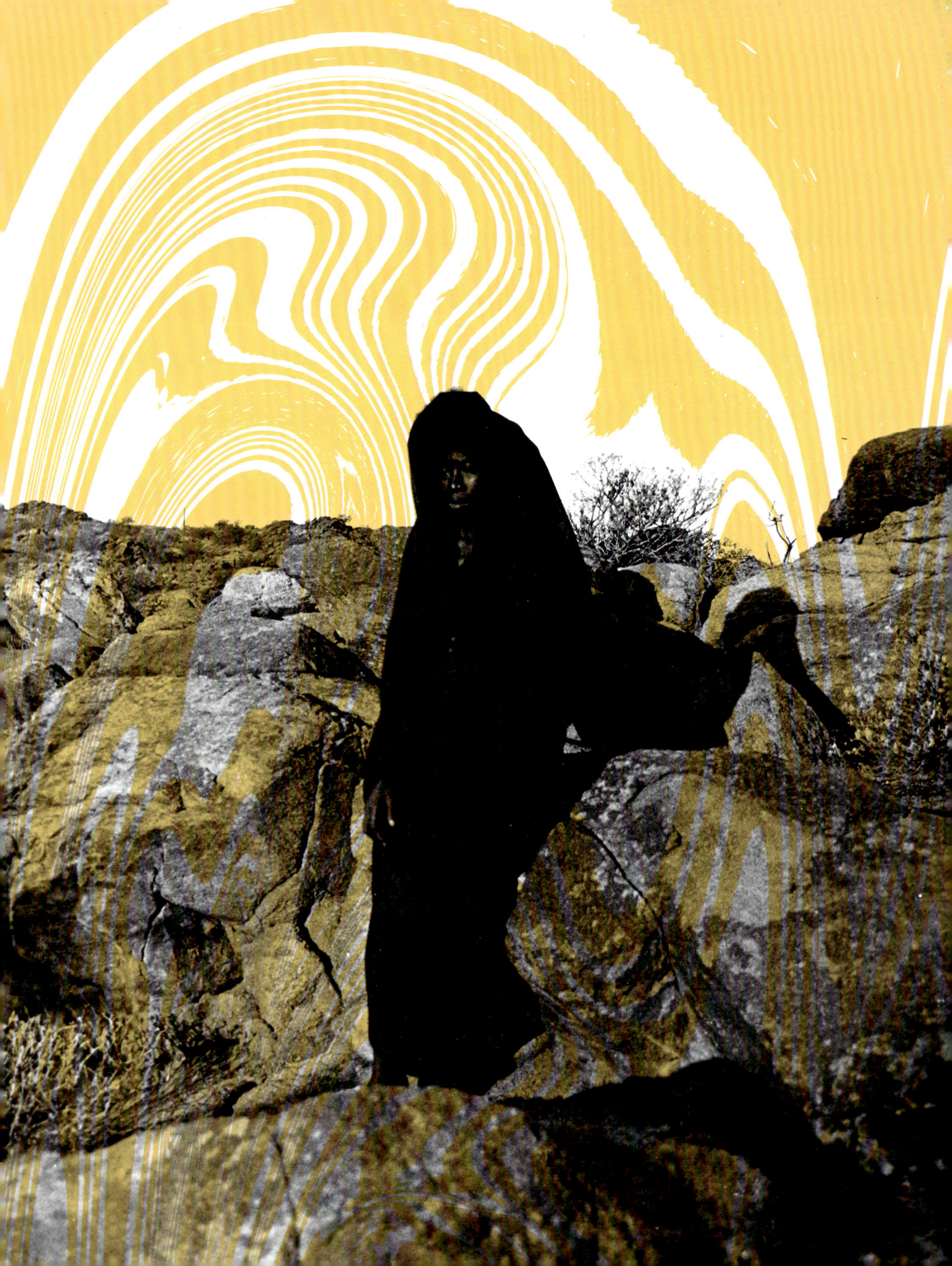

*Just left Nantes, the
former slave port . . .*

*That imported all our
wonderful spirits
to live and miscegenate
amongst these people . . .*

*I noticed they had this
ancient hotel . . .*

*As you walk through
the entrance, you see two
wonderfully dressed Africans
as part of the pillars . . .*

*Sankofa in full effect,
the past woven into the future
. . .*

*Art Energy . . .
It's made America a
little more human.*

*And less settler
oriented,
To just think that
everybody is alien, and you
can just take their things.*

*Instead of coming to
people as if they're friends,
sharing as humans do.*

*That's the beauty of
what we have to offer.*

*—Ben Caldwell
"OCTAVIA FLASHBACK SR018F"*

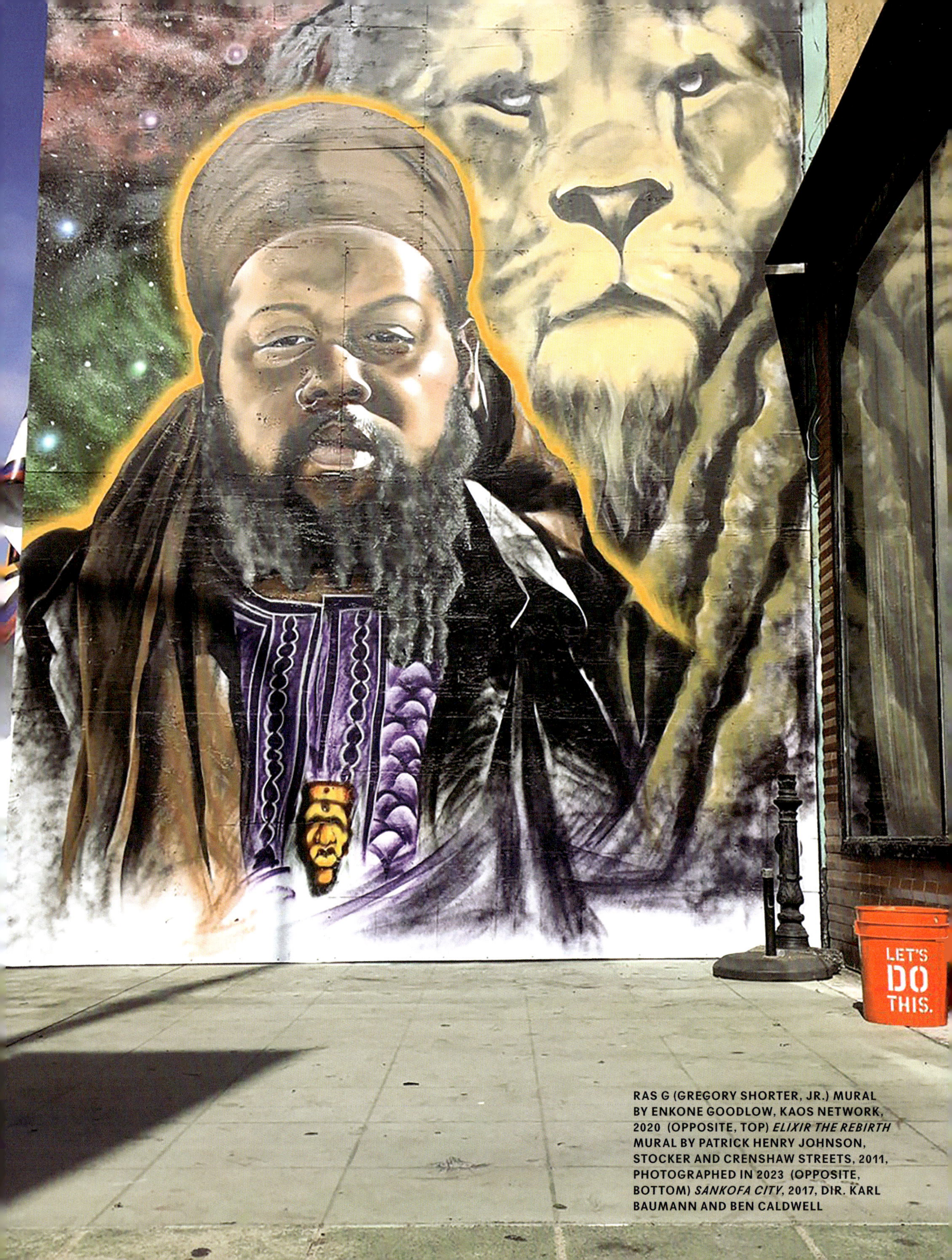

RAS G (GREGORY SHORTER, JR.) MURAL BY ENKONE GOODLOW, KAOS NETWORK, 2020 (OPPOSITE, TOP) *ELIXIR THE REBIRTH* MURAL BY PATRICK HENRY JOHNSON, STOCKER AND CRENSHAW STREETS, 2011, PHOTOGRAPHED IN 2023 (OPPOSITE, BOTTOM) *SANKOFA CITY*, 2017, DIR. KARL BAUMANN AND BEN CALDWELL

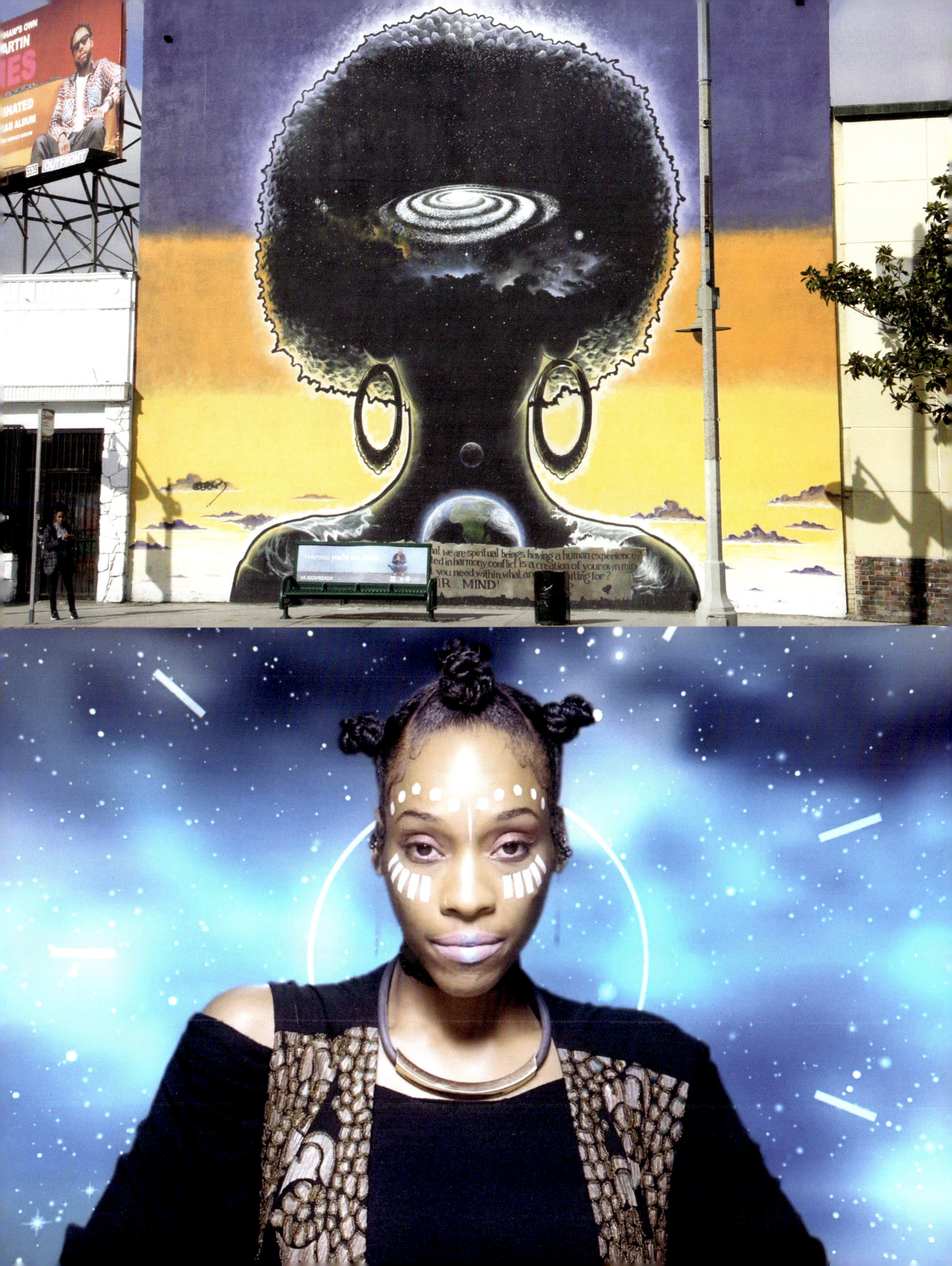
...hat we are spiritual beings having a human experience?
...ed in harmony conflict is a creation of your own mind
...you need within, what ar... ...iting for?
...IR MIND!
Veterans, you're not alone
VA.GOV/REACH

ILL LIFE,
CODA
eimert Park
POSTCARDS FROM
SANKOFA CITIES
LEIMERT PARK
WE OUT SIDE

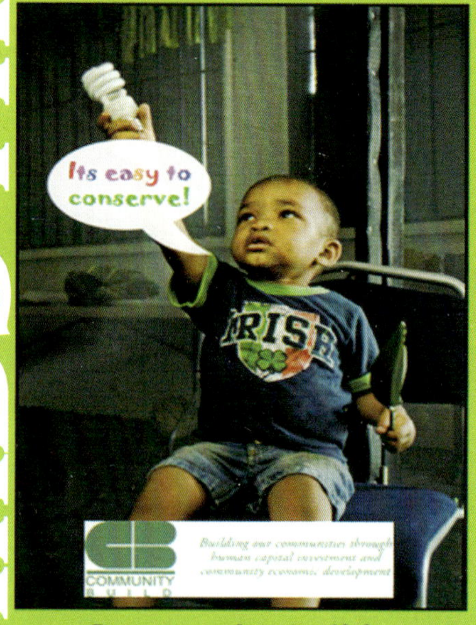
Its easy to conserve!
IRISH
COMMUNITY BUILD
Building our communities through human capital investment and community economic development
Community Build
Energy and Water Conservation in the 8th
December 9, 2011 from 6-9 pm
Art Show

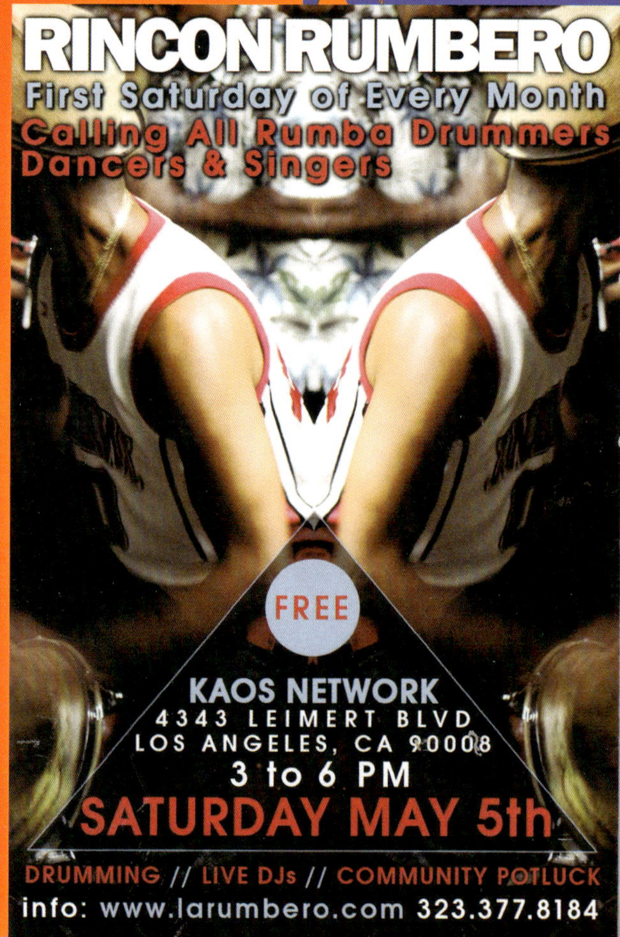
RINCON RUMBERO
First Saturday of Every Month
Calling All Rumba Drummers
Dancers & Singers
FREE
KAOS NETWORK
4343 LEIMERT BLVD
LOS ANGELES, CA 90008
3 to 6 PM
SATURDAY MAY 5th
DRUMMING // LIVE DJs // COMMUNITY POTLUCK
info: www.larumbero.com 323.377.8184

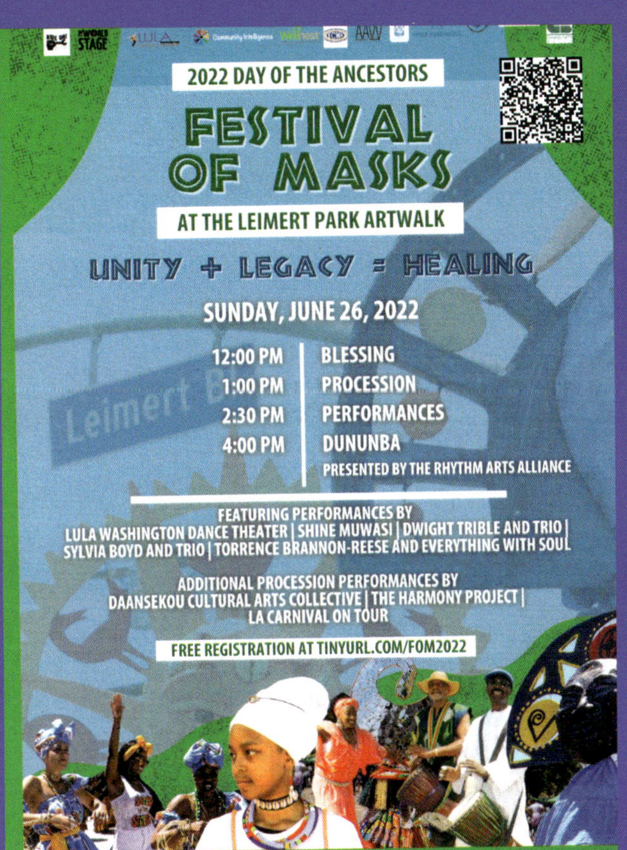

The Griot* Workshop

A great place to share and develop your story

7pm – 9pm
The 2nd Tuesday of every month
at
3335 43rd Place, Los Angeles
(at KAOS Network next to the
Vision Theatre in Leimert Park)

For more info call
Michael D. McCarty 310-677-8099

* Griot from the African tradition.
One who keeps the history & stories of
the people.

On the last Sunday of each month, Leimert Park Village hosts the Leimert Park Artwalk, a day of art exhibitions, music, fashion, food, drumming, spoken word, and local shopping. One of the key art walk events is the annual "Festival of Masks," the community's celebration of the ancestors and invocation for the South Central L.A. community. It was founded in 2011 by master percussionist Najite Agindotan, Rene Fisher-Mims (founder of the women's drum circle S.H.I.N.E. Muwasi (Sister's Healing, Inspiring, Nurturing, and Empowering in the Hands of God)), and Ben Caldwell in collaboration with L.A. Commons and its founder and director Karen Mack. Inspired by traditions of ancestor veneration like Yoruba Egungun Masquerades, the Festival of the Masks is a multicultural, multigenerational, and multimedia arts event that champions the vast identities of the African diaspora. The festival features a procession, a libation ceremony dance, and musical performances. The procession symbolizes the importance of community members taking back the streets, while the libation and blessing ceremony facilitates healing within the community. The festival begins with two months of community workshops to prepare masks, costumes, choreographed dances, and drum rhythms. It then culminates the last Sunday in June with a Blessing and then a Procession and Performance featuring Drumming, Dance, Masks, Giant Puppets, and local cultural performance groups.

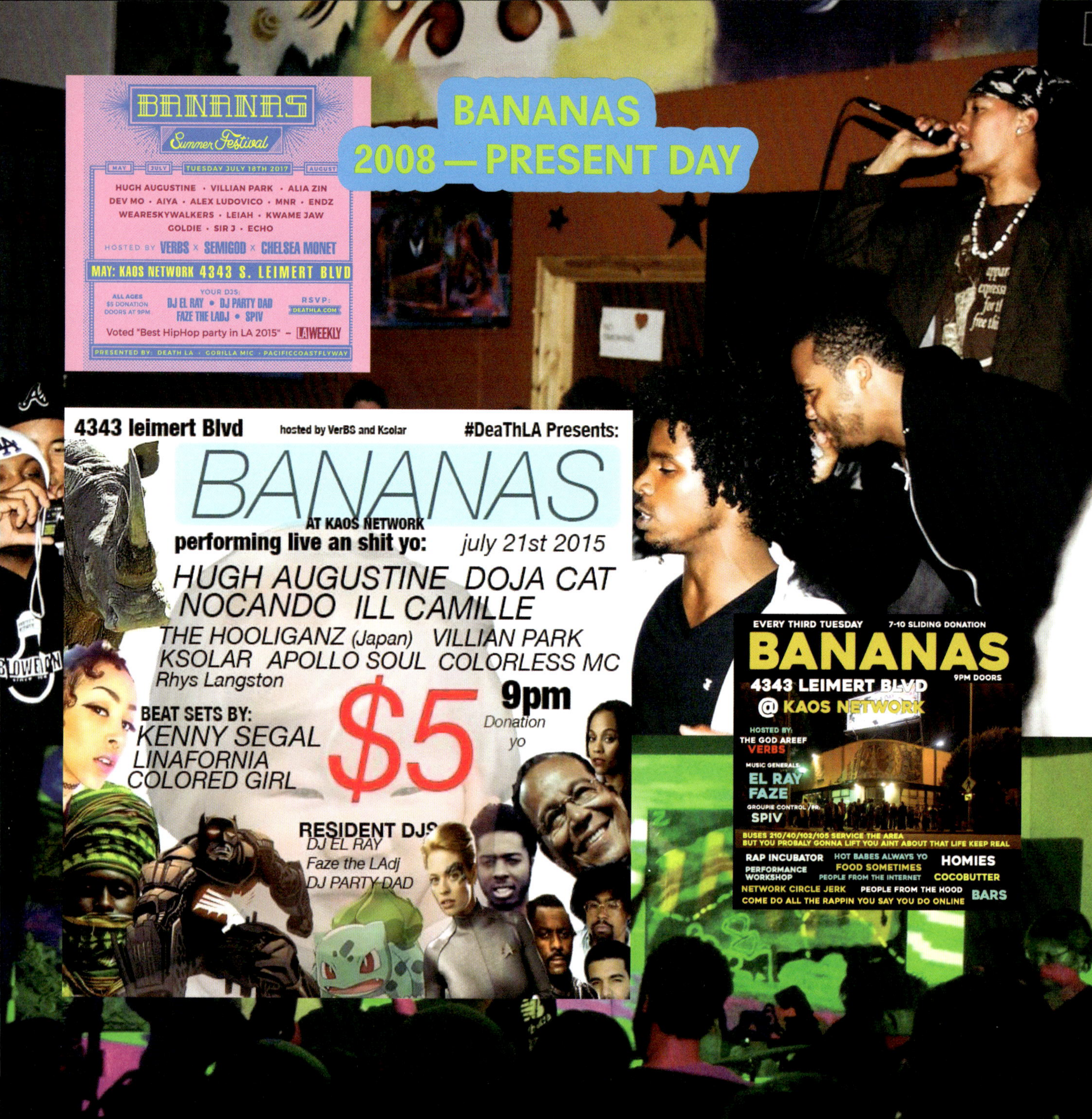

Held at KAOS Network, Bananas's monthly music show-case brings together local rappers, singers, musicians, DJs, abands, and out-of-town acts for an after-hours (10 p.m.–2 a.m.) performance workshop and open mic that features the best and brightest of L.A.'s various underground music scenes and communities. It was founded by rappers VerBS (Kyle Guy) and Gumshoe (Devin Montgomery) and has come to be a premier music series. Its monthly lineup is usually composed of both male and female hip-hop and alternative acts, and its regular attendees are always an intergenerational multiracial, multiethnic crew.

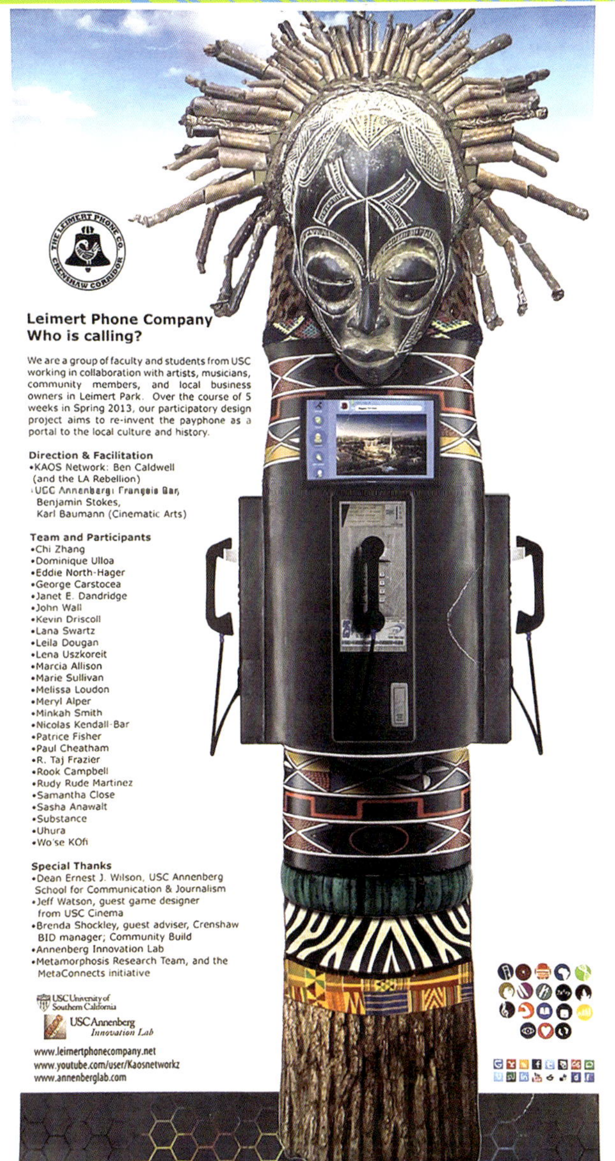

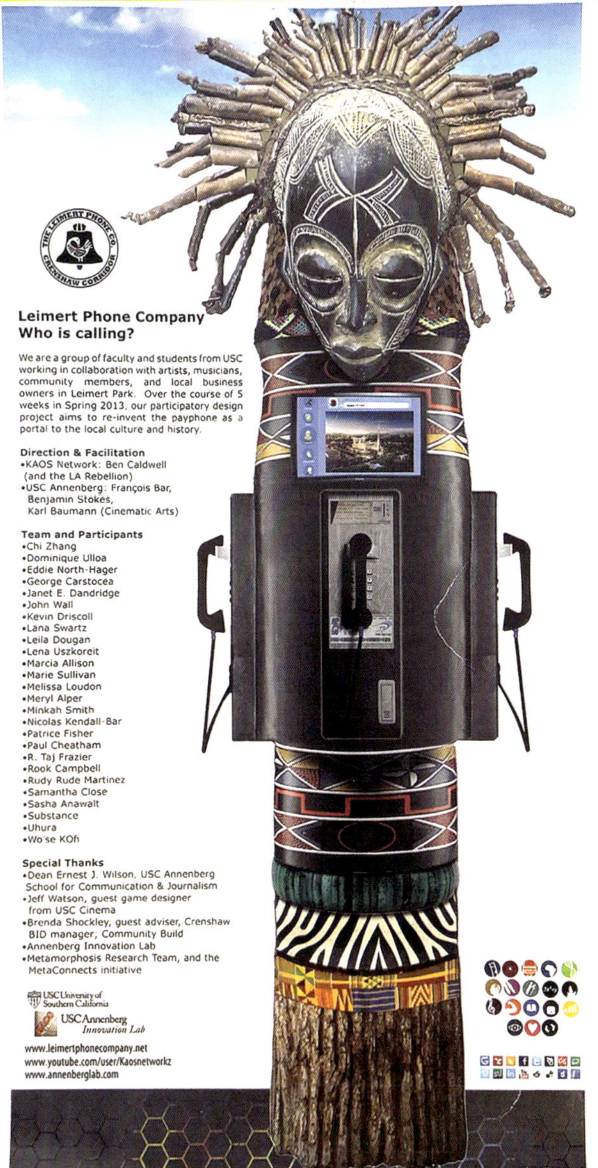

Leimert Phone Company
Who is calling?
We are a group of faculty and students from USC working in collaboration with artists, musicians, community members, and local business owners in Leimert Park. Over the course of 5 weeks in Spring 2013, our participatory design project aims to re-invent the payphone as a portal to the local culture and history.
Direction & Facilitation
•KAOS Network: Ben Caldwell (and the LA Rebellion)
•USC Annenberg: François Bar, Benjamin Stokes, Karl Baumann (Cinematic Arts)
Team and Participants
•Chi Zhang
•Dominique Ulloa
•Eddie North-Hager
•George Carstocea
•Janet E. Dandridge
•John Wall
•Kevin Driscoll
•Lana Swartz
•Leila Dougan
•Lena Uszkoreit
•Marcia Allison
•Marie Sullivan
•Melissa Loudon
•Meryl Alper
•Minkah Smith
•Nicolas Kendall-Bar
•Patrice Fisher
•Paul Cheatham
•R. Taj Frazier
•Rook Campbell
•Rudy Rude Martinez
•Samantha Close
•Sasha Anawalt
•Substance
•Uhura
•Wo'se KOfi
Special Thanks
•Dean Ernest J. Wilson, USC Annenberg School for Communication & Journalism
•Jeff Watson, guest game designer from USC Cinema
•Brenda Shockley, guest adviser, Crenshaw BID manager; Community Build
•Annenberg Innovation Lab
•Metamorphosis Research Team, and the MetaConnects initiative
USC University of Southern California
USC Annenberg Innovation Lab
www.leimertphonecompany.net
www.youtube.com/user/Kaosnetworkz
www.annenberglab.com

The Leimert Park Phone Company is an ongoing experiment in transmedia, bottom-up tech, and neighborhood storytelling. Conceived by Ben Caldwell, professors François Bar and Benjamin Stokes, and designer and filmmaker Karl Baumann, the project repurposes urban furniture (payphones, bus benches, etc.) in collaboration with community stakeholders. The goal is to create spaces and experiments that democratize the process of envisioning and building the future. The project brings together media technologists, academics, local artists, and businesses to cultivate different models for how communities in Los Angeles and other places can bridge the physical and digital, bringing social issues and gentrification into public space while still promoting sustainable development.

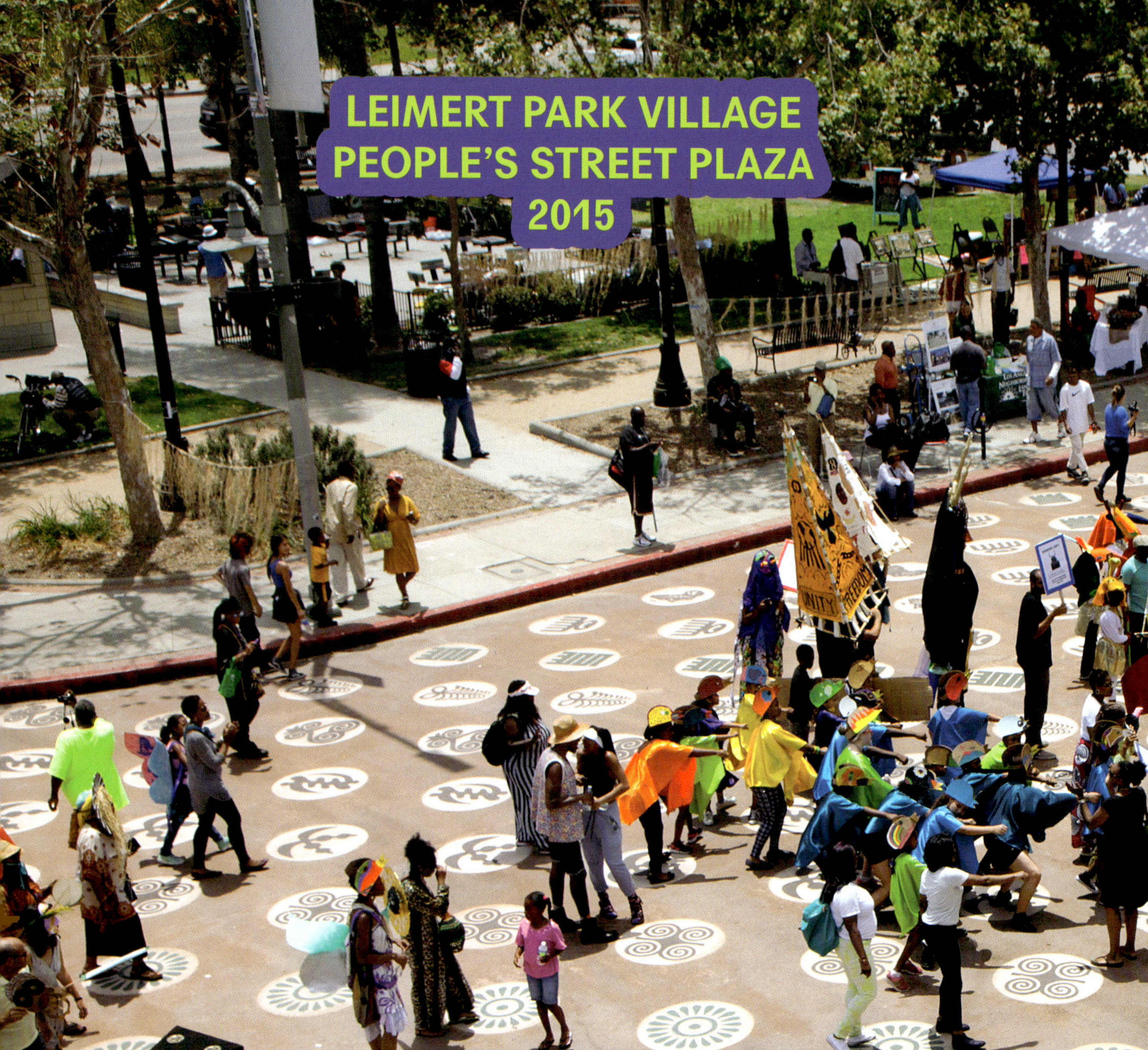

The People's Street Plaza is a closed-off strip of West 43rd Place, located directly in front of KAOS Network, the Vision Theatre, and Art + Practice, and just across from Leimert Park Plaza. The plaza grew out of discussions among local business owners and residents in which they articulated a desire for more spaces for community interactions, art activations and performances, and business vending, especially amid gentrification and the construction of a new Metro rail line. A group of these community members, educators, students, and city planners and architects ultimately came together to submit a proposal for the street to be sectioned off from car traffic as part of a Department of Transportation program that helps communities convert spaces into parklets, plazas, or bike corrals. Their application was approved. The street was closed off and decorated with cocoa-colored Adinkra symbols. These are cryptograms of the Akan people, an ethnic group in Ghana. Adinkra markings and figures symbolize proverbs and offer insights and lessons about human behavior and the world as the Akan people understood it. One of the symbols is the Sankofa bird.

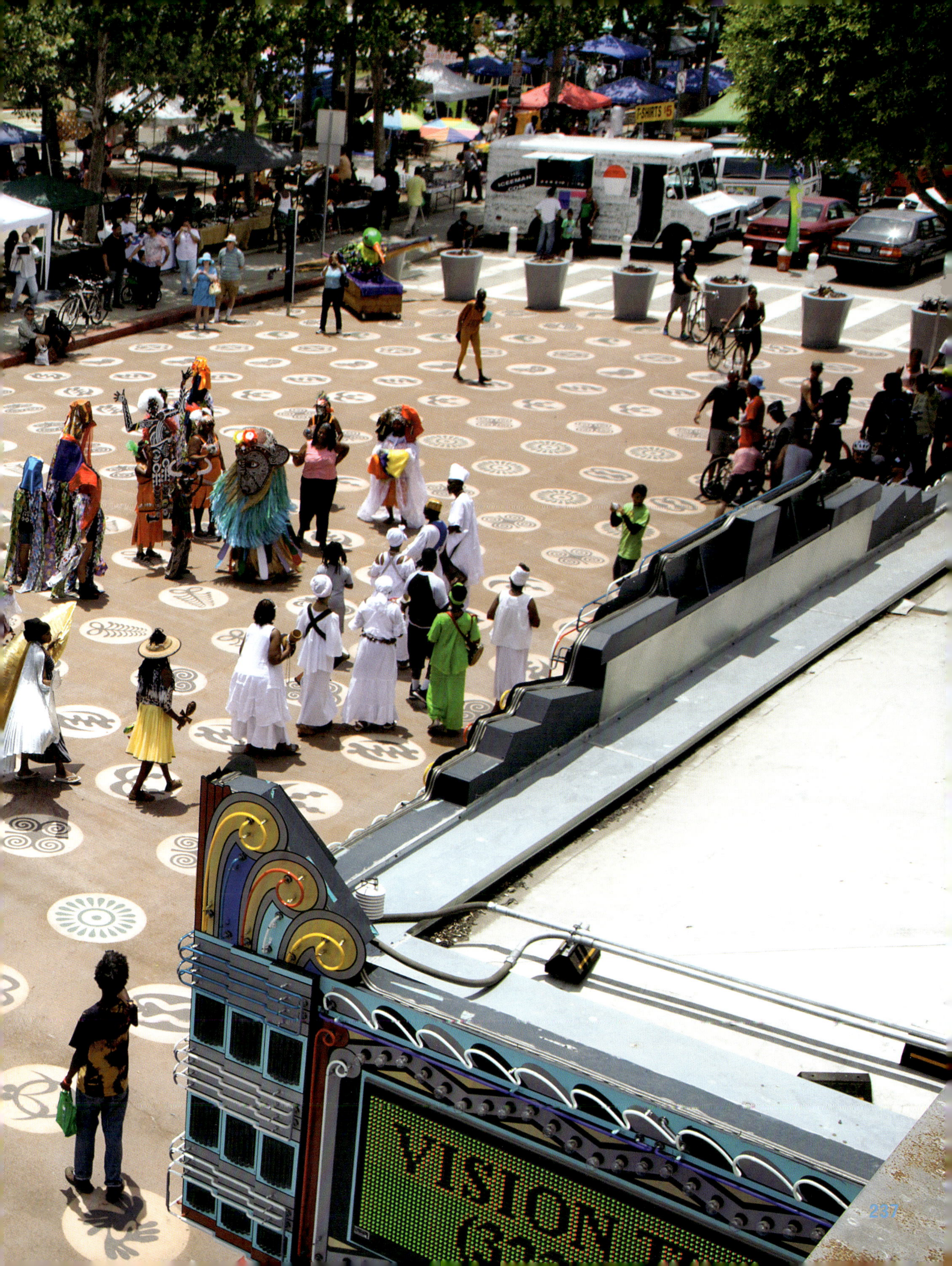
T-SHIRTS $5
THE ICEMAN.COM
VISION
237

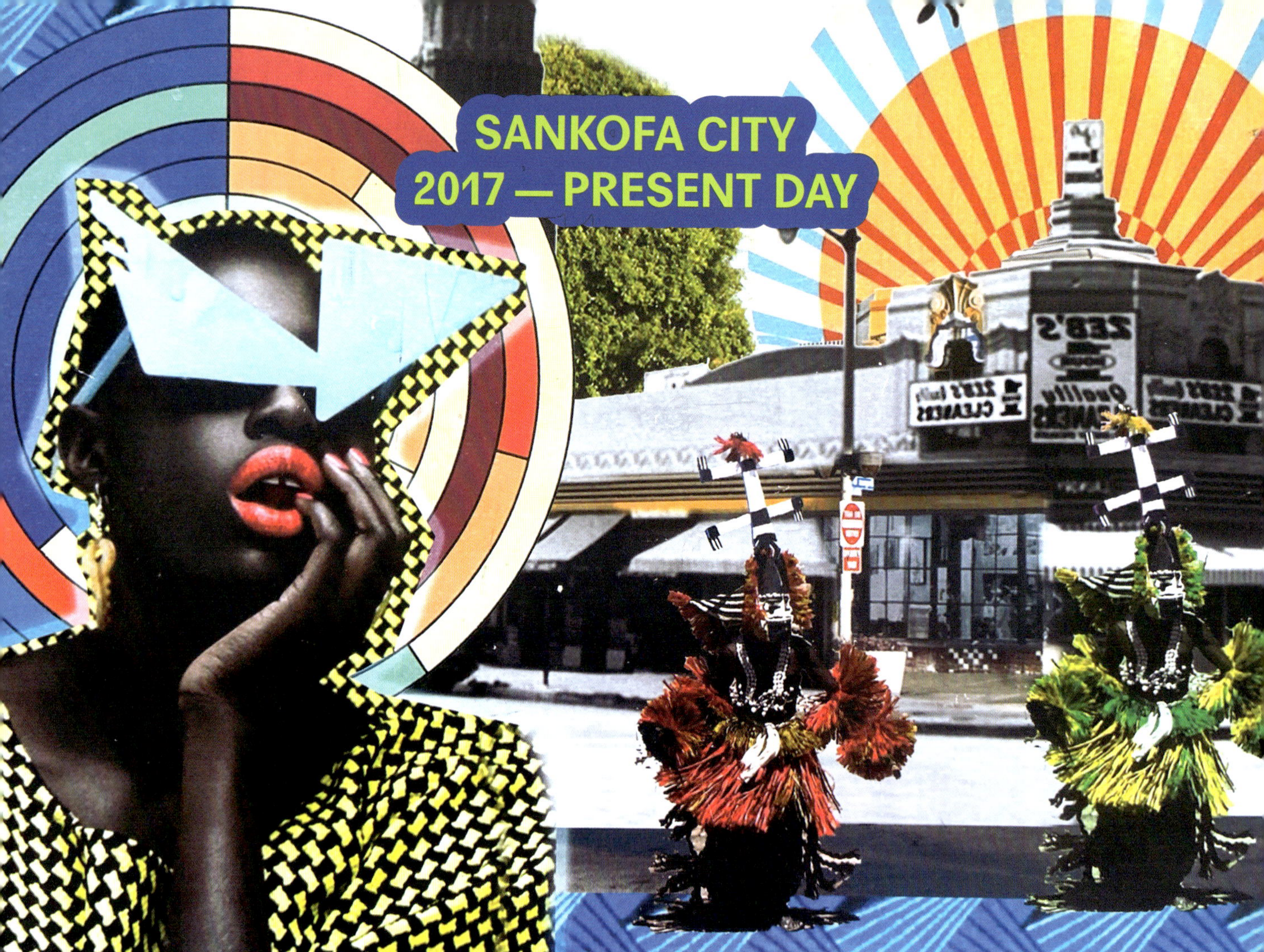

Sankofa City is a collaborative community design project created by Ben Caldwell, designer and filmmaker Karl Baumann, and creative director and designer Raul-David (Retro) Poblano. It envisions concepts and prototypes for the future of urban technology, such as augmented reality and self-driving cars. By working directly with residents, this project creates alternative models for local innovation, cultural preservation, and sustainable urban development. Considering that Leimert Park is currently the site of heated discussions about gentrification and cultural displacement, the

"Sankofa City" project complements other ongoing community planning groups by focusing on long-term strategies and imaginative solutions. Together, Caldwell and Baumann produced Sankofa City (2017), a film and interactive VR film that premiered at the 2018 Pan African Film Festival. In 2017, Caldwell and Baumann also traveled to Chicago with a group of Leimert Park Phone Company contributors (Professor Francois Bar and Los Angeles-based artist and activist janet e. dandridge) to facilitate the first Sankofa City Summer School.

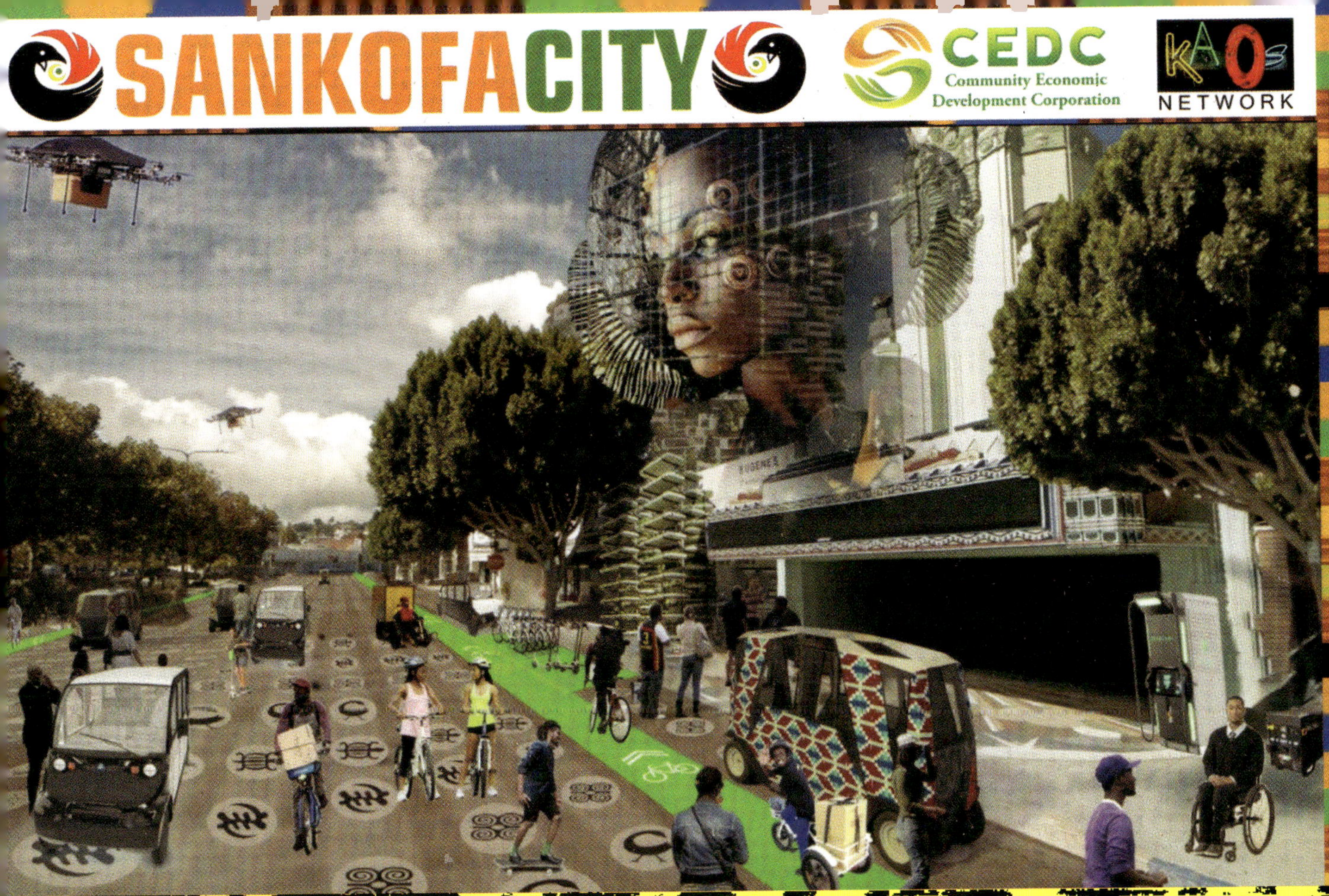

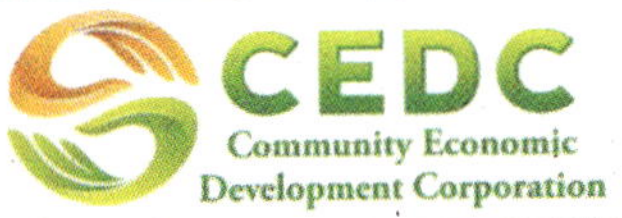
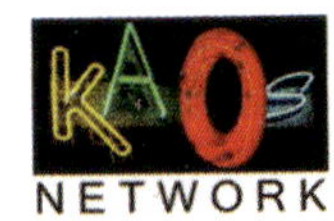

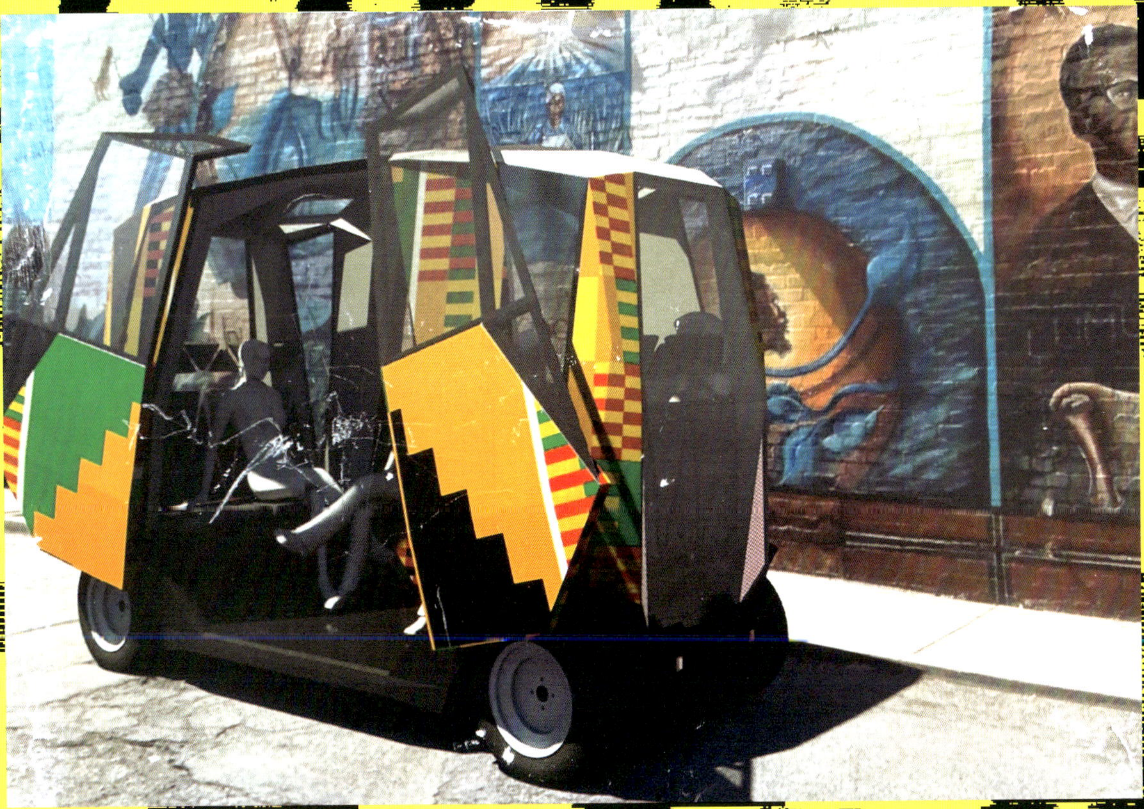

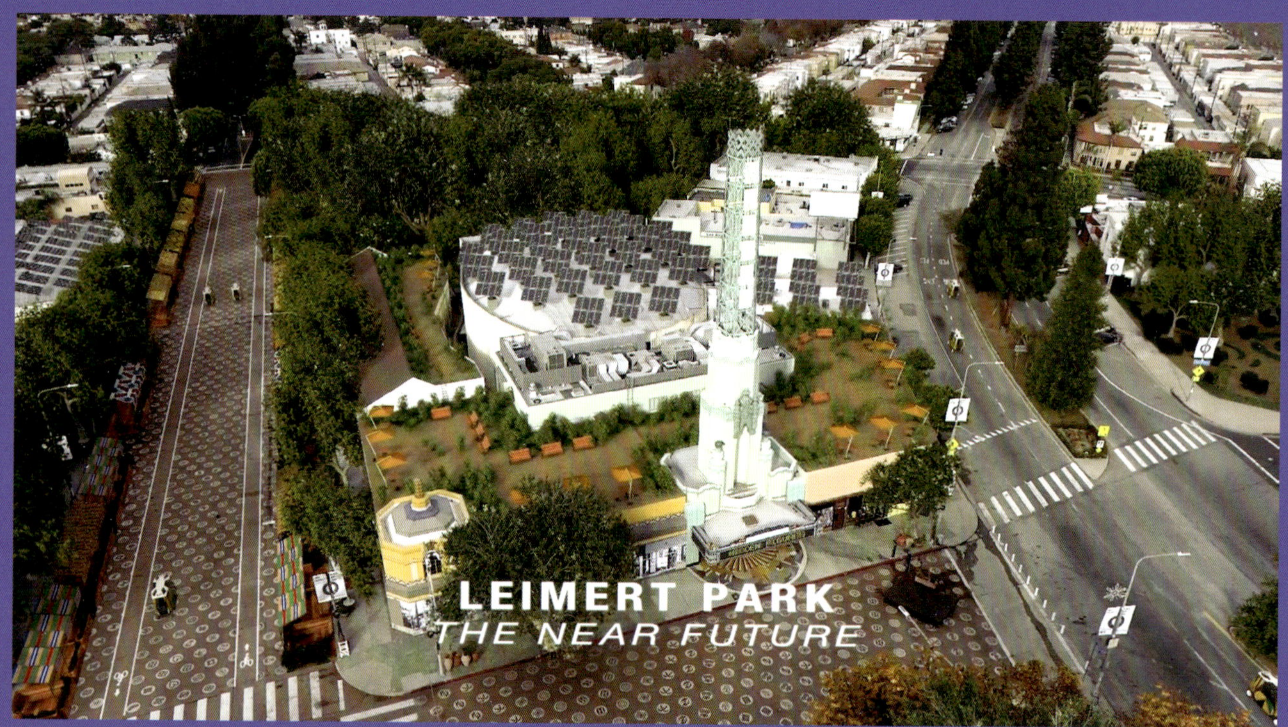

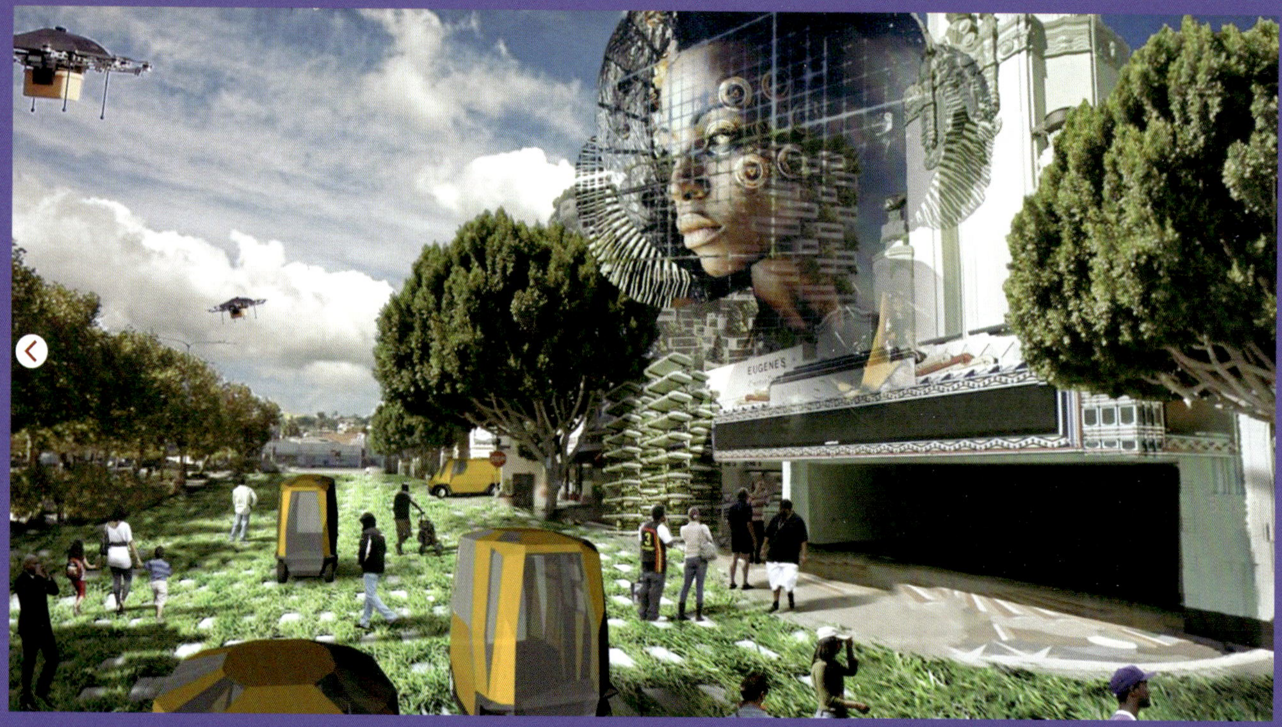

SANKOFA CITY, 2017, DIR. KARL
BAUMANN AND BEN CALDWELL

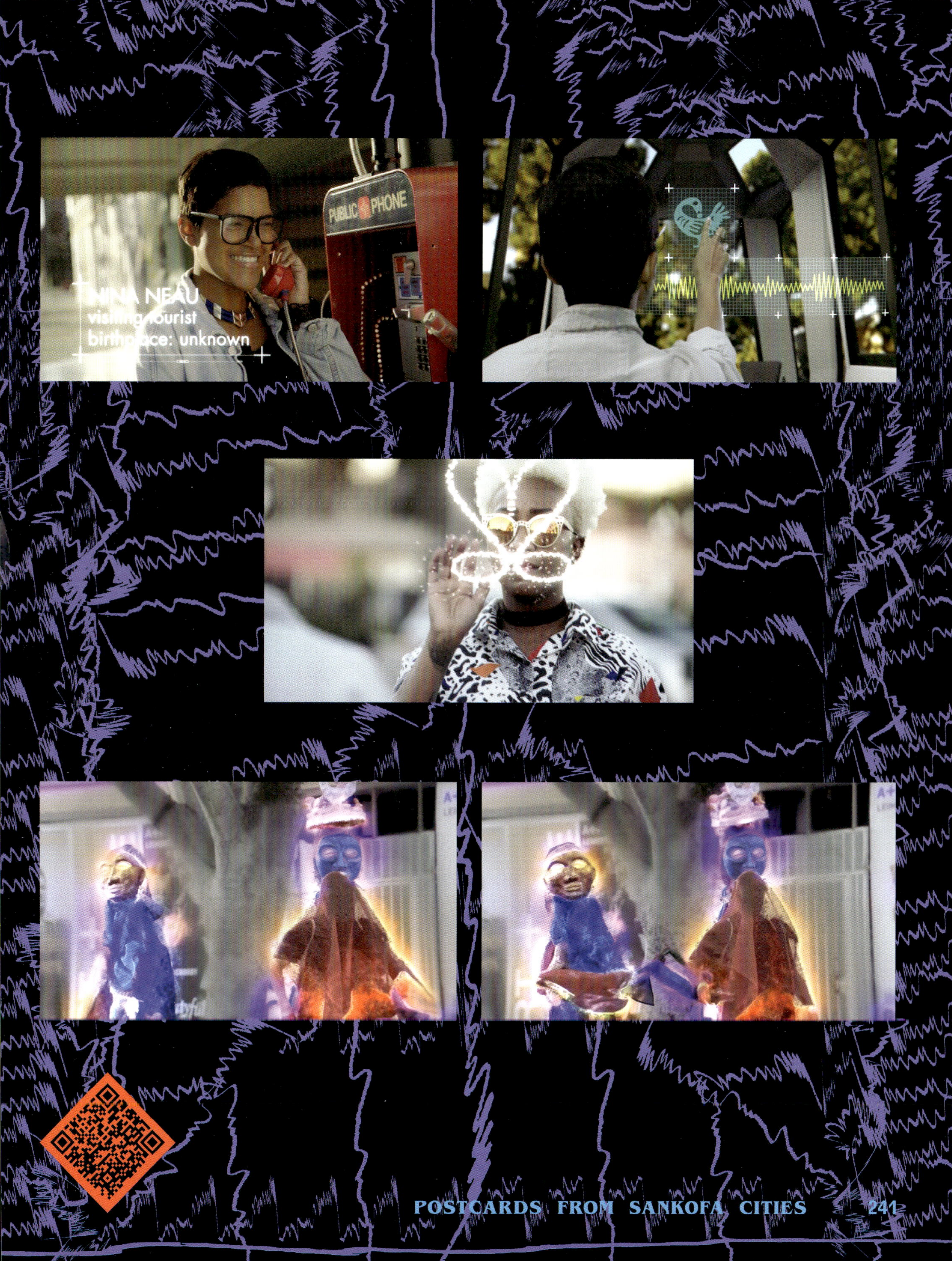

PUBLIC PHONE
NINA NEAU
visiting tourist
birthplace: unknown

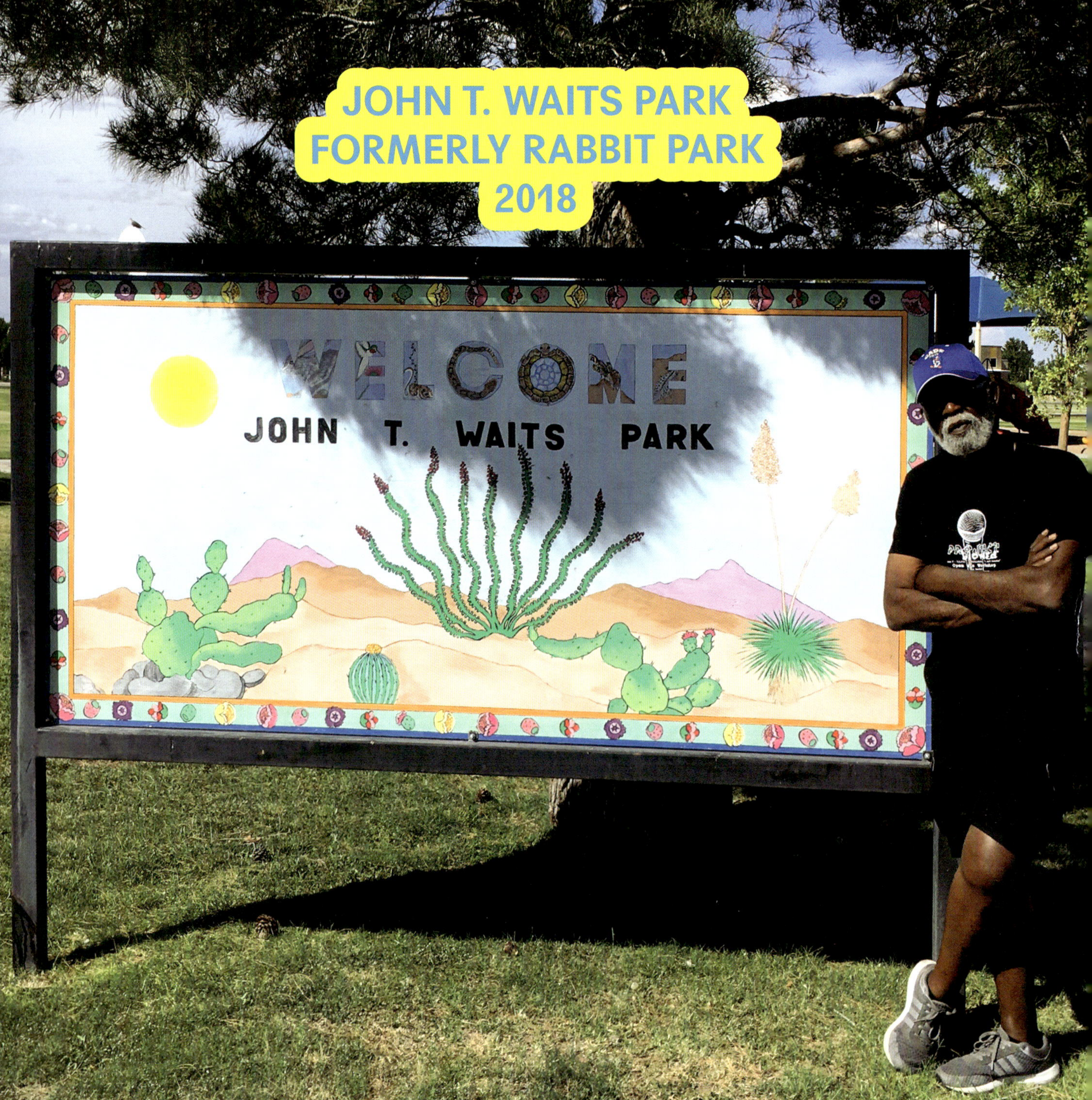

In the late 1950s, Rabbit Park was established as a sports park on the north side of Deming. There, Deming Merchants manager John T. Waits trained young ball-players. For years it was a rocky, weed-filled lot where youth played sandlot baseball. Decades after Waits's death, his former player Colonius "Pee Wee" Newton worked with the city of Deming to change the name of the park to honor Waits's legacy as a community leader in the village.

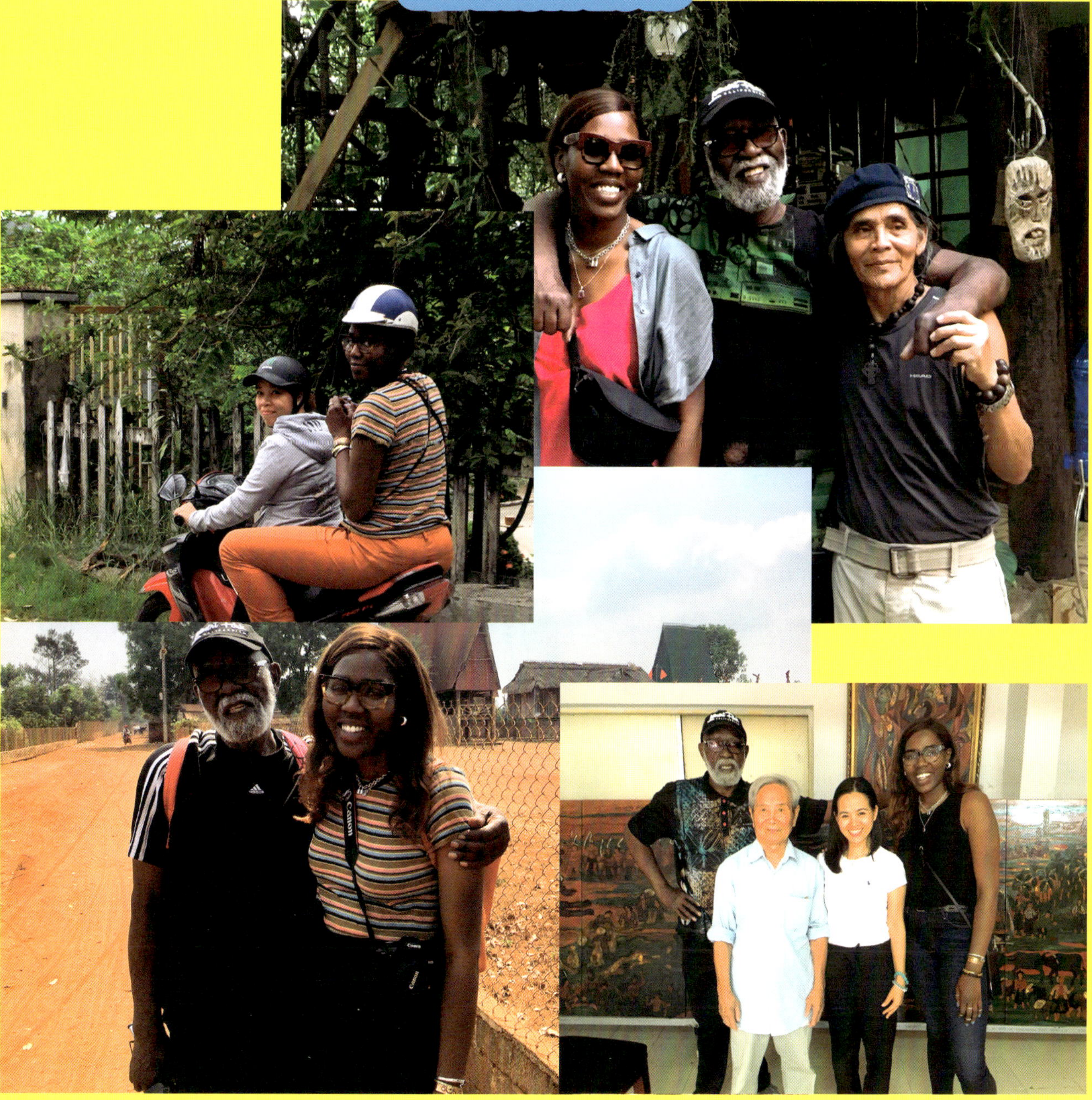

Ben traveled to Vietnam with his daughter Elizabeth. It was his first time back in the country since 1968, since his experiences there as a soldier. For two weeks, he and Elizabeth traveled to the villages and regions where he lived during his tour of duty. Ben also engaged in cultural exchanges with Vietnamese artists who had fought for the NLF/NVA, the militaries who fought against U.S. forces. It was a sobering and liberating experience.

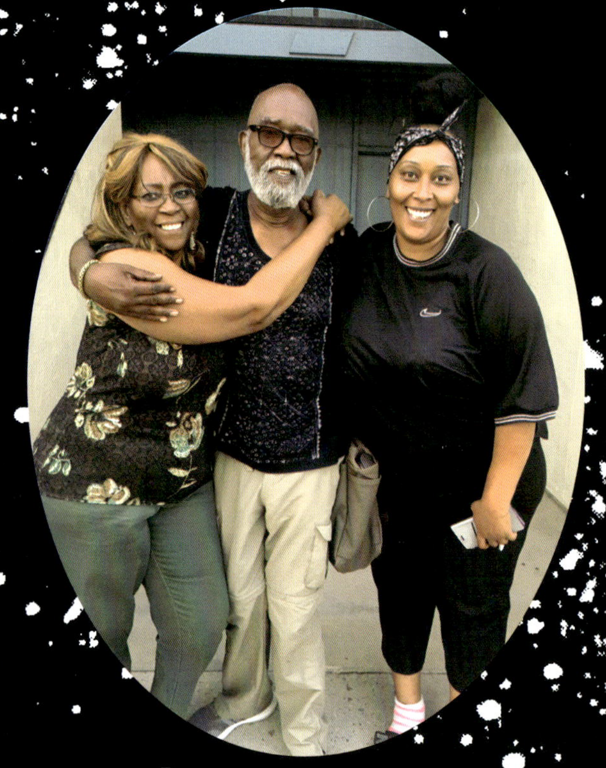

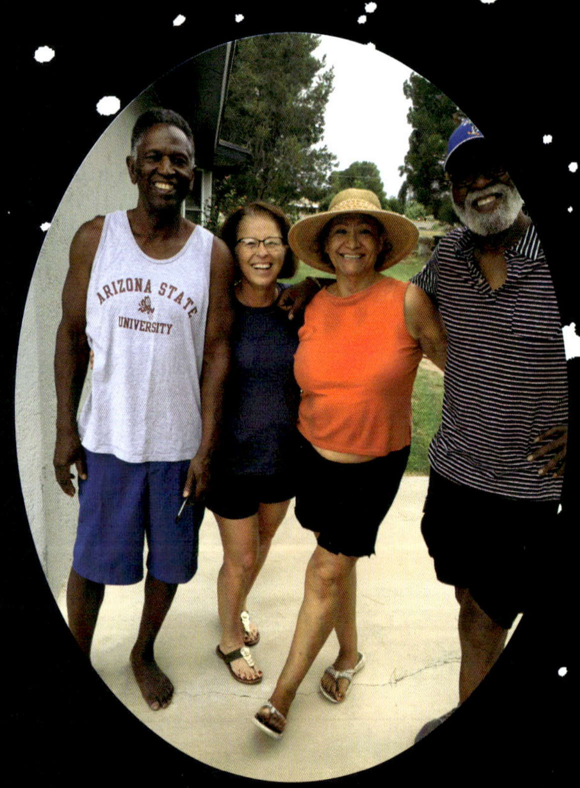

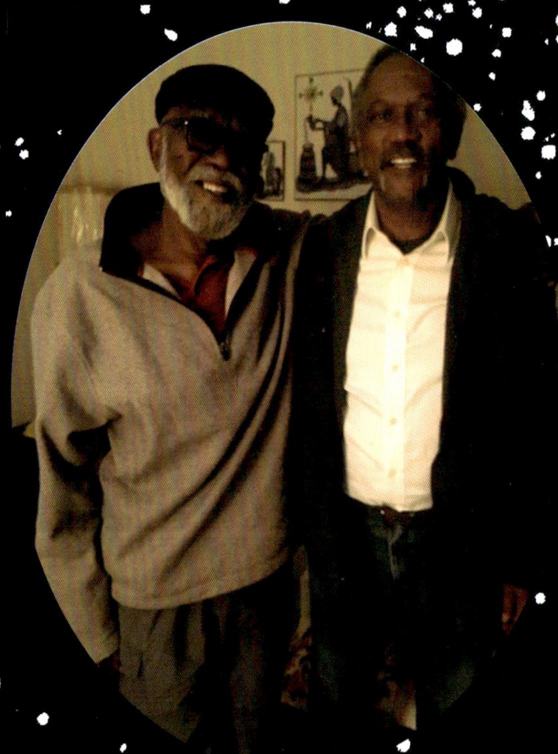

PHOTOS OF THE CALDWELL FAMILY

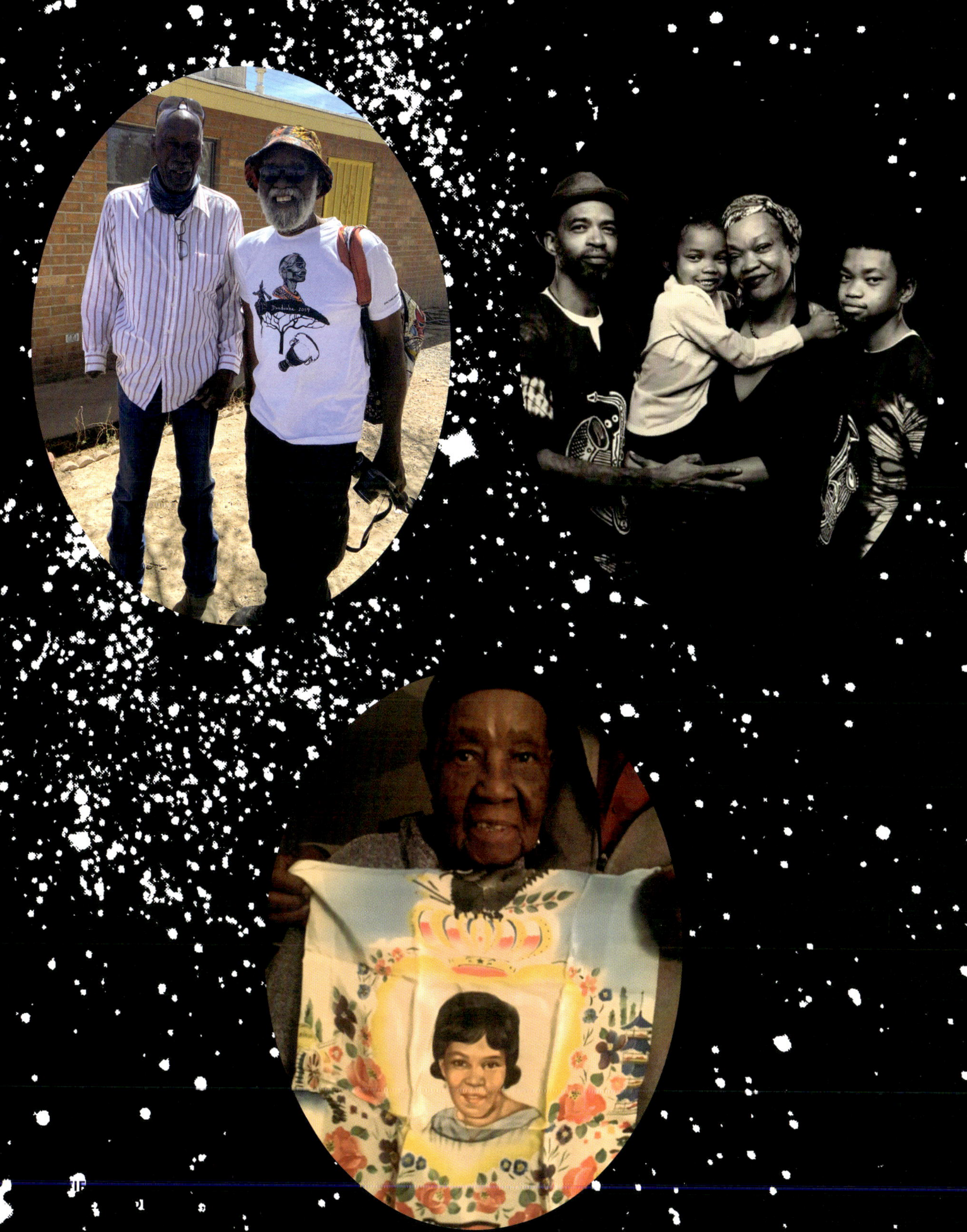

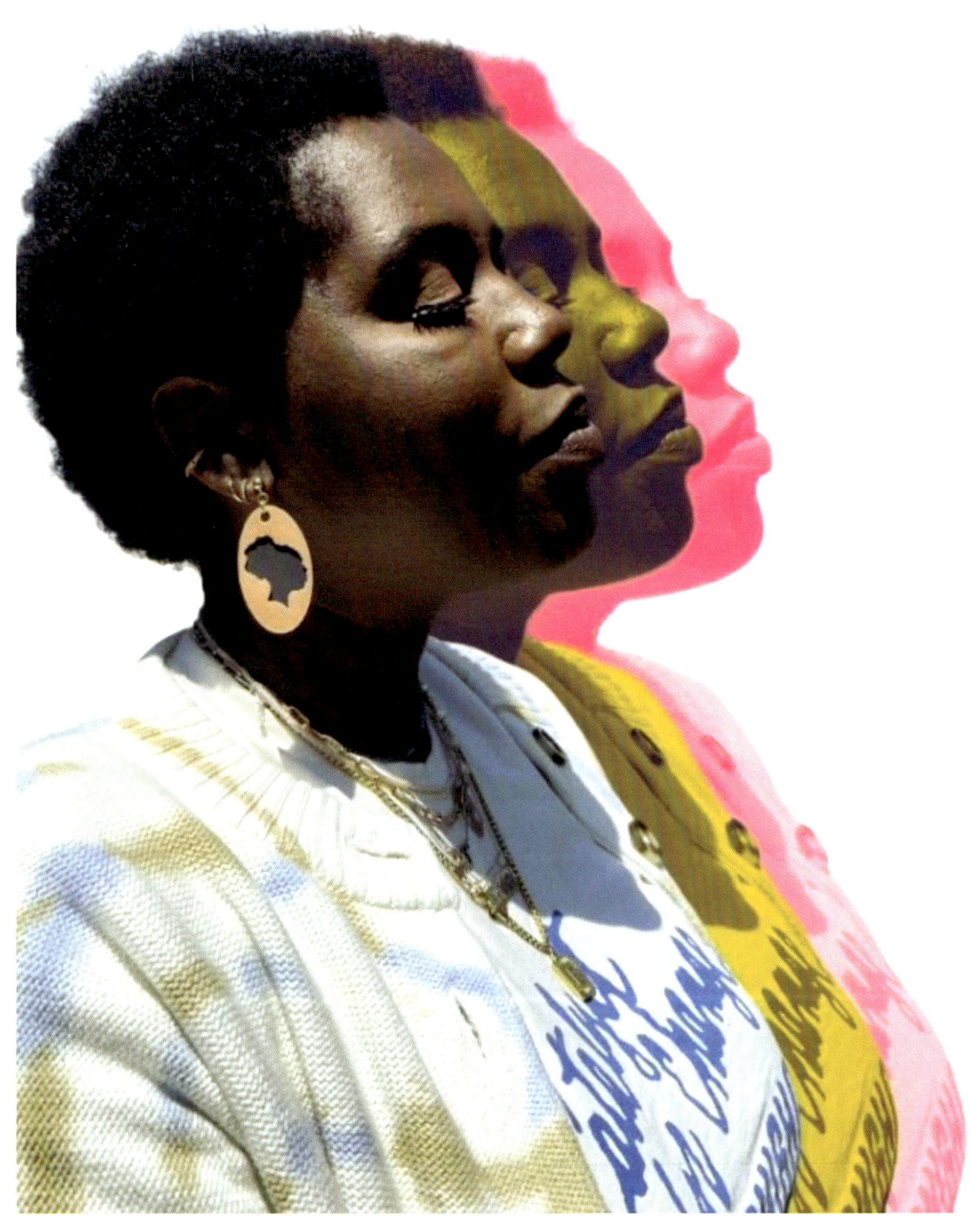

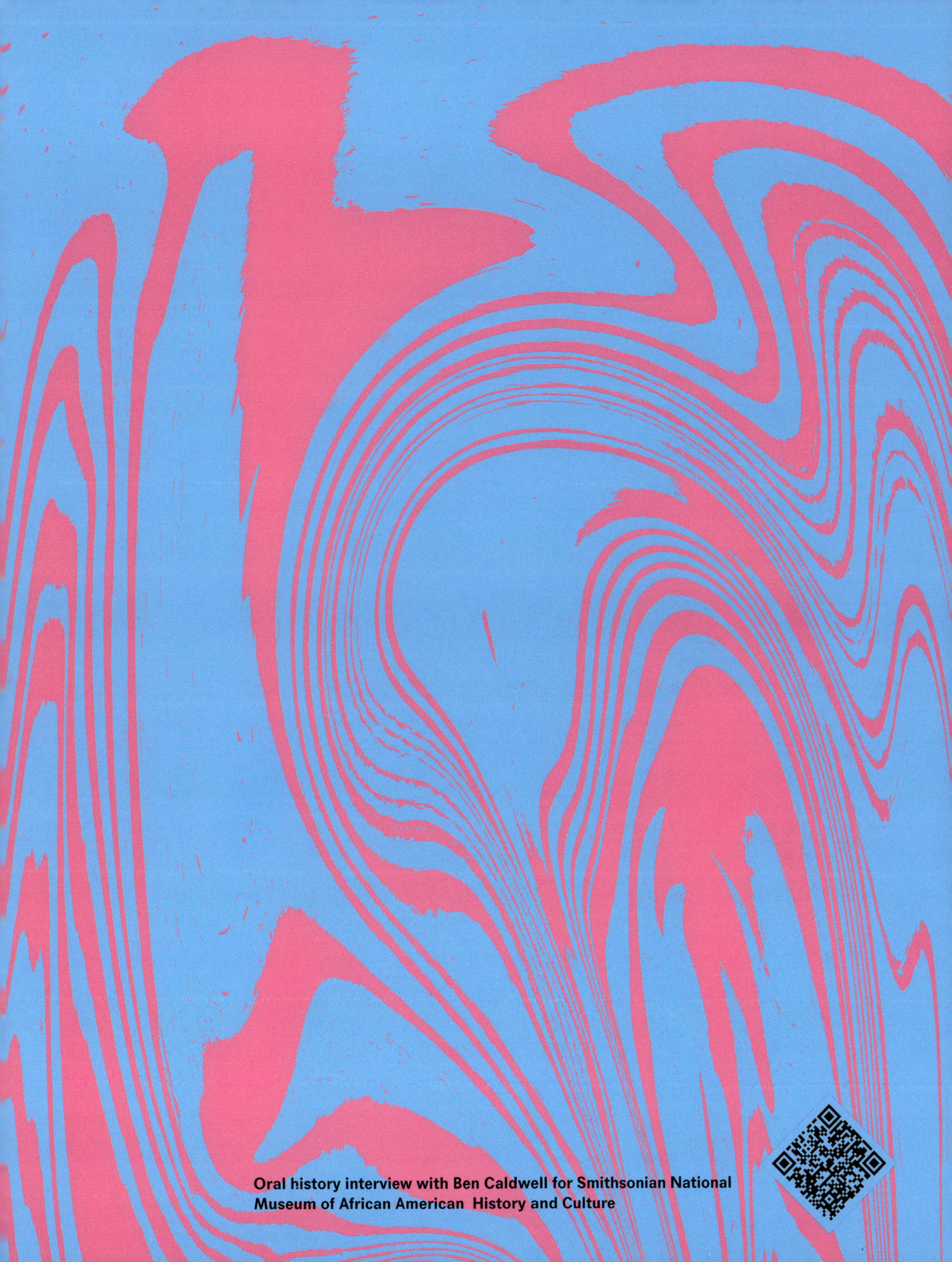

Oral history interview with Ben Caldwell for Smithsonian National
Museum of African American History and Culture

IN TRIBUTE TO

Mamie T. Caldwell
Robert Thomas Caldwell Jr.
John T. Waits
John Caldwell
Harold Caldwell
Richard Caldwell
Sonny Abegaze
William "Bill" Adams
Gregory "General Black"
Baker, aka Zefouba
Meznkhepra
Melvonna Ballenger
William "Bill" Barlow
Daniel L. Bonner aka CLEVER
Alfredo Bowman, aka Dr. Sebi
Brian Breye
Edgar "Ed" Brokaw Jr.
Fred Calloway
Shirley Clarke
Beatrice Cureton
Joseph "Joe Boy" Davis
Ivan Dixon
David Driskell
Allen Ayers Dutton
Jamaa Fanaka
Cecil Fergerson
Richard Fulton
Teshome Gabriel
Sam Gilliam
Beverly Cureton Graham
Michael Greenlee
J. Eugene Grigsby
Billy Higgins
DJ Al Jackson
Darrin Johnson, aka Meen
Green
Mazisi Kunene
Majid Mahadi
Keshaun McClendon, aka
Ganjah K/Pee Wee Jam
Dan McLaughlin
Barbara Morrison
Nicolas Markos Navarrette,
aka Gajah of Acid Reign
John Nemec
Colonius "Pee Wee" Newton
Noni Olabisi
John Outterbridge
Greg Angaza Pitts
Judson Powell
Noah Purifoy
Rose Pyles
Sherrie Rabinowitz
Derf Reklaw
John Rier
Beverly Robinson
Gregory Shorter Jr., aka Ras G
Christopher H. Smith
Lou Stovall
Horace Tapscott
Greg "Iron Man" Tate
Vantile Whitfield
Roosevelt "Rip" Woods
Michael Zinzun

Thank you for sharing your time and attention with us and creating room in your mind and spirit.

This book is firstly a tribute to Ben's family, especially his parents Mamie and Robert Caldwell and his grandfather John Waits. They laid the bricks for the work he has committed his life to.

This book began as a series of interviews and discussions between the two of us. It found its feet, however, after we traveled to New Mexico and spent time with Ben's mother and his siblings Lucinda, William, Robert, Michael, Richard, Gary, and David. They and their families opened their homes and memories to us. A deep gratitude is owed to them for this, as well as for entrusting us to share some aspects of their family's history in these pages. Of central significance were the insights shared by Robert and William, and even more the hospitality, food, and good times had with them and their loving wives Geri and Linda. This book's first chapters, moreover, could not have been written without the memories shared by Colonius "Pee Wee" Newton (RIP), John Nemec (RIP), and Ben's mother, Mamie T. Caldwell (RIP). Several days' worth of discussions with them, along with immersing ourselves in the Deming Luna Mimbres Museum and Archive, gave us the confidence to move forward.

Besides Ben's family, we honor the villages that have sustained him and enabled his life and work. This book features some of these people. But not all of them. We express immense gratitude to those who shared memories and wisdom with us: Charletta Johnson, Wesley Groves, Donald "DonKingski" Thomas, Mark Broyard, Roger Guenveur Smith, Vernon "King Oji" Vanoy, Dara Caldwell Ross, Pamela Larson, Lori Harris, Elizabeth Caldwell, Glen Williams,

Lance Caldwell (aka Sachii/Chill), Eddie Hayes Jr. (aka Aceyalone), Michael Lafayette Troy (aka Myka 9), Aaron Pointer (aka Abstract Rude), Darryl "JMD" Moore, Brian "B+" Cross, Karen Mack, Kit Galloway, and Tasha Wiggins Hunter.

Furthermore, KAOS Network is indebted to a long list of Los Angeles organizations that have used arts and media to facilitate creative exploration, community, and healing, especially for its most socially marginalized, surveilled, and economically exploited residents. Organizations like the Watts Towers Arts Center, Brockman Gallery, the Pan Afrikan Peoples Arkestra, Communicative Arts Academy, Aquarian Bookshop and Spiritual Center, Performing Arts Society of Los Angeles, The Gathering, the Mafundi Institute, the Watts Writers Workshop, the Watts Prophets, the Woman's Building, Studio Z, Inner City Cultural Center, Othervisions, LACE, EZTV, Electronic Café, On Time Offline, 18th Street Arts Center, Radiotron, Artworks 4, the Good Life Cafe, The World Stage, William Grant Still Arts Center, Fernando Pullum Community Arts Center, Lula Washington Dance Theatre, Debbie Allen Dance Academy, L.A. Commons, L.A. Freewaves, Echo Park Film Center, Plaza de la Raza, Self Help Graphics & Art, Inner City Arts, Visual Communications, L.A. Filmforum, Long Beach Museum, Community Services Unlimited, and many more.

KAOS Network was a seed that was nourished in many spaces. Two of the first educational spaces were Arizona State University's Fine Art Department and ASU's Black House Cultural Center, especially via discussions and fellowship with Chip Wheeler, Karen Truax, Adaybe, Sharon Stewart, and many others. UCLA's Graduate Advance Program

was also key, as was Howard University's Department of Radio, Television, and Film and Katherine Ruell, Katherine Arnaud, and Pearl Bowser's curation of Ben and his peers' work throughout the world. Can't forget to mention Linda Blackaby, Oliver Franklin, Woodie King, Warrington Hudlin, Ayoka Chenzira, and Cornelius Moore, who helped showcase this work throughout the U.S. And, of course, essential to KAOS's foundation is the work of Ben's community of UCLA-affiliated filmmakers (the collective often referred to as the "L.A. Rebellion"). Love and 'nuff respect to this family of artists, healers, and educators.

There would be no KAOS Network without the people who have helped run the space and left their imprint on it. People such as Joyce, Donald, and Mrs. Hart, Teddy Stewart, Damaris and Dennis Bernard, Judith Bowman, Leila Lois and Adrian Baird, Pat Bohannon, Mel Preston, Carroll Hill, Tamara Nails and Kwaku Lynn. A special thanks must also go to the Sheila and Joseph Pinkel fund.

KAOS Network has also benefited from working with numerous initiatives and institutions. This includes the CalArts Community Arts Partnership, Heart Foundation, Exceptional Children's Foundation, MobilityCouture, Community Economic Development Corporation/Institute for Maximum Human Potential, California Arts Council's Artist in Communities Program, Sci-Arc, UCLA Film and Television Archive, Social and Public Art Resource Center, Tate Modern, Festival des 3 Continents, Art and Practice, California African American Museum, Hammer Museum, The Getty, Fowler Museum, Destination Crenshaw, USC Annenberg Innovation Lab, Harvard University's Hip-Hop Archive and Research Institute, the Gray Center for Arts and Inquiry, the Black Speculative

Arts Movement, the Hip-Hop Initiative at UCLA's Ralph Bunche Center, the Universal Hip-Hop Museum, and everyone who contributed to creating the People's Street.

Big love, also, to all who contribute to KAOS Network's ethos of creative community:

Leimert Park Village businesses of yesterday, today, and tomorrow.

The artists, scholars, journalists, organizers, and intellectuals—Arthur Jafa, Charles Burnett, Lynell George, Marcyliena Morgan, Sheena Lester, Sherri Franklin, Delores Brown, Clyde Taylor, Jacqueline Stewart, Erin Aubry Kaplan, Najite Agindotan, Kenneth Wyrick, Rene Fisher-Mims, Ulysses Jenkins, Todd Darling, Heng Lam Foong, Allyson Field, Jan-Christopher Horak, Judy Baca, St. Clair Bourne, Sheila Pinkel, Nancy Buchanan, Anne Bray, Jeffrey Stewart, Reynaldo Anderson, Anna Everett, Theaster Gates, Lindsey Shields, Shamell Bell, Patrice Fisher, d. Sabela grimes.

The livest crews—Project Blowed, Funky Circle, Juju/the Soul Children, Club KAOS, Bananas, Tha Juice Joint, Five on the Black Hand Side, Revolutionary Poets Café, Kids at 43rd Place, Beat Cypher Collective, Trap Heals, We Love Leimert, SÜPRMARKT.

And, of course, the Village's nucleus—Kamau Daáood, Sika Dwimfo, James V. Burks, Marla Gibbs, B. Hall, Janie Mae Scott-Goodkin, Mark Bradford and the Art and Practice team, Torrence Brannon-Reese, James Fugate, Tom Hamilton, Ramsess, Adé Nett, Nesanet and Banch Abegaze, Anthony Jolly, Chace Infinite, the Bakewell family, the Leimert Park Village Stakeholders Collective, and many others.

Completing this book has been fun. And many people have helped us on this journey. Thank you to Sahra Sulaiman, Martha Diaz, Mona Ibrahim, Karl Baumann, Raul-David "Retro" Poblano, Azatuhi Babayan, Walter Thompson-Hernández, Susu Attar, Bee-Be Smith and Fred Johnson, Jheanelle Brown, Essence Harden, George Villanueva, Alison Trope, Ben Carrington, Cristina Visperas, Courtney Cox, Briana Ellerbe, Azeb Madebo, Caitlin Dobson, Brooklyne Gipson, Cerriane Roberson, Joshua Michael, BC Biermann, Jermaine Richards, Endiya Griffin, William "Jody" O'Keefe, Benjamin Stokes, Andrew Schrock, Beth Peterson, and Willa Seidenberg.

This book is a collaboration between two people and, moreover, two institutions: KAOS Network and the University of Southern California's Institute for Diversity and Empowerment at Annenberg (IDEA). Although the connection between our organizations was initiated nearly a decade ago, it was nurtured in profound ways due to the partnerships and friendships that were forged and facilitated by the USC RAP (Race, Arts, and Place) collective. Much love and appreciation to every member of this crew, especially Annette Kim, Francois Bar, Josh Kun, and Holly Willis. The four of you have been fundamental in supporting us and fostering the creative spirit and teamwork that takes life in this book. Additional gratitude must be expressed to the USC Annenberg School for Communication and Journalism, especially Dean Willow Bay, Director Hector Amaya, Associate Dean Allyson Hill, and Sarah Holterman.

We received institutional support via a USC Zumberge Diversity and Inclusion Research Award, several USC RAP grants, and an L.A. as Subject Residency Program collaboration which resulted in the digitization of portions of Ben's collection of archival images and ephemera. You can find "The Ben Caldwell Collection" in the University of Southern California's digital library.

Thank you to the book's designers, ELLA, led by Stephen Serrato and River Jukes-Hudson and project manager Emma Sutton. As we expected, working with you took the book to another level, another stratosphere.

Thank you to Inna Arzumanova, who read and provided beautiful and thoughtful feedback for the initial draft of this book.

Thank you to Amitis Motevalli, George Lipsitz, Kellie Jones, Danny Widener, Gerald Horne, Fanon Che Wilkins, Lin Zhang, Bill Deverell, Karen Moss, and others for reading and providing feedback to this work, and/or just supporting and nurturing it via facilitating event programming where we could work out our ideas.

What you hold in your hands is also a product of the phenomenal work of Angel City Press. ACP co-founders Paddy Calistro and Scott McAuley have demonstrated a zeal for this project since our initial conversation. We're very appreciative of their commitment to this book and their openness to our aesthetic aspirations and agenda. Furthermore, our work was greatly enhanced by ACP Editorial Director Terri Accomazzo's editing and stewardship of the book. Working with Terri was one of the best gifts of the post-production process. Her feedback and heart enhanced the quality of the book's narrative, and the clarity of our message, vision, and intent.

To anyone whose name is not mentioned here, please know, WE LOVE AND APPRECIATE YOU.

Lastly an immense thank-you and love is expressed to our families and friends.

Much love to Taj's parents, Patricia, Bonnie, and Larry, his mother-in-law, Heather, his in-laws, and the extended Frazier, Patton, Nance, Haswell, and Woods clans.

Much love to Ben's son-in-law Eddie Ross (Ero Zilla/E+RO=3), Ben's grandchildren Elan and Yana Ross, Pamela Larson, Lori Harris, and the Nedd, Harris, and Markham families, as well as Ben's extended Caldwell family members from California to Arizona to New Mexico and beyond.

And our heartfelt thanks and respect to our most beloved: Ebony, Seu, Benoît, and Satya Frazier; and Elizabeth Nozwe Caldwell and Dara Caldwell Ross. We thank God and our ancestors for you and for the lessons, joy, purpose, and fulfillment that you help to actualize for us every day. Ashé!

Ben Caldwell
Leimert Park Village

Robeson Taj Frazier
Crenshaw District

Notes

PRELUDE:
THE VILLAGE OCTOPUS

– *He is a polymath that a journalist once described.* **Rangarajan, "The Father of Leimert Park, or the Octopus."**
– *"show[s] the interconnectedness of many ideas"* and *"blur[s] the lines."* **Skoller, "Space is the Place."**
– *"media-arts sanctuary."* **George, "The KAOS Theory."**
– *"adaptive, relational way of being"* that *"see[s] the world in life-code."* **brown,** *Emergent Strategy,* **p. 2.**
– *the term also serves as a shorthand for Black community-centered practices...and Afro-speculative.* **Isoardi,** *The Dark Tree;* **Tapscott,** *Songs of the Unsung;* **Brown,** *Black Utopias;* **Neal,** *Black Ephemera.*
– *"consummate connector."* **See "The Crenshaw Continuum."**
– *"human internet."* **Interview with Wesley Michael Groves, December 5, 2018.**
– *"I was raised in New Mexico. My family was a migrant family."* **See** *L.A. Rebellion | Ben Caldwell on UCLA's "The View"*

CHAPTER 1:
TULLI HOPPIN'

– *"That portion of the country which is sure God's handiwork, if anything is."* **Coleman, "El Tisico," 252.**
– *To execute this illicit land grab, these white people.* **Horne,** *The Counter Revolution of 1836;* **Anderson,** *The Conquest of Texas.*
– *christened the area as "Falls County".* **Brawn,** *The History of Falls County;* **Old Settlers and Veterans Association of Falls County,** *History of Falls County, Texas;* **St. Romain,** *Western Falls County, Texas;* **Falls County Historical Commission,** *Families of Falls County*
– *Taylor was born in 1856.* **Ancestry.com, "1870 Census Precinct 3, Falls, Texas."**
– *After a brief and humiliating stint in the Confederate Army's Mississippi Volunteers Infantry.* **See**
– **"Compiled Service Records of Confederate Soldiers."**
– *Falls County's economy was centered.* **Tomlinson,** *Tomlinson Hill;* **LeSeur,** *Not All Okies Are White.*
– *worshiped at Zion Rock Baptist Church.* **Zion Rock Baptist Church, "One Hundred Second Church Anniversary." June 11, 1995; http://www.highbanktexashistory.com/church/; McQueen,** *Black Churches in Texas.*

– *throughout Texas, acts of barbarity and terror.* **Horne,** *The Counter Revolution of 1836;* **Caldwell and DeLord,** *Eternity at the End of a Rope;* **Marlin Bicentennial Heritage Committee,** *Marlin 1851-1976,* **17.**
– *live performances of Henry "Ragtime Texas" Thomas.* **Tomlinson,** *Tomlinson Hill,* **221-25**
– *Songs like this were part of a work-song tradition.* **Barlow,** *Looking Up at Down,* **56-78; Jackson,** *Wake Up Dead Man;* **Woods,** *Development Arrested;* **Davis,** *Blues Legacies and Black Feminism.*
– *Keeping time, or better put, keeping in time.* **Jackson,** *Wake Up Dead Man,* **33. Kae,** *Keeping Time.*
– *"The boll weevil is a lil' bug, from Mexico."* **Federal Writers' Project, "Oral History of John Love," 28.**
– *"I know why that boll-weevil came."* **Federal Writers' Project, "Oral History of John Love," 27–8.**
– *Falls County's total number of farms.* **Brawn,** *The History of Falls County;* **Old Settlers and Veterans Association of Falls County,** *History of Falls County, Texas.*
– *It had formed in Mexico's Bay of Campeche.* **Kelley, "Brazos River"; Dalrymple, Major Texas Floods of 1936; Tannehill, "Tropical Disturbances of 1936."**
– *"The water was deep enough."* **See "Highbank Texas| Photos & Stories of Early Day Settlers."**

CHAPTER 2:
DEM'(ING) FOLKS

– *to help build the base.* **St. John,** *World War II Bombardiers,* **9-15; "WWII Ghosts at Nearby Luna County Deming Airport"; Penn, "Records of Military Agencies"; Shaw,** *Locating Air Force Base Sites History's Legacy; Deming Army Airfield.*
– *Black troops were not included.* **Osur,** *Blacks in the Army Air Forces During World War II,* **124.**
– *Previous eras had seen small waves of Black migration.* **Glasrud,** *African American History in New Mexico;* **Billington.** *New Mexico's Buffalo Soldiers;* **Anton, "Racial Ambiguity in the Borderlands."**
– *A. C. Rist alleged that he saw a member of the boys' group stealing* **apples. See "Assault to Kill Charge is Filed"; "Charge Local Man with Shooting Boy for Apple 'Hooking'"; "(One Thousand Dollars) $1000 is Sought in Shooting Suit."**
– *Harold's mangled body was discovered near the railroad tracks.* **See "Train Kills Three Youths"; "Charles City**

Couple Dies in Auto Crash"; "Services Set for CCC Boys."**
– *And he developed a rap sheet of petty crimes.* **See "Gambling House Charges Ignored"; "Claim 'Chicken Jar' Used for a Weapon"; "Franklin Grants Parole to Youth, 19".**
– *he was arrested and sentenced to ten years.* **See "Charge 3 with Robbing Man"; "Three Youths Held in Robbery Case"; "Robbery Charge: 3 Youths Given 10-Year Sentence."**
– *Deming, his hometown, was a creation of the railroad industry.* **Krol,** *Deming (Images of America);* **Reynolds,** *SWNM History;* **The Luna County Historical Society, Inc.** *The History of Luna County.*
– *Take the Apaches.* **Cook, "The Last Apache "Broncho."**
– *The Mimbres peoples, on the other hand.* **Roth,** *New Perspectives on Mimbres Archaeology;* **Hegmon, "Experiencing Social Change: Life during the Mimbres Classic Transformation."**
– *Central to Spanish conquistador and Anglo American militarial /colonial settlement of the Southwest.* **Mitchell,** *Coyote Nation.*
– *more commonly known as "Esteban" and "Estevanico."* **Goodwin,** *Crossing the Continent;* **Herrick,** *Esteban.*
– *However, such history lessons were not the norm.* **Reynolds,** *SWNM History.*
– *The town's power structure was a microcosm of the broader region.* **Barrera,** *Race and Class in the Southwest;* **Mitchell,** *Coyote Nation;* **Glasrud,** *African American History in New Mexico;* **Reynolds,** *SWNM History;* **Knox, "Racial Integration in the Public Schools of Arizona, Kansas and New Mexico"; Foley,** *From Mexicans in the Making of America,* **113.**

CHAPTER 3:
I KNOW YOU [BUFFALO SOLDIER]

– *"We used to talk about how the birds can do these extraordinary maneuvers."* **Kelley,** *Thelonious Monk,* **196.**
– *uprisings in Tucson and Phoenix after the Tucson police arrested a fourteen-year-old Black teen.* **"Arrest of Negro Boy Starts Melee in Tucson."; Fernandez, "Tucson Race Riot,"; "29 Killed, Thousands Injured as Race Riots Spread to 12 U.S. Cities."**
– *The 4th Division was in the final throes of OPERATION FRANCIS MARION.* **MacGarrigle,** *United States Army in Vietnam* **Combat Operations,** **287–310.**
– *the more than 300,000 Black troops that served in Vietnam.* **Lucks, "African American soldiers and the Vietnam War"; Phillips,** *War! What Is It Good*

For?; **Cortwright,** "Black GI Resistance During the Vietnam War."

‒   *One day I went and asked her for my own garden.* **X with Haley,** *The Autobiography of Malcolm X,* **8–9.**

‒   *A helicopter sent in to evacuate several Marine casualties and wounded soldiers had been shot down.* **Telfer,** *U.S. Marines in Vietnam,* **125–147.**

‒   *In November they fought at Đ k Tô.* **Okendo,** *Sky Soldier;* **Lung,** *The General Offensives of 1968-1969;* **Murphy, Dak To; Eggleston, Dak To and the Border Battles of Vietnam, 1967–1968.**

‒   *the quiet intimate life and relations that surrounded him.* **Quashie,** *The Sovereignty of Quiet.*

‒   *15,000 Montagnards continued to live in the areas.* **MacGarrigle,** *United States Army in Vietnam Combat Operations,* **307-308; Montagnard Foundation,** *History of the Montagnard/ Degar People.*

‒   *The professor, Allen Ayers Dutton.* **Corcoran Gallery of Art, "Strange But True."**

CHAPTER 4:
EMANCIPATE THE (I)MAGE

‒   *he was drawn into a collective of emerging filmmakers.* **Field, Horak, and Stewart,** *L.A. Rebellion;* **Masilela, "The Los Angeles School of Black Filmmakers"; Pines and Willemen,** *Questions of Third Cinema.*

‒   *"It's about becoming more comfortable getting to a place where there are no answers."* **Phoenix Community Alliance, "Allen Dutton Photography Exhibition."**

‒   *photography as a process of "conscious discovery".* **White,** *Mirrors, Messages, Manifestations* **and "Equivalence: The Perennial Trend."**

‒   *Ben determined that his films would create a visual poetics.* **Field, "Rebellious Unlearning."**

‒   *"to change the ritual"* by *"way of emancipating the image."* **See "Ben Caldwell Oral History Interview Conducted by Allyson Field and Jacqueline Stewart."**

‒   *"'I and I' is a word that goes back us far as Sanskrit, as far as Egyptian mythology."* **UCLA Film and Television Archive, "L.A. Rebellion | Ben Caldwell on UCLA's "The View."**

‒   *"The structure that we know of now."* **UCLA Film and Television Archive, "L.A. Rebellion | Ben Caldwell on UCLA's "The View."**

‒   *several attendees questioned Ben's cinematic point of* view. **Flaherty Film Seminar Archive, "Post-Film Discussion."**

CHAPTER 5:
GEORGIA AVE × LEIMERT PARK

‒   *What they got was a militarized city manned by the LAPD.* **Davis,** *City of Quartz;* **Felkner-Kantor,** *Policing Los Angeles.*

‒   *"It is naive to believe that the viewing of a single movie."* **Scarupa, "The Image Messengers."**

‒   *"video as a process art form."* See **"Shirley Clarke: An Interview" and Gurian, "Thoughts on Shirley Clarke and The TP Videospace Troupe."**

‒   *Don's crew was part of a city-wide multitude.* **Cross,** *It's Not About a Salary;* **Chang,** *Can't Stop Won't Stop.*

CHAPTER 6:
HOLLYWATTS

‒   *It was part of a citywide ecosphere where performance art.* **Burnham and Durland,** *The Citizen Artist.*

‒   *Ben's visual images "suppl[ied] a third rhythmic force" to the performance.* **Sullivan, "Stage Review.**

‒   *innovative set and video design were also influenced by Mabou Mines.* **Fischer,** *Mabou Mines.*

‒   *Los Angeles's tradition of Black assemblage art and freeform jazz and funk musicianship.* **Jones,** *South of Pico;* **Jones and Carby,** *Now Dig This!;* **Isoardi,** *The Dark Tree;* **Widener,** *Black Arts West.*

‒   *"an intimate portrait . . . that spoke to those who will inhabit the 21st century."* **Haile, "Events, Roger Guenveur Smith."**

‒   *"an evocative portrait drawn from the orator's insightful, beautifully articulated observations."* **Santiago, "Roger Guenveur Smith's One-Man Show."**

‒   *"a mesmerizing production."* **McCoy, "'Creole Mafia' Proves Controversial."**

‒   *"These young men are clever writers."* **Koehler, "Stirring up an Indefinable 'Creole."**

‒   *"subtle satirical jab at the theater of multicultural identity."* **Kreiswirth, "'Creole Mafia' Makes Its Point with a Sharp Wit."**

‒   *"an important theatrical triumph."* **Hobbes, "Editorial Opinion."**

CHAPTER 7:
ENTER THE KAOS

‒   *Blowed was an echo of the "Good Life."* **DuVernay,** *This is the Life;* **Morgan,** *The Real Hiphop;* **Lee,** *Blowin' Up;* **Myka 9,** *My Kaleidoscope.*

‒   *"creative response to the arrival of the Orwellian year."* **Galloway and Rabinowitz,** *Electronic Café.*

‒   *"Chaos is everywhere."* **Abraham,** "Chaos and Life, Interview, 1990."

‒   *one of several storefront businesses to help rejuvenate the Village's cultural life.* **Washington,** *Performing Africa;* **Lindsay,** *Leimert Park;* **Vargas,** *Catching Hell in the City of Angels.*

‒   *there were somewhere between 57,000 and 61,000 gang members in L.A.* **Gates and Jackson, "Gang Violence in Los Angeles."**

‒   *There were more than 3,300 gang-related murders in L.A. during this period.* **Smith, "Gangs Continue to Terrorize L.A. Residents."**

‒   *"murderous arc."* **Davis,** *City of Quartz,* **270.**

‒   *there were more than 6,327 drive-by shootings.* **Hutson, "Drive-by Shootings by Violent Street Gangs in Los Angeles."**

CODA:
POSTCARDS FROM SANKOFA CITIES

‒   *"You don't realize when you're doing what you love that you're mentoring someone."* **See** *Medusa (Monae Smith) Interview by Mako Fitts and Michelle Habel-Pallan.*

Bibliography

Abraham, Ralph. "Chaos and Life, Interview, 1990: Interview with Rebecca McClen and David Jay Brown." *IS Journal*, vol. 9, 1990, pp. 3, 7–8.
Abraham, Ralph and Yoshisuke Ueda. Editors. *Chaos Avant-Garde, The: Memoirs of The Early Days of Chaos Theory.* World Scientific Publishing Company, 2001.
Ancestry.com, United States Federal Census, Ancestry.com Operations, Inc., 1997–2018.
Anderson, Gary Clayton. *The Conquest of Texas: Ethnic Cleansing in the Promised Land, 1820-1875.* University of Oklahoma Press, 2019.
Anton, Jacqulyne. "Racial Ambiguity in the Borderlands: New Mexico's African American Soldiers, 1860–1922," *History in the Making,* Vol. 12 Article 11, 2019.
Arkatov, Janice. "Creole Culture, Italian Farce Take the Stage." *Los Angeles Times,* 1 Dec. 1991.
"Arrest of Negro Boy Starts Melee in Tucson." *The Washington Post, Times Herald,* 25 July 1967.
"Assault to Kill Charge is Filed," *The Des Moines Tribune,* 28 July 1930, p. 3.
Bailey, Ralph. "Noteworthy Student Shot in His Car, Dies." *Los Angeles Sentinel,* 23 Apr. 1987, p. A5.
Barlow, William. *"Looking up at Down": The Emergence of Blues Culture.* Temple University Press, 1989.
Barrera, Mario. *Race & Class in the Southwest: A Theory of Racial Inequality.* University of Notre Dame Press, 1979.
"Ben Caldwell Oral History Interview Conducted by Allyson Field and Jacqueline Stewart," *L.A. Rebellion Collection,* UCLA Film & Television Archive, Los Angeles, June 14, 2010.
Ben Caldwell Oral History Interview Conducted by David P. Cline in Los Angeles, California. Directed by David P. Cline, 2013, https://www.loc.gov/item/2015669176/.
Bicentennial Heritage Committee. *Marlin, 1851–1976.* 1976.
Billington, Monroe Lee. *New Mexico's Buffalo Soldiers, 1866-1900.* University of Colorado Press, 1991.
Blacks in the Army Air Forces During World War II: The Problems of Race Relations. DIANE Publishing, 1977.
Bradford, Gary. "Featured Filmmaker Answers Call of Art, Not Hollywood." *Pittsburgh Press,* 12 June 1980.
Brawn, Walter W. *The History of Falls County.* Baylor University, 1938.
Brazos Flood at Waco, September 27, 1936. Baylor University. The Texas Collection.

brown, adrienne m. *Emergent Strategy.* AK Press, 2017.
Brown, Jayna. *Black Utopias: Speculative Life and the Music of Other Worlds.* Duke University Press, 2021.
Broyard, Bliss. *One Drop: My Father's Hidden Life: A Story of Race and Family Secrets.* Back Bay Books, 2008.
Burnham, Linda Frye, and Steven Durland. *The Citizen Artist: 20 Years of Art in the Public Arena/ an Anthology from High Performance Magazine 1978–1998.* Critical Press, 1998.
Caldwell, Clifford R., and Ron DeLord. *Eternity at the End of a Rope: Executions, Lynchings and Vigilante Justice in Texas, 1819-1923.* Sunstone Press, 2015.
Chang, Jeff. *Can't Stop Won't Stop: A History of the Hip-Hop Generation.* St. Martin's Press, 2007.
"Charge Local Man with Shooting Boy for Apple 'Hooking'," *The Des Moines Register,* 28 July 1930, p. 2.
"Charge 3 with Robbing Man: Police Say Suspects Have Admitted Guilt," *The Des Moines Register,* 2 Nov. 1938, p. 3.
"Charles City Couple Dies in Auto Crash: Fatal Wrecks Occur at South Amana and Hubbard," *The Des Moines Register,* 17 June 1935, p. 1.
Cheng, Meiling. "Highways, L.A.: Multiple Communities in a Heterolocus." *Theatre Journal* (Washington, D.C.), vol. 53, no. 3, 2001, pp. 429–54.
"Claim 'Chicken Jar' Used for a Weapon," *The Des Moines Register,* 13 July 1934, p. 11.
Chideya, Farai. "Viewing Los Angeles Through a Creole Lens." *The New York Times,* 21 Jan. 2016.
Coleman, Anita Scott. "El Tisico." *The Crisis,* vol. 19, no. 5, Mar. 1920, pp. 251–53.
Cook, Leah. "The Last Apache 'Broncho': The Apache Outlaw in the Popular Imagination, 1886–2013." *History ETDs,* July 2014, https://digitalrepository-.unm.edu/hist_etds/16.
"Compiled Service Records of Confederate Soldiers Who Served in Organizations from the State of Mississippi," *Fold3.com,* National Archives Catalog 586957, https://www.fold3.com/image/84986478
Cortwright, David. "Black GI Resistance During the Vietnam War." *Vietnam Generation,* vol. 2, no. 1, Jan. 1990.
Cross, Brian. *It's Not About a Salary: Rap, Race, and Resistance in Los Angeles,* Verso, 1994.
Dalrymple, Tate. *Major Texas Floods of 1936.* US Government Printing Office, 1937.
Davis, Angela Y. *Blues Legacies and Black Feminism: Gertrude 'Ma' Rainey, Bessie Smith, and Billie Holiday.* Vintage Books, 1999.
Davis, Mike. *City of Quartz: Excavating the Future in Los Angeles.* Verso, 2018.
Deming Army Airfield: Army Airforce Flying Training Command. Army and Navy Publishing Co., Inc., 1943.
Diawara, Manthia. editor. *Black American* Cinema. Routledge, 1993.
Dutton, Allen. *Real to Surreal.* Self-published, 2014.
---. *Strange But True: The Arizona Photographs of Allen Dutton,* Corcoran Gallery of Art. 2000
---. *Arizona Then & Now* Self-published, 1981.
Eggleston, Michael A. *Dak To and the Border Battles of Vietnam, 1967–1968.* McFarland & Company, Inc., Publishers, 2017.
"Exhibition Walkthrough With Ben Caldwell and Jheanelle Brown," *Art + Practice,* Feb. 26, 2019.
Exum, Cynthia E., and Maty Guiza-Leimert. *Leimert Park.* Arcadia Publishing, 2012.
Falls County Historical Commission. *Families of Falls County.* Eakin Press, 1987.
Federal Writers' Project. *Oral History of John Love.* 17 v. in 33. mounted photos. 28 cm., https://lccn.loc.gov/41021619. Library of Congress.
Felkner-Kantor, Max. *Policing Los Angeles: Race, Resistance, and the Rise of the LAPD.* The University of North Carolina Press, 2018.
Fernandez, Maritza. "Tucson Race Riot." *Black Past,* 25 Mar. 2018, https://www.blackpast.org/african-american-history/tucson-race-riot-1967/.
Field, Allyson Nadia, et al., editors. *L.A. Rebellion: Creating a New Black Cinema.* University of California Press, 2015.
---. "Rebellious Unlearning: UCLA Project One Films (1967–1978)." *L.A. Rebellion: Creating a New Black Cinema,* University of California Press, 2015.
Fischer, Iris Smith. *Mabou Mines: Making Avant-Garde Theater in the 1970s.* The University of Michigan Press, 2010.
Foley, Neil. *Mexicans in the Making of America.* Belknap Press, 2017.
"Franklin Grants Parole to Youth, 19," *The Des Moines Tribune,* 7 Jan. 1938, p. 22.
Galloway, Kit, and Sherrie Rabinowitz. *Electronic Café: A Manifesto for the Original 1984 Electronic Café Network Project.* 1983, http://www.ecafe.com/museum/about_festo/84manifesto.html
"Gambling House Charges Ignored," *The Des Moines Register,* 31 Dec. 1936, p. 3.
Gates, D. F., and R. K. Jackson. "Gang Violence in Los Angeles." *Police Chief,* Nov. 1990, pp. 20–22.

George, Lynell. *A Handful of Earth, A Handful of Sky: The World of Octavia Butler.* Angel City Press, 2020.

---. "The KAOS Theory: Ben Caldwell's Multimedia Sanctuary Provides a Cultural Bridge." *Los Angeles Times,* 23 Jan. 1996.

Getty Foundation, Sponsor, and Pacific Standard Time. *L.A. Rebellion Oral History Interviews, 2010–2011.* 2010, pp. Pacific Standard Time Art in L.A. Recordings, 2008–2012.

Glahn, Philip, and Cary Levine, "The Future Is Present: Electronic Café and the Politics of Technological Fantasy," *Art Journal,* no. 3, Fall 2019.

Glasrud, Bruce A., editor. *African American History in New Mexico: Portraits from Five Hundred Years.* University of New Mexico Press, 2013.

Goodwin, Robert. *Crossing the Continent 1527-1540: The Story of the First African-American Explorer of the American South.* Harper, 2008.

Greenstein, M. A. "Skin Test." *Artweek,* vol. 24, no. 22, 18 Nov. 1993, p. 17.

Griffin, Farah Jasmine. *"Who Set You Flowin'?": The African-American Migration Narrative.* Oxford University Press, 1995.

Grigsby, J. Eugene. *Art & Ethnics: Background for Teaching Youth in a Pluralistic Society (Trends in Art Education).* W. C. Brown Co, 1977.

"Guenveur Smith Takes Highways to Creole Heaven." *Los Angeles Sentinel,* 28 Nov. 1991, p. B7.

Gurian, Andrew. "Thoughts on Shirley Clarke and The TP Videospace Troupe." *Millennium Film Journal,* vol. 42, Fall 2004.

Gustafson, C. A., editor. *SWNM History: A Collection of Old West Stories 1300-2000: Featuring Deming, New Mexico & Highlights of Neighboring Towns.* JReynolds Photo & Computer Works, 2012.

Haile, Mark. "Events, Roger Guenveur Smith: Frederick Douglass Now." *High Performance,* vol. 14, Spring 1991, p. 42.

Hegmon, Michelle, et al. "Experiencing Social Change: Life during the Mimbres Classic Transformation." *Archaeological Papers of the American Anthropological Association,* vol. 27, no. 1, 2016, pp. 54–73.

Herrick, Dennis F. *Esteban: The African Slave Who Explored America.* University of New Mexico Press, 2018.

"Highbank Texas| Photos & Stories of Early Day Settlers." *History of Highbank, Texas,* http://www.forttumbleweed. net/highbank.html and http://www. highbanktexashistory.com/.

Hoang, Ngoc Lung. *The General Offensives of 1968-69.* General Research Corporation, 1978.

Hobbes, Dwight. "Editorial Opinion: Politically Correct Theater Critics Allowing Bad Black Art to Slide By." *Minnesota Spokesman-Recorder.*

Horn, Barbara Lee. *Ellen Stewart and La Mama: A Bio-Bibliography.* Greenwood Press, 1993.

Horne, Gerald. *The Counter Revolution of 1836: Texas Slavery & Jim Crow and the Roots of U.S. Fascism.* International Publishers, 2022.

Human Rights Watch. *Repression Of Montagnards: Conflicts over Land and Religion in Vietnam's Central Highlands.* United Nations High Commissioner for Refugees, 23 Apr. 2002.

Hunt, Darnell M., and Ana-Christina Ramón, editors. *Black Los Angeles: American Dreams and Racial Realities.* New York University Press, 2010.

Hutson, H. Range, et al. "Drive-by Shootings by Violent Street Gangs in Los Angeles: A Five-Year Review from 1989 to 1993." *Academic Emergency Medicine,* vol. 3, no. 4, 1996, pp. 300–03.

Isoardi, Steven L. *The Dark Tree: Jazz and the Community Arts in Los Angeles.* University of California Press, 2006.

Ivereem, Esther. "Young Artists Take Stage for Black History Month. Sidebars: A Guide to Black History Month." *Newsday,* 2 Feb. 1990, pp. 1, 14–15.

Jackson, Bruce, editor. *Wake up Dead Man: Afro-American Worksongs from Texas Prisons.* Harvard University Press, 1974.

Jenkins, Ulysses, et al. *Ulysses Jenkins: Without Your Interpretation.* Institute of Contemporary Art, University of Pennsylvania, 2021.

John, Philip A. St. *WWII Bombardiers.* Turner Publishing Company, 1998.

Jones, Kellie. *South of Pico: African American Artists in Los Angeles in the 1960s and 1970s.* Duke University Press, 2017.

Jones, Kellie, and Hazel V. Carby. *Now Dig This! Art & Black Los Angeles, 1960-1980.* Hammer Museum; University of California; DelMonico Books/Prestel, 2011.

Keeping Time. Directed by Darol Olu Kae, 2023.

Kelley, Dayton. "Brazos River." *The Handbook of Waco and McLennan County, Texas,* Texian Press, 1972, pp. 35–36.

Kelley, Robin D. G. *Thelonious Monk: The Life and Times of an American Original.* Free Press, 2010.

Knox, Ellis O. "Racial Integration in the Public Schools of Arizona, Kansas and New Mexico." *The Journal of Negro Education,* vol. 23, no. 3, 1954, pp. 290–95.

Koehler, Robert. "Stirring Up an Indefinable 'Creole' Dish." *Los Angeles Times,* 7 Dec. 1991.

Kreiswirth, Sandra. "'Creole Mafia' Makes Its Point with a Sharp Wit." *The Daily Breeze/News-Pilot,* 5 Nov. 1993.

Krol, Laura V. *Deming.* Arcadia Publishing Library Editions, 2012.

Krout-Hasegawa, Ellen. "Theater Picks of the Week: Inside the Creole Mafia." *LA Weekly,* vol. 15, no. No. 24, 14 May 1993.

L.A. Rebellion | Ben Caldwell on UCLA's "The View" (c. 1979). Directed by UCLA Film and Television Archive, 2013, https://www.youtube.com/ watch?v=SLe8bvBxEn0.

Lee, Jooyoung. *Blowin' Up: Rap Dreams in South Central.* The University of Chicago Press, 2016.

Leimert Park: The Story of a Village in South Central Los Angeles. Directed by Jeanette Lindsay, 2006.

LeSeur, Geta J. *Not All Okies Are White: The Lives of Black Cotton Pickers in Arizona.* University of Missouri Press, 2000.

Lornell, Kip, and Charles C. Stephenson. *The Beat! Go-Go Music from Washington, D.C.* University Press of Mississippi, 2009.

Lucks, Daniel. "African American Soldiers and the Vietnam War: No More Vietnams." *The Sixties,* vol. 10, no. 2, July 2017, pp. 196–220.

MacGarrigle, George L. *Combat Operations: Taking the Offensive: October 1966 to October 1967 (United States Army in Vietnam).* 1998.

Mahoney, John C. "It's Certainly Space." *Los Angeles Downtown News,* 20 Jan. 1986.

Marlin Chamber of Commerce. *Marlin, 1851-1976.* Bicentennial Heritage Committee, 1976.

Masilela, Ntongela. "The Los Angeles School of Black Filmmakers: *Black American Cinema,*" Routledge, 1993, pp. 115–25.

McCoy, Franklin Milton. "'Creole Mafia' Proves Controversial." *Los Angeles Sentinel,* 28 Oct. 1993.

McQueen, Clyde. *Black Churches in Texas: A Guide to Historic Congregations.* Texas A&M University Press, 2000.

Medusa (Monae Smith) Interview by Mako Fitts and Michelle Habel-Pallan, Women Who Rock Digital Oral History Project, University of Washington, 5 May 2012, https://content.lib.washington.edu/ wwrweb/transcripts/Medusa.pdf

Milbauer, John A. "Population Origins and Ethnicity in the Silver City Mining Region of New Mexico, 1870-1890." *International Social Science Review,* vol. 60, no. 4, Fall 1985, pp. 160–65.

Mitchell, Pablo. *Coyote Nation: Sexuality,*

Race, and Conquest in Modernizing New Mexico, 1880-1920. **University Of Chicago Press, 2005.**

Morgan, Marcyliena H. *The Real Hiphop: Battling for Knowledge, Power, and Respect in the LA Underground.* **Duke University Press, 2009.**

Murphy, Edward F. *Dak To: America's Sky Soldiers in South Vietnam's Central Highlands.* **Presidio Press, 2007.**

Myka 9, *My Kaleidoscope.* **Lulu Publishing, 2022.**

National Gallery of Art (U.S.), et al., editors. *Alfred Stieglitz: The Key Set—Volume I & II: The Alfred Stieglitz Collection of Photographs.* **National Gallery of Art; Harry N. Abrams, 2002.**

Neal, Mark Anthony. *Black Ephemera: The Crisis and Challenge of the Musical Archive.* **New York University Press, 2022.**

Okendo, Lawrence D. *Sky Soldier: Battles of Dak-To.* **L.D. Okendo, 1988.**

Old Settlers and Veterans Association of Falls County, *History of Falls County, Texas,* **1947.**

"(One Thousand Dollars) $1000 is Sought in Shooting Suit," *The Des Moines Tribune,* **16 Oct. 1930.**

Penn, Lisha H. *Records of Military Agencies Relating to African Americans from the Post-World War I Period to the Korean War.* **National Archives and Records Administration, 2006.**

Phillips, Kimberley L. *War! What Is It Good For?: Black Freedom Struggles and the U.S. Military from World War II to Iraq.* **The University of North Carolina Press, 2012.**

Phoenix Community Alliance, "Allen Dutton Photography Exhibition." Website no longer available.

Pines, Jim., and Paul Willemen, *Questions of Third Cinema.* **British Film Institute, 1989.**

Quashie, Kevin E. *The Sovereignty of Quiet: Beyond Resistance in Black Culture.* **Rutgers University Press, 2012.**

Rangarajan, Sinduja. **"The Father of Leimert Park, or the Octopus."** *KCET,* **12 Sept. 2014, https://www.kcet.org/ shows/departures/the-father-of-leimert-park-or-the-octopus.**

Reeve, Frank Driver and Alice Ann Cleaveland. *New Mexico, Land of Many Cultures.* **Pruett, 1969.**

"Reviews: Inside the Creole Mafia." *Los Angeles Magazine,* **Dec. 1993.**

Richards, David. **"The Worlds of Roger Smith."** *The Washington Post,* **3 Nov. 1996.**

RIP Woods: The Man, The Artist, The Teacher. **Directed by Dee Woods, https:// vimeo.com/78722120.**

"Robbery Charge: 3 Youths Given 10-Year Sentence," *The Des Moines Tribune,* **23 Nov. 1938.**

Robertson, Gil L. *Family Affair: What It Means to Be African-American Today.* **Agate Publishing, Incorporated, 2009.**

Ross, Michael E. **"Puncturing a Sacred Myth: Review of Christopher Columbus 1992."** *San Francisco Chronicle,* **27 Sept. 1992, pp. 32–34.**

Roth, Barbara J., et al., editors. *New Perspectives on Mimbres Archaeology: Three Millennia of Human Occupation in the North American Southwest.* **The University of Arizona Press, 2018.**

Santiago, Chiori. **"Roger Guenveur Smith's One-Man Show / Frederick Douglass' Words, Ideals Revived / Show Ushers in Black History Month."** *San Francisco Chronicle,* **19 Jan. 1992, p. 22.**

Sawyer, Amanda. **"1936 Flood."** *Waco History,* **https://wacohistory.org/items/ show/63.**

Scarupa, Harriet Jackson. **"The Image Messengers: Filmmakers at Howard."** *New Directions,* **vol. 10, no. 3, Apr. 1983.**

"Services Set for CCC Boys: Third Train Victim is Identified," *The Des Moines Register,* **18 June 1935.**

Shaw, Frederick. *Locating Air Force Base Sites: History's Legacy.* **2004.**

"Shirley Clarke: An Interview." *Radical Software,* **vol. 2, no. 4, 1973, pp. 25–27.**

Skoller, Jeffrey. **"Space Is the Place: Review of John Akomfrah's Film the Last Angel of History."** *Afterimage,* **Dec. 1997, p. 14.**

Smith, Leef. **"Gangs Continue to Terrorize L.A. Residents."** *The Washington Post,* **16 Sept. 1992**

Smith, Leo. **"Updated Message."** *Los Angeles Times,* **14 Jan. 1993, p. VCJ 14.**

Snowden, Don. **"Ben Caldwell's 'Fresh' Approach to Film Making."** *Los Angeles Times,* **8 Jan. 1998.**

---. **"Cultural Spring in Crenshaw: Arts Transform Degnan Boulevard."** *Los Angeles Times,* **3 Oct. 1992.**

Society, The Luna County Historical. *The History of Luna County.* **1978.**

St. Romain, Lillian S. *A History of Western Falls County Texas.* **Texas State Historical Association, 1951.**

Stevens, Tad. *The Stage: Creole Hee Haw.* **Unknown publication.**

Stewart, Jacqueline, and Ben Caldwell. **"Money, Land, Film, Future: In Conversation."** *Portable Gray,* **vol. 1, no. 1, Sept. 2018, pp. 15–26.**

Sullivan, Dan. **"Stage Review: 'Piecemeal Serves up 8 Statements."** *Los Angeles Times,* **21 Mar. 1986, p. 11.**

Surence, Matthew. **"Inside Creole Mafia' at Solo Mio Festival."** *The Oakland Tribune,* **16 Sept. 1993.**

Tajima, Renee E., and Tracey Willard. **"Nothing Lights a Fire Like a Dream Deferred,"** *The Independent,* **Vol. 7, No. 10, November 1984, pp. 18–21.**

Tannehill, Edgar W. **"Tropical Disturbances of 1936: September 1936."** *Monthly Weather Review,* **vol. 64, no. 6, Sept. 1936.**

Tapscott, Horace. *Songs of the Unsung: The Musical and Social Journey of Horace Tapscott,* **Duke University Press, 2001.**

Telfer, Gary L., et al. *U.S. Marines in Vietnam: Fighting the North Vietnamese 1967.* **History and Museums Division, Headquarters, U.S. Marine Corps, 1984.**

The 23rd Annual Flaherty Seminar, Tape 10: August 30, 1977, "Post-Film Discussion with Ben Caldwell, Sally [Hechel], Paul Trejo, David Feingold," in Robert Flaherty Film Seminar Archive 1949–2011, Subseries A: Audio Recordings, Box 6, Media ID: 326.0282, Fales Library and Special Collections, Elmer Holmes Bobst Library, New York University.

"The Crenshaw Continuum." *Deep Routes,* **3, 21 July 2020, https://www. dublab.com/archive/metro-art-dublab-present-deep-routes-episode-3-the-crenshaw-continuum-07-21-20.**

"The Good Life: L.A. Hip-Hop's Untold Story." *Hip-Hop Wired,* **7 July 2009.**

"The History of Falls County." *Marlin Texas,* **https://marlintexas.com/ falls-county-history/.**

The Montagnard Foundation. *History of the Montagnard/Degar People: Their Struggle for Survival and Rights Before International Law.* **The Foundation, 2001.**

"Three Youths Held in Robbery Case," *The Des Moines Tribune,* **28 October 1938, p. 6.**

This is the Life. **Directed by Ava DuVernay, 2008.**

Tomlinson, Chris. *Tomlinson Hill: The Remarkable Story of Two Families Who Share the Tomlinson Name - One White, One Black.* **Macmillan, 2014.**

"Train Kills Three Youths: Bodies Found Early Sunday Near Tracks," *Centerville Daily Iowegian,* **17 June 1935, p. 1.**

"Twenty-Nine Killed, Thousands Injured as Race Riots Spread to 12 U.S. Cities: 11,500 Federal Troops in Detroit." *The Jerusalem Post,* **26 July 1967.**

Vargas, João Helion Costa. *Catching Hell in the City of Angels: Life and Meanings of Blackness in South Central Los Angeles.* **University of Minnesota Press, 2006.**

Washington, Giavanni ReShae. *Performing Africa: Memory, Tradition, and Resistance in the Leimert Park Drum Circle.* **University of California Los Angeles (UCLA), 2013.**

Waters, Frank. *Mexico Mystique: The Coming Sixth World of Consciousness.* **1st ed, Sage Books, 1975.**

White, Minor. **"Equivalence: The Perennial Trend."** *PSA Journal,* **vol. 29, no. 7, 1963, pp. 17–21.**

---. *Mirrors, Messages, Manifestations.* 2nd ed., Aperture, 1982.

Widener, Daniel. *Black Arts West: Culture and Struggle in Postwar Los Angeles.* Duke University Press, 2010.

Wilson, Stephen. *Information Arts: Intersections of Art, Science, and Technology.* MIT Press, 2002.

Woods, Clyde Adrian. *Development Arrested: The Blues and Plantation Power in the Mississippi Delta.* Verso, 1998.

"WWII Ghosts at Nearby Luna County Deming Airport." *First Aero Squadron Foundation*, 8 Dec. 2015.

X, Malcolm, and Alex Haley. *The Autobiography of Malcolm X.* 1965. Ballantine Books, 1992.

Yearwood, Gladstone Lloyd, editor. *Black Cinema Aesthetics: Issues in Independent Black Filmmaking.* Center for Afro-American Studies, Ohio University, 1982.

Zion Rock Baptist Church. https://sites.rootsweb.com/~txfalls/Churches/Church_Webpages/ZionRockBaptistChurch.html.

ABOUT THE AUTHORS

ROBESON TAJ FRAZIER is a writer and associate professor in the Annenberg School for Communication and Journalism at the University of Southern California and director of the Institute for Diversity and Empowerment at Annenberg (IDEA). He is the author of *The East is Black: Cold War China in the Black Radical Imagination*, producer of the documentary film *It's Yours: A Story About Hip Hop and the Internet*, and host of the PBS Digital Studios production, *Hip Hop and the Metaverse*.

BEN CALDWELL is an arts educator, independent filmmaker, and founder of KAOS Network, a multimedia arts/tech accelerator center located in Leimert Park, a historic and cultural hub of Los Angeles. A native of New Mexico, Caldwell earned an MFA in film and television at UCLA, taught at Howard University and California Institute of the Arts, and is a senior fellow in the University of Southern California's Annenberg Innovation Lab. Caldwell's work has been shown nationally and internationally, including at the Tate Modern, Festival des 3 Continents, and the Lisbon & Estoril Film Festival.

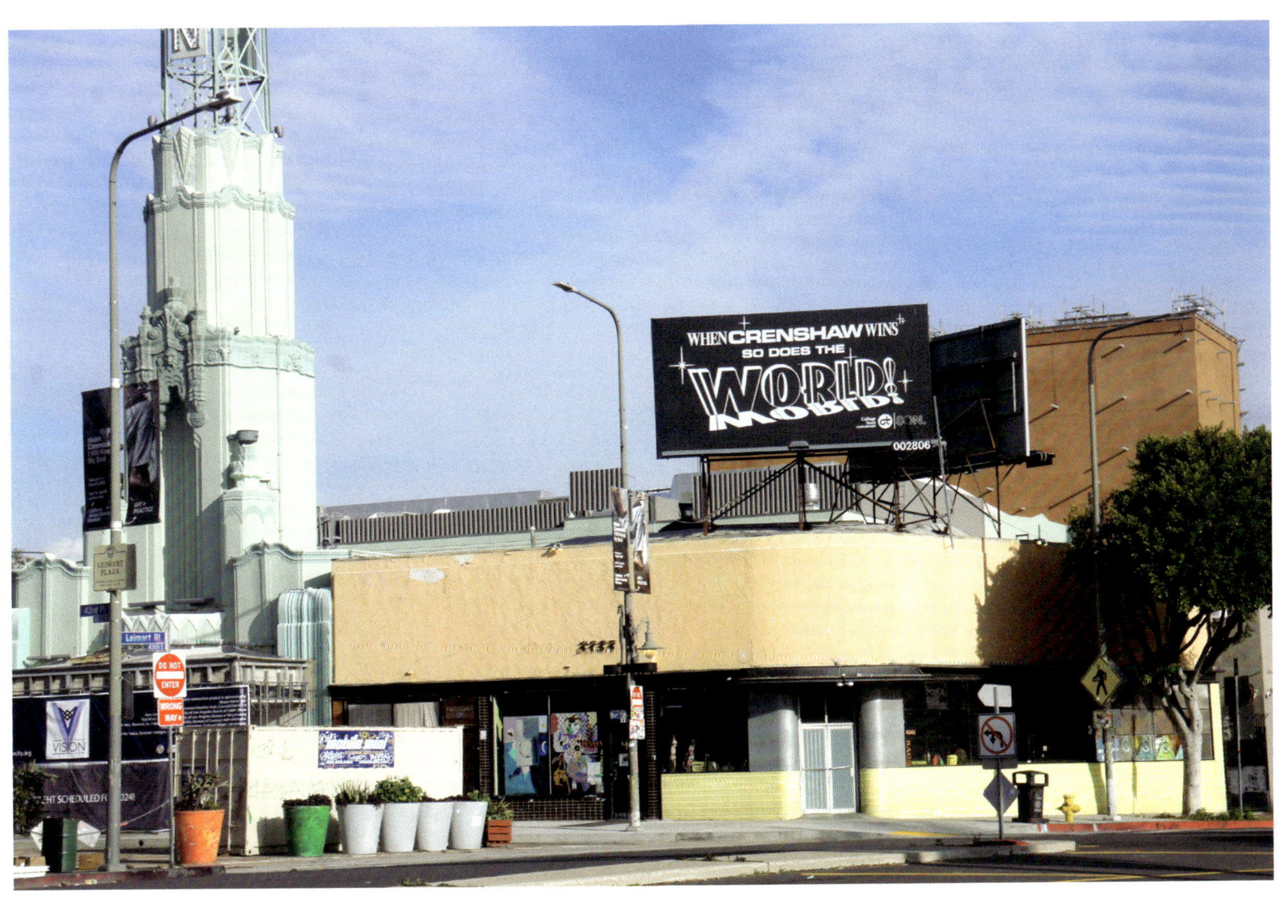

KAOS Theory: The Afrokosmic Ark of Ben Caldwell

By Robeson Taj Frazier with Ben Caldwell
Foreword by Arthur Jafa

Copyright © 2023 Robeson Taj Frazier and Ben R. Caldwell

Design by ELLA

10 9 8 7 6 5 4 3 2 1

ISBN-13 978-1-62640-117-4

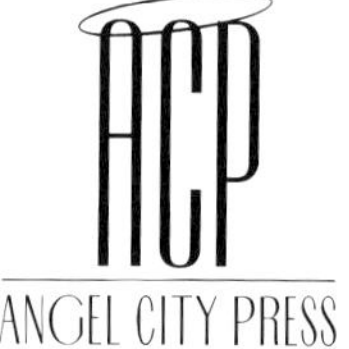

Published by Angel City Press
www.angelcitypress.com

Printed in Canada

All images are from the Ben Caldwell Collection except as noted below:

Baylor University Library, The Texas Collection, Acree Family Papers, photograph by Fred Acree: 35, bottom
Broyard, Mark: 170, bottom
Cross, Brian "B+" : 218, 221
Emory University, Stuart A. Rose Manuscript, Archives, and Rare Book Library, African American Photograph Collection: 40, bottom; 43, top; 47
Frazier, Robeson Taj: 18; 231, top; 242; 255
Guy, Kyle "VerBS": 234
Hardin-Simmons University, Jesse Wallace Williams Map Collection: 24
Johnson, Charletta: 133
Kitizawa, Yosuke: Endpapers front and back, 2; top; 12, 17, 19
La MaMa Archives / Ellen Stewart Private Collection: photograph by Carl Brunn: 183
Library of Congress, Farm Security Administration— Office of War Information Photograph Collection: photographs by Dorothea Lange, 29 top and bottom; 30, bottom; photograph by Russell Lee, 36
Los Angeles Sentinel: 161; 220, top
Los Angeles Times: 224
Simmons, Jim: 236
Southern California News Group: 163
State Historical Society of North Dakota, Vernon K. Lykken Collection: 44, top; 61
University of North Texas Libraries, The Portal to Texas History, and the Private Collection of T. B. Willis: 30, top.
USA Today Network: *Deming Headlight*: 73, top

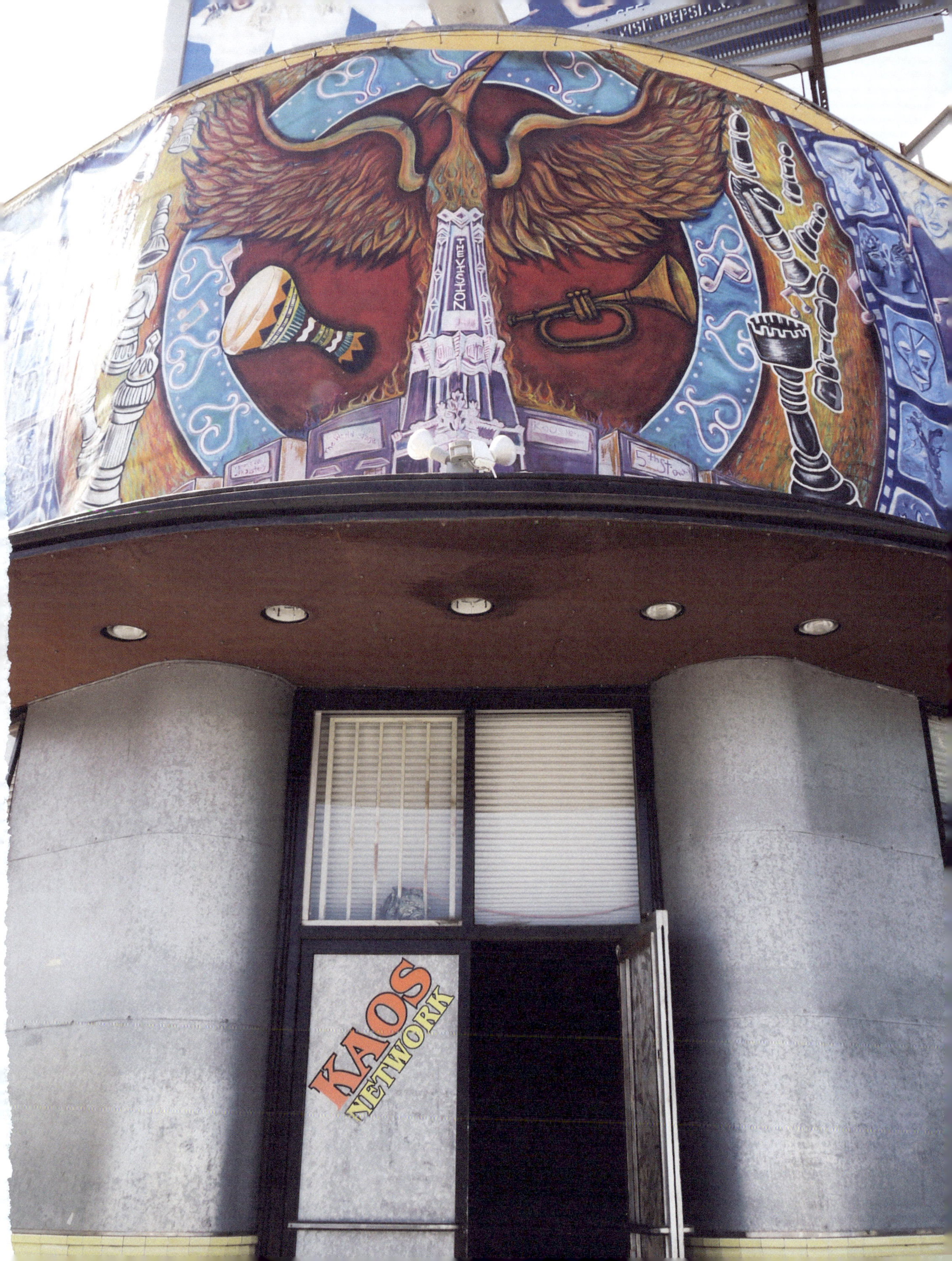

THE VISION
KAOS
NETWORK

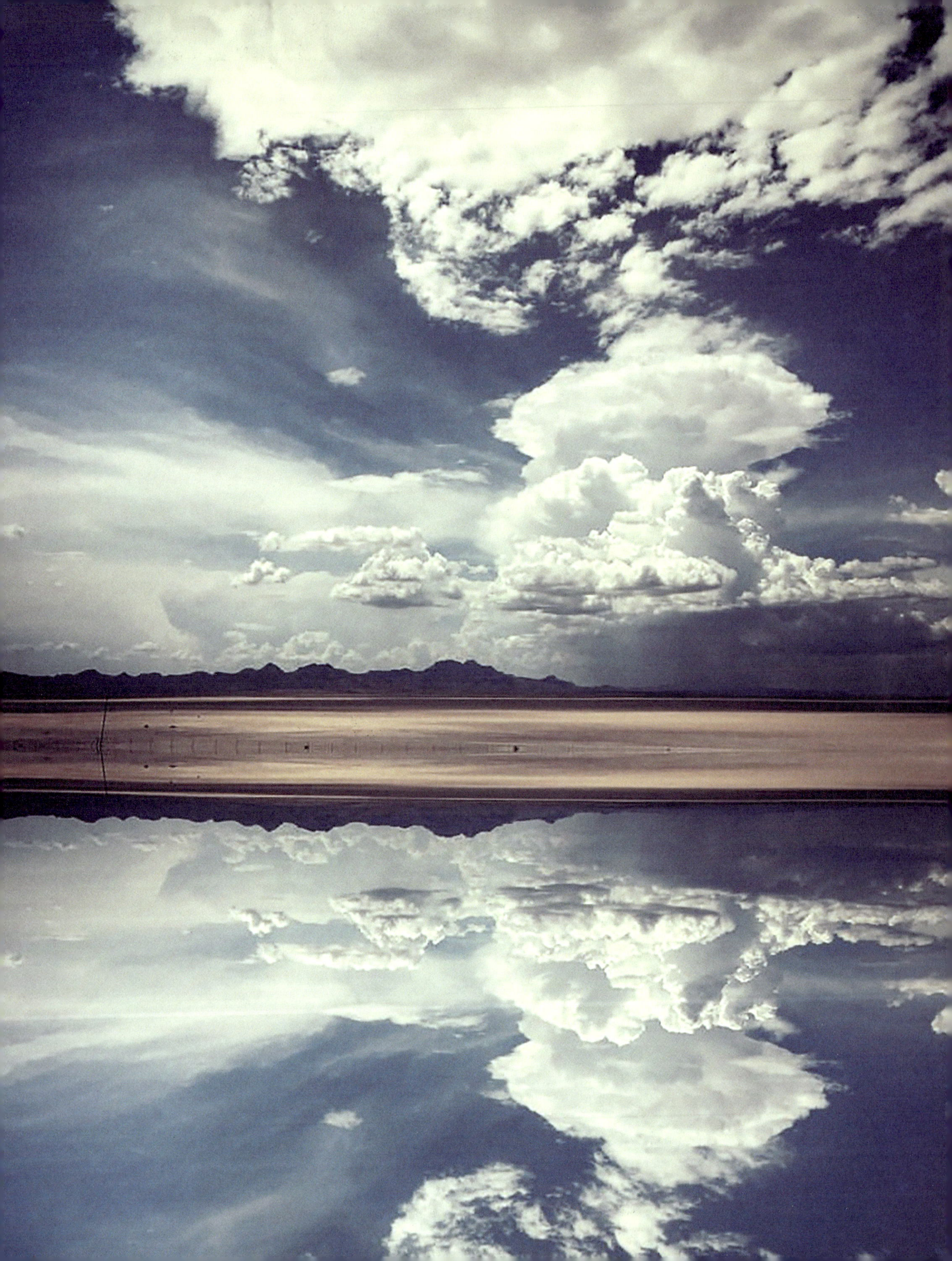